HINDUISM

HINDUISM

HINDUISM

A Religion to Live By

NIRAD C. CHAUDHURI

DELHI
OXFORD UNIVERSITY PRESS
CALCUTTA CHENNAI MUMBAI

Oxford University Press, Great Clarendon Street, Oxford OX2 6DP

Oxford New York
Athens Auckland Bangkok Calcutta
Cape Town Chennai Dar es Salaam Delhi
Florence Hong Kong Istanbul Karachi
Kuala Lumpur Madrid Melbourne Mexico City
Mumbai Nairobi Paris Singapore
Taipei Tokyo Toronto

and associates in

Berlin Ibadan

© Nirad C. Chaudhuri, 1979
First published in Great Britain by Chatto & Windus, Ltd., and
in the United States by Oxford University Press, Inc., 1979
First issued as an Oxford University Press paperback,
Oxford and New York, 1980,
by arrangement with Chatto & Windus, Ltd.

Oxford India Paperbacks 1996
Third impression 1998

ISBN 0 19 564013 6

Printed at Pauls Press, New Delhi 110020
and published by Manzar Khan, Oxford University Press
YMCA Library Building, Jai Singh Road, New Delhi 110 001

QUEST OF HINDUISM

Me dit un jour le grand Chiron —

Cherchez-vous les dieux, ô Macarée! et d'où sont issus les hommes, les animaux et les principes du feu universel?

Mais le vieil Océan*, père de toutes choses, retient en lui-même ces secrets, et les nymphes qui l'entourent décrivent en chantant un chœur éternel devant lui, pour couvrir ce qui pourrait s'évader de ses lèvres entr'ouvertes par le sommeil.

Les mortels qui touchèrent les dieux par leur vertu ont reçu de leurs mains des lyres pour charmer les peuples, ou des semences nouvelles pour les enrichir, mais rien de leur bouche inexorable.

*   *   *

Les dieux jaloux ont enfoui quelque part les témoignages de la descendance des choses; mais au bord de quel océan ont-ils roulé la pierre qui les couvre, ô Macarée!

LE CENTAURE
Maurice de Guérin

* Ouranos = Varuna

EXPLANATIONS

The book contains many Sanskrit words which are essential to an exact definition of the concepts of Hinduism. But at their first occurrence and frequently in important contexts an approximate English translation has been given. Therefore a special glossary has not been provided. However, certain explanations are called for.

1. It must be understood that the word 'Hinduism' is only a convenient term for the religious beliefs and practices of the Hindus, and was never used by them. Even the word 'Hindu' was not used by them to designate themselves except when, under Muslim rule, they employed this Muslim term for this purpose. Etymologically the word 'Hindu' means the same thing as 'Indian'. At first, even the British used the word 'Gentoo' for the adherents of the Hindu religion.

2. Three words of similar sound will be found in the book: 'Brahmin', 'Brahman', and 'Brāhmanic'. The first word means a man of the Brāhmana caste, and has been adopted in the English language in the spelling given. The second word 'Brahman' means the absolute entity which is the ultimate reality in Hindu religion and philosophy. The word 'Brāhmanic' means that part of the Hindu religion which has come down from early Indo-Aryan times.

3. The transliteration of the Sanskrit into the Roman alphabet in this book follows the standard system in the citations, but in the text diacritical marks are given only when there is a possibility of mistaking the exact word. Besides, *ch* and not *c* is used for the English *ch* sound (i.e. as in *chat*). Also *sh* is used for the cerebral *ṣ*. In the citations from old English books the spelling of the original has been retained.

4. Except in special cases, no references to the sources of information have been given, although in the case of citations the title of the book and the name of the author have been mentioned.

CONTENTS

Explanations   *page* vi
Acknowledgements   ix
Preface   xi
Introduction   What is Hinduism?   I

Part One
HISTORICAL

Chapter One   History of Hinduism: Its Methodology   27
Chapter Two   Historical Data about Hinduism   42
Chapter Three   Indo-European Core of Hinduism   64
Chapter Four   What happened in India   84

Part Two
DESCRIPTIVE

Chapter One   Sources for Description   103
Chapter Two   Regional and Social Diversity   122
Chapter Three   Intrinsic Diversity   144
Chapter Four   Priesthood and Sects   164
Chapter Five   Religious Control of Hindu Life   186

Part Three
ANALYTICAL

Chapter One   Some Special Features of Hinduism   215
Chapter Two   The Cults of Siva and Durga-Kali   237
Chapter Three   The Cult of Krishna   255
Chapter Four   Gain from Religion   294

Epilogue   Hindu Spirituality   311
Bibliography   331
Index   333

ACKNOWLEDGEMENTS

I would first thank Lord Weidenfeld for having asked me to write a book on Hinduism for the series *History of Religion*, published by his House. I had always intended to do so on my own, but was kept at bay by the magnitude and complexity of the subject. Had I not been specially urged, I would perhaps have put off such an undertaking until it was too late. His House did not feel able to publish it because I failed to deliver it within the stipulated time. Nevertheless, I am grateful to Lord Weidenfeld for being the begetter of the original suggestion.

I am indebted to Professor H. G. Güterbock of the University of Chicago, the leading authority on Hittite language, for putting me on the track of the very recondite literature on the Hittites. To two books I would acknowledge special indebtedness, they are Georges Dumézil's *La Religion Romaine Archaïque* and Father E. des Places' *La Religion Grecque*. A good deal of the erudition aired by me is due to them.

Hugo Brunner has laid me under a deep obligation not only by his readiness to help the writing of the book, but also by going through the drafts at every stage in its production over three years and making suggestions for improvement. I am obliged to Angela Blackburn for editing the book with meticulous care for the press and bringing to my notice many faults in the wording of the text, and to Elsa Summers for preparing the final copy. But my obligation to them, and to Hugo Brunner, extends beyond what was imposed on them. I have been encouraged by the fact that two highly educated women and a man have not only found the book not boring but have even enjoyed it, though they knew nothing about Hinduism, for books on the religion repel *normal* Occidentals.

As before, I am obliged to the staffs of the Indian Institute of the Bodleian Library and London Library for their courtesy. The Kipling Estate managed by A. P. Watt & Son has given me permission to quote from the story: *The Bridge-builders*, for which I am grateful.

ACKNOWLEDGEMENTS

Finally, I could not have carried out the research needed for the book in England for seven years without financial support from many sources. My publishers, more especially, have been very patient and generous. I shall set down what I owe to all these helpers on another occasion. Here I shall only put on record that for writing this book I also received a grant from the Arts Council of Great Britain.

N. C. C.

PREFACE

This book attempts to give a description and interpretation of the religion of the Hindus as practised and experienced by them. It is not a summary of their mythology, dogmas, and rituals as found in the texts. Information from them has been included in the description only when there was reason to believe that it related to actual practice at some historic period. The emphasis is throughout on the religious psychology and behaviour of the Hindus. The methodological principles on which the historical account and the descriptions offered are based are set out in the initial chapters of Part I and Part II. In Part III some important features are examined in greater detail.

The book is addressed to those who, either in India or in the outside world, take an intellectual interest in Hinduism in all its greatness and strangeness as the product of a particular kind of mind in a particular environment. It is not meant for those who go to Hinduism from some personal emotional pressure, or to put it more bluntly, for those who seek in Hinduism what they feel they do not find in the religion into which they were born, or simply an anodyne for psychological malaise. I have had to say some hard words about Hinduizing Occidentals.

Yet I have not written the book on the assumption that the religion can only be a subject of detached intellectual interest, without implications for life as lived in the present age. For one thing, no one can deal with India, or understand the social and cultural life of the people of the country, without a knowledge of Hinduism, which has influenced the behaviour even of non-Hindus. Next, religion still remains a great issue for mankind, even though it is in a shambles in the contemporary world, and Hinduism is a great religion of a particular kind. An account of it might lead to a better understanding of the religious urge in man, which is innate.

I am actuated by this conviction, although I had lost faith in the tenets of Hinduism and indeed in all established religions long ago. On account of this conviction, I have read and thought

about the religion and also other religions all my life, and I have
observed the practice of Hinduism at first hand. This book, put
in its final shape on the day I completed my eightieth year, is the
product of that life-long preoccupation. However, the study of
Hinduism is in such a confused state that my account of it must be
regarded as very tentative, only as the starting point of a new
approach to it.

NIRAD C. CHAUDHURI

Oxford
23 November 1977

INTRODUCTION

WHAT IS HINDUISM?

THIS introduction is meant to be an overture to the account of Hinduism offered in the body of the book. Actually, I had intended to set down my view of the essential character of the religion quite explicitly in an epilogue, instead of leaving it to be inferred from the incidental remarks made in the course of describing its beliefs and practices. But after nearly completing the book I decided to transfer the essay to its beginning and make that a prologue. Here was a case which could illustrate Pascal's dictum that the last thing an author discovers when writing a book is what to put first.

The reason for it was imperative. Hinduism is a human phenomenon of immense magnitude and is overpowering not only by reason of that, but also owing to its bewildering diversity. Even in dealing with the far less varied Greek religion, Father E. des Places, S.J., observed in his book *La Religion grecque* (1969): 'Elle a si peu d'unité qu'on en parle plus justement au pluriel, comme je l'ai fait précédemment après d'autres, en intitulant l'exposé: "Les Religions de la Grèce antique". Et pourtant la religion occupe dans la vie grecque une place considérable et constante.' Hinduism can be described as many religions with greater aptness, and it also pervades Hindu life as lived in the world in every nook and cranny.

In dealing with Hinduism, many writers have tried to overcome the difficulty of coping with the endless and confusing diversities in it by being selective and giving an exposition of only those features which in their view contain its religious message. But the religion cannot be divided up in this way, and to be selective about it is to falsify its true character. Despite its all-too-obvious inconsistencies, Hinduism is one whole. Even those features in it which seem to have no connection with religion, as understood today, stem from its basic character as natural offshoots.

On the other hand, to describe all its varied features exhaustively is out of the question in a book of one volume. Therefore the method least open to objection would be to include all the

1

features which make Hinduism the kind of religion it is, only reducing them to a small scale. This also will have its disadvantage, for a summary presentation of all its characteristic features is bound to throw the apparent inconsistencies of Hinduism into higher relief. Thus, whatever the method, the modern reader will have one difficulty or another in following any account of the religion which purports to show it as what it really is. To avoid this it is necessary to prepare him in advance for what he is going to meet, and to make him realize that Hinduism is a special kind of religion which has to be met on its own terms. This is what this introduction aims at doing.

The Western Approach

In reading about Hinduism the reader must emancipate himself from the prepossession created by the current conception of religion. It is of European origin, but has been adopted even by modern Hindus under the influence of Western thought. It was shaped by Christianity, but partly also by Judaism and Islam, all of which constitute a particular family of religions.

Christian thought has given to the word 'religion' a meaning in all modern European languages which the Latin word *religio*, from which it is derived, never had. Even to the Latin word the Christian Fathers gave one etymological meaning, and the classical Latin writers another. For instance, Tertullian derived it from the verb *ligare* — to bind, but Cicero from *legere* — to collect, gather together. Lactantius said that religion was a bond of piety between man and the Divinity. It is this conception of religion into which Hinduism will not fit. It is based on a wholly different idea of the need for religion and its function.

Furthermore, the serious student of Hinduism will also have to break with the whole Western tradition about the religious life of the Hindus which has been in existence for centuries, and strangely enough continues down to this day. The tradition originated with the Greeks and Romans, and by the third century of the Christian era it seems to have popularized a vague idea in the eastern parts of the Roman empire that the Hindus were endowed with all kinds of esoteric knowledge. Thus Plotinus, the creator of Neo-Platonism, wished to become acquainted with the philosophical ideas of the Persians and Indians in order to develop the line of philosophical and mystic thinking into which he had been led by the teaching of the philosopher Ammonius. Accordingly, he accompanied the Emperor Gordian in his campaign against Persia, but had to give up his quest and come back when the Emperor was killed in Mesopotamia.

It would be interesting to find out what notions Plotinus had about the religious and philosophical speculations of the Hindus. The teachings of Zoroaster were known to the Greeks and Romans, but it is improbable that they had any exact knowledge of Hindu philosophy, which was not systematized in the third century A.D. All that can be said is that Plotinus, like many others in the Graeco-Roman world, may have been familiar with the notions about India current in that world. These were all descended from the accounts given by the companions of Alexander the Great in his invasion of the Punjab and reproduced by Strabo, Pliny, Arrian, Plutarch, and other classical writers. As will be seen later, they gave very little information about the religion of the Hindus, but related stories about the Gymnosophists (naked philosophers) and the Brahmins. These men became stock figures in all classical accounts of India, and stories about them became a pendant to the legend of gold-digging ants recorded by Herodotus.

But the more sensational stories about India and her wise men are to be found in the collection of legendary writings known as the Alexander Romance, which is a folk epic about Alexander the Great. The earliest work in it was written in Ptolemaic Egypt, probably in the third century B.C., by an Alexandrian, whom modern scholars call Pseudo-Callisthenes. There were later Latin versions of this Greek work, and also many Latin tracts about the Brahmins written in the Middle Ages. All these finally consolidated the reputation of the Hindus for esoteric knowledge in Europe. Curiously enough, there are writers even of our time who are naïve enough to take these writings seriously.

As there was no direct communication between India and Europe until the end of the fifteenth century, the ideas about Hindu religion and philosophy which are found in the works of classical writers held the field down to that age. Even in the succeeding centuries realistic accounts of Hindu religion and philosophy were given only by the Christian missionaries who went to India, while the theoretical scholars stuck to the legends.

Of this contrast, a good illustration can be given. Henry Lord, an English clergyman who wrote the very first book on Hinduism based on first-hand knowledge in any European language, said that the Hindus might have got their idea of transmigration of souls from Pythagoras. On the contrary, Thomas La Grue, a French scholar who annotated the second book on Hinduism published in Europe (whose author was Abraham Roger, a Dutch missionary), wrote in his introduction that the Brahmins 'were people who are usually said to be endowed with extraordinary judgement, and with a science or knowledge which is perfect; to whom even Pythagoras and Plato were not ashamed to go in search of wisdom and knowledge; it is even held that they borrowed much of their philosophy from them.' La Grue's adherence to the classical tradition is also revealed in other ways: e.g., he gave the title *La Porte ouverte, pour parvenir à la connoissance du paganism caché* to the French translation of the book by Roger; referred to all the classical writers on India as his authorities; spoke of the Gymnosophists; and in his notes brought in Hermes Trismegistos many times.[1]

This legend of Hindu wisdom and esoteric knowledge, which filled a vacuum created by ignorance, has to be accounted for. The explanation of its beginnings is easily given. It was created by the Greeks who had gone to India with Alexander, and left accounts of the Gymnosophists or naked philosophers. In them the Greeks were meeting men who claimed to be philosophers, a type very well known to them, and who yet struck them as being very strange in their behaviour.

What appeared so to them could not have been the nudity by itself, for they were used to that in their athletes; nor the matted hair, ashes and paint on the body, and the dirtiness, for they were becoming used to such things by seeing the antics of the Cynics; they must have been overwhelmed by the combination of these traits with attitudes which did not go with them: an overbearing air of superiority, a gravity which was not consistent with their appearance, total absense of humour or malice in their exhibition of unconventionality, and a self-confidence which would not even condescend to air any contempt for worldliness.

The impact of such behaviour may easily be imagined. In admitting the superiority of other men over themselves, ordinary

[1] For Lord and Roger, see p .104ff.

human beings are swayed, not by the content of the mind, but by a behaviour which creates an impression of greatness by virtue of its abnormality. The fact is that the more rational a set of men are, the more ready are they to succumb to an assertive irrationality. The Hindu ascetics who ostensibly seemed to be philosophers to the Greeks created such a confrontation.

They were assertive and exhibited an intense desire to domineer over their fellow-men, and yet they were wholly egocentric and indifferent to everybody. They employed both speech and silence with equal effect as instruments of self-assertion: they poured out rigmarole which gave an impression of profundity, and at the same time affected a taciturnity which had the same effect. Above all, they could sink into unconsciousness and yet seem to have attained to the highest state of consciousness. The basic aim of Hindu mystical life, which is to convert all inward experience into physical states perceptible to the senses, was so far realized by them as to intimidate most rational minds. The Hindu Sadhus were pythons of the psychic world, whose slumbrous coils contained, and at the same time hid, the force of a battering ram in the head.

How even a powerful and practical European mind could be influenced by the behaviour of Hindu religious men can be illustrated by what Warren Hastings wrote in a letter to the Chairman of the East India Company, in which he recommended the publication of the translation of the *Gita* into English by Charles Wilkins.[1] He was trying to disarm in advance any objection on the score of the obscurity of the text, which might repel the Western mind. To lead to this he first described a personal experience. 'I myself was once,' he wrote, 'a witness of a man employed in this species of devotion[2] at the principal temple of Banaris. His right hand and arm were enclosed in a loose sleeve or bag of red cloth, within which he passed the beads of his rosary, one after another, through his fingers, repeating with the touch of each (as I was informed) one of the names of God, while his mind laboured to catch and dwell on the idea of the quality which appertained to it,

---

[1] See p. 107 for particulars of the book.
[2] The manner was explained by Hastings in these words: 'It is required of those who practice this exercise, not only that they divest their minds of all sensual desire, but that their attention be abstracted from every external object, and absorbed, with every sense, in the prescribed subject of their meditation.'

and shewed the violence of its exertion to attain this purpose by the convulsive movements of all his features, his eyes being at the same time closed, doubtless to assist the abstraction.'

This is, of course, the well-known *dhyana* (meditation) of Hindu devotees, in which they have to visualize the physical manifestation of the god or goddess as given in a ready-made formula. But Warren Hastings connected the behaviour of the man he saw with the last admonition of Krishna to Arjuna in the *Gita* and quoted the couplet: 'Hath what I have been speaking, O Arjoon, been heard *with thy mind fixed to one point?* Is the *distraction* of thought, which arose from thy ignorance, removed?'[1] (Italics by Hastings himself.)

Then he offered an explanation of what he saw which shows what concessions a very intelligent European was ready to make to Hindu religious behaviour. He wrote:

> To those who have never been accustomed to this separation of the mind from the notices of the senses, it may not be easy to conceive by what means such a power is to be attained; since even the most studious men of our hemisphere will find it difficult so to restrain their attention but that it will wander to some object of present sense or recollection; and even the buzzing of a fly will sometimes have the power to disturb it. But if we are told that there have been men who were successively, for ages past, in the daily habit of abstracted contemplation, begun in the earliest period of youth, and continued in many to the maturity of age, each adding some portion of knowledge to the store accumulated by his predecessors; it is not assuming too much to conclude, that, as the mind ever gathers strength, like the body, by exercise, so in such an exercise it may in each have acquired the faculty to which they aspired, and that their collective studies may have led them to the discovery of new tracks and combinations of sentiment, totally different from the doctrines with which the learned of other nations are acquainted: doctrines, which however speculative and subtle, still, as they possess the advantage of being derived from a source so free from every adventitious mixture, may be equally founded in truth with the most simple of our own. But as they must differ, yet

---

[1] I give the *sloka* in the original:

Kaccid etac chrutam, Pārtha,
tvayai 'kāgrena cetasā
kaccid ajñāna saṃmohaḥ
praṇaṣtas te, Dhanaṃjaya?

The *Gita*: 18.72

more than the most abstruse of ours, from the common modes of thinking, so they will require consonant modes of expression, which it may be impossible to render by any known terms of science in our language, or even to make them intelligible by definition.

This shows that Warren Hastings was fully aware of the difficulties in the way of explaining Hinduism in terms of Western thought—which have never been overcome—but it also shows how far a rational mind of the eighteenth century was ready to go in meeting Hinduism. The next step was taken by the Romantic Movement which was ready to go much further.

The Romantic Movement was driven by a passion to extend the limits of the human mind by wandering as far as possible in time and space, and more especially by roaming in twilight areas of knowledge which fostered dreaming. Thus it was as natural for the Romantics to turn to India as to the Middle Ages. They did so all the more because at the end of the eighteenth century India was beginning to be known, and the knowledge about Hindu civilization was just sufficient to swell out the sails but not to put a ballast of cargo in the hold.

Thus Friedrich Schlegel could write: 'It is in the East that we must look for the supreme Romanticism.' His *Essay on the Language and Wisdom of the Hindus*, published in 1808, was compared by James Darmesteter to the manifesto on literature issued by Joachim Du Bellay on behalf of his fellow-poets of the Pléiade. Baron von Eckstein declared that for superior minds the literature of the East was going to be what Greek literature was for the scholars of the sixteenth century. J. J. Ampère noted that more and more the vast and mysterious East was soliciting and attracting all minds. Edgar Quinet gave the heading 'Oriental Renaissance' to a chapter in his book on religion.

All this fervour was worked up from very scanty information about the civilization and religion of the Hindus. It was only the researches of the Orientalists over the next one hundred years which were to make them properly known. But it was the early enthusiasm rather than the facts made available by the scholars which created the Western legend of Hindu spirituality. Anything less like Hindu spirituality than the ideas about it held by Hegel or Schopenhauer can hardly be conceived. But the legend persisted and, taken up in recent times by Hindu propagandists, it still colours the general conception of Hinduism. The exposition

7

given by specialists, which is very competent so far as it goes, runs along a parallel channel into which only fellow-Orientalists go.

But the continuing influence of the legend has a different implication today from what it had in the last century. Then it did no harm. On the contrary, one might even say that it did some good by stimulating the European spiritual consciousness by its catalytic action. In the present enfeebled state of Western life and culture, the so-called Hindu spirituality has become a mirage to lure those Europeans who have become so de-vitalized that they feel the Western heritage of religion, ethics, and intellection as an unbearable burden.[1] They cannot see that if the esoteric wisdom attributed to the Hindus could do any good to anybody they themselves would not have been in the state of mental inertness from which they were aroused only by the Western ideas which came to India with the establishment of British rule. That they had survived even in that state as a community was due to the *real* Hindu religion, which is not what these Occidentals imagine it to be.

Besides the interest at the highest mental level, there was also, of course, throughout the West in the nineteenth century the attraction of Hindu charlatanry and mumbo-jumbo for the superstitious, who thought they could get from Hinduism what was not to be had from Christianity. This is comparable to the lure of the Cabala in the eighteenth century. This kind of attraction also continues, and has become more insidiously dangerous because it operates on all that is weak, unsettled, and morally debased in the West. After losing the mental stability and spiritual confidence which came from Christianity many people in the West are coming round to think that they can find a substitute in certain things in Hinduism, e.g., Yoga. Also, they have undermined repose and happiness in their daily life by a manner of conducting it which is almost devoid of sanity, and are taking recourse to the same Yoga and also to Vaishnavism, which is in no way better than taking to drugs. Worst of all, the contemporary sensuality in the whole of the West is seeking vicarious satisfaction in the erotic aspects of Hinduism, and this is encouraging the production of a literature which cannot be distinguished from pornography. Compared with the style of these works, even

[1] Aldous Huxley furnishes a pitiful example of this.

8

Casanova's confirmed habit of employing words connected with religious worship like *autel, sanctuaire*, and *libation* is less unpleasant, for that was quite honestly blasphemous.

Any writer, more especially if he is a Hindu, will have to reckon with these Western demands in presenting Hinduism today. Some Hindu writers are actually writing to meet such expectations, each choosing which he would satisfy. Thus one ladles out Vedanta to the intellectually debilitated, another Yoga to the physically degenerate, and a third Tantra to the erotomaniac who has not the courage of his lechery. So, there is a good deal of deliberate misrepresentation of Hinduism. Yet it is not easy to do something different. An honest writer can, of course, ignore the dubious interests, and in any case he will not pander to them. But he cannot ignore the idealistic expectation, the sincere interest in Hinduism inspired by the Western religious sentiment, for by so doing he will puzzle many readers and also create emotional and intellectual resistance.

The notions about Hindu spirituality current in the West, though mythical, are too firmly established to be merely ignored or dismissed out of hand as false. They can be counteracted only by presenting a true view of Hindu spirituality, that is, the element in Hinduism which roughly corresponds to what is known as spirituality in the West. There is also another Western notion about Hinduism which must be dealt with. It is the idea that the profoundest part of Hinduism is an esoteric religious experience. This is wrong. Therefore the real nature of Hindu esotericism will also have to be explained. But the discussion of both is being reserved for the epilogue to the book. In this introduction only the open aspect and the basic function of Hinduism will be set forth.

Worldly Character of Hinduism

Hinduism differs fundamentally from Christianity in this, that for its followers it is not an alternative to the world, but primarily the means of supporting and improving their existence in it. Of course, as in all other religions, so in Hinduism there is belief in another world, in life after death, and in all the supra-mundane things which form the staple of every religious system. The Hindus also make a distinction between *this* world *(iha-loka)* and the *other* world *(para-loka)*, between things which belong to *here (aihika)* and those that belong to *there (pāratrika)*. They also speak of salvation *(moksha)*. But the unworldly aims of the religion when put against the worldly have hardly any weight.

As to the notion of salvation, it is wholly unreal and unattractive—a mere talking point, as indeed the verbiage about it shows. Salvation is never the object of the religious observances and worship of the Hindus. The main object is worldly prosperity, and this absorption in the world has made the doctrine of rebirth in it the most appealing and strongly held belief among all the notions put forward by them about existence after death. They so loved the world that they made the possibility of leaving it for good even after many cycles of birth as remote and difficult as possible.

Albert Schweitzer had the insight to perceive this, and said that Hinduism was not a religion of world negation. Actually, the religion is for the world, and there is no unworldliness in it. At the same time, the world is also for religion and the two cannot be separated. Therefore in Hindu society every worldly activity is under the control of religion, and everything religious is involved in the world.

This has not only been recognized, but emphasized by all Western writers who have learnt about it at first hand. For instance, W. J. Wilkins, a missionary who has written a very accurate book on Hinduism,[1] felt compelled to say in 1887:

> It may appear strange to some readers to see several subjects treated in this book which professes to be an account of the Hindu religion; but it must ever be borne in mind that, with the Hindu, religion is not a thing for times and seasons only, but professes to regulate his life in all its many relations. It orders ceremonies to be performed on behalf of a man before he is born, and gives instructions to his descendants, which they must follow in order that his happiness may be secured after death. It regulates the ceremonies attendant on his birth, his early training, his food, and its cooking, his style of dress and its manufacture, his employment, marriage, amusements—his whole life from before his birth, until generations after his death. Religion seeks to regulate not only the private life of the Hindu, but also his domestic and national relations, and no contingencies are possible for which it has not provided laws. To treat, then, of the ordinary life of the Hindu is to describe the Hindu religion.

[1] See p. 110 for particulars of the book. The observation is on p. vi.

INTRODUCTION

How Hinduism controls Hindu worldly life will be described at some length in its proper place later in the book.[1] What is called for in this preliminary indication of the character of the religion is an explanation of the mingling of religion and worldly matters. Before the coming of European ideas no Hindu perceived that the two were separate things. It was only when modern Hindus acquired the notion of a distinction between secular and religious matters from European theology and philosophy, that they thought an apology was necessary. But instead of remaining on the defensive they opened an offensive, declaring that the intermingling of religion and worldly life proved the superiority of Hindu culture over the European.

The Hindu Argument

The Europeans, the modern Hindu said, cut up life into fragments, because their *method* was analytical, whereas the Hindus preferred synthesis. So, the modern Hindu took up the stand that life must be treated as an indivisible whole, and must not be cut up to be labelled spiritual in one part and secular in another, or social, economic, cultural, political, and so on. This view was put forward aggressively against all European critics of Hinduism. Not even the *Action Française* was more assertive about its doctrine of *nationalisme intégrale* than were the neo-Hindus of the late nineteenth century about an integral Hinduism, and this apologia continued up to the second decade of the twentieth.

The inseparability of the secular from the religious was argued at the highest level by Bankim Chandra Chatterji (1838–94), the great Bengali writer who can be regarded as the most powerful Indian mind of the nineteenth century. In an exposition of Hinduism, written in Bengali and published in 1888, he quoted a passage from an article of his own written in English.

> With other peoples [he wrote], religion is only a part of life; there are things religious, and there are things lay and secular. To the Hindu, his whole life was religion. To other peoples, their relations to God and to the spiritual world are things sharply distinguished from their relations to man and to the temporal world. To the Hindu, his relations to God and his relations to man, his spiritual life and his temporal life are incapable of being so distinguished. They form one compact and harmonious whole, to separate which

[1] See p. 186ff.

into component parts is to break the entire fabric. All life to him was religion, and religion never received a name from him, because it never had for him an existence apart from all that had received a name. A department of thought which the people in whom it had its existence had thus failed to differentiate, has necessarily mixed itself inextricably with every other department of thought, and this is what makes it so difficult at the present day to erect it into a separate entity.

Holding such views, Chatterji was bound to consider any form of culture which was secular in the sense of being independent of religion as no true culture. He put forward this view in the same book in the form of a Platonic dialogue between a Guru (not of the type familiar in the West today) and his disciple:

Disciple So, I am to understand that the cultivation and exercise of all our bodily and mental faculties is religion, and not to do that is to be irreligious.

Teacher Religion is a very big subject. It cannot be summed up in a few words. But let us assume it is so.

D. Why, this is the European doctrine of culture!

T. Culture is not a European thing. It is the essence of Hinduism.

D. How can that be? There is no equivalent even of the word *culture* in any Indian language.

T. We run after the word, and not the thing, and that is why we have come to this pass. What do you think the four stages of life of the twice-born are?

D. A system of culture?

T. Indeed, and so much so that I doubt if European advocates of culture like your Matthew Arnold have the capacity to understand it. It is latent in the devotion of the wife to her husband as god, in the life of chastity and abstinence of the widow, in all the observances and injunctions of the routine of religion, in the rules of the Tantras, in Yoga. If ever I am able to make you understand this doctrine of culture, you will find that the purest and the most heart-winning spiritual message which is declared in the *Gita* is based on this notion of culture.

D. What you say does indeed make me eager to hear more about this doctrine of culture. But, so far as I can see, the European doctrine of culture seems to be atheistic. It might even be held that the Godless philosophy of Comte is based on that doctrine of culture.

T. Very true. The European doctrine of culture is Godless. Of course, I cannot be sure whether it is incomplete and immature because of this, or Godless because it is incomplete and immature. But Hindus are men of faith and devotion, and therefore they have placed their doctrine of culture at the feet of God.

(Translated from Bengali)

This would show that the new Hindu intellectual could hoist European rationalism with its own petard. But the argument was not of the Hinduism which was known through the ages. How foreign this mode of thinking was to the traditional Hindu can be judged from the fact that, in the Bengali book, Chatterji did not give a Bengali translation of the passage quoted from his English article, on the ground that its argument would not be understood by many of his Bengali readers. It is also significant that in the dialogue the word 'culture' and the phrases 'doctrine of culture' and 'system of culture' were in English, though embodied in a Bengali sentence. What Chatterji did was simply to turn round the garment of Hinduism to show that Hindu worldliness was really religious. This was scoring a debating point against the European critics of the religion, but not explaining its real nature.

Orthodox Doctrine and Behaviour

Such arguments were unnecessary when the Hindu world was not challenged by the European. Thus the most authoritative texts of Hinduism simply defined the position, and all Hindus accepted it. I shall quote only what the *Gita* says about the relationship between the gods and men, because in a book whose central doctrine is totally opposed to the Vedic ritualistic tradition, which is the basis of the worldliness of Hinduism, the unquestioning admission of the orthodox position is very significant. It says:

> After creating living beings with sacrifices the Creator (Prajapati) said of old: You will procreate yourselves through this—let this be the Cow of Wishes for you. With this you will prosper the gods and let the gods prosper you. From this mutual prospering you will attain the highest welfare. Prospered by sacrifices, the gods will give you the enjoyments you desire. Those who enjoy their gifts without giving them their dues are surely thieves.[1]

---

[1] Saha-yajñaḥ prajāḥ sṛṣṭvā/ puro 'vāca Prajāpatiḥ: (The *Gita*: 3. 10–12)
anena prasaviṣyadhvam/ eṣa vo 'stv iṣṭa-Kāmadhuk.
Devān bhāvayatā 'nena/te devā bhāvayantu vaḥ
parasparam bhāvayantaḥ/ śreyaḥ param avāpsyatha.
Iṣṭān bhogān hi vo devā/ dāsyante yajñabhāvitāḥ
tair dattān apradāyai 'bhyo/ yo bhuṅkte stena eva saḥ.

HINDUISM

Ritualistic worship is the practical discharge on the part of the Hindu of this contract of mutual help. For example, goats, sheep, and buffaloes are sacrificed to the Goddess Durga at her annual worship, and the goat is told: 'The goddess will be pleased to receive your flesh mixed with blood.' When the head has been cut off, it is taken to the image of the goddess with some blood, and the goddess is apostrophized: 'Thou who art fond of sacrificial meat, O great goddess! accept the blood of the beast with its flesh.' The same procedure is followed with the buffalo, and it is told before its head is cut off: '*Om!* O hero, forgive the pain which you will feel from the stroke of the scimitar, for you will attain heaven (literally, *Gandharva-loka*).'[1]

Since the goddess has been given her due, the worshipper (actually the priest on his behalf) feels entitled to utter this prayer:

Om! Give me long life, give me fame, O goddess! give me good fortune. Give me sons, give me wealth, give me all things desirable.

She is also asked to give immunity from blindness, leprosy, poverty, diseases, great bereavements, loss of friends and relatives, and all distressing situations. Then comes the thanksgiving:

Om! The man who has placed you on his head will have his kingdom well-founded, his good fortune will remain firm, ruling the world will be within his power. I am blessed that I have done my duty, my life has attained to its fulfilment because you, Great Goddess! have come to my dwelling.

After discharging all his obligations to the gods in order to get what he wants, the Hindu will offer renewed offerings when he has got it. For instance, if a child is ill the mother will take this vow: 'O Mother! Save my child and I will sacrifice a pair of goats to you.' And she will most conscientiously fulfil it if the child recovers. Gratitude is expressed to a god or goddess even if any kind of property is acquired by a man solely by his own efforts. A new house is not entered without a religious ceremony, and in very recent times I have seen offerings sent to the 'very awake' (*jāgrata*) Kali of Kalighat in Calcutta after the purchase of an Austin car. Hinduism is a social contract between two acquisitive communities.

[1] For the effect of the goat and buffalo sacrifice on the worshippers and spectators see my *Autobiography of an Unknown Indian* (1951), pp. 65–7.

14

The Hindus were also capable of feeling resentment against their gods if they failed to perform their part of the contract. The Abbé Dubois noticed this in the south, and there is no reason to doubt his account of observed facts. In his famous work on Hindu manners and customs he wrote: 'When they [the Hindus] are displeased with their idols they do not scruple to upbraid them fiercely to their faces, at the same time heaping the grossest insults upon them, with every outward gesture and sign of anger and resentment. In fact, there is no limit to the blasphemies, curses, and abuse which they hurl at them under the circumstances.' He added:

If a person of high position has a grievance against the gods, he sometimes revenges himself by having the doors of their temples stopped up with thorns and brambles, so that no one can enter to worship or offer sacrifices.

After giving these particulars Dubois commented:

As a matter of fact, their religious devotion increases or diminishes in proportion to the amount of profit they expect to make out of it, and it also depends on the amount of publicity surrounding them. Those deities who do not contribute towards the welfare of the votaries here below receive very careless and perfunctory worship.

However, it has to be pointed out that Dubois was writing about the Brahmins of the south of his times, when they were hardboiled, cynical, and arrogant. He himself quoted a Hindu proverb to explain their irreverence: 'A temple mouse fears not the gods.' Generally speaking, the Hindus blamed themselves instead of the gods, and assumed that if they had not got what they wanted that was due to some fault of their own not perceived by them.

The worldly orientation of the entire religious life of the Hindus can be seen in its manifold expressions, but it cannot be said that, according to their belief, the material and moral order of the universe is in any way maintained by their religion or their gods. What is clear is that the Hindu gods could give to their worshippers what the world contained, but had no part to play in maintaining the existence of the world, nor were they responsible for the moral behaviour of men. In fact, help from religion was sought for all purposes, moral or immoral. Religion and morality ran along parallel courses.

Bankim Chandra Chatterji gave a very interesting illustration of this from his personal experience:

> We know of a landowner [he wrote in a Bengali article published in 1884] who is a Brahmin and a very strict Hindu. In winter as in summer he gets up very early in the morning and takes his bath [in cold water—it has to be added]. After that he performs his daily worship for many hours with the utmost scrupulousness. He feels as if he is stunned by a blow on the head if there is even a slight interruption of it. He takes only one vegetarian meal during the day and that in the afternoon. Then he attends to the business of his properties. At that time his mind becomes wholly intent on the problems of ruining one or other of his tenants, depriving an unprotected widow of all her possessions, cheating his creditors, securing false witnesses to send some innocent person to jail, or concocting evidence to win his cases, and his efforts in all these directions are successful. Yet we also know for certain that he is wholly sincere in his devotion to the gods and Brahmins and that there is no hypocrisy whatever in that. Even when faking a document he utters the name of Hari [i.e. Vishnu, the Preserver], and he believes that this will make the fraud effectual.

It should be remembered that Bankim Chandra Chatterji was also a magistrate of long experience and with a very distinguished record. But being the exponent of a new kind of Hinduism, he asked the question: Is this man a real Hindu? And he answered it with a 'No'. None the less, the landowner he described was a typical traditional Hindu. In India even thieves and robbers worshipped their special deity for success in their ventures.

This separation of morality from religion has, however, a long history behind it. There is clear evidence that in the earliest stage of the Hindu religion, order in the universe, both in its material and moral aspect, was in charge of the dual gods Mitra and Varuna. The name given to this order was *rta*, which meant 'straight', both literally and figuratively. But the idea had receded into the background even at the stage which the *Rig-Veda* stands for. Later Hindu mythology, too, gives instances of the intervention of Vishnu in successive crises for gods and men. The late legend of the ten incarnations of Vishnu embodies the idea of the dependence of the cosmos on one god for its preservation and survival. But Hindu mythology, as will be explained more fully later, was never any part of the Hindu religion as practised. So, in the fully developed form of Hinduism as religion, the role of the gods, even of the major ones, in preserving the cosmic order is never emphasized, though their capacity to give or withhold all desirable things in the world is always asserted.

The existence of the world, especially of moral order in it, without which even material order could not survive, was dependent on an abstract entity which was moral rather than religious. It was Dharma, which was certainly descended from the old notion of ṛta. Of course, in Hindu mythology the god of death, Yama, is the guardian of Dharma, and he is therefore called Dharma Raja, King of Dharma, corresponding roughly to the Greek god Hades. But this also existed as a purely mythological idea, and Dharma in its full ethical aspect never became concrete as an anthropomorphic god. The abstract Dharma became identified not only with order, but also with righteousness, and was thought of as a power which acted by itself without being associated with any god of the Hindu pantheon. Thus the moral life of the Hindus became detached from their religious activities and observances. But in Hinduism no aspect of life is fully separated from any other, and therefore, Dharma, too, formed part of a very wide and vague religious consciousness.

All this may create the impression that the intermingling of religion and worldliness in Hinduism is wholly sordid. Undoubtedly many of the motives behind the religious observances of the Hindus are so. But there is more to it, because all kinds of worldly prosperity have been given an aura of sanctification in Hinduism. Furthermore, it was not for monetary and other gains alone that the Hindus turned to religion. It supported their life in the world in every way, and conferred tangible as well as intangible benefits. What these were and are will be described in the book.

The Religion in Relation to Its Followers

The explanation for the intermingling of religion and worldly life still remains to be given. But to make that easier to understand, something more should be said about the relationship between the divine and the human order in Hinduism. It has been seen that it is based on a contract, which is at the bottom of the worldliness of the religion. But in this contract the two contracting parties are not on the same footing, because the worshippers are not wholly free. The Hindu's relationship with his gods contains an element of coercion, which is very much like that which exists between a modern democratic State and its citizens. The political position is that, though the citizens have the right to create the agents of the State, they have no power to create or remove the State itself or to check its exercise of power. In every way the State is an intangible and irremovable authority which is obeyed because it has created the psychological readiness to obey. In nothing is the power of the modern State seen to be more absolute than in the submission to its power to impose taxes, which no tyrant of the past ever possessed to such a degree. All that the people get from the State in return is the maintenance of conditions in which he can live securely, and, in addition, they can receive social benefits like unemployment allowances and old age pensions, as well as medical benefit. The Hindu also gets such things from his religion and obeys it.

But the Hindus never felt this coercion in any human sense. They not only spent money for religious purposes voluntarily, but actually regarded the acceptance of their gifts by the gods as a favour—*prasada*, pleasure of the god, as they called it. This feeling was all the stronger among them because the Hindu gods, in the forms in which they were worshipped for centuries, had no tyrannical, malevolent, or fearful character for their worshippers. No Hindu god or goddess, except a minor and local goddess of third rank, has been represented as pursuing any human being with the vindictiveness of Hera, Athena, or Aphrodite. Indra, the only god who is shown in Hindu mythology as a lecher seducing the wives of the sages, lost the status of a worshipped deity long before historic Hinduism appeared. Siva is the god of destruction in mythology, but in worship he is the god who guarantees welfare and safety, and is easily pleased. Kali, so terrifying in her image as killer of demons, is a mother full of love and mercy. What characterizes the god–man relationship in Hinduism is benignity on one side and devotion on the other.

Inseparability of the Natural and the Supernatural

The simple explanation of the worldliness of Hinduism is that for all Hindus their religion is a supernatural overlay on the natural world, and the two cannot be separated. Its ultimate derivation is from primitive life, in which the two mingle in every conceivable way. But in its Hindu version the primitive belief has come via the original Indo-European outlook, which also never distinguished religion from the rest of life. That was why neither the Greeks nor the Romans had any specific word for the whole complex of their religious beliefs, practices, and experiences.

The supernatural permeated the life of the Hindus and influenced all their activities so thoroughly that it became an additional environment of their existence. Moreover, this supernatural comprised not only their impersonal pantheism, their peculiar monotheism and their anthropomorphic polytheism, but also magic, auguries, and the like. In this they were both similar and dissimilar to the Greeks and Romans.

Originally, neither the Greeks nor the Romans made any distinction between religion and superstitition. The Greek word *deisidaimon* (employed in the superlative by way of praise by St Paul at Athens) at first meant one who fears the *daimones*, that is, fears the gods as they should be feared, and is therefore respectful of his religion and zealous in his practices. But later it acquired a pejorative meaning, which was equivalent to being superstitious in the modern sense. The case of the Romans is more interesting. They had two words *religio* and *superstitio*, from which the modern words in the European languages have descended. At first they overlapped. But from the first century B.C. the two drifted apart, and *superstitio* became pejorative.

The Hindus did not have any equivalent of the Greek word, nor of the two Latin words. Also, they did not develop any sense of there being two aspects to their religion, one religious and the other superstitious, for the simple reason that they never acquired the notion of superstition. But without having the words, they had an attitude towards all their religious observances which might be described by the Latin word *religio* in it old meaning. Derived from *legere* and not *ligare*, the word meant — to have scruples, hesitation, or diffidence vis-à-vis the gods or supernatural forces. In Latin the opposite of *religion* is *neglect*. That is to say, religion consists in not neglecting the promptings of scruples. For the Hindus these scruples did not come from inside, like those coming to the Greeks from what they called *aidos*, their equivalent of conscience, but from an awareness of a watch on their actions and behaviour from the outside, as if invisible beings all around were looking out for failure in being scrupulous, so as to punish any negligence. The Hindus have a word for the failure. It is *dosha*, which means offence or stumbling in a religious sense. Even when in their intellectual attitudes they had become philosophical, religion meant for them consciousness of the strength of scruples and abstaining from acts about which they had scruples.

Among the Hindus the feeling of awe in the presence of invisible powers, which is one of the elements of religiosity, came from their awareness of the powers immanent in the world in which they lived, who demanded scruples. Of course, this meant that, in the ultimate analysis, Hinduism was a very highly evolved form of animism, which made no distinction between a material and a spiritual world.

Sanctification of Worldliness

The worldliness in Hinduism did not also make the Hindus irreligious in the modern sense, because at the same time they sanctified worldly prosperity in a very striking way. There are two very curious facts to note about this sanctification. In the first place, the Hindus had no word for holiness. The Greek language had two words for complementary aspects of holiness, namely, *hieros* and *hagios*. Latin equally had two, namely, *sacer* and *sanctus*. But Sanskrit had none. Linguists have connected the Greek *hagios* with the Sanskrit verb *yaj-*, to sacrifice. The Latin *sacrificare* in its etymology means *to make sacred*; *yaj-* has no such association.[1] Yet the notion of the 'sacred' or 'sanctified' is present in every act of Hindu life. Conception, birth, eating, dressing, going on a journey, building a house, all have to be sanctified. In short, it might be said that Hinduism, in spite of its worldliness, has not merely seven sacraments like the Roman Church, but a whole series of them.

Secondly, the gods through whose cults worldly life is sanctified, have no sanctity by themselves. As seen in Hindu theogony and mythology, they are all human beings on a heroic scale, with all

---

[1] I am aware that the derivative adjective *Yajata*, which in the Vedas is often applied to the gods and which literally means 'those who are worthy of sacrifices', has been given the meaning of 'holy' or 'divine' in modern Sanskrit dictionaries. But I am unable to discover why. In any case, it is not a word in common use.

the human failings in godly measure and also power, but no virtue. It is only when they are brought into relationship with man through the cults which are meant to sanctify worldly life, that they acquire sanctity or holiness, that is, godliness in the religious sense. This is true of all the gods of the great cults.

The sanctification of worldliness is best seen in the cult of Lakshmi, the goddess of wealth and prosperity. In recent times her worship has become very mercenary, but in its typical form the worship of Lakshmi was never sordid. She was Sri, grace of the world, the embodiment of beauty in a sanctified form. Therefore the most gracious festival of the Hindus, the Dipavali (Dewali), or the festival of light, was specially hers. The notion of sanctified beauty covered not only its aesthetic expression, but also the moral. Thus a young girl who was lovable by reason of her character was always called Lakshmi, even though she might be plain. Even a good boy was called a Lakshmi boy.

The religious or sanctified complexion of worldly life of the Hindus is very clearly seen in the application to it of the adjectives of moral grading which are used by them to evaluate all phenomena. They traditionally recognize three moral attributes: *sattva* (purity, goodness, and repose in combination), *rajas* (majesty, power, splendour), and *tamas* (darkness, uncleanness, baseness). The worldly life which is commendable by reason of its affiliation with religion can have either the first quality or the second. The second quality of splendour is as legitimate in religion as the first, which implies abnegation. It might be added that Hindu women wear their most gorgeous clothes and valuable jewellery at religious festivals, as at weddings and other social occasions. Not only are these not considered to be opposed to the religious spirit, it is even unbecoming to be before a god or goddess on these occasions in everyday clothes.

Conclusion

To sum up, Hinduism in its fundamental aspect is a civilized amplification of the primitive man's way of living in the world by accepting the conditions which he believes are inexorably laid down by the supernatural spirits who really own and govern it. It is also an elaboration of the primitive man's corollary to the main proposition that by accepting the conditions it is possible to establish a relationship of mutual dependence which will be stable. In modern terms, the collaboration between man and the supernatural spirits might be called religious feudalism based on the principles of fealty, service, and protection.

But above this elemental aspect of Hinduism there is another which is not less fundamental. This has been created by the geographical environment and historical evolution of the Indo-Aryans. This process is not, however, unique, for it was seen among three other Indo-European ethnic groups, namely, the Romans, the Greeks, and the Persians. All the Indo-Europeans who moved out of their original habitat with cultures already crystallized, had to face the problem of adjusting their institutions and more especially religion which sustained their worldly life to the new environments. They did so in four different ways in Italy, Greece, Persia, and India, and brought into existence four distinct cultures. These were bound to differ in obedience to the particular conditions set by each environment.

The Greeks came to the eastern Mediterranean region where there already were highly developed cultures and religions. These modified the original features of their religion to such an extent that scholars dealing with the Greek religion in its developed form have not been able to recover all of them. But this transformation did not change the basically Indo-European character of the religion.

The Romans retained more of the original heritage through a very tenacious conservatism, combined with a certain degree of adaptability. They found nothing in Italy which could drastically modify their archaic religion, though they borrowed certain things from the Etruscans. The real impact of outsiders was felt by them when on account of their political expansion they came in contact, first, with Hellenism, and after that with the cultures and religions of Asia and Egypt. Syncretization with Hellenism was easy, and a good deal of it was assimilated into their old religion. But the more exotic religions were adopted as parallel cults. Thus the religion of the Roman empire corresponded to the organization of the empire itself. It became a heterogeneous religion for a heterogeneous empire, with a central religion which corresponded to the political imperium, and other religions as *federati*, so to speak.

The Persians shaped their religion in a different way, but that too was influenced by political circumstances. They did not find any religion in Persia which could disturb their Indo-European polytheism. But they had an internal religious revolution which did away with the polytheism. Whether this was due to the presence in adjacent areas to the west of the more or less exclusive monotheism of the Semites cannot be determined. In any case, the new monotheism became the national religion for the Iranians, and a means of retaining their identity in their multi-racial and multi-cultural empire, with its tolerance of all other religions in it.

The case of the Aryans in India was wholly different. In the first place, they became completely cut off from the polytheism of other Indo-Europeans not only by immense distances, but by the intervening monotheism of the Persians which was very assertive. On the other hand, they found nothing within India with which they could strengthen their culture in isolation. They had to face the difficult problem of surviving with their culture in an environment which was hostile in every way. For this they had to create a way of life which would serve multiple purposes: resist the enmity of the aboriginal inhabitants whom they looked upon as savages, as well as the temptation to fraternize with them; compensate for the decline of vitality inevitable in a tropical environment; check erosion of morale; and withstand the destructive impact of the environment on their institutions.

This security could not come from their social life, which itself had to be saved. It could also not come from political activity, because they were thoroughly incompetent in politics. In this they were wholly different from the Romans and the Persians, and even worse than the Greeks. There were no alternative secular ideals on which they could fall back. They had none. Indeed, in that age no human group had a secular pattern of life. Furthermore, they never developed any intellectual faculty except in dealing with religion, and that too was of a very special kind even in its own field.

These handicaps would have created serious difficulties in the way of social and cultural survival even in a favourable geographical environment. But the environment was wholly hostile, because in India nature in all its aspects was in arms against man. Therefore to win the battle against nature they had to seek the help of the supernatural in everything. A pattern of life had to be created in which the supernatural would be able to reinforce human strength.

This was done with an amazing thoroughness. The original Indo-European religion was developed in such a way as to become a strong and comprehensive way of life, covering every aspect of human existence. This was accomplished in part by internal development, forcing the old religion to a lush growth, and also by borrowing from outside which added new features to it. Naturally, in this effort to survive many experimental ways were taken which have remained blind alleys; certain aberrant lines were also taken which have not been discarded, but are only ways of escaping by avoiding the problems; nevertheless, a massive norm was also established which, by becoming Hinduism at its widest and most general, has become the framework of worldly life in India. It still sustains life at a level of confidence maintained by few religions in the world. Historically, the great achievement of the Hindu religion is that it has enabled Hindu society and culture to survive through vicissitudes which have destroyed other societies and cultures contemporaneous with it.

In addition, the religion has created what must be regarded as the true nationalism of the country. It is this which gives appropriateness to the name of *Hinduism*, which foreigners have given to the religion of the Indo-Aryans, for whom their religion was nameless. The word *Hindu* was originally only a geographical term, employed by the Persians to designate the inhabitants of the country which is known to the outside world as India. And the words 'India' and 'Indian' are only Greek and Latin adaptations from the Persian word. But since the inhabitants could never in any aspect of their life be separated from their religion the word 'Hindu' became religious, and the national identity became the same as adherence to a religion. The fusion is the only real guarantee behind the national identity of Indians. If Hinduism disappears at any time, the inhabitants of India will, unless they acquire identities derived from other religions like Islam or Christianity, cease to have any distinctive identity.

PART ONE

HISTORICAL

Chapter One

HISTORY OF HINDUISM:
ITS METHODOLOGY

ANY writer wishing to give an account of the historical evolution of Hinduism must begin by taking the reader into his
confidence about the method he is following in order to do this.
If he does not, he would be guilty of practising something very
much like deception by trying to pass off as genuine history what
at best can only be a speculative reconstruction, and that too of
decreasing validity as he goes backwards. Indeed, in strict honesty,
he should be ready to confess that a full and continuous history of
the religion cannot be written at all. There can be no doubt that
the origins of Hinduism go back to a very distant past. But nothing
is known about what it was like in practice in India until the
beginning of the Christian era, and even for about five hundred
years after that our knowledge of it is fragmentary. It has to be
frankly recognized that it is not possible to give a continuous
account of the development of Hinduism from its beginnings to its
present form.

Nevertheless, a particular kind of history of the religion has
been offered by almost every writer who has dealt with it. In
constructing it these writers have depended on the texts of Hinduism, which are very numerous. They have analysed the character of the dogmas, myths, and rituals in the various texts and on
the basis of the analysis divided them into homogeneous blocs.
These, they have placed in a relative chronological sequence like
archaeological strata, and after that even gone forward to assign
absolute dates to the stages. The result has been the erection of a
conventional history of Hinduism, divided nowadays into three
broad but distinct stages, namely, the Vedic, the ancient, and the
modern.

In view of the existence of this kind of history, it would be odd
if no attempt was made in this book to give an account of the
evolution of the religion. But a new version of it would not be
justified unless that aimed at describing a process which could
be presumed to have taken place in actual fact. However, this calls

for a wholly different method. What that can and should be cannot be explained without first examining the method so far adopted because reliance on it has prevented scholars from seeing that there was an alternative one whose soundness was obvious.

The historical approach to Hinduism has been of two kinds — one with an apologetic motivation, and the other objective and intellectual. The first made its appearance only in the nineteenth century among the Hindus themselves under the impact of European learning. Before that the Hindus had never thought of justifying their religion, nor considered it historically. They accepted it as something which had always been what it was and will be for evermore. They regarded their religion as an integral part of a complete way of life and interwoven with it. This way of life, they called the *Sanatana Dharma* — the established, permanent, and eternal way of life.

Therefore they submitted to their religion as an indivisible whole, however varied and even incongruous its doctrines, injunctions, and rituals might be. Actually, in ancient times the Hindus were so indifferent to the discrepancies that they were able to attribute most of their basic texts to one legendary author, the sage Vyasa. According to Hindu traditions he was the author of the *Mahabharata*, the *Puranas*, and of the philosophical treatise, the *Brahmasutra*. He could not be regarded as the author of the Vedas as well only because they were considered to have been revealed and not composed by any human being. So he was described only as the editor of the Vedas, and given the title of Veda-Vyasa, the arranger of the Vedas.

The impact of Western thought and scholarship, which brought the historical attitude to modern educated Hindus, made it impossible for them to go on regarding all their religious texts, doctrines, and practices as an integral whole. Moreover, Christian religious notions brought to them the idea, utterly foreign to Hinduism, that monotheism and polytheism were mutually exclusive, and also its corollary that polytheism was a corruption of religion. Thus in nineteenth-century India the historical attitude and the urge for religious reform became fused.

Between them they made the reformers give up what might be called Hindu 'fundamentalism' and formulate a cut-and-dried historical view of the religion. This was partly inspired by the work of European scholars on the Vedic texts and partly by the basic monotheism of the Hindus themselves. Simply stated, the reforming view held that originally Hinduism was a pure mono-theistic religion, whose true doctrines were to be found in the Upanishads, but that after being swamped by Buddhism, it reap-peared in the seventh or eighth century A.D. in a grossly polytheistic form. This, they called Puranic Hinduism.

This view of Hinduism, which was no more sound history than the orthodox view, has become outmoded even among the Hindus, for religious reformation is no longer a living cause with them. In its place those modern Hindus who take an intellectual interest in their religion have become disciples of the Western specialists on Hinduism. Naturally, those Hindus who write on their religion have also adopted the method of the Western scholars. Therefore it is this method which has to be examined.

It has been mentioned that the history of Hinduism has been divided by these scholars into three stages, the Vedic, ancient, and modern. Of their descriptions of these, only that of the modern stage can be said to conform to any historical reality, for it has been compiled mostly from direct observation. But modern Hin-duism has never appealed to academic scholars. They have con-cerned themselves with the older forms, and left the description of the last stage to the Christian missionaries or British adminis-trators.

In giving their description of Hinduism as well as for recon-structing the history of the religion these scholars have depended almost wholly on the texts. It is this dependence which is open to objection. On the face of it, there would seem to be every reason to draw on them, and since their volume is immense to neglect them would be to deprive oneself of the most ample body of source material. But in this matter the Hindu texts differ materially from the Judaic, Christian, and Islamic scriptures, which furnish the basis both of devotion and practice in these religions.

Not so in Hinduism. A Hindu religious text may or may not be the basis of practice or even faith. Whether it is, has to be proved, not merely by the existence and survival of the text, but by independent evidence as to its use. I shall give two instances to illustrate this.

The *Rig-Veda* is regarded as the original revealed source of their religion by all Hindus. It is still recited with the strictest conformity with the rules for doing so. But it has no connection with any practised cult. Even in the age which the *Mahabharata* describes, it had become difficult to understand, as certain statements in it indicate. Apart from the epic itself, the *Hari-Vamsa*, which is a Vaishnava text interpolated in it, compares frogs croaking together in the rainy season to pious Brahmins reciting the *Rig-Veda* with their disciples. The writer of the *Hari-Vamsa* could not be accused of blasphemy because even the *Rig-Veda* itself has this simile.

The position of the *Gita* is even more striking. It is fervently read by devout Hindus every day and is recited at religious ceremonies, especially at those connected with death. There is no text, even among those which constitute the *Sruti* or the corpus of revealed scriptures, which is held in greater veneration. None the less, its specific doctrines have no place in the practice of Vaishnavism as it has been ever since it became a popular cult. Although such a statement would sound paradoxical I would say that the more highly regarded a text is in theory the less it is followed in practice.

But after assuming that the texts do reflect practice the scholars have gone forward to base their account of the historical development of Hinduism on them by arranging them, as has already been said, in a chronological sequence, both relative and absolute. This is wholly unsound because not one of these texts, unless it is very late, i.e. later than the twelfth century A.D., can be assigned to a definite date. No serious writer on ancient Indian history has ever disputed this fact.

Yet there is a conventional chronology of the texts, even the most ancient. I shall illustrate the method by which it has been arrived at with the same two examples, namely, the *Rig-Veda* and the *Gita*. The *Rig-Veda* is rightly considered as the *terminus a quo* of Hinduism. The only external evidence for placing it in a particular age is linguistic. The Sanskrit in which it is written is akin to the Old Persian of the *Gatha* portion of the *Avesta,* which is generally supposed to go back to the early part of the sixth century B.C. But no one dreams of bringing down the date of its composition so low. That is not unreasonable, because if Buddha lived in the sixth century the Vedas could not have been composed in the same age. But they could conjecturally be placed two or three hundred years earlier without disregarding the linguistic evidence, for dialects of the Gathic type might have been current over that space of time. But even 800 B.C. is not regarded as a probable date of the *Rig-*

Veda. At first European scholars were inclined to fix upon 2000 B.C. rather than 1000 B.C. as the approximate date of the book. Then they established the convention of assigning it to any time between 1500 B.C. to 1200 B.C., and this still holds good. These dates are, of course, scoffed at by orthodox Hindus, for whom the composition or revelation of the Vedas even a million years ago is not too fanciful. Even some European scholars have suggested 4000 B.C. as the date of the *Rig-Veda* on the strength of certain astronomical data found in it. This hypothesis, however, has not found acceptance.

But the conventional date of 1500–1200 B.C. for it is also pure hypothesis, for which there is no evidence whatever. It has been assumed on the basis of another hypothetical date, that of the arrival of the Aryans in India. No archaeological data have been found in India to fix the date of this event, and the only way of introducing some certainty into this speculation is to correlate the coming of the Aryans into India with the Aryanization of Iran, for the Indo-Aryans must have been a branch of the Iranian Aryans, and they must have separated from their kinsmen after living for a period of time in Persia. Even fifty years ago very little was known about the migration of the Aryans to that country, but recent archaeological excavations have made it possible to suggest an approximate date, which is around 1000 B.C. or a little later.

But usually this correlation is not given much weight, and the Sanskritists and historians of India have stuck to their date of 1500–1200 B.C., which they had adopted before the recent archaeological excavations in Iran. Why this particular date was preferred can only be explained by supposing that even Western scholars dealing with India were unconsciously swayed by the fantastic chronology of the Hindus, but being incapable of swallowing that camel, selected instead a smaller animal which would more easily go down their throat. Moreover, the German Romantic movement, as has been pointed out, influenced Indology, and its tendency was to regard the civilization of the Hindus as the oldest civilization, because nothing was then known of the historic existence of the old Egyptian and Mesopotamian civilizations. Altogether, all Indologists *a priori* feel shy of assigning late dates to anything Hindu.

Since the *Rig-Veda* is the earliest text of Hinduism, its exact date would not have mattered if that had not become the fixed point from which to calculate the dates of later texts in terms of absolute chronology. This has been done by means of guesswork as to the length of time which was needed to transform the older notions into the new, for instance, to change Vedic religious feeling into Upanishadic feeling.

For the later texts another fixed point was adopted, and it still remains the basis of the relative as well as absolute chronology of many important texts. This is the date of Buddha. It is generally accepted that Buddha lived between *c.* 550 B.C. and 480 B.C. and therefore Hindu texts are assigned to dates before or after him according as these, in the opinion of the scholars, show or do not show knowledge of Buddhism. The fallacy of this procedure lies in two assumptions: first, that the ideas which seem to be Buddhistic could not have existed as Hindu ideas before the appearance of Buddhism; and, secondly, that all Buddhist ideas go back to Buddha — nobody makes such an assumption in respect of Zarathustra, Confucius, Lao-tzu, or Christ.

To turn now to the *Gita.* S. N. Das-Gupta, the author of the most exhaustive history of Hindu philosophy, states in volume 2 of his work (1932) that the *Gita* should be assigned to times before Buddha because it does not show any knowledge of Buddhism. On the contrary, R. C. Zaehner in his edition of the treatise (1969) says: 'It seems certain, however, that it was written later than the classical Upanishads with the possible exception of the *Maitri* and that it is post-Buddhistic.' K. N. Upadhyaya, who in his *Early Buddhism and the Bhagavadgita* (1971) offers the most thorough discussion of the date of the *Gita*, says on his part: 'We can reasonably conclude that the *Bhagavadgita* was composed sometime between the fifth and fourth century B.C., when the growing impact of Buddhism besides that of the Upanishads had made it essential for the orthodox tradition to resuscitate itself and vindicate its position.' It is not possible to imagine a greater incomprehension of the religious message of the *Gita* than to regard it, as this writer does, as a reassertion of Brahmanic orthodoxy against the doctrines of the Upanishads and of Buddhism.

The most surprising part of the methodology of the scholars when dealing with Hindu texts is the monotonous lament about the impossibility of fixing the dates of their composition, rounded off by attributions to a definite date or a period of time which is either a century or even many centuries. And this is done without

giving any reason whatever. Zaehner in his edition already referred to observed: 'As with almost every major text in India, no
firm date can be assigned to the *Gita*.' But he concluded his brief
discussion of its date by declaring: 'One would not be far wrong
if one dated it at some time between the fifth and second century
B.C.' Why these centuries and these only? Radhakrishnan also
admits the difficulty of assigning a date to the book, but he too
does so. 'Its date,' he says, 'may be assigned to the fifth century B.C.'

No less remarkable are the observations of Franklin Edgerton
on this question. He has edited the *Gita* for the Harvard Oriental
Series, and his is the most authoritative edition (1944) of the book
published so far. In it he writes:

> We do not know its author's name (indeed, almost all the early
> literature of India is anonymous). Nor can we date it with any
> accuracy; all that we can say is that it was probably composed
> before the beginning of our era, but not more than a few centuries
> before it. We do know this: it was preceded by a long literary and
> intellectual activity, covering perhaps a thousand years or even
> more, and reaching back to the hymns of the *Rig-Veda* itself, the
> oldest monument of Hindu literature.

(F. Edgerton, *The Bhagavad Gita*, vol. 2 (39th of the series), p. 5.)

The point to note is that one thousand years of speculation on
religious matters is postulated on the basis of the very texts which
as every Sanskritist confesses, cannot be dated. Coming from so
eminent a Sanskritist as Edgerton, such statements justify my
remark that Western Orientalists have succumbed to Hindu
chronological fantasies. They dare not proclaim themselves even
as agnostics.

In the absence of external evidence, the main reliance of the
scholars for establishing the date of the texts has been on a comparison of ideas. Now, to try to fix the date of one idea by noting
its similarity or dissimilarity to another idea whose date itself has
not been established by any kind of evidence, is a procedure whose
unsoundness need not be pointed out. Of course, in the light of
the conclusions of the science of Comparative Religion, which
includes the study of primitive religions, it can be said that certain
religious notions are simpler or cruder than others, and by this
sort of evaluation they can also be placed in a chronological
sequence. But it would be a mistake to make chronology dependent on qualitative analysis in every case. A simple idea is not

necessarily older than a complex idea, and what it may lead to if this relationship is assumed in every case may be illustrated by an example from recent Indian history. If the religious ideas of Mahatma Gandhi, which were put in writing by him after 1914, were taken by themselves and compared with the ideas of Swami Vivekananda, the Hindu reformer who died in 1902, the conclusion would be irresistible that Gandhi lived many centuries before Vivekananda, and was probably a contemporary of Kabir, Tulsidas, or Tukaram.

The comparative method would at best permit the formulation of a taxonomy, so to speak, of religious notions, and extended to Hindu ideas it would do the same thing within a smaller field. But to base chronology on it would be unsound as a method when independent historical evidence does not prove the currency of the idea or ideas in a particular age. In the case of Hinduism such a procedure would be more unsound still because in Hinduism very crude practices have always remained current side by side with what might be described as the highest type of religious experience. Yet the comparative method has been employed not only to establish the chronology of the beliefs and practices, but even to fix the dates of the texts. The assumption seems to have been that ten uncertainties, unlike zeros, add up to one or even more dogmatic certainties.

If this is the state of the chronology of the religious books, that of the legal and literary works is no better. The books of sacred law which are collectively known as the *Dharma Sastra* are very large in number and they have been studied thoroughly down to very recent times by a special class of Hindu learned men known as Smartas. These books are the sources of Hindu law, and their injunctions are binding on all Hindus in regard to moral and social conduct. From the beginnings of their rule the British in India became aware of their prestige and authority, and they also adopted them as the source of Hindu civil law as administered by their courts. The first compilation of rules from the *Dharma Sastra* in English was made by N. B. Halhead with the help of many Hindu pundits and printed in London in 1776. But the books were all regarded as of equal authority, and no attention was paid to their dates, though attribution to a legendary sage added to the authority of a particular treatise.

The historical approach to them was left, as in the case of the religious books. to modern scholars, and the same method was applied by them to date the legal treatises. Generally, however, very early dates were not assigned to them, except to those written in archaic Sanskrit. Recently, a noted Indian scholar, P. V. Kane, has published an elaborate work in five volumes entitled *The History of Dharma Sastra*.[1] But it is really an epitome of Hindu sacred law, and not a history. All that Kane has to say about chronology is this: 'The important question is to find out when formal treatises on *dharma* began to be composed. It is not possible to answer this question.' Nevertheless, he goes on in the manner made familiar by the historians of Hinduism to suggest speculative dates without giving any reason. He says that some of the older *Dharma Sastras* might go back to a period between 600 B.C. and 300 B.C., and by the second century B.C. they had attained a position of supreme authority on the conduct of all Hindus. Such opinions do not take the discussion of the chronology of the Hindu legal treatises very far.

The case with Sanskrit secular literature, i.e. the whole body of poetry, drama, and stories, is somewhat better, because Western historians of this literature and their Hindu disciples have not been under any emotional compulsion to adopt fanciful dates. Sanskrit secular literature is also large in volume, though not as large as the sacred literature. The largest work is, of course, the epic *Mahabharata*, and after that comes the *Ramayana*. These two are quasi-religious, especially the *Mahabharata*, and therefore in dating them the religious precedent has been followed. But with remarkable courage Western scholars have refused to place Sanskrit literature properly so called before the fifth century after Christ.

But none of these works can be dated accurately or for that matter even approximately. The time when the greatest Sanskrit poet, Kalidasa, flourished cannot be determined. He has been placed in the first century B.C. as well as the seventh century A.D., and two hundred years of discussion has not resulted in an agreed date. The only dependable chronological fact about him is a reference in an inscription of the seventh century. The same uncertainty exists about the date of the next great poet, Bhavabhuti. He is supposed to have lived in the eighth century on the strength

---

[1] This work, originally published from 1930 to 1962, is now being revised, and the first revised volume came out in 1968.

of a reference in a late historical work in Sanskrit. The dates of the other well-known poets, too, are uncertain. The only writer in classical Sanskrit whose date is certain is Banabhatta, the author of *Harshacharita* and *Kadambari*, and this is due to his connection with the historical king Harsha. The relative dates of the poets have been established on the basis of their references to one another.

Since with a small number of exceptions the Hindu religious texts are in classical Sanskrit, as also are the two epics, the chronological discussion about them could have been placed on firmer ground if we knew when this form of Sanskrit gained currency. But here, too, the scholars have adopted the method of fixing one date by relating it to another conjectural date. In fact, the history of classical Sanskrit, so far as it has been written, has been dealt with very casually. It has been assumed that this form of Sanskrit must be contemporaneous with the most authoritative grammar of the language, namely, that attributed to Panini, whose date is supposed to be the fifth century B.C.

It is perfectly logical to assume that an elaborate grammar of a language must be of the same age as the language itself in its fully developed form. But it is not logical to determine the age of a language on the strength of the hypothetical date of its grammar, instead of fixing the date of the grammar itself by first establishing the existence of the language by independent evidence. The date of the fifth century for Panini faces the student of classical Sanskrit with the fact that at least seven centuries lie between the composition of an elaborate grammar of the language and its expression in literature. This fact can be got round only by taking back the whole of classical Sanskrit literature to the supposed date of Panini, which no scholar has ventured to do. Why was the Paninian grammar written if not for helping composition in classical Sanskrit? It would seem that the whole question of the relationship between the grammar and literary composition in this form of Sanskrit will have to be examined afresh. Actually, the date of Panini had been fixed partly by assuming hypothetical dates for Katyayana and Patanjali, the two commentators on his grammar.

Yet it was possible to arrive at greater certainty about the appearance and general use of classical Sanskrit by other means: first, by giving proper consideration to its character; and, secondly, by making use of epigraphic data. No Sanskritist disputes the proposition that classical Sanskrit was never a naturally spoken language, but a made up or synthetic language adopted for a special purpose. This is implied by its very name, *Samskṛta*, which means 'put together', 'artificially made', 'perfected', or 'refined'. It was primarily a written literary language, but was also used as a spoken language by the learned or educated elements in Hindu society for pan-Indian religious, political, and cultural communication.

On the other hand, the language which was colloquial among the educated and the only language spoken by the unlearned even in the higher classes of Hindu society was known as Prakrit, the name itself meaning 'natural' and by extension 'popular'. In all Sanskrit plays even queens speak only in Prakrit, and the conversation between a king and his consort is bilingual. The literary convention of making common people speak in Prakrit should be linked with the fact that all the early Buddhist texts are in a particular form of Prakrit, namely, Pali.

The mere fact that such an artificial language was created would suggest what it was meant to do and why it became necessary. There can be no doubt that it was meant to neutralize the effect of the natural linguistic evolution of the Indo-Aryans which threatened to destroy the unity of their community and culture. To put the matter more explicitly, the linguistic evolution brought into existence different dialects in different regions of India and as time passed the differences became so great that the inhabitants of one region could not understand the spoken language of another region. It was to re-establish the original intelligibility that classical Sanskrit was created. It succeeded in maintaining the unity of the Hindus at the highest cultural level.

Epigraphic data enable us to see this process at work and furthermore to determine when it began and was completed. Naturally, a fairly long period of time was needed. The earliest epigraphic evidence on languages employed in India comes from the inscriptions of Asoka, which were inscribed in the third century B.C. and are found all over the Indian subcontinent from the borders of Afghanistan in the north to Mysore in the south, and from Orissa in the east to Kathiawar in the west. The language of all these inscriptions is a particular kind of Prakrit. It would not have been used unless it was understood and in common use all over

India. Its employment in this way also suggests that India was more homogeneous in language in the third century B.C. than in any subsequent age.

Asokan inscriptions have a vital bearing on the history of classical Sanskrit. It is inconceivable that this language could have been in general use or spoken by a considerable number of people and yet not even one Asokan inscription has been inscribed in it. The only argument which can be put forward against this conclusion is that Asoka was preaching Buddhism or at least Buddhistic ethics to the masses and so he did not see the necessity of putting his message in the language of learned and cultured Hindus. But this argument cannot be admitted as valid for two reasons: first, when Sanskrit began to be widely used the Buddhists employed it like the Hindus. Indeed, among the extant literary works in classical Sanskrit Asvaghosha's life of Buddha might be the very first. Secondly, Asoka himself showed the utmost anxiety that his teaching should be understood by all classes of his subjects, and over the whole of his dominions.

The care taken by him to make his message intelligible to all can be judged from the conformity to local pronunciation and script in inscribing the same Magadhan texts in the different regions of India. For instance, in the word *Raja* the consonant *r* is used only in the west, whereas the softer *l* is used in the east. Again, in the extreme north-west the script of the inscriptions is not the Brahmi, which is written from left to right, but Kharoshthi, which follows the right-to-left mode of the Middle East and is also more cursive.

Even more remarkable is the fact, which has only been recently discovered, that for those people who at the time lived in Afghanistan, his message was given in Greek as well as Aramaic. One of the Greek inscriptions is a translation of the Kalinga Edict, and the Greek of the inscriptions is not inferior in style to the classical Greek of Greek literature. In such circumstances neglect of Sanskrit by Asoka, if the language was widely used, would be contrary to all his practice. So, the absence of Sanskrit in his inscriptions should be taken to indicate that it was not in general use in his time.

Coming to the next stage, classical Sanskrit does not appear in inscriptions for some two centuries after Asoka. In certain inscriptions of the first century B.C. a few words are in Sanskrit, and one inscription found in the region of Ayodhya is in that language. In fact, this is the first inscription in Sanskrit. Since it mentions the sixth successor of Pushyamitra Sunga it has been placed in the first century B.C.

Employment of classical Sanskrit in its fully developed form is first attested by an inscription dating from the year 72 of the Saka era, this being equivalent to A.D. 150. It records the repair of a dam originally built by Chandragupta Maurya, and also contains a panegyric in verse which can be regarded as the first literary composition in classical Sanskrit. It is at Girnar in Kathiawar, and was inscribed by Rudradamana, the Saka Satrap of Ujjayini, on the same rock on which the Fourteen Rock Edicts of Asoka were also found. It is significant that Rudradamana employed classical Sanskrit in a region where about four hundred years before him Asoka had used only Prakrit. This definitely proves that in the second century A.D. Sanskrit was replacing the dialects. Even so the language did not replace Prakrit everywhere. It continued to be used in inscriptions for something like one hundred years or even more after this date. But from the fifth century classical Sanskrit is seen to be the dominant language in the inscriptions.

These facts would justify certain conjectures regarding the origin and use of classical Sanskrit, and nothing but conjecture is possible. It may be assumed that soon after their arrival in India the Aryans relegated Vedic Sanskrit and its modified forms to sacerdotal use alone. Thus for that purpose it had to be kept alive with effort. The meticulous treatises on Vedic phonetics and metres suggest that the old language could no longer be pronounced naturally, and those who recited them had to be taught the sounds and rhythms of the language with great care. This was very important; in fact, imperative because being in one aspect magical incantations, the hymns and formulas had to be vocalized correctly in order to be effectual. The relationship between this Sanskrit in sacerdotal use and the language employed in general life in the centuries before the Christian era might be compared to that which subsisted between Hebrew and Aramaic among the Jews in Palestine in the age of Jesus.

But while this old Sanskrit continued to be taught and read for its specialized purpose, the spoken language seems to have been a more or less uniform dialect all over Aryanized India. This uniformity was likely to continue so long as the memory of expansion from the central region of Indo-Aryan life remained living. But with the consolidation of the settlements in the different regions variations in the common dialect were bound to appear. The resultant unintelligibility, as has been stated above, led to the creation of Sanskrit for maintaining the uniformity of culture and religion. The process must have been conscious.

The new Sanskrit may have been created by expanding the archaic Sanskrit of the religious texts and also by a phonetic and orthographical upgrading of the words in Prakrit. This would not have presented a difficult problem to the ancient Hindus because in order to study the Vedas they had already created an advanced phonology. Of such an enterprise modern Hebrew furnishes a well-known historical example. By the fifth century A.D. this newly created language became the standard language of the Hindus for their highest cultural expression. It might be added that classical Sanskrit served this purpose among orthodox Hindus, who would not employ English or Persian, down to the beginning of the twentieth century.

If this conjectural reconstruction of the history of classical Sanskrit has any validity it would have clear implications for the chronology of the Hindu religious texts, because with the exception of the Vedas and their ancillary treatises, they are all in classical Sanskrit. Therefore in their present form none of them can be earlier than the fourth century A.D. This would apply to the Upanishads as well, with perhaps two exceptions. It would follow from this that they cannot be drawn upon to write a history of Hinduism or even to describe its practices before the time of their redaction in their extant form. It would be risky to trace the evolution of Hindu beliefs and practices with their help even over the succeeding centuries because their exact chronological relationship cannot be determined.

Of course, the lateness of the extant texts does not mean that the dogmas and practices which are found in them are all equally late. On the contrary, many of them must have been current for many centuries before the final compilation of the books. But the difficulty is to ascertain what is old and what is new in them. As has already been pointed out, ideological analysis cannot bring greater certainty into the chronological speculation. Therefore dependence on the texts for writing a history of Hinduism has to be given up. But the data found in them can be utilized to fill out a chronological outline established by dependable historical evidence.

This I have sought and found in five classes of sources, which are also those utilized for writing the political history of ancient India. These are the following: (1) inscriptions; (2) art objects; (3) religious buildings; (4) accounts of foreign travellers; and (5) works of secular Sanskrit literature.

The inclusion of classical Sanskrit secular literature among the historical sources for writing about Hinduism may appear surprising after what I have said about the uncertainty over the dates of the literary works. But they can prove two things: first, the actual practice of a cult, for if a writer describes a religious ceremony it can be assumed that it was performed in the age with which he is dealing; secondly, that all the practices mentioned by these writers as current may be placed in a period beginning from the fifth or sixth century A.D. Even this would be a gain.

I have collected what information about the religious life of the Hindus is to be found in these sources. Furthermore, since they are or can be correctly dated I have constructed a chronological framework of Hinduism with the help of these data. However, one very important fact has to be kept in mind about these sources. None of them go back to an age earlier than the third century B.C. or the end of the century before that. What implication this has for a history of Hinduism will be discussed later. For the present I have to summarize the information found in the sources. This is done in the next chapter.

Chapter Two

HISTORICAL DATA
ABOUT HINDUISM

IN this chapter I shall summarize the information on the religious beliefs, cults, and rituals of the Hindus which can be gathered or just gleaned from the classes of evidence mentioned at the end of the previous chapter. But in doing so I shall not go beyond the seventh century of the Christian era except in special cases, because by that time the general character of the religion seems to have been established, and most of its major features as seen in recent times had made their appearance.

Epigraphic Data

Of all the kinds of evidence which establish the actual existence of Hindu cults, beliefs, and practices, the most dependable is that provided by the inscriptions, whose dates are in many cases given, and even when not, can be approximately determined by the style of the script. What the inscriptions prove with absolute certainty is that every Hindu belief or practice must have appeared before the date of the inscription in which it is mentioned.

As it happens, the only evidence which establishes any kind of antiquity for the Hindu gods, as a matter of certainty and not mere supposition, is epigraphic. It has, however, been found, not in India but in Asia Minor. The reference is in a tablet in Hittite cuneiform and written in the Akkadian language, discovered at Boghazköy. The document is an adjunct to a treaty between the Hittite king Suppiluliuma and his son-in-law, the Mitannian king Kurtiwaza, and it contains a long list of the gods of the peoples who were parties to it. The date of the tablet must be some year within the reign of Suppiluliuma, which according to K. Bittel extended from 1370 B.C. to 1335 B.C.

The gods are invoked to witness the conclusion of the treaty and guarantee its observance. The gods of the Mitannians are named in these forms: *Mi-it-ra, U-ru-ua-na, In-da-ra,* and *Na-sa-at-ti-ia-an-na.* It is evident that these names correspond to Mitra, Varuna, Indra, and Nasatyau of the Vedic pantheon. The following anathema is also pronounced against the Mitannians: 'If you, Kurtiwaza, the prince, and (you) the sons of the Hurri country do not fulfil the words of the treaty may the gods, the lords of earth, blot you out, you (Kurtiwaza) and (you) the Hurri men together with your country, your wives, and all that you have.'[1]

There is also a close linguistic affinity between the Mitannians and the Indo-Aryans in respect of language, and its evidence is to be found in four tablets in cuneiform, which contain the so-called 'Horse Treatise' by a Mitannian named Kikkuli. These, too, were found at Boghazköy. The Treatise contains words in a number of languages, and the following are akin to Sanskrit: *Aika-vartana* (= *Ekavartana* in S., meaning one turn), *Triu-vartana* (= *Tryavartana* in S., meaning three turns), *Panza-vartana* (= *Panchavartana* in S., meaning five turns), *Sapta-vartana* (= *Saptavartana* in S., meaning seven turns), *Nau-vartana* (= *Nava-vartana* in S., meaning nine turns); also *Asua* (= *Asva* in S., meaning horse).[2]

The significance of the theogonic and linguistic data furnished by these tablets, scanty as they are, has been discussed by many distinguished scholars in all the connected fields with meticulous erudition, and as is usual among scholars working on very insufficient data they have rejected one another's conclusions with fierce intolerance. The point at issue is whether the analogies are to be accepted as indicating a direct ethnic, religious, and linguistic connection between the Mitannians and the Indo-Aryans, or merely a distant collateral relationship.

To put it more explicitly, the question is whether the gods mentioned in the Boghazköy inscriptions are merely proto-Aryan or later and identical with the Indo-Aryan gods of similar names who are found in the *Rig-Veda*, but who first made their appearance in history in upper Mesopotamia. The issue is the same with the linguistic analogies.[3]

---

[1] For the original document see *Keilschrifttexte aus Boghazköy* (1916–68). Translation by A. Goetze is in *Ancient Near Eastern Texts relating to the Old Testament*, edited by J. B. Pritchard. 3rd edition (1969), p. 205.

[2] For the 'Horse Treatise' see *Hippologica Hethitica* by Annelies Kammenhuber (1961).

[3] The arguments on both sides have been summarized in an article entitled 'The Aryan Gods of the Mitanni Treaties' by Paul Thieme of Tübingen in the *Journal of the American Oriental Society*, vol. 80 (1960), pp. 301–17. Thieme inclines to the view that the gods were Indic. The same view is taken by R. Hauschild in *Über die frühesten Arier im Alten Orient* (1962).

The dispute is, however, too finespun. It is obvious that with only four names and six words absolute certainty cannot be arrived at. But it is also extremely improbable that the similarities in both cases could be mere distant parallelisms. A commonsense view would assume a close connection. In fact, Dumézil was the first to point out the analogy between enumeration of the gods in the tablet and in *Rig-Veda* 10:125–1b.c.

I feel that it is not unreasonable to assume that a people very much like the Aryans of India formed the ruling aristocracy among the Mitannians of upper Mesopotamia, and also that the history of the Hindu gods should begin with the list of the gods of the Mitannians in the Hittite treaty. But no other mention of these gods or any Hindu god is to be found in any inscription anywhere for about twelve hundred years after this.

The next epigraphic mention of a Hindu god occurs in India, and it is found in an inscription by a Greek, and not a Hindu. It is the Garuda pillar inscription at Besnagar, which has been assigned to the end of the second century B.C. This is about one hundred years later than the famous Asoka inscriptions, which are the earliest and largest body of inscriptions to be found in India. But those inscriptions do not mention any Hindu god, though they refer to Brahmins.

The Besnagar inscription is in Prakrit, the popular spoken language of ancient India, and it records the erection of the pillar in the following words: 'This pillar with a Garuda capital *(Garuda-dhvaja)* of the god of gods *(deva-devasya)* Vasudeva has been erected by the devotee of the Blessed One *(Bhāgavatena)* Heliodorous, son of Dions.' This Heliodorous was the envoy of the Greek king Antialcidas at the court of an unknow Hindu king. The inscription is decisive proof of the existence of the cult of Vishnu as identified with Krishna, as early as the second century B.C.

From this time down to the fourth century after Christ, references to Hindu gods, cults, and rituals are to be found in inscriptions over the whole of India. They are not indeed numerous, but they furnish fixed points for working out the chronology of the cults and practices. These early inscriptions are also almost all in Prakrit or the popular language, and very rarely in Sanskrit.

The earliest and most important of them is the Nanaghat cave inscription which has been assigned to the first century B.C. on palaeographic grounds. It proclaims a queen's obeisance to Dharma, Indra, Baladeva, Vasudeva, Surya, Chandra, and the four guardians of the world, viz., Yama, Varuna, Kuvera, and Vasabha, and records gifts as well as performances of Vedic sacrifices. The gifts are to Brahmins, and one gift consisted of 11,000 cows and one elephant. The sacrifices referred to are the *Rk*, *Agnyadheya*, and *Analambhaniya*.

The other inscriptions of this epoch provide evidence for various cults and practices. The name Sivarakshita (protected by Siva) is found in an inscription from the time of the Parthian king Azes (*c.* first century A.D.). The name Sivasena is also found. Both indicate the existence of the cult of Siva. The existence of the Vishnu-Krishna cult is more directly testified. An inscription of the first century A.D. records the building of a gate *(torana)* to Vasudeva. A later inscription (A.D. 278–9) contains an explicit homage to Vishnu in the words: 'Obeisance to the Blessed *(Bhagavat)*, Supreme God of Gods *(Deva-parama-Deva)*, Ancient Spirit *(Purāna-Purusha)* Narayana.' This is from Nagarjunakonda.

As to religious practices, one inscription of the first century A.D. refers to Benares as a holy place. Inscriptions from Nasik from the time of Nahapana, the Saka Satrap (beginning of the second century A.D.) records gifts to Brahmins and also refers to feeding them ceremonially. Lastly, another inscription from Nagarjunakonda (A.D. 273–4) mentions the following Vedic sacrifices: *Asvamedha*, *Agnishtoma*, *Agnihotra*, *Vajapeya*.

Reference to the deities and rituals become more numerous with the advent of the Gupta dynasty (*c.* A.D. 320). However, these become adequate only after the accession of the third king of the dynasty, Chandra Gupta II (376–415), while by the seventh century—the latest limit for this summary—the information derived from the inscriptions shows that the cults and practices of Hinduism as known in recent times are fully established. I give below a summary of the data from the inscriptions of this period instead of setting them forth inscription by inscription.[1]

Among the deities Vishnu comes first. The other names under which he is mentioned are those traditionally given to him, and

[1] The main, though not the sole, collection from which the information is drawn is Fleet's *Corpus Inscriptionum Indicarum*, vol. 3, 'Inscriptions of the early Gupta Kings and their Successors' (1888).

some of them are specifically the names of Krishna. All his mythological relationships and attributes are given in their traditional forms. He is the husband of Lakshmi (Sri), younger brother of Indra, lord of the serpent Ananta or Sesha; he has four arms, and bears the wheel or discus, the club, the bow Sarnga, and wears the jewel Kaustubha and a garland; his mount is the bird-man Garuda; he lies in the ocean and sleeps for four months; he became incarnate as Varaha (boar), as Nrisimha (man-lion), as Vamana (dwarf), and he destroyed many demons; he is the supporting pillar of the three worlds. Some special and significant attributes of Vishnu are also mentioned. In one inscription he is hailed as creator, preserver, and destroyer and so on, not simply as preserver. In three inscriptions the earth is described as belonging to Vishnu or as being the female principle in Vishnu in an embodied form—*Bhur-vaishnavi*.

In many inscriptions Vishnu is God *par excellence*, and is mentioned simply under the name of Bhagavat (the Divine or Blessed One) without any specific name. It should be noted that the term *Bhagavata* always denotes a worshipper of Vishnu, and that the two most authoritative texts of Vaishnavism are entitled *Srimad-Bhagavad-Gita* and *Bhagavata Purana*.

Krishna is referred to under this name and also as Vāsudeva (son of Vasudeva). He is shown in his epic, mythological, and divine characters. Of the identification of Vishnu and Krishna more will be said later.

Lakshmi under the alternative name of Sri (grace) is referred to as the wife of Vishnu.

The inscriptions of this age show that a fully developed cult of Vishnu was in existence, for many kings and chiefs proclaim themselves as worshippers of Vishnu under his various names, among which are also the names of Krishna.

In addition, the building of temples and other monuments to Vishnu is recorded. There is an inscription of A.D. 423–4 which says that a minister named Mayuraksha built a place for Vishnu which was as high as the mount Kailasa in order to proclaim his great devotion *(bhakti)* to the god. Another inscription records that a chief named Chakrapalita who had offered his life at the feet of Govinda *(Govinda-padārpita-jīvana)* has also built a house for Vishnu under the name *Chakrabhṛt* (bearer of the discus) in A.D. 437–8. To give some more examples, on the Iron Pillar of Mehrauli near Delhi whose date and attribution are uncertain, but which has been assumed to have been erected by one of the early Guptas, is inscribed that the column was erected as the standard of Bhagavan Vishnu, and the place is called Vishnupada or feet of Vishnu. The other temple of Vishnu, described as *bhavanottama*, 'the excellent house', was built by Adityasena of the family of the Guptas of Magadha at a place near modern Gaya, probably in the seventh century.

The cult of Siva is also seen as fully developed, and as an alternative to that of Vishnu. It presents exact parallelisms. Just as the devotee of Vishnu described themselves as *Parama* or *Atyanta-Bhagavata*, those of Siva called themselves *Parama-Mahesvara*. It has to be explained that Siva as the supreme God is always referred to as Isa, Isvara, or Mahesvara, that is, Lord or Great Lord, whereas Vishnu is referred to as Bhagavat (the Blessed or Divine One). The appellation of Siva as the Lord *par excellence* has persisted down to this day.

He is referred to under all his familiar mythological names: Bhutapati, Hara, Isa, Isvara, Mahadeva, Mahesvara,, Paramesvara, Pasupati, Pinakin, Sambhu, Sarva, Sthanu, Sulapani, Tripurantaka, Visvanatha, etc. All his physical attributes are seen to be as they are in mythological books. He has tawny and matted hair, and the moon on his forehead. All his mythological associations are also mentioned in the inscriptions: he is the husband of Devi or Parvati and father of Kartikeya; he rides the bull Nandin; he reduced the god of love to ashes.

It would seem that Siva also had shrines in this period. The king Anantavarman records that he had a marvellous image of Bhutapati (Siva) installed in a cave. There is also reference to the *linga* as his symbol. The Vakataka king Pravarasena II (*c.* end of the fifth century A.D.) says in one of his inscriptions that he gave great satisfaction to Siva by carrying his *linga* on his shoulder. Finally, as with Vishnu so with Siva, the character of the deity is that he is a complete God, and not as in Hindu theory only a god of destruction. In the Mandasore inscription of Yasodharman (*c.* middle of the sixth century) Siva is described as the creator of the world *(Bhava-srj)* and its continuator as well.

The cult of his wife Parvati is also seen side by side. In the inscriptions she is referred to as Devi (the goddess or lady), Bhavani, or Katyayani. The name Durga, under which she is worshipped as the mother goddess *par excellence*, is not found, but the character of the goddess is seen to be identical, for as Bhavani and Katyayani she is described as the killer of the demon Mahishasura. The Maukhari king Anantavarman says in his Nagarjunakonda inscription that he has set up an image of Katyayani in a cave in the Vindhya hills, and that she is seen with her foot (jingling with an anklet) on the head of Mahishasura. He also records that he has made the gift of a village for her service.

One inscription dating from A.D. 423–4, the same in which the minister Mayuraksha says that he erected an image of Vishnu, also shows that a form of Sakta worship, i.e. worship of the mother goddess as the embodiment of power, existed, and that it was some sort of prototype of the later Tantric cult. The word *Tāntra* (adjectival form of *Tantra*) is found, and the inscription says that the minister has built a terrible abode of the Mothers *(Mātram)*, who shout with joy and stir up the oceans with winds raised by magical ceremonies *(tantrodbhuta-prabala-pavanodvārtita' ambhonidhinām)*. It adds that this abode is full of the female evil spirits called Dakinis. I have not found the name Kali in any inscription of the period.

Besides these major cults there was also a cult of the sun as a god. There is an inscription which gives a very interesting and elaborate description of the building of a temple to the sun in A.D. 437–8 by a guild of silk-weavers at Dasapura. The building *(bhavana)* is said to be noble, spacious, and incomparable, and with a high steeple *(sikhara)*.

Gods and goddesses for whom there were no major cults, but whose names are familiar from mythology, are also mentioned in the inscriptions. Among them are Varuna, Indra, Sachi, Yama, Kuvera, Kartikeya, Kama, Rati, Chandra, and others. Even the monkey god Hanuman is mentioned. The attributes and associations given to them in the inscriptions are identical with those given in the Puranas.

The origin of the Vedas has already become legendary in this age, and the sage Vyasa is referred to as the arranger of the Vedas. However, Vedic studies are referred to as an active sacerdotal occupation, and what is more important Vedic public sacrifices are shown by the epigraphic references to be common in all these historic centuries, among them even the *Asvamedha*, the supreme sacrifice of the conqueror, is referred to again and again from the first century B.C. to much later centuries. But this only testifies to the continuation of the Vedic *Karmakanda* (ritualistic injunctions) in an age in which the Vedic religious beliefs had become wholly obsolete. Actually, one inscription of Chandra Gupta II states that Samudra Gupta restored the Asvamedha or horse sacrifice which had been in abeyance for centuries. The mythological information as a whole found in the inscriptions is also identical with what is found in the texts. There is no difference whatever.

Representation in Art and Sacred Buildings

Representation of the deities in art supplements the data from the inscriptions bearing on the development of all Hindu cults. However, the expression of Hinduism in art is very much later than that of Buddhism. The legends of Buddha began to be illustrated in sculpture at least from the second century B.C. In contrast, the Hindu gods and goddesses do not appear in art on any noticeable scale before the fifth century A.D. and even then the examples are not numerous. But as soon as the Hindu gods and goddesses appear in sculpture, they are seen to be very much like what they have been in recent centuries. They also conform to the Puranic forms which have been supposed to be later developments from a hypothetical earlier form of Hinduism. There is, however, no archaeological evidence to prove the historical existence of any other form of Hinduism. For instance, even the small number of representations which have come down from the period before the fifth century show that the cult of Siva, Vishnu, and Sakti (or Durga) are fully developed in the forms in which they have been seen in recent times. As it is not possible to mention all the representations of the Hindu deities found in sculpture, only those which are important for the establishment of the chronology of the cults are included in the following summary.

The earliest representations are not in sculpture, but on small objects like seals and coins. The iconographical interpretation of the signs or figures in the very early objects of this class is very doubtful. I shall therefore only mention those in which the identification is certain.

Two very early examples of representation are on coins. One of them, assumed to date from the third century before Christ, shows the well-known motif known as Gaja-Lakshmi, i.e. the goddess of wealth and prosperity flanked on either side by an elephant with the trunk raised as if in salute. This design is found on other coins dating from the second century B.C. down to the first century A.D. and it was also repeated on other kinds of objects, e.g. lamps.

In a coin from the environs of Ujjayini, assigned to the first or second century, Siva appears for the first time, but the clearest representation of the god is on a copper seal found at Sirkap in north-western India, dating from the first century A.D. Most of the early representations of Siva come from the extreme north-west of India, and are assigned to the epoch of the Scythians, Kushanas, and other foreign rulers. The outstanding school of Indian sculpture of this period, generally known as the Mathura school, provides very few examples of Hindu iconography, though the representation of Buddhist legends in it is very impressive.

Representation of Hindu deities in Indian sculpture becomes noticeable only from the so-called Gupta period, whose commencement is placed early in the fourth century A.D. But the extant examples of major sculpture are all later than A.D. 400, and even these are not very numerous. Appearance of Hindu gods in sculpture becomes really impressive only after the middle of the seventh century. None the less, the examples from the Gupta age establish that the three Hindu cults of Siva, Vishnu, and Durga were already developed to a point at which they became standardized.

An early coin of this period, with the figure of the first Gupta monarch Chandra Gupta I (A.D. 320-45), shows on the reverse the figure of a goddess seated on a lion. This does not depict Durga as she is in the later standardized iconography, but the deity may be assumed to be the goddess. A later coin of the reign of Kumara Gupta (A.D. 414-55) shows another seated goddess, who cannot be identified. But the representation of the Hindu war-god Kartikeya and of Ganga (the river Ganges deified), as found on the coins of this period, are of the standard type. Clearly, by the end of the fifth century the gods of Hindu mythology and cults had received their well-known iconographical forms.

This is also the conclusion which can be drawn from sculpture in the round and in relief. A very important group, dating from the early part of the fifth century, is to be seen outside the caves of Udayagiri, near Bhopal. Architecturally, the caves are not notable. But the representation of the major gods and of mythological themes at this place are of great historical importance, for the figures are the earliest examples of standard Hindu iconography. There is a remarkable high relief showing Vishnu with his four arms and the familiar adjuncts. There is also a great relief—one of the largest in India—depicting the boar incarnations of Vishnu. The existence of the cult of Siva in the familiar form is proved by a remarkable *linga*. It has the face of the god with his three eyes carved on it. The cult of Durga is seen in its full development in two representations of her as Mahishamardini or slayer of the demon Mahisha. The postures are different in the two figures, and this fact indicates that the iconography of this episode in the mythology of Durga had not become standardized. But the theme was.

Another important group of sculptures, from a slightly later date is at Eran, not very far from Udayagiri. The most notable figures from this site are those of two incarnations of Vishnu, namely, the Varaha or boar, and Nrisimha or man-lion.

Figures connected with the cults of Siva and Durga are to be seen at a third site in the same area, namely, Badoh Pathari. One set of figures in relief show the Sapta Matrikas or Seven Mothers connected with the cult of Durga, and there is another figure showing Siva in his special form of Virabhadra. Besides these there are at other places detached figures of Vishnu, Siva, and other gods. As the dates are not certain it is not necessary to mention individual examples. However, those whose dates are reasonably certain establish the existence in the fifth century of the major Hindu cults in the form in which they are known even today.

One point should, however, be made clear in connection with these representations. The pieces belonging to this epoch appear to be illustrations of mythology, and not images of gods meant for worship in temples. In fact, it is very difficult to say which images were placed in the sanctums for actual worship.

The sacred buildings which have survived intact or in ruins have to be considered next. These duplicate the evidence supplied by the inscriptions and works of art, and reveal the same historical development or state of the religion. However, the buildings consecrated to Hinduism are not only much later than the earliest

Buddhist monuments, they are later even than the reliefs or statues in the round of Hindu divinities.

The remains of the earliest structure which can be regarded as a temple has been found not in India but in Afghanistan. They were discovered at a place called Surkh Kotal in 1951 by Schlumberger, who was then the head of the French archaeological mission at Kabul. The ruins do not show the structure to be wholly like a Greek temple, but it had hypostylar features. In it was also found a long inscription of Kanishka in Greek letters, but not in the Greek language. The language is Etio-Tokharian, the ancient Indo-European dialect of Bactria.

There is no agreement as yet about the character of this temple. Schlumberger regarded it as a fire temple of the Persian type. But André Maricq thinks that it is a temple to King Kanishka as god, that is, a temple for some kind of imperial cult, like that of the Roman emperors.

The date of the temple also cannot be determined because the date of Kanishka is itself uncertain. But there can be no doubt that it is the earliest structure in India or in any adjacent country which can be regarded as a temple.

If one could be more certain about the cult for which this temple was built, it would have been possible to fix the date of image worship in temples in India and adjacent regions as early as the second century A.D. But the certainty is absent, and therefore the remains at Surkh Kotal can be regarded only as evidence for the erection of a structure which is undoubtedly a temple and the earliest one found so far in the Indian region.[1]

Nor are the remains found in India proper of greater help in dating the beginnings of image worship in temples, because they are all later than the inscriptions and the sculptures which mention or indicate that kind of worship. The earliest of these remains have not been regarded as earlier than the late fourth or early fifth century A.D. The two temples which have survived more or less intact in their structure, though damaged, can at the earliest be assigned to the latter half of the fifth century. But some scholars have placed them in the seventh century.

Both these temples are dedicated to Vishnu. One of them is at

---

[1] *Proceedings of the British Academy* (1961), Albert Reckitt archaeological lecture by D. Schlumberger, 31 May 1961, pp. 77–95. *Journal Asiatique,* vol. 246, pp. 345–440: 'Inscription de Surkh-Kotal', André Maricq.

Deogarh in the area of the Udayagiri monuments. It is built of stone, and has some fine sculptures on it. The second temple is in the Gangetic plain at Bhitargaon and is built of brick. In fact, it is the earliest brick temple found in India. Owing to its location it has an added importance, for it is the only early temple surviving in the central region of Hindu culture, all the other early remains are in the outlying regions. The absence of temples in this region is due to the fact that over the whole of the Gangetic plain the temples were systematically destroyed by the Muslim conquerors. The result of this destruction will be considered later.

The reason for the survival in these cases seems to be that all these temples were small structures. The sanctum of the temple at Deogarh is only nine feet nine inches square, while that of Bhitargaon is fifteen feet square. All that is established by these remains is that by the end of the sixth century worship in temples had become well established. However, it cannot be said that even then the temples were very impressive in size or style.

Information from Foreign Accounts

Of the foreigners who have left accounts of India the Greeks were the earliest, and the Chinese, who naturally felt an interest in the land of Buddha and wished to learn about his doctrines at first hand, came many centuries later. However, the most detailed description of the religious beliefs and sciences of the Hindus is to be found in the work on India of the great Muslim scholar Alberuni, who compiled it at the beginning of the eleventh century. Though it is a very important source for the state of Hinduism in that age, it has not been drawn upon for this chapter as it is much later than the chronological limits set for it.

Information which the Graeco-Roman world had about India was derived, as has been said already, from the Greeks who accompanied Alexander the Great (327–325 B.C.) in his expedition to India, and also from Megasthenes who represented Seleucus at the court of Chandragupta Maurya (c. 300 B.C.). But none of the original accounts, including that of Megasthenes, have survived. They are all found in extracts incorporated in the writings of later Greek and Roman authors, the most important of whom are Strabo (c. 63 B.C.–c. A.D. 23), Arrian (c. A.D. 96–180), and Plutarch (c. A.D. 46–120).

The information on religion in these accounts does not amount to much, and what is given comes mainly from Strabo and Arrian who wrote on the authority of Megasthenes. The Greek legend was that Dionysos had conquered India and also that Herakles had gone towards that country. So, what the Greeks saw of religion in India was connected by them with both. Strabo (*Geography* Bk 15.1.58) cites Megasthenes as saying that in the mountainous regions the people were votaries of Dionysos, whereas on the plains they honoured Herakles. Arrian (*Indica* 8.4, 11.12) on the same authority mentions Mathura as the place where Herakles was held in special honour. No Hindu gods are mentioned by these or any other classical authors, but the Greek names obviously suggest Siva and Krishna as the Hindu deities. However, it is not possible to infer from these references whether the cults of Siva and Krishna were already in existence in the age with which Strabo deals. The Greek verb is *tim-ao*, which means to honour, esteem, or worship. In any case, the existence of the mythology of Siva and Krishna seemed to be suggested, and also the later connection of Siva with the Himalayas and of Krishna with Mathura.

These two classical authors as well as others give information about the social aspects of the Hindu religion. Their accounts of the various groups of religious men are often confused, but broadly speaking their descriptions agree with what is known from Indian sources as well as observation. In the first place, the Hindus are distinguished from the Buddhists. The Hindu priestly order is called the *Brachmanes* and the Buddhist the *Garmanes* by Arrian, i.e. the *Brahmanas* and the *Sramanas* in Sanskrit. After that an account is given of the system of education of the Brahmins, which conforms to the first or Brahmacharya stage of Hindu life of their sacred law. But the Greeks were most struck by the Hindu philosophers, especially by those whom they called Gymnoso-phists or naked philosophers. Alexander, according to these writers, had both friendly and unfriendly dealings with them.

In dealing with the Hindus who specially devoted themselves to religious life, the classical authors made a distinction between those who lived as recluses in their hermitages in the woods, and those who wandered from place to place and practised extreme asceticism. The former were obviously the sages *(Rishis)* of the epics and classical Sanskrit literature, and the latter the sadhus who are so conspicuous a feature of Hindu religious life even today. With their matted hair, uncouth appearance, and nudity they were equally conspicuous to the Greeks. The classical writers also noted the prevalence of religious and philosophical discussion among religious men, and gave examples of some of the opinions expressed. One author, Quintus Curtius Rufus even said that the Hindu philosophers were fond of wrangling, quarrelsome, foolish, and boastful. But generally the Graeco-Roman world looked upon them as the repositories of esoteric knowledge and wisdom.

The Chinese travellers take up the story much later. All of them wrote from their own observation of religious life as it was when they came to India. There were three famous pilgrims who came to learn at first hand about Buddhism. The first was Fa-Hien, who travelled throughout India from A.D. 399 to A.D. 414. The second, Hiuan-tsang, or Yuan-Chwang, was in India between A.D. 629 and A.D. 645, i.e. during the reign of Harsha. The third Chinese, I-Tsing, came a little later, arriving in India in A.D. 671 and returning in A.D. 695.

The account given by Fa-Hien is very curious. Although he visited India when the Gupta dynasty was at the height of its power with Chandra Gupta II on the throne, and went not only to the places sacred to Buddhism, but also to the centres of Hindu culture like Mathura, Kanyakubja, and Pataliputra (assumed to be the capital of the Gupta Empire), he does not mention any great king by name, nor does he refer to anything like an imperial system in which one king exercised suzerainty over others. He presents the picture of a large country divided into small kingdoms. He does not describe Hindu cults, and in his account there are very few references to temples. He speaks more than once of the rivalry between the worshippers of the Devas (i.e. the Hindu gods) and the Buddhists, but does not give details of Hindu beliefs and practices. As to temples, one notable reference is to a Deva temple in Jetavana at Sravasti which was erected opposite a Vihara (Buddhist monastery) and was more than sixty cubits, or ninety feet, high.

This neglect of things Hindu may be explained by the fact that, being a pious Buddhist, Fa-Hien was interested only in his own religion and did not record anything about Hinduism or Hindu kings. But the book is also a traveller's account, and in respect of one region at least, the Madhya Desa (Middle Country) around

Mathura, he gives a short description of the system of government. The absence of all allusions to the imperial Guptas is thus surprising.

The paucity of Fa-Hien's references to temples also requires explanation for he must have seen them wherever they existed. Whether this could mean that at the beginning of the fifth century temples were neither numerous nor very impressive cannot be stated with certainty. But such a supposition would be justified by the fact that very few remains of Hindu temples have come down from the fifth century. As has been mentioned above, the surviving buildings are overwhelmingly in outlying areas and not on the Gangetic plain. It is quite possible that whatever sacred structures from early times existed in that region have disappeared along with the monuments of later periods. In any case, if the temple cult existed in the fifth century, Fa-Hien does not show that it had a very impressive expression.

In contrast, Yuan-Chwang, who visited India about two hundred and twenty-five years later, presents a wholly different picture. He not only speaks about Harsha and his political power and refers to other things, agreeing broadly in his account with the version of Harsha's life given in *Harsha-Charita*; he also records the existence of Hindu temples and gives their number wherever he saw them from the Punjab to Assam, together with the number of Buddhist *viharas*. For instance, he says that at Kanyakubja on the Ganges (which Fa-Hien also visited), there were splendid temples of Surya (the Sun god) and of Mahesvara (Siva). At Prayag (modern Allahabad), according to him, there was a celebrated temple and near it a spreading tree — clearly the Akshaya Vata or the indestructible banyan tree of our times. In his description of Varanasi (modern Benares) Yuan-Chwang mentions there were 100 temples in the whole district and 20 in the city itself. He also specifically mentions that the chief deity of Benares was Siva (which he also is today), and that there was a life-like image of him, awe-inspiring in its majesty. Of course, he also describes the Buddhist holy place of Sarnath (about eight miles from Benares) and also records the existence of a *stupa* (tumulus) built by Asoka (the Dhameka Stupa, which still stands there).

Yuan-Chwang's description of the kingdom of Kamarupa is very interesting. He says that under its Hindu king, Vaskaravarman, an ally of Harsha, the religion of the kingdom was Hinduism, and that such Buddhists as lived in it practised their religion secretly. From all that Yuan-Chwang says it would appear that a great development of the material expression of Hinduism had taken place between the time of Fa-Hien and Yuan-Chwang unless we assume that Fa-Hien deliberately kept silent about Hinduism and Hindu monuments.

Not less interesting is Yuan-Chwang's description of the holy character of the Ganges, which he emphasizes. He writes of a place which he calls the Ganges Gate (clearly modern Hardwar) —the Gate of Siva—where the river debouches into the plain), and says that it is a place of great religious merit where sin and guilt are extinguished. He also emphasizes the sacredness of the confluence of the Ganges and the Jumna at Prayag (modern Allahabad), and it is still sacred. He writes that every day numbers of people arrive at the confluence to drown themselves in its sacred waters in the hope that they might be reborn in heaven. He adds that even monkeys and other wild creatures do this. He also noticed the presence of hermits practising their austerities on the bank of the rivers near the confluence. They are still to be seen at this spot.

I-Tsing, the third pilgrim from China, records nothing about Hinduism. That may be due to the fact that his book, apart from a short summary of his journey, is an account of Buddhist doctrines and practices as he found them in India. He was not concerned with Hinduism or other aspects of Hindu life.

Information from Secular Literature

The value of the data about Hinduism which can be found in secular literature in Sanskrit and Prakrit is lessened by the uncertainty about the dates of the books. As has been seen, neither the two epics nor the works of the greatest Sanskrit poets can be assigned to particular dates. The stories of the epics must have been current from fairly early times, but they could not have received their present form before the third century A.D. Secular poetry is later.

Apart from the two epics, which form a special category, I have examined the works of Kalidasa, who is certainly the earliest of the ancient Indian poets whose writings have survived and whose date I have assumed to be either the late fifth or sixth century A.D. After him I have consulted the works of Bharavi,

Bana, Dandin, Subandhu, and Magha, i.e. all the poets who may be presumed to have lived before the eighth century. Besides them, I have gone to Bhavabhuti, generally assigned to the eighth century, and to Sri Harsha, author of *Naishadha Charita*, who comes later. In addition, I have consulted the important poetical anthology in Prakrit, the *Gatha Saptasati*.

The two epics, whenever they were put into their present form, embody the legends of the early existence of the Aryans in India. Of these two, the *Ramayana* certainly describes a stage of that existence which is earlier than that described in the *Mahabharata*. But compared with the *Ramayana* in its extant form the *Mahabharata* is more archaic in the treatment of the stories and in the atmosphere it creates. However, this difference does not affect their value as sources for a history of Hinduism, because both give religious and mythological information·of the same type.

To consider the mythology first. The *Ramayana* is itself partly a mythological story, and the *Mahabharata* can be regarded as an almost complete corpus of Hindu mythology. The first point to note is that the mythology of the epics is, in spite of differences in detail, identical with what is found in the specifically mythological books, the Puranas. Again, the mythological stories and legends which furnish the staple of the themes in secular literature in Sanskrit properly so called, are also identical in their substance with those of the epics and Puranas. Thus the Puranas, the epics, and the later plays and poems present one coherent body of mythology as against Vedic mythology. This mythology is the Hindu mythology proper, and it has remained unchanged to this day. This is also the mythology referred to in the inscriptions and depicted in art.

But though the themes are identical, the spirit in which they are treated in late Sanskrit secular literature, is wholly different from that of the epics. The distinction has to be pointed out because an overwhelming number of subjects in the later plays and poems are taken from the epics. The themes are, so to speak, humanized and even sentimentalized. This is all the more significant because the epics and the later works of literature are written in the same classical Sanskrit, although the diction and metres in the epics are much simpler. The later poets treated the themes which they took over with a more complex artistry.

More important is the difference in the emotional quality. The mind of the heroes and heroines is more primitive in the epics and their behaviour is not only more frank and assertive but also flamboyant. In classical Sanskrit literature the same characters and incidents become more subdued, complex, and sophisticated. The difference is greater than that which exists between a Greek mythological story as found in Homer or Hesiod and in Sophocles or Euripides. Indeed, Kalidasa's Sakuntala is as different from the Sakuntala of the Mahabharata as is Tennyson's Oenone from the original Achaean maiden. A very striking example of the contrast is furnished by Bhavabhuti's treatment of the later life of Rama and Sita in his *Uttara-Rama-Charita* when set against his source in the seventh canto of the *Ramayana*. The same contrast can be seen in every play or poem in classical Sanskrit literature. Despite the difference of treatment the secular literature, together with the epics and the Puranas, has presented one solid block of Hindu mythology, which the Hindu has always regarded as the only historical background of their life and religion.

In regard to religion as distinct from mythology, secular Sanskrit literature exhibits conformity with as well as departure from the epics, and this dichotomy is extremely important for the history of Hinduism. Naturally, information about religion in literature is only incidental. It is also so in one of the epics, the *Ramayana*. The *Mahabharata*, however, contains more information and presents a very full picture of the life of the sages in the hermitages. In both, the religious rites are of the Vedic type, but none of them refer to temples or image worship. The secular books, when they present religion, describe Vedic rituals as well as image worship in temples.

To be more specific, when the subjects of the poems and plays of classical Sanskrit literature are the stories from mythology and legend, the religious doctrines and practices described conform to the older ritualistic system of Hinduism, and neither temples nor image worship is introduced, although when these books were written these certainly existed. The only description I have read in classical Sanskrit literature of a king of the epic cycle being represented as worshipping before an image in a shrine is of Nala in *Naishadha Charita*. But this work is very late, and the exception found in it is not significant. The earlier poets seem to have been aware that to introduce temples and image worship in the stories taken from the epics would be an anachronism.

On the other hand, when the story belongs to the age of the poet, the cults and rituals of his own times are not excluded. This difference of treatment is exhibited by the same writer. For instance, in Bhavabhuti's *Uttara-Rama-Charita*, which adapts a story from the *Ramayana*, there is no reference whatever to temples or images. But in the same poet's *Malati-Madhava*, whose plot is contemporaneous with the writer, temples of Siva and Kali as well as their cults are found. Besides, in the prologues and introductions of plays and poems, in which the poets speak for themselves and for their age, they give expression to current doctrines. For example both in his *Sakuntala* and *Raghuvamsa* Kalidasa invokes Siva as the monotheistic deity of the Saiva cult, and not as the Siva of mythology.

To sum up, in dealing with religion, classical Sanskrit literature conforms to the inscriptions which are concerned with actual historical events. At the same time, it must not be forgotten that the more elaborate Hindu inscriptions are also literature in their way, and not simply official records of historical deeds, achievements, conquests, or gifts of the monarchs. In fact, in form they are the epigraphic counterparts of poetry in the books. All the major inscriptions are in verse, and they employ the same diction and figures of speech as are found in classical Sanskrit literature.

Conclusions from the Historical Evidence

The information provided by any one of the five classes of historical evidence on Hinduism considered in this chapter, is not sufficient on its own, or for that matter in combination with others, to permit the construction of a full picture of the religion, although these are the only data which prove what was actually practised. But in spite of their small volume they are valuable in two ways: first, they furnish a dependable chronological framework into which the elaborate but undatable description in the religious texts can be fitted. Next, they clearly indicate what Hinduism was like in the sixth, the seventh, or the eighth century A.D. The facts from all these classes of evidence are consistent with one another, and they also create an impression of homogeneity.

But the data on the religion as it was before the fifth century A.D. are very scanty. Though this may not justify a definite view, it may be assumed that the paucity of evidence probably reflects an incubating period for Hinduism. To be more explicit, it suggests that from the third or second century B.C. to the fifth century A.D. Hinduism was evolving towards the historic form which it took at the end of the period. But the information, despite the scantiness, shows quite clearly that the Hinduism revealed by it is the same religion which is seen in its more fully developed form after the fifth century.

Now, what is even more significant for the history of Hinduism is the fact that the Hinduism which is attested by admissible historical evidence to have existed in and after the fifth century is also the Hinduism as it was in the nineteenth century, or even in my young days. In other words, the beliefs and practices of the religion have remained substantially unchanged from the fifth century to the present day. Certainly, new features have been added and some old ones modified, but nothing that existed at the beginning of the eighth century has become obsolete.

The mythology has remained virtually unchanged, for it is the same in classical Sanskrit literature and in the literature in the modern Indian languages. Only, having been brought down to a popular level in the latter, it has become more or less crude. As to beliefs and practices, Hinduism from that age down to the present shows the continuation of rituals derived from the Vedic traditions with worship according to the later cults, which have always been its basic feature. The infrastructure of the religion, if the word can be employed in this connection, has not been affected by any subsequent change. The cult of the three supreme deities, Siva, Vishnu-Krishna, and Sakti (the Mother Goddess) have flourished side by side as they are still doing. The only new development is the transformation of the cult of Vishnu-Krishna into the cult of Radha and Krishna, which is as puzzling doctrinally as it is historically. Otherwise, Hinduism has remained the same despite an immense proliferation of variations and offshoots. What can be said of trees is also true of the religion; new branches or twigs and the falling and coming of leaves do not make a new tree.

The Hinduism whose existence is established as a reality by historical evidence, is also defined as to its character by the same evidence. That is, what is known as Hinduism today is not an ancient religion. Not to speak of the Egyptian, Babylonian, or Assyrian religions, it is not even as old as the Greek religion known to Plato. As a fully developed religion, Hinduism does not belong to any time before the fifth century A.D. This is in line, however, with what is fully established in respect of the historic existence of Hindu civilization. It is not an old civilization, but contemporaneous with the late Roman and Byzantine, and thus Hindu civilization and historic Hinduism are coeval.

But it is equally certain that this historic Hinduism is not the only Hinduism which has existed in time. If nothing else proved that, the Boghazköy inscription does. Unfortunately, nothing definite is known about the Hindu gods for more than a thousand years after that, though the presumption that they continued to be worshipped is justified by the existence of the Vedic literature. Usually, some form of Vedic religion is assumed to be the most primitive form of Hinduism practised in India. But this religion as described by the specialists in this field is a reconstruction mainly from the *Rig-Veda*. The whole hangs, so to speak, in the air of very rarefied scholarship. The reconstruction itself may not be correct, and if it were, it might not be the whole of the archaic Hinduism from which the historic Hinduism was descended. Moreover, a part of the Vedic religion might have been already developed before the Aryans came to India, and, last of all, we do not know when they came and brought the religion with them. Altogether, whatever preceded the appearance of historic Hinduism must be regarded as the prehistory of the religion.

None the less, there is no doubt that this prehistory bequeathed a solid legacy which became the foundation of the historic Hinduism. It was embodied in a voluminous literature in archaic Sanskrit, and the link between the archaic and the historic remains unbroken. First, the later Hindu pantheon is a development of the Vedic, and all the gods of the older religion have remained gods in the new, and if in every case not in cults, at least in mythology. Secondly, the whole of the Vedic system of rituals has continued both in the public and the private practice of the religion. For example, the three most important events in a Hindu's life, initiation, marriage, and funeral—which naturally have a religious character—are conducted according to Vedic rituals even today.

In addition, there are two extraordinary facts which illustrate the dominance of the prehistoric or archaic Hinduism over the historic Hinduism. In the first place, it is the texts of archaic Hinduism, including even the most formal and arid treatises on ritual, which are accepted as the only revealed scriptures of Hinduism, and not even the most authoritative and venerated texts of the later cults have this status, even though they enunciate the doctrines and practices of the living cults.

Next, even more surprisingly, the only obligatory religious duties of a Hindu are those which are laid down in the old ritualistic literature. In contrast, all the doctrines and rites of the later cults are left to option. No injunction compels a Hindu to believe in any of the gods of the later cults or to go to a temple to worship them. The universal and impressive observances of the later Hinduism are dependent on a free, personal choice by all Hindus. In a word, the Hindus practise their historic religion only *ad libitum*.

It is as if the historic and living Hinduism was an elaborate cadenza to an unplayed composition, on which the Hindus have been improvising variations in near and distant keys without feeling that they are being unorthodox. This behaviour springs from their unwavering loyalty to the archaic religion embodied in the Vedas as the *fons et origo* of all their life in India.

The submission to a lost past can only be regarded as the compulsion of a fossilized historic memory, which makes them cherish the religion which they brought with them when they migrated to India. It continued to influence their life and religion unconsciously all through, and became the foundation of the superstructure which they raised in India. The nature of this heritage and foundation has to be considered next.

Note

In addition to the facts given on p. 43, names of the Mitannian kings should be taken into account. Their meaning can be determined with the help of Vedic Sanskrit, for instance: Artatama = Ṛta-dhāma (abode of Ṛta); Parsashatar = Para-sastar (chastiser of enemies); Tushratta = Tvish-ratha (he who has a splendid chariot); Aitagama = Eta-gama (he who has the gait of an antelope; Biryawaza = Vīrya-vāja (he who has valour).

Chapter Three

INDO-EUROPEAN CORE
OF HINDUISM

THE earliest form of Hinduism, which I have described as prehistoric by applying the criterion of true historicity, is really the Indo-European core of the religion, and its Indo-European character is only one aspect of the general Indo-European complexion of the life and culture, as well as the institutions, of the ancient Hindus.

The most important proof of the affiliation is, of course, linguistic — the well-established fact that all the languages of northern India, both ancient and modern, belong to the Indo-European family. Since language is the vehicle of all mental activity, it may be assumed, *a priori,* that when a people speak a language closely related to others, there will be some affinity between them and the speakers of the other languages in mental cast and basic features of cultural life.

In writing about Hindu culture some writers have under–rated the importance of the Indo-European character of the north Indian languages on the ground that the languages of south India are not Indo-European, but Dravidian. This has been a red herring across the true historical trail of Hindu civilization since the middle of the nineteenth century. Before that no Hindu of the south thought that he was in any way different from a Hindu of the north in culture and religion. In actual fact, the linguistic difference between the south and the north in India has no significance whatever for cultural history, although the geographical situations have had some.

Even the linguistic distinction has been grossly exaggerated. The south Indian languages are Dravidian only in syntax and the workaday part of the vocabulary. All the words which embody cultural notions in them are Sanskritic or translations of Sanskrit or Prakrit words into Dravidian forms, just as many German words which constitute the vocabulary of culture are only etymological equivalents of words in Greek or Latin. Besides, all along Sanskrit has been the basis of the highest culture of the south, and in recent times Sanskrit was better understood and more thoroughly studied there than in northern India. To cut the matter short, there is not a single element in the culture of any civilized human group in south India which is not Aryan-Brahmanic.

Why this pan-Indian Aryan-Brahmanic culture of peninsular India came to have a composite linguistic medium at the popular level is easily explained. The Aryan colonists from the north who took civilization to the south spoke their own language (some kind of Prakrit) originally. This is testified by the Asokan inscriptions in Mysore whose significance has already been explained. At the same time, in the south as in the north, the sacerdotal language must have been Sanskrit. But as the great mass of the aboriginal people over whom the colonists from the north dominated spoke some form of the languages which are now classified as Dravidian,[1] they too adopted these partially. There are two familiar parallels for this kind of adoption: the Normans in England took over the Anglo-Saxon grammatical forms and words, and in India the Turks, Mongols, and Persians went over to the syntax and vocabulary of Hindi. This has no relevance to the cultural situation. There are, of course, differences in the cultural expression between the north and the south. But these are due to local evolution, and are in no way more basic than the regional variations in the Hindu culture of the north. In fact, popular Hinduism in the Gangetic plain differs to a greater degree from higher Hinduism than does any form of Hinduism in the south. Linguistic differences have played no part in the cultural differentiation.

Concept of Indo-European

The really important question which arises in determining the original character of Hinduism is different, namely, whether the concept of Indo-European can be extended from language to culture, social life, and institutions. This question arises from the fact that there is no evidence for the existence of an original and undifferentiated Indo-European culture which can be regarded as the prototype of the separate cultures of the peoples speaking

[1] This supposition is justified by the fact that in central India the aboriginal Gonds speak a language which has been classified as 'Dravidian', in which case it must be close to the primitive Dravidian dialects of the south.

the Indo-European languages, viz., the Greeks, Italians, Celts, Germans, Slavs, Iranians, and Indians. But the existence of a common and original Indo-European culture, however rudimentary, is not more problematical than the existence of a common Indo-European language. Actually, the proto-Indo-European language has been reconstructed by working backwards from the words common to the historic languages of the same family, and the existence of such a language has not been denied in theory.

A linguistic ancestor like this could have had its counterpart in a cultural ancestor, and it has already been stated that its existence can be assumed a priori. But there are facts in addition to inference to establish it as a reality. A fair number of words have been found in countries from India to Ireland which embody concepts and whose Indo-European primitive forms have been determined. These show that the proto-Indo-European language was rich in ideas. Even when the words, which express ideas and are common to a number of modern historic Indo-European languages, have not been taken back to the proto-Indo-European stage, the mere fact of some of them being common to Celtic or Latin on the one hand and Sanskrit on the other would suggest a common origin for the ideas, for later borrowing is inconceivable.

Both kinds of words have been brought together by Émile Benveniste, and after studying them he has established a vocabulary of Indo-European institutions relating to economy, family, social life, power, law, and religion.[1] It is, however, Georges Dumézil who has established the common religious heritage of the Indo-European peoples. In a long series of books he has set forth the common features in the religions of the people who spoke the Indo-European languages in ancient times. No student of Hinduism today can neglect his work.

When trying, however, to establish the basic Indo-European character of Hinduism, it is necessary to be very clear about the classes of evidence on which the demonstration is to rest. I am depending on three kinds of facts: first, words of the Hindu religious vocabulary which either go back to the proto-Indo-European language or have analogues in European languages; secondly, certain notions and concepts in Hinduism which could not have originated in the geographical environment which India provides but could only have come from some cold region; lastly,

[1] Émile Benveniste, *Le Vocabulaire des institutions indo-européennes*, 2 vols. (1969).

certain rituals and beliefs in Hinduism which show a clear similarity with those of the Greeks, Romans, Celts, Germans, Scandinavians, or Slavs.

Religious Vocabulary

To begin then with the linguistic facts. A number of basic words of Hinduism, like words denoting personal relationships and certain other features of human life, go back even to the oldest proto-Indo-European stage, when the separate languages of the different branches of the Indo-Europeans had not appeared. Coming to the differentiated stage, Sanskrit shows closer affinity with two Western groups than with the other Indo-European languages. It has been recognized for a long time that the Celtic and Italic groups on the one hand and the Indo-Iranian on the other have a number of common words in respect of liturgy and ritual. The connection between the Indian and the Western world is best illustrated by the words for 'king', whose office was a quasi-religious institution. It is *ri* in Hiberno-Celtic, *rix* in Gallo-Celtic (as in Vercingetorix, 'warrior king'), *rex* in Latin, and *rāj (an)* in Sanskrit.

These words have been taken back to a reconstructed Indo-European root *reg*, meaning 'to move in a straight line', with the extension 'to direct in a straight line, lead, rule', and from this a lengthened-grade form *rēg*, meaning 'tribal king' has been reconstructed in the old Indo-European. All this is inference from the usually accepted etymology of the Latin word *rex*. It is supposed to be derived from the verb *regere*, 'to direct', from which *rectus*, etc., are also derived. This would connect the idea of kingship with the notion of order in the universe, which in Sanskrit is *r̥ta*. But in Sanskrit the true derivation was lost, and the word *rāj (an)*, instead of being connected with *rta*, was derived by Sanskrit grammarians and lexicographers from the verbal root *rāj*, which means 'to shine'. That is, the word for 'king' was assimilated in its verbal significance to the word for 'god', namely, *deva*, which is the noun form of the root *div*, 'to shine'.

But such general similarities are not all. There are more specific religious words which are homologous in Sanskrit and the old European languages. The most important of these is, of course, the primary word for 'god', which in Sanskrit is *deva*. It goes back to proto-Indo-European times, and is descended from one of the most firmly established verbal roots of the original Indo-European language. This root is *deiw*, meaning 'to shine', and the word for a god is *deiwos*, meaning 'those who shine'. The word survived in Germanic as *Tiwaz*, in Old English as *Tiw* or *Tig*, and in Old Norse as *Tyr*. In Sanskrit, *deva*, Latin *deus*, and Greek *theos* the old form of the word is supposed to have remained virtually unchanged. Between Greek and Sanskrit there is the well-known homologue between *Zeus pater* and *Dyaus pitr*.

Equally well established is the Indo-European character of one of the most important words in Hindu ritual, namely, *hav (an)*, which means 'to pour libations', and from which the word *hotr* — the priest who pours the libation — is derived. The original Indo-European root for pouring is *gheu*, which has given *khein* to Greek, *fundere* to Latin, and *geotan* to Old English.

A third important word in the Hindu religious vocabulary is *sraddhā*, which means 'faith' and from which the word *srāddha*, the Hindu religious ceremony of showing respect to dead ancestors, has come, and this word is also Indo-European. Its Latin homologue is *credere*, 'to believe', of which *credo* is the most familiar derivative. The Sanskrit word has its corresponding form in Avestan, it is *zrazda*, and bears the same meaning. Even the word *Veda* goes back to the Indo-European root which in its various forms have given 'wisdom' and 'wit' to English, 'vision' to English as well as to the Romance languages, and *idea* to Greek. These examples should be enough to illustrate the descent of the Hindu religious vocabulary from the original Indo-European language as it was before the different groups of the dialects developed.

Worship of Light

I shall next consider the derivation of two of the most basic features of the Hindu religious consciousness which could not have originated in India, but must have come from some cold region, as I have already stated; or to be more specific, from the assumed original habitat of the people who spoke the Indo-European languages, that is, the Eurasian plain from the Danube to the Volga. These features are worship of light and worship of fire.

An ecstatic attitude to light is the most striking feature of the most rarefied religious sentiment of the Hindus. It might be called mysticism in a loose way. Again and again we find an exultant veneration of light, in which light is identified with *Atman*, the Oversoul, which is the final reality or even the only real existence, and light is regarded as the only manifestation accessible to the senses of an entity which otherwise is attributeless. The best-known example of this feeling is the prayer in the *Brihadaranyaka Upanishad*:

> A-sato mā sad gamaya,
>   tamaso mā jyotir gamaya,
>   mṛtyor mā(a)mṛtam gamaya.

> Lead me from non-being to being,
> Lead me from darkness to light,
> Lead me from death to immortality.
>
> *Br. Up.* 3.28

And certainly the most exultant and beautiful identification of *Atman* with light is to be found in the famous verse of the *Katha Upanishad*:

> Na tatra suryo bhāti, na candra-tārakan-
>   nema vidyuto bhānti, kuto(a)yamagniḥ,
> tameva bhāntam anubhāti sarvam-
>   tasya bhāsā sarvam idam vibhāti.

> There the sun shines not, nor the moon and stars,
> Nor those lightnings, not to speak of fire,
> It's only when he shines that after him shine all,
> It is his refulgence which makes all things shine.

This answer is given in reply to a question whether the *Atman* itself shines or only reflects light received from other sources. Simply put, the statement means that the Oversoul does not need to be lighted up by any known source of light, but is its own source of light and all else only reflects its light. There is an extraordinary resonance in this verse, and it convinces not by the meaning of the words alone, but by the passion with which they seem to be charged. In contrast, Saṃkara's comment on this verse in his *Vashya* of the Upanishad is pedestrian construing. Clearly, by his time the exultant mysticism of the old Aryan had become mere philosophizing or even logic-chopping.

The actual Sanskrit words employed in referring to light also have a deep significance. The common Sanskrit word for light is *aloka*, 'that by which one sees'. It is not used in religious contexts, where the words are *jyoti* or *bhas,* which mean the radiance or refulgence of light, i.e. its dazzling luminosity. The employment of the word *jyoti* without any philosophical association is also found in the *Rig-Veda* and other Vedas.

Such a sense of light and the elaboration of this sensation into a spiritual experience could never have originated in India, where light becomes glare by eight o'clock in the morning. In northern India, the region in which Hindu culture reached its full development, even at morning and evening light is only soft, and never luminous. The whole idea of refulgence as a source of joy would be foreign to India. One would naturally associate it with the aurora borealis. Perhaps such an association of ideas made a great and very conservative Hindu scholar put forward the theory that the Rig-Vedic Aryans had come from the Arctic region, which was absurd. But the feeling could be acquired further south, though only in a climatic zone where snow falls. I realized this from a personal experience, and I hope an account of it will not be considered more irrelevant to a theory of the origin of the worship of light by the Hindus than Newton's observation of the falling apple and Watts's of the boiling kettle.

At the end of 1970 I was working on this book in a village near Oxford, and on Christmas night it began to snow. Till then I had never seen snow, and I felt excited. Up to bed-time snow fell only in flakes like down, and the fall was not heavy. But when I woke up the next morning very early I saw a very bright light coming through a chink in the curtains, as if there was a brilliant moonlit night outside. The illusion of moonlight was so strong that I ran to the south side of the house to look at the setting full moon, completely forgetting that I had seen the crescent moon the previous day and knew that the new moon was only two days away.

Of course, there was no moon, and the sky was one unbroken pall of grey. No light was coming from anywhere above, for neither the house nor the cypress before it was casting any shadow. At last I realized that the light was rising from the ground, which was covered with snow. It was a mass of dazzling white, and its radiance was stretching to the sky. I wondered how a reflecting surface could throw up light when there was none perceptible to the eye from any source above. But the light must have been present in the sky, and the snow-covered ground was reflecting it with an incredible intensity. The snow seemed to have converted the earth, which is only a reflector of light, into a source of light in itself.

This refulgence, which was the product of a strange reversal of roles between the sky and the earth, at once gave me an explanation of the feeling for light in our Upanishads. The realization was so decisive that I at once sent an article to a paper in India offering an explanation of the verses of the Upanishad I have quoted above. I put forward the theory that the Indo-Aryans had formulated their association between light and religion from what they saw on the snow-covered plains of their original home, probably in south Russia, and took it with them to India where it was an intrusion.

There is also in Vedic literature another beautiful evocation of light, which is poetic and religious at the same time. This is found in all the descriptions of Ushas (personified dawn), corresponding to Aurora in Latin and Eos in Greek, as the anthropomorphic embodiment of the first appearance of daylight. Now, the physical phenomenon as described in a personified form in the *Rig-Veda* is not normally seen in northern India, where dawn is a reddish flush without radiance. Something like the Vedic dawn can be seen in Bengal and other parts of India where the monsoons are strong. But the Vedas were put in their final shape almost certainly in the Punjab, or in the region between the Sutlej and the Jumna, and not in eastern India. Thus it would seem that the image of the Vedic Ushas was brought into India by the Aryans from a region where such mornings are a visible climatic phenomenon.

There is, however, one association with light in Vedic literature which must be an Indian extension of the original notion of light derived from a cold northern region. It is the very unexpected association of light with night. In the religious and ethical writings of the Hindus darkness *(tamas)* is associated with all that is low and degraded in human nature, and *tamas* is declared to be the lowest *guna* or attribute of nature. But this *tamas* is not an attribute of night. In the religious consciousness of the Hindus there is no place for the Christian notion that night is the time when the powers of evil are abroad.

The Sanskrit word for night is *rātri*. In a personified form, night as Ratri is described in Vedic literature as the sister of Ushas

(Dawn), who is the destroyer of darkness. As the *Rig-Veda* has it, 'the two are twins *(yāmia)*, and are robed in different colours — for one bright and for the other black. The Dark and the Red are two sisters *(svasārau)*.' This combination is deliberate, and not accidental or casual. In the *Rig-Veda* the word *svasr* (sister) is applied thirteen times to deities, and in eleven cases it is applied either to Ushas or to Ratri. These are an inseparable couple. In the dual *svasārau*, the word is applied five times, three times to Ushas and Ratri, and twice to the earth and the sky. Both Ushas and Ratri belong indivisibly to *Rta*, the righteous order of the universe.

The occurrence of another word is also significant. It is *Vibhāvari*, 'the radiant'. In the earlier contexts it means 'dawn', but was later extended to stand almost exclusively for the starlit sky. Those who have seen the starlit sky of northern India will have no difficulty in understanding how a word first applied to dawn came to be used for night. At first it stood for light at its most luminous, and afterwards for light at its softest.

Last of all, attention must be drawn to a significant contrast. In the whole of Sanskrit literature there is no pleasant association with the sun's rays or light. The word for direct sunlight, which is connected only with heat, is *raudra*, which as an adjective means angry, fierce, terrible. What is always emphasized is the oppressiveness of the heat of the sun. A woman who has exposed herself to the sun is described as a wilted flower. That the Hindu wedding can never take place in daytime, is surely connected with the general attitude to daylight. This is a product of India, and the Sun god of Hinduism, who is drawn by seven horses, is a god from a different world.

Worship of Fire

Another feature of Hinduism which connects it with a cold climate is the supreme place held in it by fire. This is particularly noticeable in the earliest stage. In the *Rig-Veda* the hymns to Agni, i.e. personified and deified fire (= *ignis* in Latin, *ognji* in Old Slavonic, and reconstructed as *egnis* in the original Indo-European), exceed those addressed to all the other gods with the sole exception of Indra. Agni derives his importance from his connection with sacrifices. But the place fire occupies in ritual will be dealt with later, when considering the similarities between Hindu and Roman religious rituals. Here only the Hindu's idea of fire and his veneration for it will be described.

For man everywhere fire has three aspects: the destructive, the useful, and the comforting. The most obvious of these is the first, which must have been perceived before the others, and the Hindus were perfectly conscious of that. Some Rig-Vedic verses speak of fire's awful anger, and describe how it shears off great forests as if with a razor. But this aspect became submerged in the general feeling of the beneficent utility of fire as a means of production.

The *Kausitaki Brahmana* of the *Rig-Veda* (1.1) actually describes how the dangerous and the benign aspect of fire were separated. At first, the book says, both the gods and men were in the world. But in migrating to heaven the other gods asked Agni to remain on earth to be the overseer of the world on their behalf. Agni questioned how that could be since he was dangerous and therefore was not honoured by men. What happened after that I give in the actual words of the *Brahmana*:

> The gods said, 'The dread forms of thee as such we deposit apart, and then thou be here for man with that form of thine which is auspicious, helpful, and worthy of sacrifice.' Then in the waters they placed his blowing form, in the wind the purifying, in the sun the bright. Then with his auspicious, helpful, and sacrificial forms he burnt here for men. These indeed are the forms of Agni.

It is difficult to discover what personified and deified fire is not from the references to him in Vedic and other early religious texts of the Hindus. Agni is the immortal who has taken up his abode with mortals as their guest; he is the domestic priest who comes with dawn; he is the most adorable of sacrificers; he is a great sage; he is the wise man among the foolish; he is father, king, ruler, banner, and outward manifestation; he is a brilliant guest in every house; he is friendly to mankind and despises no man; some of his worshippers claim a hereditary friendship with him. As a god, fire is addressed with a bewildering variety of admiring and affectionate appellations.

Agni's relations with his worshippers is always benevolent. His worshippers prosper, they become wealthy, and they live long. Agni is the deliverer and friend of man, the man who comes to him with fine horses, gold, and a chariot full of riches. He watches with a thousand eyes over the man who brings him food and nourishes him with libations. He gives riches, which he abundantly commands. He also confers immortality and is its guardian and Lord.

The highest godly functions are assigned to Agni. He is called the divine monarch, and is declared to be as strong as Indra. His greatness exceeds that of heaven, and all the worlds. He knows the recesses of heaven, the divine ordinations, and the races of gods and men, as well as the secrets of mortals.

All these are only a selection from the attributes of Agni singled out in the Hindu scriptures for praise. Such an enthusiasm and admiration for fire could not have been the product of a tropical country. The Hindu ascetics who sit on fire to inflict self-motification on themselves exhibit the natural, geographically conditioned approach to it. The old religious attitude of the Hindus to fire is akin to that of the Romans and Persians. In all of them this must have come from a common habitat.

Ritual

The elaborate rituals of the Vedic religion, which have continued in a more or less modified form down to this day and which constitute the most obligatory part of the religion of the Hindus, furnish the most decisive evidence for its Indo-European character. However, these cannot be traced to their origins, but can be demonstrated at one remove by comparing the Brahmanic rituals with the Roman. This in no way weakens the evidence because in respect of ritual both the Hindus and the Romans were extremely conservative and tenacious, so that even when the beliefs and cults were transformed, the rites remained true to type. Moreover, there can be no question of the similarities being the result of later contacts. These must be referred back to a common origin in a prehistoric past.

The parallelisms are very striking, and the first of these is seen in the rite of sacrifice. The *yajna* is the major rite in Hinduism, so is *sacrificium* in Roman religion. In Hinduism the Creator himself began the work of creation with a sacrifice. The purpose of sacrifice among both the peoples was the same. Primarily, it was to obtain and secure worldly welfare of every kind. But, in addition, there is in both the idea of some kind of magical efficacy, and, above all, the notion of consecration. The Latin word *sacrificare* exactly means that, i.e. 'to make something sacred'. Though the Brahmanic word does not mean the same thing, the texts throughout suggest that sacrifice is the means of raising all that is profane to the sacred plane. It is not only that the status of the sacrificial victim is changed by it, this happens also with the status of the man on whose behalf the sacrifice is performed. The victim establishes the connection between the profane and the sacred, and the sacrificing priest represents both the sacrificer and the gods.

There is also a striking similarity between the Brahmanic and the Roman sacrifice as regards the species of animals to be sacrificed, with only one difference. The sacrificial animals of the Hindus, arranged according to their importance in respect of the result from the sacrifice, are the following: man, horse, bull, ram, and goat. For animal sacrifice the Romans had the horse, bull, ram, and hog (instead of goat). The Roman sacrifice of *suovetaurilia* was similar to the Vedic *Sautramani* sacrifice to Indra.[1] There was some difference between the Hindus and the Romans in respect of human sacrifice.

In Hindu rituals a man was sacrificed because he was the first among animals, and thus he had precedence over the other animals.[2] The Romans excluded human sacrifice from the national cults. But there is historical evidence for the practice among them. The last human sacrifice in public in Rome took place in 216 B.C. after the disaster of Cannae, where a Roman army was annihilated by Hannibal. Usually, at Roman human sacrifices a couple (a man and a woman) were sacrificed. But in 216, due to the gravity of the crisis, two couples—two Gauls and two Greeks—were sacrificed. It is believed by scholars that the practice continued secretly, and in any case it was formally interdicted by a *senatus consultum* of 97 B.C. But popular superstition regarded the vanquished gladiator as the sacrificed animal. In Hinduism, human sacrifice in more than one form continued till perhaps the middle of the nineteenth century, and during British

---

[1] The comparison is elaborate, for which see Dumézil, *Tarpeia* (1947), pp. 117–58.

[2] *Satapatha Brahmana* has it: 'Sa etān panca paśun apaśyat—puruṣam, aśvam, gām, avim, ajam . . . Puruṣam prathamam alabhate, puruṣo hi prathamaḥ paśunām . . .' There was human sacrifice in both Norse and German religions.

rule common people would never believe that a bridge was successfully built without human sacrifice.[1]

The second parallel between Hindu and Roman ritual is to be found in the separation between private and public rites. In Rome the two were placed in two categories: *sacra privata* and *sacra publica*. Among the Hindus the injunctions for the domestic rites were laid down in the *Grihya Sutras* (from *griha = domus*) and for the public in the *Srauta Sutras*. In their different ways both were equally important. The domestic rites ensured the safety and welfare of the home in both societies, and in both it was the head of the family—*grihapati* of the Hindus and *pater familias* of the Romans—who was in charge of these duties. It is unnecessary to give details of the public rites. They were equally ceremonious and gorgeous in both societies.

The object of propitiation in both were the great gods of each people, so far as the public rites were concerned, and the procedure varied for the different gods as also did the names of the sacrifices. In the private rites the objects of the sacrifices were the gods or spirits who were specially associated with private life. They were not identical in the two societies, but their nature was similar. The Roman private sacrifices were concerned with the *Penates, Lares, Genius*, and also *Manes*. The Hindu domestic rites were five in number: they were called the 'five sacrifices', and were performed for five classes of beings: the gods, all living creatures, the ancestors, men as a special group of living creatures, and the Vedas, as personified things. All these had to be offered oblations with unfailing and meticulous regularity. The performance of the domestic rites could be a heavy burden, but neither the Hindus nor the Romans could neglect them for this reason. As the Romans said, the *privatus* who failed became *impius*.

Moreover, both societies laid the strongest possible emphasis on the correctness of the invocations, utterance of the incantations faultlessly, appropriate gestures, and also adornment of the sacri-

[1] I am not speaking here of human sacrifice as seen among the aboriginals or criminal tribes and communities, but of the sacrifice in connection with certain cults by either the Tantric Kapaliks or by very wealthy people to ensure the permanence and increase of their wealth. As to the association with bridge building, see Kipling's story of *The Bridge-Builders*. In any case, deaths by accident during construction were always regarded as a *quid pro quo* exacted by the divine river. The lascar Peroo said in the story: 'As for the bridge, so many have died in the building that it cannot fail.'

ficial animal. In Rome the animal was often decorated with bands and had the horns gilded, among the Hindus it had to be bathed and decorated with vermilion and garlands. (*paśum snāpitam sinduramālyādyalaṃkṛtam*).The place of sacrifice, whether permanent or temporary, was sacred to both the peoples, and at the time of sacrifice, among both, there had to be silence (*Favete linguis!*) or music.

Another parallel between Hinduism and Roman religion is seen in the domestic religious obligations laid down by both. These were, first, the performance of a series of prescribed rites for the main events of a man's life from birth to death, and, secondly, the service of regular oblations to the departed ancestors. With both the peoples, the first group of rites were almost sacraments. With both, a period of seven or eight days after the birth of a child in the family were unclean days, and a purification ceremony was performed at the end of the period. Among the Romans, as among the Hindus, the initiation and marriage were very important. The Romans had these features in their wedding ceremony: joining of hands; invocation of the gods of the household and of the conjugal goddesses, especially Juno; sacrifice; and circumambulation of the altar presenting the right side. These are similar to what is done in the Hindu ceremony. The Hindus had ten of these ceremonies, some details of which will be given later.

As to dead ancestors, they had to be remembered in both societies with analogous rites, which consisted in offering oblations at regular intervals, and also on important occasions. For instance, no Hindu wedding could take place unless it had been preceded by oblations to the dead ancestors, which were known as *ābhyudayika*. Among the Hindus, as among the Romans, the continuity of the service to the dead had to be maintained from generation to generation, and therefore the continuation of the male line of descent was essential. The Romans in their attitude to their dead ancestors always assumed that the *manes* weighed on the living with the burden of an undefined disquiet. This was the case with the Hindus as well. That, due to some cause not within their control, the oblations for the ancestors might cease, was a terror with the departed as well as their living descendants. This was called the calamity of *pindalopa*.

But the most striking resemblance between Hinduism and the Roman religion is to be found in regard to fire — in the ritual obligation to maintain fire both in public and private life. For the Romans, the hearth, which they called *focus*, was the centre of the home. Its shape was round, and it is supposed that this conformed to the shape of the primitive mud hut. From this the modern meaning of the word as 'a central point' has been derived. There was also a portable hearth called the *foculus*.

The hearth among the Romans was the most holy and necessary feature of the home. Its fire was regarded as divine. It was the duty of the master of the house to maintain the fire in the hearth continuously, and it could not go out without harm for the family. Furthermore, every day and for every meal there had to be sacrifices to it. At the new moon, first quarter, and the full moon, it was festooned with flower garlands. At night the fire was covered with cinders and re-lighted in the morning.

Among the ancient Hindus, too, the establishment and maintenance of the household fire was a strict religious obligation. The inauguration of a new household, which naturally was coincident with marriage, was marked by the lighting of a new fire by its master, the newly married man. He thus became *sāgnika* (possessed of fire) and attained to the status of a householder *(grihapati)*, recognized both by religion and society. The fire had to be maintained perpetually, and if the householder went on a journey the responsibility for doing that passed to his representative. On the death of a householder, his son re-lighted it. In the home oblations were offered on it.

In both societies the public fires were equally important. Among the Hindus the whole contract between men and the gods rested on the fire sacrifices. Their cessation meant its collapse, and as a result dire calamities in the worldly order. In ancient times the Hindu kings saw to it that the great public sacrifices were performed frequently and with due splendour. Among the Romans it was the Republic which had this responsibility. The State had its eternal fire, which was tended by the Vestals. It could not go out without endangering Rome. There were in addition fires in or before the temples.

There was also a close relation between the public and the private fire among both peoples. The two fires could never be disassociated. This connection was most clearly seen in the fire sacrifices of the Hindus. The arrangements for the *yajnas* in the open were strictly prescribed. The two fires had to be at two ends of an east-to-west axis, and the public fire was at the eastern end, the distance between the two depending on the caste of the sacrificer. The public fire was called the *āhavaniya* and the private *gārhapatya*. In this arrangement there was also a third but minor fire, placed to the south of the axis and called the *dakshināgni*. The Romans had the first two fires in the same form, and the third in a somewhat different form.

The shape of the altars for the fires was both important and significant. In the Hindu arrangement the private fire was circular and the public rectangular, and the southern fire was semicircular, with the diametrical line to the north.

The Romans maintained this convention of shapes, as was seen in its most striking exhibition in the Forum Romanum. The eternal Vestal fire was the private fire of the whole nation, and therefore its temple was circular. Built under Augustus, reconstructed by Julia Domna, wife of Septimius Severus, and recently restored, it stands adjacent to the Atrium of the Vestals in the Forum. The public fires were in or just outside the great rectangular temples. The shapes and arrangements were symbolic. Among the Hindus it was explicitly stated: the private fire was the earth and this world, and the public the sky and the other world. The explanation was the same in the case of the Romans.

Religious Concepts and the Pantheon

The Indo-European character of Hindu religious concepts can be demonstrated by means of comparisons, not only with Rome, but all the Indo-European peoples before they adopted Christianity as their religion. The subject is, however, very large, and is, in fact, the whole content of comparative mythology combined with comparative religion, each of which has an immense literature. Here only the most important common elements will be set forth, and that, too, has to be done very briefly.

The most primitive Indo-European notion of a divine order is perhaps the idea of the bright sky as a non-anthropomorphic deity. The Greek Zeus Pater, the Latin Jupiter, and the Sanskrit Dyaus Pitr, all embody it. The original Persian religion also appears to have been of this kind, to judge by what Herodotus had to say about it, and on this subject he was hardly likely to have gone wrong. He wrote:

I am aware that the Persians practise the following customs. They are not in the habit of erecting images, temples, or altars; indeed, they charge those who do so with folly, because, I suppose they do not like the Greeks hold the gods to be of human shape. Their practice is to climb the highest mountains and sacrifice to Zeus, by which name they call the whole circle of the sky. They sacrifice also to the sun and moon, the earth, fire, and water, and the winds. These and these alone are their original objects of worship.[1]

A. B. Cook in his great book *Zeus* observes:

Personally I should not refuse the term *religious* to the attitude of reverential fear with which I suppose early man to have approached the animate sky. Indeed, it would not be absurd to maintain that the pre-anthropomorphic conception was not in some respects the higher, because more true than the later anthropomorphism.[2]

The description of Herodotus suggests that the Persians shared the general Indo-European attitude of regarding all natural phenomena as divine. This feeling is certainly responsible for creating many gods of the Hindu pantheon. The deification of natural phenomena, which is so pronounced a feature of Hinduism, was also present among the Greeks. All Indo-European peoples, including the Greeks, Hindus, and others, deified not only the great natural phenomena, but also smaller ones like rivers and streams.[3] This lies behind not only the Hindu pantheism, but also the animism which is so strongly felt in the religion.

In one respect early Hinduism, i.e. Vedic Brahmanism which continued as a parallel strand in later Hinduism, went back to an older stratum of the Indo-European religion than did Greek or Roman religion. This is seen in the fact that the earliest Hindus knew neither temples nor images, and were like the Germans in respect of giving locations on earth to their gods and rites. They always worshipped in sacred or sanctified places. The Germans also did that. Tacitus related that they did not confine their gods within walls, and did not make images of them, but consecrated forests and groves, and invested them with that hidden power (*secretum*), which they saw only with the reverence of their eyes.

[1] Herodotus Bk. I, Ch. 131 (Cook's translation).
[2] A. B. Cook, *Zeus* (1914), vol. I, p. 13.
[3] On a Syracusan gold coin of *c.* 460 B.C. the river Arethusa is shown as a goddess. In the same manner the rivers Yamuna and Ganga in India had their iconography.

The Romans and the Greeks also had these feelings, but since they had taken over temples and image worship from the Egyptians and the peoples of Asia, the deification of nature remained in their religion as a secondary, but also a living element.

The shift from the non-anthropomorphic, deified nature to the anthropomorphic took place naturally. It transformed the deified sky, the sky god, and endowed it with a special relationship with the earth as mother. And the process was extended to form an anthropomorphic pantheon. The whole process is similar in Hinduism, Roman religion, and Greek religion, but its date cannot be determined.

The completed process is to be seen among all the Indo-European groups, namely, the Hindus, Greeks, Romans, Germans, and Scandinavians, all of whom have analogous pantheons. The analogy is indisputable, but it would be a mistake to try to establish very precise identifications. It is well known, even though traditionally identifications between the Greek and Roman gods and goddesses were accepted, that they are not exactly the same. Zeus is not wholly Jupiter, Hera Juno, Athena Minerva, Hermes Mercury, and so on. The Vedic pantheon presents clear parallels with the Greek, Roman, German, and Scandinavian, but these cannot be regarded as identifications. For instance, Zeus, Jupiter, Odinn, Wotan, Thor present similarities with Indra, but they are also different in important respects. The divergences are certainly due to particular evolution after the dispersion of the original community.

However, as anthropomorphic gods, they present common human characteristics, irrespective of the pantheon to which they belong. All the gods and goddesses are heroic men and women, with all the virtues and failings, especially amorousness, of the heroic age. They are intoxicated with power, domineering, jealous, combative, sensual. These traits are to be found as much in the *Mahabharata* as in the *Iliad*. But in respect of the character and behaviour of the gods the picture drawn in the Hindu epics and Puranas is closer to that found in Norse mythology than in the Greek or Roman. There are strange analogies in details. Freyja, the goddess of fertility and very lascivious as such, exhibits an excitability as the mistress of Odinn which is like that of Indrani (Sachi) with Indra in the *Rig-Veda*. She also rides in a chariot drawn by cats, which is symbolic because they are so prolific. The

Hindu goddess of fertility, Sasthi, also rides them. There is also an analogy between the story of the seizure of mead by Odinn and the story of the quarrel between Indra and the Nasatyau, which was ended by cutting a monster named Mada (which means wine or alcohol) to make alcohol, just as the blood of Kvasir was brewed into mead. It is only in the Indo-European pantheons that the divinities have these aristocratic human characteristics. In the Mesopotamian and Egyptian pantheons, and especially the latter, the gods and goddesses have an altogether different character: they are supra-human, majestic, inscrutable, grave, and yet benign with a faint suggestion of a smile on their lips.

But the basic oneness of all the Indo-European pantheons is to be found not in these similarities in details, which are numerous, but in the structure and organization of the society and hierarchy of the gods and goddesses. In regard to this I have fully accepted the theory of Dumézil that all these pantheons have a tripartite organization reflecting the organization of the Indo-European communities. Taking the social organization of the ancient Hindus as the full development of the original Indo-European pattern, he says that all these societies had a tripartite structure, consisting of two classes, the priests and the warriors, and the masses, i.e. the people in general represented in Hindu society by the caste known as the Vaisyas, who carried on the general economic activities of the society.[1] As can be easily seen, this division is functional. In the same way, according to Dumézil's theory, the pantheon, i.e. the society of the gods, is tripartite or divided into three classes — the sovereign gods who control the world by magical powers, the warrior gods who fight the demons and other enemies of the divine and human orders, and the economic gods who maintain the economic activities and also ensure the continuation of the species. Dumézil has worked out this pattern in all the known Indo-European societies and their pantheons.

His theory has been rejected by some scholars, more especially in Britain. But the rebuttal is very unconvincing, and it does not

---

[1] The worst mistake about Hindu social organization is to regard the Vaisya caste as a trading caste on the strength of present practice. In the *Dharma Sastras* and certainly also in practice in ancient times the Vaisyas pursued three vocations, namely, agriculture, trade, and cattle-raising (*krishi, vanijya, goraksha*, as the *Gita* has it.) Even the name *Vaisya* is derived from *Vis* which means 'the populace in general'.

seem to me that Dumézil's opponents have taken full stock of his theory. Certain scholars have pointed out that a tripartite division of society is not exclusive to the Indo-Europeans, but can be found among other people. This is only to draw attention to the obvious. The really important consideration is that the three divisions are worked out most thoroughly and have remained most stable in the Indo-European societies. It is seen not only in the organization of Hindu society but also in the organization of the British parliament on the basis of three orders, which is paralleled in the French States General. Even more important is the fact that it is only in Indo-European societies that the entire pantheon reflects human society. Nowhere else has any pantheon been created in the image of the worshipping society. In the Hindu pantheon of even a late age these three classes of gods were grouped into classes known as the Adityas, Rudras, and Vasus.

It is only in the association of a god with a particular function that the Indo-European societies differ, and not in the fundamental grouping. For instance, Zeus and Jupiter present features analogous to those of Indra, but they cannot be regarded as the Greek or Roman counterparts of the Hindu god even in their earliest forms. Their later evolution was wholly different. But the distribution of the functions among the individual gods is the result of a very complex process, conditioned by many unknown factors. What cannot be ignored is the broad unity of the patterns of the pantheons. This is analogous in all of them. And indeed no serious scholar has disputed the original Indo-European character of Hinduism. But its evolution after the arrival of the Aryans in India has been differently viewed. So, that process has to be considered by way of concluding the discussion of the historical development of Hinduism.

Chapter Four

WHAT HAPPENED IN INDIA

TO conclude the historical investigation of Hinduism an attempt will be made to indicate in a very sketchy outline the evolution which the religion of the Indo-European colonists underwent in India from their first arrival down to the Muslim conquest. This is a period of something like two thousand years, the first thousand of which must be regarded as prehistoric. In speculating about the development of Hinduism during this stage the historian has no archaeological data, but only a body of texts attributed to this period. But it must be remembered that this account is wholly conjectural. Besides, the account of the development of Hinduism offered here is more concerned with the types of religious experience than with chronology.

The first difficulty is to discover what the very starting point was. With what beliefs and practices did the Aryans come to India? The conventional answer to the question is that they had the Vedic religion. Now, the so-called Vedic religion is itself only a theoretical reconstruction from the four Vedic *Samhitas* and the *Brahmanas*, and it cannot be regarded as a coherent religion practised at any particular point of time. Even the *Rig-Veda* by itself shows a good deal of stratification. Some of the beliefs found in it could only have originated after the settlement of the Aryans in India, others belonged to their pre-Indian existence, and were already obsolete when they came into the country. The whole of the Vedic corpus shows greater heterogeneity. The *Rig-Veda* suggests rituals which are not identical with those in the formal ritualistic treatises, the *Brahmanas*, and the *Brahmanas* differ among themselves. So the Vedic corpus must be regarded as a canonical embodiment of beliefs and practices which had developed over a fairly long period of time.

Nor should the ideas and rites which have been described as the Indo-European core of the religion in the last chapter be taken as the starting point, for the account consisted of only a selection made from features found in the texts as well as practices which could be traced back inferentially to a hypothetical Indo-European past, and which at the same time remained living for ages in India.

Nevertheless, the Vedic literature certainly gives some idea of the beliefs and practices of Hinduism in the early centuries of Aryan colonization. This primitive Hinduism is very different from what is revealed by the historical evidence summarized in Chapter 2. But this transformation, fundamental as it might seem, is neither unnatural nor exceptional in the history of religion. The archaic Roman religion was not the Roman religion of the Empire; Buddhism did not remain the simple teaching of Buddha; the Zoroastrian cult is not the creation of Zarathustra; Taoism is not the doctrine of Lao-tse; finally, Christianity *today* contains much more than the original teaching of Jesus and even that of the Apostles. Hinduism underwent far more drastic changes. The only religion in the world which has remained very close to the first message of the founder is Islam.

The Way of Knowledge—its Origin

The first change that the Indo-European form of Hinduism underwent since its unknown origins was the shift from a non-anthropomorphic concept of the supreme deity to an anthropomorphic concept. This must have taken place very early, probably in Persia, because the existence of an anthropomorphic polytheism there is attested by indications which have survived in Zoroastrian literature. The change did not totally destroy the old notion of a non-anthropomorphic deity symbolized by the bright sky and daylight, but the survival took three different forms in three religions—the Greek, the Persian, and the Hindu.

The Greeks made the Zeus who was identified with the sky and daylight wholly anthropomorphic, but placed him in the ether, and gave him a special name, Zeus Aitherios. In Hellenistic art Zeus Aitherios was represented with a blue nimbus, blue globe, and blue mantle. Zeus also retained his association with light as Zeus Lykaios (connected with light rather than with wolf, though there was also a special wolf-Zeus). The Greek philosophers, however, seem to have remained attached to the idea of impersonality. Heraclitus used the term Zeus Aitherios as the equivalent of the serene sky. The impersonal idea was pursued by other philosophers in different ways, e.g. by the Stoics and the Eclectics.

D

In Persia the pre-anthropomorphic sky-god certainly became Ahura Mazda, who is ambivalent between anthropomorphism and impersonality.

The Hindus took a different line altogether. They did not abandon the pre-anthropomorphic deity at all, but put him in a parallel channel of their religious life with their anthropomorphic polytheism. This is the famous Way of Knowledge or *Gnosis* (*Jnana Marga*), in which a formless, attributeless, eternal, and infinite deity is the object of mystical contemplation. In other words, the notion of *Brahman* or *Atman* was the continuation of the old non-anthropomorphic idea, and so far as the Way of Knowledge survives among the Hindus it has remained non-anthropomorphic.

This makes the individual soul in the *Jnana Marga* basically different from what it is in Christianity. In the latter, even when liberated from the body, it remains a psychological person, an individual entity. The idea that there was a soul (*psyche* or *anima*) residing in the body and quite distinct from it, originated at the human end, and after the death of the man in whose body it was residing it became only a disembodied projection of the same human personality, which remained quite distinct from the Divine personality. The human, in fact the bodily origin of the notion of soul is clearly indicated by the words in the Christian vocabulary which stand for a non-corporeal psychological person, viz., *nephesh* in Hebrew, *ruach* in Aramaic, *pneuma* in Greek, *spiritus* in Latin, *ghost* in the old English sense. All of these had the primary meaning of breath.

Not so in the Way of Knowledge of Hinduism. In it the idea of the individual human soul originated at the cosmic end, and was a reduction of the notion of an Oversoul, which itself came from the conception of an all-pervasive non-anthropomorphic divinity. The human soul was only the microcosm of an infinite macrocosm, and its separate existence was like the confinement of a part of the atmosphere within a pot. Moreover, when it left the human body it also ceased to have any separate existence. Actually, it ceased, not only to be a psychological entity, but also to have any attributes accessible to the human mind. The conception of the soul in the rest of Hinduism is so confused and contradictory that it is hardly possible to say what it is or is not.

It is clear from the tone of its literature that the Way of Knowledge was truly religious in origin and remained religious for a long time. It may have been so in the age of the *Gita*, which proclaimed a personal God of love, for Krishna is made to reconcile the Way of Knowledge with the Way of Love. In the twelfth chapter of the book the following dialogue takes place between him and Arjuna:

> *Arjuna:* There are those who worship you with love, and there are others who worship the imperishable and unmanifest. Of these, who are the better in religious discipline?
>
> *Krishna:* I hold them to be most disciplined who worship me with supreme faith, but they also attain me who worship the imperishable, undefinable, unmanifest, omnipresent, unthinkable, immovable, and unchanging.[1]

But the mystical contemplation or realization of the imponderable *Atman* (the unmanifested ultimate reality) came to an end in religious life and passed into philosophy. The transition was completed in any case by the time of Samkara (usually placed at the beginning of the ninth century), as can be seen from the position he took about 'It' in his commentaries on the Upanishads. One example may be given. It is his interpretation of the famous stanza which describes the means of attaining the *Atman* (literally, how 'It' is *obtainable* = *labhya*). The *Mundaka Upanishad*, in which the stanza occurs, says that 'It' cannot be obtained by *pravachana* (discussion or instruction), nor by *medhā* (intellectual capacity), nor by *bahu śruta* (much hearing of the sacred texts): 'It' reveals 'Its' form *(tanu)* only to that man whom 'It' chooses *(vṛnute)*. Now, no ambiguity is left by the grammatical construction of the sentence that it is the *Atman* which both chooses and reveals. That is to say, no human effort can ensure 'Its' attainment, and whether 'It' will be realized by any human being depends on 'It' alone.

But not so for Samkara. By one of those extraordinary distortions of grammar and lexicon which is usual with him, he interprets the passage to mean that the *Atman* is attainable by a man if he is eager enough in seeking knowledge. One would not say that Samkara's opinion is only intellectual and not religious — but still,

[1] Here the purport is given. For the whole dialogue see *Gita*, 12.1–5. I give the original of the crucial lines:

> Ye tv akṣaram anirdeśyam/ avyaktaṃ paryupāsate,
> sarvatragam acintyaṃ ca/ kūṭastham acalaṃ druvam . . .
> te prāpnuvanti mām eva . . .

the *Atman* is brought within the reach of human effort, human will, and human aspiration. This is a break with the entire Upanishadic mysticism.

When this stage was reached the Way of Knowledge (*Jnana Marga*) of the Hindu religion was bound to pass out of religion, and became the preserve of philosophy. If, in spite of that, the Way did not become purely intellectual that was because, having sprung from religion, Hindu philosophy never became wholly free from it. This fact has led most students to treat Hindu philosophy as if it were a part of Hindu religious life, and to include philosophical discussion in the treatment of the religion.

Polymorphous Monotheism

Thus Vedic ritualism and Vedic mysticism seem to have continued side by side, and we know nothing of any new development until a new type of cult with Siva and Vishnu-Krishna as alternative deities is seen emerging in the first century B.C. But, though the process cannot be described, its outcome is known. When completed, it resulted in the creation of gods who were not at all like the personal gods of the Greek and Roman religions. Siva and Vishnu-Krishna of this new Hinduism are not to be compared even to the supreme gods of these two pantheons, Zeus and Jupiter. The two Hindu gods were more like the monotheistic God of the historic religions, and had some of their attributes. But there were also two very important differences. First, instead of one, there were two gods of the monotheistic type, either one of which could be chosen by a votary as his personal god. Secondly, there was no obligation on any Hindu to worship any of them: he was as free to adopt the monotheistic type of cult as he was to select the god for it. But after the adoption, which was usual in practice though not obligatory in doctrine, one or other of these gods became for the worshipper a monotheistic god in a very real sense. I would call this cult polymorphous monotheism, a very special form of monotheism created by the Hindus.

The two gods who figured in it were only minor gods in the Rig-Vedic pantheon. None the less, they supplanted its major gods, e.g. Mitra, Varuna, Indra, Vayu, or Agni. But at some stage a third divinity was added to the two, and it was the Mother Goddess (Durga or Kali), who could be chosen by the worshipper

as his special monotheistic deity. When exactly she became the
third in the polymorphous monotheism cannot be determined. In
any case, these three cults, though not obligatory, are the main
features of historic Hinduism. Of course, the Vedic rituals continued as their obligatory accompaniment. As these three cults
are described at length in the third part of the book, their evolution and character need not be discussed at this point.

But some observations might be made about the order of their
appearance. It seems certain that in this polymorphous monotheism, the cult of Siva or Saivism emerged first, and the Vishnu-
Krishna cult or Vaishnavism came afterwards as an imitation and
duplication. The earlier appearance of Siva is indicated in the
first instance by the fact that it is he alone among the Hindu gods
who is called Isa or Isvara, which means 'the Lord', and also
Mahesvara or Paramesvara, meaning 'Great Lord' or 'Supreme
Lord'. Though after its appearance the Vishnu-Krishna combination became as important a monotheistic entity as Siva,
neither Vishnu nor Krishna was ever called a rival Lord, but was
referred to as Bhagavan (conventionally translated as the 'Blessed
One'), and their followers were called Bhagavatas or Vaishnavas.

That the cult of Siva preceded that of Vishnu-Krishna seems
also to be borne out by the *Mahabharata*, whose testimony is particularly significant. It must be borne in mind that the monotheistic Vaishnava cult is not that of Vishnu alone, but of Vishnu
combined with Krishna, and this Krishna is as much the hero of
the *Mahabharata* as the Pandavas. Yet the epic throughout represents him as a man, a heroic and exceptional man, but still a
human being and not a god. What is even more significant is that
there are many passages in the book which relate incidents in
which Krishna is shown as worshipping or begging favours from
Siva. He declares himself to be a devotee of Siva as the Supreme
Lord, and sees a vision of him as the Lord of the universe which is
like the vision which Arjuna had of Krishna in the *Gita*. Furthermore, Krishna receives eight boons from Siva: (1) steadfastness
in righteousness, (2) destruction of all his enemies in battle, (3)
great renown, (4) great strength, (5) discipline *(yoga)*, (6) amia-
bility, (7) close proximity to Siva, and (8) one thousand sons. This
makes Krishna a suppliant, indeed a very human suppliant to
Siva as God. Such passages could not have occurred in the
Mahabharata if, when the epic was given its final shape, Siva had

not already become a kind of monotheistic god, and Krishna remained a man.[1]

Image Worship in Temples

With the introduction of the new cults of Siva and Vishnu-Krishna, to which was added the cult of the Mother Goddess, Hinduism entered the historic period of its existence. The cults took a few centuries to become fully developed, but by the beginning of the Christian era the first two had taken root. With this also came the greatest revolution in the history of Hinduism — the introduction of image worship in temples, which the religion had not known before. To the outside world and even to non-Hindus in India, Hinduism is identified now with idolatry and temples. Yet the religion had existed without them for one thousand years at least.

Something has already been said about the relationship between the old Hinduism without image worship and the new Hinduism with it, but two points might be repeated; first, not a single text of the revealed scriptures of the Hindus refers to images or temples, and even the epics do not; secondly, like adherence to the cults of Siva, Krishna, or Durga, worship of images in temples is wholly optional.

In addition, attention has to be drawn to two aspects of image worship in temples which show that this new expression of Hinduism has remained, in spite of its universal adoption, only a domiciled foreigner and has flourished apart from the deepest and most natural religious sentiment of the Hindus.

First, the liturgy of worship of the images in temples has not been made religious in the sense Hindu sacrifices and devotions are so. The whole routine of daily worship in temples is only a replica of the daily life of the Hindu king. The god or goddess is awakened in the morning with music or praise, then bathed, dressed, and adorned. After that the deity receives food, and then he gives audience to his subjects, hears their applications, grants their requests figuratively. The applicants, of course, bring

---

[1] Like all the books embodying Hindu legends and traditions, the *Mahabharata* is not consistent. In a passage following the one summarized here Mahadeva praises Krishna. But though this panegyric gives a few of the attributes of Siva to Krishna, on the whole the praise is given to the Vishnu of mythology.

their tribute and presents. Then the door is shut for the midday meal and siesta. In the afternoon the god comes to the audience chamber again, but only to be entertained. The whole routine of evening worship is entertainment, in which dances are included. Formerly, many temples had, of course, dedicated woman dancers. The gods also go out like the kings for periodic excursions or visits, and even set out on campaigns. The gods and goddesses also wear costumes and ornaments which are exactly like those of Hindu royalty. In short, there is nothing unworldly in the worship of images in temples. It is based on the Hindu quality of *rajasika*, or regality. The *sattvika*, which is the quality of holiness, has no place in it.

Secondly, and more significantly still, Hindu theorists and apologists have never accepted image worship wholeheartedly. On the contrary, they have asserted that it is not the real Hindu religion. They have consistently represented it only as a substitute for the real thing for simple and uneducated people, to whom the highest expression of Hinduism is too abstruse and thus incomprehensible. This apology I have read and heard all my life.

But it must not be assumed that this line has been taken only in response to the challenge of Christian or secular European ideas in the nineteenth century. It is much older, and is seen fully developed as an argument during Muslim rule which was imposed on India in the thirteenth century. The Muslims charged the Hindus with idolatry — *butparasti* — but instead of being ashamed, the Hindu counter-attacked. I shall give an example of this from an old Bengali poem written around 1750, in which the poet sets forth an argument between the Mogul Emperor Jehangir and a Bengali Brahmin to prove the superiority of Hinduism.

The Emperor says that Hindus make idols of clay, wood, and stone and, by infusing life into these by means of spells, only worship evil spirits. He asks: 'Who can save a people who give life to things made by man and what can be the future life of those who put vermilion on trees and pitchers and call these goddesses?'[1]

The Brahmin replies: 'Clay, wood, or stone, all things movable or immovable contain God according to the Puranas as well as

---

[1] It is as if the Bengali poet had read St Paul and put his denunciation of idolatry in the mouth of the Muslim Emperor.

the Quran. He who makes images of Him with these only makes the intangible God tangible. He who contemplates only the intangible without the help of the tangible drops the gold and only ties an empty knot in his scarf.'

Writing more than eight hundred years before this about the highest Hindu conception of God in his famous book on India, the great Muslim scholar Alberuni wrote:

> The beliefs of educated and uneducated people differ in every nation; for the former strive to conceive abstract ideas and to define general principles, whilst the latter do not pass beyond the apprehension of the senses . . . The Hindus believe with regard to God that he is one, eternal, without beginning and end, acting by free will, almighty, all-wise, living, giving life, ruling, preserving; one who in his sovereignty is unique, beyond all likeness and unlikeness, and that he does not resemble anything nor does anything resemble him . . . This is what educated people believe about God . . . If we now pass from the ideas of the educated people among the Hindus to those of common people, we must say that they present a great variety. Some of them are simply abominable, but similar errors also occur in other religions.

Clearly, Alberuni was giving the Hindu view of the relationship between monotheism and polytheism. There is no doubt that in the highest Hindu religious consciousness there were always reservations about giving a material form to God or the gods and to worship the divinity in images. This is paralleled among the Greeks and Romans, and deprecation of image worship in temples can be found in the opinions of the philosophers. This is cited by later Christian writers.

Clement of Alexandria quoted two lines of verse from a fragment attributed to Euripides: 'What house built by carpenters could immure within it the divine body?' To Zeno the Stoic, both Plutarch and Clement attributed the following opinion, set down in almost identical words: 'No one should build temples, for no temple is either precious or holy, no structure made by a mason can be that.' The disapproval is extended to statues *(agalmata)*. A passage in Plato's *Laws* was also interpreted as a disapproval of temples. In it he said: 'When the ground and the hearth of the home have been consecrated to gods why should there be a second consecration (in a temple?) for them?' Cicero put the same opinion in Latin as follows: 'Terra igitur, ut focus, domicilium sacrum deorum omnium est. Quocirca ne quis iterum idem consecrato.'[1]

In any case, Eusebius of Caesaria, the historian of the Church, definitely thought that there was no idolatry in the early stage of the Greek religion. Thus he wrote in his *Demonstratio evangelica*:

> In ancient times mortals turned only to the heavenly bodies and ignored idols . . . This is what I proved in the *Praeparatio evangelica*, where I have demonstrated that the most ancient of men did not make use of statues carved by hand . . . So it is time that the Greeks recognized this themselves on the strength of their own texts and admitted that idolatry and the cult of invisible spirits were recent superstitions, absent in the religion of the ancients.

The revulsion from image worship at the highest level of Greek, Roman, and Hindu religious and philosophical thinking, discreetly expressed as it was, was still real, and sprang from a sensation of *malaise*. The reason was the same with all the three people: they were Indo-Europeans with an Indo-European legacy in religion. No Indo-European people made images of their gods, nor worshipped them in temples, though they had created anthropomorphic pantheons. But the anthropomorphism had not affected the basically pantheistic character of their religion, derived from a strong feeling for nature. Their gods were very largely nature gods, and for this reason more appropriately worshipped at sacred spots or in groves. Such gods could not be easily brought into man-made buildings.

Yet anthropomorphism, which created psychological images of gods, was bound to create the desire to give to the psychological image a material form and thus lead to idol worship. This latent tendency in the anthropomorphic Indo-European religions found practical expression first among the Greeks, because they were in close contact with the countries which not only practised image worship in temples, but had also given an overpowering grandeur to their cults. The centres of this type of cult were in Egypt and Mesopotamia, and the mere artistic effect of the Egyptian material embodiment of religion must have been overpowering to a nation with such artistic sensibility as the Greeks. Thus Greece became the source of diffusion of the temple cult among all Indo-European

[1] *De Legibus* 4. 18. 45.

peoples. The Romans took it over from the Greeks. But the Germans were too far away and too primitive to adopt it. The Persians were in direct contact with Mesopotamia and with Egypt as well. But they were protected against the temple cult by their exclusive monotheism. The Hindus, too, were at first too distant to be influenced by it.

But the invasion of Alexander brought the Greeks to the north-western regions of India,[1] and exposed the life and culture of the Hindus to Hellenic influences in many things. The invasion itself was only an episode, but its effects were lasting. First, under the Seleucids the Greeks settled in the whole area as far to the north as the Oxus, and after Persia was lost to the Parthians by the Seleucids, they remained in the Punjab and Afghanistan under local kings, and they kept up their Hellenism for about three hundred years. This Greek presence was a potent cultural influence on the Hindus.

The Greek influence on Hindu culture has always been discounted by Indian scholars from purely nationalistic sentiment. But there can be no doubt that this influence was real. How strongly entrenched Greek culture was in this area can be judged from the fact already referred to that Asoka found it necessary to have his religious message inscribed in Afghanistan in the Greek language. The Greek of the Asokan inscriptions was not a pidgin dialect, but the classical Greek employed by the Greek philosophers. For instance, in order to translate the word *dhamma (dharma)* of the Magadhi Prakrit (the normal language of his inscriptions all over India) his translator used the Greek word *eusebeia*, which is employed even by Plato. It means, on the one hand, 'giving to the gods their dues', and, on the other, also embodies notions of social justice like respect for oaths, filial piety, consideration for parents, and awareness of the fallibility of human beings. These were exactly the virtues Asoka wanted to preach.

Moreover, it was not in language alone that the region was Hellenized. It was more so in the material expression of culture. Thus the Greek colonists not only gave a new artistic representation to Buddhism, but also imported Hellenistic works of art from Egypt, western Asia, and Greece. They must also have had temples,

[1] Geographically, the sub-continent of India extends to the Hindu Kush, and thus in the past it included cis-Hindu Kush Afghanistan.

and it is no accident that the oldest remains of a temple of the Hindu type has been found in Afghanistan.

Furthermore, it should be remembered that the Indo-Aryan culture was extremely weak in material expression, and it acquired that expression only through contact with the Persians in the first instance, and then with the Greeks. This is admitted frankly in Sanskrit literature in respect of architecture. Whenever any marvellous building is mentioned, it is attributed to the Danavas, who are of course the Persians. The adoption of the Greek material expression would naturally follow the imitation of the Persians. There can be no doubt that temples and images were taken over by the Hindus from the Greeks who had settled in what is now Punjab and Afghanistan. This would be perfectly consistent with the general development of architecture and sculpture in ancient India.

Other Developments

After the adoption of temples and images, the next great change in the religion of the Hindus is seen in the introduction of a wholly new feeling for the monotheistic gods. This is the famous Way of Love *(Bhakti Marga)*, which means disinterested surrender of self to a personal god of love. This was so foreign to all the previous religious traditions of the Hindus that it can be reasonably set down to an external influence. This new kind of devotion was first seen in the worship of Krishna, but was extended to Siva as well as the Mother Goddess.

From this point onwards, with one exception, Hinduism developed under its own motive power, that is, along a line of evolution which amplified what had already been received or created. In this process all the three cults of the monotheistic type of gods, namely, those of Siva, Krishna, and the Mother Goddess, reached their full expression. Of these, the cult of Siva remained the least changed. The cult of the Mother Goddess underwent greater changes, and, as it would seem, absorbed one foreign influence. But the cult of Krishna underwent what was virtually a revolution as a result of pressures inherent in the Hindu mind as it had developed in India. All these changes will be discussed in the third part of the book.

Hinduism and the Aboriginals

Those who are familiar with what is said about the evolution of
Hinduism in most of the books current on the subject will have
noticed a silence in this chapter which they will consider very
strange. It is the absence in the account I have just given of the
broad lines of development of the religion, of any reference to the
influence which the religions of the aboriginals of India exercised
on it. There has grown up a definite school of historians of
Hinduism, especially at the popular level, which regards the full-
grown religion as the product of an interaction between the Indo-
European religion of the incoming Aryans and the religion of the
aboriginals of the country. The cults of Siva and Durga, more
especially, have been regarded as borrowings in some of their
aspects from the aboriginals.

The reason for my exclusion of this view from my account is
simply that I consider it as wholly unfounded, and I am con-
vinced that no such interaction ever took place. On this subject
a very significant difference is found between academic Western
scholars and the British administrators who have written about
Hinduism or Hindu social customs. The latter have always
singled out the Hinduization of the aboriginals as the most important religious change in India, observing what the aboriginals
were doing under their eyes. I have already quoted Lyall's view of
it. In my boyhood I came to know of one such case of Hinduization and was very proud of it. The Khasis of Assam never showed
any tendency to adopt Hindu beliefs or rites, and they were converted to Christianity in large numbers. But one Khasi of good
education and social position became a Hindu and performed the
worship of Durga in the orthodox Bengali manner. He even adopted
a Bengali name, Jivan Ray. Historians of ancient India, too, have
put forward the view that many of the Hindu dynasties of central
India were of aboriginal origins. In fact, it is the builders of the
famous temple group of Khajuraho who have been thought to be so.

Why some historians of Hinduism took the alternative view
that the aboriginals influenced the incoming Aryans has its explanation. What is really surprising is that they should have put
forward this opinion after reading Sanskrit. If the whole of Sanskrit literature, sacred or profane, makes one thing clear it is that
there was one line no Hindu could cross, and that was the line

which separated the Aryan in India from the non-Aryan. The two ethnic nouns even acquired moral connotations: to be *Arya* (Aryan) was to be noble and honourable, and to be *Anarya* (non-Aryan) was to be base and dishonourable. The non-Aryans were beyond the pale of Hindu society, and therefore untouchable. The Aryan Hindus regarded them with fear, hatred, contempt, disgust, but at times these feelings were mixed with some admiration for their physical strength, frankness, and joyousness. It is impossible even to imagine that with such pride of race as they always showed the Hindus would borrow anything from the non-Aryans to create their fully developed way of life. It is easier to believe that the Americans of the United States have created a new Christianity by borrowing ideas from the Red Indians, or that the Boers in South Africa have a religion which is a mixture of Christianity and the practices of the Zulus or Hottentots.

The historical ground for rejecting the theory of adoption from the aboriginals is that no scrap of evidence exists to prove the existence of any kind of developed religion among the aboriginals of India. There are references to their religious practices in Sanskrit books, but these show the religion of the aboriginals to have been very much what the British administrators observed it to be.

The theory of the adoption of features from the aboriginal religions by the Indo-European Hindus owes its origin and currency to wholly adventitious reasons, which are emotional predispositions and not intellectual conclusions. To begin with, those who took interest in the early form of Hinduism, that is, the Vedic religion, were German and very romantic. They totally refused to believe that a fellow-Aryan people could have practised human sacrifice, worshipped the phallus, or been given to magic and spells, and so they attributed all that they regarded as degrading in the practice of Hinduism to the non-Aryan aboriginals.

What was really surprising was that they even ignored the chthonic and sexual features in the *Rig-Veda* itself, and seemed to be unaware that all the Indo-European peoples had both human sacrifice and phallicism. With greater knowledge of the Greek, Roman, German, and Norse religions there is now not the slightest reason to derive any Hindu practice, however degrading it might seem to idealizers, from the aboriginals. Yet the myth of aboriginal influences still dogs the history of Hinduism.

The second contribution to the theory of an intermingling of

97

Aryan and non-Aryan elements in Hinduism came from the missionaries. They found that the strongest resistance to conversion to Christianity was coming from the high-caste Hindus, more especially the learned priests who had their conservatism nourished by Sanskrit. Quite rightly they saw in that language the source of the ideological resistance to Christianity. Therefore they began to propagate the idea that some of the popular languages of India were not Indo-European but Dravidian or Turanian. One missionary even went to the length of saying that the Bengali language was more Turanian than Indo-European, which was of course absurd. In addition to them some British administrators, who became amateur anthropologists, put forward the theory that the Bengali people were not Aryan, but Dravido-Mongol.

The latest contribution to the myth was made by Bengali intellectuals in my young days, and that was due to a cultural conflict which had developed in Bengali society. Throughout the latter part of the nineteenth century the Bengali intelligentsia was divided between liberalism and conservatism. At first the liberal movement with its ideas of religious and social reform carried everything before it, and the traditional conservatives could not resist the liberals. But towards the end of the century a wholly new kind of Hindu conservatism appeared in Bengal. Basing their doctrines on the work of the European Orientalists, they gave a new interpretation to Hinduism, and justified polytheism, image worship, and all the practices of traditional Hinduism, rationalizing them with arguments taken from Comparative Philology and Comparative Religion. In this new Hindu movement, the notion of an Indo-European family of languages with its racial suggestion fortified the old Hindu pride of being Aryan. As a result, on the popular level an Aryan legend was created and believed in, which was as grotesque as the Aryan doctrine of the Nazis. This movement became dominant in Bengali life by 1905. To counteract this, the Bengali liberals trotted out a theory that the Bengalis were not Aryans at all, and as a corollary to it they also put forward the idea that a good deal of Hinduism was non-Aryan. As Bengali thinking very powerfully influenced all historical notions held by Anglicized Indians, the theory of an intermingling of Aryan and non-Aryan elements in Hinduism has become part of a progressive credo in India. Historically, it does not deserve any consideration.

Role of the South

One very important aspect of the later development of Hinduism
has finally to be noted. It is the part played in the process by south
India from the ninth century onwards. From that time all the
new speculation, exegesis, and movements originated virtually in
the south. What had happened in the Gangetic plain to shift Hindu
thinking to the south is not clear, but in any case religious life and
thought seem to have become wholly static in it. On the other
hand, the south created not only the philosophy of the Vedanta,
but also a new religious feeling manifested both in Saivism and
Vaishnavism. Another interesting aspect of the geographical shift
is that in contrast with the north, where all the religious and
philosophical texts had fictitious or eponymous authors, mostly
the legendary sages, in the south these were composed by
definite historical persons. The anonymity of Hinduism came to
an end.

Naturally, this process was completed by the Muslim conquest,
which destroyed the Hindu political and intellectual aristocracy
in the north. Henceforth, in the south alongside of the Hindu
political power, there also flourished the Hindu intellectual power.
The task of maintaining Hinduism by exegesis was taken over by
the scholars of the south, who might be likened to the Byzantine
scholars who continued the study of Greek literature. The Vedas,
the Upanishads, and all the major texts of Hinduism, including
the *Gita*, found new commentators in the south, and it is the interpretations offered by these scholars which remain the most authoritative all over India. The only region in northern India where
scholarly study of the Hindu philosophical and legal systems was
continued was Bengal with the adjacent district of Mithila or the
northern portion of Bihar.

Nevertheless, movement and innovation in religious life did not
cease in the Gangetic plain. But it assumed a popular character
which made Hinduism of the old Aryavarta (the land of the
Aryans) very simple. The outcome of the process was the creation
of a popular devotion and popular sects. Thus there was a reversal
of the roles of the north and the south in respect of the historical
development and continuity of Hinduism. Aryavarta, the old
centre, lost its lead, and transferred that to its colonial extension.
The north became simple, and crude in its simplicity, but both the

south and Bengal remained sophisticated, but tending towards fossilization.

In concluding this attempt at giving an indication of the historical development of Hinduism, I would repeat that the account given in this part of the book stops at the Muslim conquest of India at the end of the twelfth century. Hinduism continued to grow and change, and the process is still going on. But at the point chosen for concluding the historical survey, the structure of Hindu religious life was fully erected, and the later changes only extended it without in any way modifying the character of the system.

PART TWO

DESCRIPTIVE

Chapter One

SOURCES FOR DESCRIPTION

TO give a description of Hinduism is not as difficult as to reconstruct its history. But this, too, has its problem, which is to make the account what it ought to be. First and foremost, the description must correspond to a reality and not be merely an epitome of the immense amount of information on mythology, doctrines, and rituals contained in the texts. After that it must show Hinduism not only in its fully developed state, but also at its most typical.

The most obvious way of fulfilling both the conditions would be to show the religion as it is today, if not in all its variations, at least in its major features which are common to the whole of India. But this description will not be that of its unimpaired expression. During the last fifty years or so the religion has been subjected to so many disruptive influences, partly from the cultural impact of the West and partly from economic changes, that many of its observances have disappeared and the devotion it inspired and evoked has become very much weakened.

This is particularly true of the educated, upper-class Hindus who live in the great cities and constitute the cultural élite. The hold of Hinduism on them is somewhat like that of Christianity on the Western urban intelligentsia, though almost all of them remain more or less superstitious. In the villages, among rural folks, the religion is still living and strong, but very simple. Besides, even in that world so many cultural, economic, and demographic changes are taking place that Hindu outlooks and practices are undergoing a sort of erosion. Thus any description of Hinduism based on observation of the contemporary state of Hinduism would give an incomplete and faded picture. Above all, the fervour and joy of Hindu religious life will be seen in a much weakened form.

Logically, the alternative would be to describe Hinduism as it was before the Muslim conquest at the end of the twelfth century, when the Hindus were politically independent and their culture had reached its full development. But even for the period of four centuries from the eighth, which was not included in the historical part of this book, the sources are so scanty that it is not possible to give a reasonably complete and systematic account of the actual religious life of the Hindus. The same inadequacy faces the student for the six centuries of Muslim rule. We have some knowledge of the new popular religious movements and of the preachings of the popular prophets, but virtually none about the higher levels of religious life.

So one has to face the paradoxical situation that in order to give a more or less systematic description of Hinduism one has to come down to the age when European observers began to write about the religion. Their accounts not only show which of the beliefs and rituals laid down in the texts were to be found in actual practice, but also supply information which cannot be found in them. But as the writings on Hinduism by foreign writers who observed it at first hand did not become large enough in volume till the nineteenth century, a systematic description of the religion based on them would only show what it was like in that century.

European Accounts

However, Europeans began to write about Hinduism long before that date. Actually, the earliest books by them date from the seventeenth century. Three early accounts deserve particular attention, and the earliest of them is the first extant account of Hinduism by a European writer. Naturally, these writers were all Christian priests or missionaries, who could be expected to take an interest in Indian religious life and also to be the most competent Europeans to write on it.

The first book was by an English clergyman, and was published in London in 1630. His name was Henry Lord, and he was attached to the English commercial establishment at Surat on the western coast of India. The Gujarati Hindus of this region belonged mostly to the Bania or trading caste, and therefore Lord gave to his book the title: *A Discoverie of the Sects of the Banians*, and further explained its scope by adding: 'Containing their History, Law, Liturgie, Casts, Customs, and Ceremonies—Gathered from their Bramanes, Teachers of that Sect: As the particulars were comprized in the Books of their Law, called Shaster: Together with a display of their Manners, both in times past, and their present.'

Though the book was not as exhaustive as this description suggested, it covered, despite its restricted title of *Banian Religion*, the whole range of Hindu beliefs and mythologies so far as Lord knew them, and he regarded himself as a discoverer in this field. He was very much struck by the appearance of the Gujarati Hindus who worked for the East India Company or transacted business with it, and he wrote:

> A people presented themselves to mine eyes, cloathed in linen garments somewhat low descending, of a gesture and garbe, as I may say, maydenly and wellnigh effiminate; of a countenance shy and somewhat estranged, yet smiling out a glosed[1] and bashful familiarity . . .

He continued:

> Truth to say, mine eyes, unacquainted with such objects, tooke up their wonder and gazed; and this admiration, the badge of a fresh travailer, bred in mee the importunity of a questioner. I asked what manner of people these were, so strangely notable and notably strange? Reply was made. They were Banians, a people forraigne to the knowledge of the Christian world; their religion, rites and customs sparingly treated of by any, and they no less reserved in the publication of them: but some opinion they derived from the philosopher Pythagoras, touching transanimation of soules. It was thought the novelty would make the discovery thereof grateful and acceptable to some of our countrymen: that some of my predecessors had become scrutinous to bring to light this religion; but whether deterred with fictions chymeraes, wherewith Banian writings abound, that might make it unworthy of acceptation, or the shyness of the Bramanes, who will scarce admit a stranger to conversation, the worke was left to him that would make a path through these impediments.

Lord said that Thomas Kerridge, President of the factory, urged him to make up the omission, and that he was compiling his book from the manuscripts of the Hindus with the help of interpreters, especially 'out of booke of theirs called the *Shaster*, which to them is their bible, containing the grounds of their religion in a written word'.

The second description was written by a Dutch priest and missionary who lived for many years on the coast of Coromandel and adjacent regions. His name was Abraham Roger, and his

[1] Variant of *gloze* = to shine or gleam *(O.E.D.)*.

book in Dutch was published at Amsterdam in 1651. A German translation followed in 1663, and a French with copious notes in 1670. The general title of the book as given in French is: *La Porte ouverte, pour parvenir à la connoissance du paganism caché ou la vraye représentation de la vie, des mœurs de la religion, & du service divin des Brahmines, qui demeurent sur les costes de Choromandel, & aux pays circonvoisins*. The annotator was Sieur Thomas la Grue, Maistre és Arts et Docteur en Medecine. This book is much fuller and more accurate than that of Lord, and in compiling it Roger was helped by a Brahmin named Padmanabha. The book also contains a translation of one hundred aphorisms of Bhartrihari, and is illustrated by many line-engravings showing the burning of a Hindu widow, incarnations of Vishnu, and also what must be regarded as the first representation of the story of Hindus throwing themselves under the car of Juggernaut.

The third description also comes from a Dutchman, Philip Baldaeus, 'Minister of the Word of God in Ceylon'. It formed the last part of his lengthy account of the coasts of Malabar and Coromandel as well as Ceylon, and was published in Amsterdam in 1672. An English translation was published in Amsterdam in 1704, and it was reproduced in the third volume of *Churchill's Collection of Voyages and Travels*, brought out in 1745. The description of Hinduism was stated to be 'a most circumstantial and compleat Account of the Idolatry of the Pagans in the *East Indies*, the *Malabars, Benjans, Gentives, Brahmans*, etc. Taken partly from their own *Vedam*, or Law-Book, and authentick Manuscripts; partly from frequent Conversation with their Priests and Divines: With draughts of their Idols, done after their Originals.' The engravings made specially for this collection are extremely fine and accurate, and therefore a valuable supplement to the description.

The lay interest in Hinduism naturally began to show itself with the establishment of British power in India, and as it happened the earliest lay account came from the man who was also the author of the sensational account of the Black Hole. He was John Zephaniah Holwell. Holwell boasted about his knowledge of the religion of the Hindus, of his efforts to collect information, and of his manuscripts. But his account is both crude and full of mistakes.

More competent laymen began to follow him. Their interest in Hinduism was the result of administrative necessity. British rule was extending over large parts of India, and in order to govern the country the British administrators had to acquire knowledge of the laws, customs, and social institutions of the inhabitants, both Muslim and Hindu. This also meant knowledge of the two religions because among both Hindus and Muslims, and more especially among the first, all secular matters were connected with religion. For this reason Warren Hastings, with all his heavy political duties, took a good deal of interest in the promotion of Oriental learning. Thus he wrote a long letter of recommendation to the Chairman of the Court of Directors of the East India Company in favour of an English translation of the *Gita* by Charles Wilkins, a servant of the Company—which was also the first authentic translation of a Sanskrit religious text into any European language.[1] In this letter he said that he, as Governor-General of India, encouraged Oriental studies among the servants of the Company for three reasons:

I. He believed that the permanency of the Company's dominion in India depended more on the virtue than the ability of its servants and that cultivation of language and science will form the moral character and habits of the service.

II. 'Every accumulation of knowledge, and especially such as is obtained by social communication with people over whom we exercise a dominion founded on the right of conquest, is useful to the state: it is the gain of humanity: in the specific instance which I have stated, it attracts and conciliates distant affections; it lessens the weight of the chain by which the natives are held in subjection; it imprints on the hearts of our own countrymen the sense and obligation of benevolence.'

III. Last of all, knowledge of Hindu culture was likely to bring a change in the attitude of the British people to Indians. As Hastings put it:

It is not very long since the inhabitants of India were considered by many, as creatures scarce above the degree of savage life; nor, I fear, is that prejudice yet wholly eradicated, though surely abated. Every instance which brings their real character home to observation will impress us with a more generous sense of feeling for their

[1] '*The Bhagavat-Geeta*, or a Dialogues of Kreeshna and Arjoon; in eighteen lectures, with Notes. Translated from the original in the *Sanskreet*, or ancient language of the *Brahmans*, by Charles Wilkins, Senior Merchant in the service of the Honourable the East India Company, on their Bengal Establishment.' (London, 1785.)

natural rights, and teach us to estimate them by the measure of our own, but such instances can only be obtained in their writings: and these will survive when the British dominion in India shall have long ceased to exist, and when the sources which it once yielded of wealth and power are lost to remembrance.[1]

Administrative necessity also gave rise to a genuine scientific interest in Hinduism and this in its turn created the scholarly competence which was needed to deal with it. The foundation of the Asiatic Society of Bengal in 1784 marks the beginning of serious studies. Thus from the last years of the eighteenth century a series of essays and books on Hinduism began to be written both from direct observation and study of the texts. H. T. Colebrooke, a civil servant of the East India Company, was the first man to provide a reliable account of Vedic literature, and he also described current aspects of Hinduism.

The second official who contributed to the knowledge of Hinduism was Horace Hayman Wilson, who went to India as a surgeon, became the Master of the Calcutta Mint, and made himself the leading English Sanskrit scholar of the age. Afterwards he became Boden Professor of Sanskrit at Oxford, which was the first professorship of the language to be established in England. He wrote about Hinduism as a scholar, and his essays provided some of the earliest and most reliable accounts of Hinduism as practised. Gradually the religious interest among the administrators widened into the ethnographic and sociological as well. But, as has been said, Hindu social life being inseparable from religion, the sociological works of the officials also remain indispensable for a study of Hinduism.

On their part, the missionaries continued to write about Hinduism. Their interest was natural, because they could not preach Christianity in India without some knowledge of the religion of those whom they wanted to convert, and also without acquiring the ability to read and speak the languages of the Hindus. In fact, the Boden Professorship of Sanskrit at Oxford was endowed to serve the cause of conversion. Colonel Boden of the East India Company's service gave £25,000 for this purpose, 'being of opinion that a more general and critical knowledge of the Sanskrit language will be the means of enabling his countrymen to proceed

[1] C. Wilkins, *The Bhagavat-Geeta*, pp. 12–13.

in the conversion of the Natives of India to the Christian Religion, by disseminating a knowledge of the sacred scriptures amongst them, more effectually than all other means whatever'. In India, even in later times when the Hindus were asked to read the Bible, they asked the missionaries to read the Hindu sacred books first.

Apart from serious works on Hinduism from both administrators and missionaries there were also a fair number of books on it to cater for the popular interest in the religion in the West, which was ready to fasten on all that was curious, sensational, or charlatanesque in the religion. These books do not deserve serious consideration. Unfortunately, however, it was such accounts rather than the scholarly works which moulded the popular idea of Hinduism in the West. The stories of the car of Juggernaut, the Suttee, the bloody sacrifices, the lechery of Krishna and of his worshippers, etc., travelled far, even to the United States. So, when in 1858 a Bengali Brahmin who had adopted Christianity went to Boston to learn about Unitarian Christianity, he was told about Suttee, hook-swinging, and Juggernaut, and was also asked: 'Do the Hindu mothers throw their babies into the Ganges now?' This man, whose name was Joguth Chunder Gangooly (properly transliterated Jagat Chandra Ganguli) and who wrote a book on Hinduism, commented: 'I am quite amused to see the little school boys and girls in America, who seem to know more about Hinduism than I do.' However, if such accounts have not done any good to Hinduism they have also not done much harm.

Value of Missionary Writing

As the books on Hinduism written by the missionaries constitute the most exhaustive source of the religion as practised it is necessary to appraise them correctly. Throughout the nineteenth century two trends were seen side by side in their writings, one polemical and the other objective. Some of the polemical books or pamphlets were ferociously denunciatory. But even the denunciation has considerable historical value, because if the missionaries had to fight Hinduism they could not afford to be inaccurate as to facts, whatever might be their interpretation. They often gave information about certain repulsive facts about the religion which were an integral part of it, but which those who wished to show it in a favourable light avoided with a timid discretion which amounted to suppression of truth. The denunciation is also historically important because it provoked the modern Hindu apologia, and in spite of being contested publicly gave a direction to the efforts at reform.

But the great majority of the missionary writers did not feel called upon to pronounce judgements, and thought that it was in their interest to see Hinduism as it was and when writing about it to provide correct information. Besides, the missionaries who wrote scholarly works felt that to describe Hinduism accurately was the best means of controverting it by implication, and even of discrediting it. It is curious to note how this attitude was foreshadowed even by Lord, whose book was published in 1630. In his final conclusion he did indeed include a paragraph of 'censure on the material parts of this relation', but substantially his was a detached attitude based on his confidence in Christianity. As he wrote:

> Thus, worthy reader, thou hast the summe of the Banian religion, such as it is; not voyd of vaine superstitions, and composed forgery, as well may be judged by the precedent discourse, wherein, as in all other heresies, may be gathered how Sathan leadeth those that are out of the pale of the church, a round, in the maze of errour and gentilisme. I might leave the particulars to thy censure, as well to thy reading.

He thought that his book might settle his readers in the solidness of their faith which was purged of such levities. But he appears to have felt sorry for the Banians so misled by their priests, for on the title-page of his book he quoted Isaiah 9:16: 'The leaders of this people cause *them* to err; and *they that are* led of them *are* destroyed.' At the same time he hoped that the 'novelty of this relation may make it gratefull to any, who like an *Athenian* desireth to hear something strange or new.' The point of view of the modern missionaries was set down very clearly by W. J. Wilkins of the London Missionary Society, who in 1887 published a very accurate description of Hinduism as seen in northern India in his time.[1] He wrote in its introduction:

> In this book, as in my former one, I have abstained from comment on the character of these practices; my work here is rather that of

[1] Wilkins, W. J., *Modern Hinduism* (1887). The previous work to which he refers is *Hindu Mythology, Vedic and Puranic* (1882).

a chronicler than of a preacher. In writing of the mythology of the Hindus I felt that the most powerful refutation of Hinduism was a fair statement of what their books themselves teach concerning the character and conduct of the beings whom they worship as divine; and in describing the everyday life of the Hindus, which is the practical outcome of such worship, there seems to me to be but little necessity for comment.

It must not be forgotten, however, that this very objectivity of the missionaries in writing about Hinduism has been condemned by modern Hindus as propaganda against Hinduism. These Hindus are profoundly suspicious of all books on Hinduism written even by Western academic scholars. Any description or interpretation which does not conform to the recently formulated Hindu apologia, which is more political than religious, will be condemned as misrepresentation or even denigration of the religion. And all the modern Western apologists of Hinduism will be produced as witnesses against those who try to write objectively.

The realistic approach, which has been generally that of the missionaries when they have given formal accounts of Hinduism, is even more suspect. For example, the Abbé Dubois' famous *Hindu Manners, Customs, and Ceremonies* (published in 1817 in English from the first French draft, and more fully in 1897 from the final French manuscript), has always been regarded by the Hindus as missionary propaganda against Hinduism. Yet the book is very valuable for the immense amount of information it gives about the state of Hindu society and religion in south India at the end of the eighteenth and beginning of the nineteenth century. There is no book like it for any other part of India.

The only point which can be made against this book and also later works on Hinduism by the missionaries is that they all ignore the higher religious sentiment and thought which can be found in the doctrinal texts, especially the Upanishads, expositions of which have been given by academic scholars. But the missionaries were concerned with a different world of religion altogether, and in that world even the Hindus who practised their religion devoutly, completely ignored the rarefied region. For what might be regarded as the workaday world of Hinduism, the missionary works supply information which no student can do without. Moreover, any mistakes or misrepresentations that there might be in their writings can always be corrected by anyone who has personal knowledge of Hinduism as practised. But the charge of misrepresentation is mostly on the score of attitudes.

Complementary Hindu Writing

The information supplied by the missionaries and administrators can be supplemented from what the Hindus have written about their religion themselves. But their formal presentation is either polemical or apologetic. Before the nineteenth century the Hindus took their religion for granted, they lived in it like fish in water, and so they felt no need to have it preached to themselves. But, when in that century the impact of Western ideas either created an external threat for it or fostered doubts about it in their own minds, explanatory or justificatory writing naturally made its appearance. The first Hindu to produce this kind of apology was the reformer Ram Mohun Roy (? 1772–1833), who on the one hand preached Hindu monotheism on the basis of the Upanishads and, on the other, carried on controversies with the Christian clergy in India. But the re-examination of Hinduism begun by him did not gain force till the end of the century, when a full-blown apology was produced as part of a movement which might be called the Hindu Counter-Reformation and which was a reply to the Brahmo movement, the Hindu Protestantism.

The amount of factual information given about Hinduism in the writings of these reformers was not large, and does not exceed what is given by the European writers. Nor is the information always accurate or precise. In regard to interpretation they read into Hinduism many things which were not in it, and could never be. At its popular level these neo-Hindu apologetics were extremely crude and childish. But at the highest level they were both plausible and competent. What they attempted to do was to make Hinduism consistent with the European thought of the age, especially with the conclusions of comparative religion and even anthropology. The general tendency of this school of exposition was to rationalize the religion, which in itself might be regarded as its de-Hinduization. Therefore, the whole of the apologetic writing by modern Hindus is better utilized to give an account of the reforming movments than to describe the religion as it actually was.

However, this does not mean that the student is left wholly

without information from other Hindu sources. For one thing, it can be seen that certain Hindu texts are being fully used in current practice. Therefore these can be drawn upon to describe the rituals as they are actually performed. In addition, secular literature in modern Indian languages contains descriptions of worship and experiences which have no apologetic intention. This is particularly true of Bengali literature. Books in verse and prose, written both before and after the establishment of British rule, can supply vivid and realistic details of religious life. Even incidental references to Hinduism are extremely valuable. There are also books which describe traditional Bengali life, in which religion is an ever-present element. Though at times the descriptions are idealized, there is no illegitimate idealization.

Personal Observation and Enquiry

A supplementary source would be personal enquiry. But in seeking information from Hindus a foreign student has to be very wary. In the first place, the Hindus have always been very unwilling to give information about their religion. They have regarded it as the heritage and privilege of those who were born in it. As early as the early eleventh century, Alberuni, whose description of India has been referred to before, wrote: 'They [the Hindus] are by nature niggardly in communicating what they know, and they take the greatest possible care to withhold it from men of another caste among their own people, still more, of course, from any foreigner.'

All the early writers on Hinduism, beginning with Lord, also noticed this reserve, as has been seen in the extracts quoted from them. But the most striking reference to it is to be found in Dubois' preface to his book, in which he describes the attitude of the Brahmins from whom all his information about the religion had to be obtained.

All persons who have visited India or who have any notion of the character of the Brahmins, of the high esteem in which they hold themselves, and of the distant *hauteur* with which they treat the common people, will be able to appreciate the difficulties which anybody must encounter who would become intimate, or even acquainted, with these proud personages. The hate and contempt which they cherish against all strangers, and especially against

Europeans; the jealous inquietude with which they hide from the profane the mysteries of their religious cult; the records of their learning; the privacy of their homes: all these form barriers between themselves and their observers which it is almost impossible to pass.

However Dubois added: 'Nevertheless, by much diplomacy and perseverance I have succeeded in surmounting most of the obstacles which have turned back many others before me.' He also described his method. 'I made it my constant rule,' he wrote, 'to live as they did. I adopted their style of clothing, and I studied their customs and methods of life in order to be exactly like them. I even went so far as to avoid any display of repugnance to the majority of their peculiar prejudices. By such circumspect conduct I was able to ensure a free and hearty welcome from people of all castes and conditions, and was often favoured of their own accord with the most curious and interesting particulars about themselves.' Above all, it must not be forgotten that he wrote his book after living more than twenty years in India in this fashion.

The difficulties in the way of gaining reliable information about their religion from the Hindus, especially from highly educated Hindus, are not less today than they were in Dubois' time, though they are of a different kind. Unless they are very traditional and orthodox, present-day Hindus will be more communicative than secretive, but those who will be ready to give information will generally mislead foreigners both consciously and unconsciously. Most of them are thoroughgoing chauvinists and are interested in propagating a particular version of Hinduism agreeing with the Western myth about it. They are also ignorant and unfamiliar with the original sources. To spread these ideas about Hinduism has even become a commercially profitable activity. Moreover, those Europeans who will be ready nowadays to live in India like Dubois will have become such converts to Hindu charlatanry in advance that they will only be confirmed in their conversion. Some of the information which research workers collect in their field-work in India seems to me, when it is derived from statements made in answer to questions, to have been given with the intention of leg-pulling.

Nationalistic Hindus even suspect fellow-Hindus whom they look upon as unorthodox. A university lecturer in Calcutta refused to give me information about the routine of worship in the famous

Kali temple at Kalighat unless I gave him an undertaking not to show irreverence to Hinduism. He even paid me a left-handed compliment by saying that he was demanding this because a clever writer like me could hold anything up to ridicule.

But it has also to be added that in the past the reluctance was due to a sincerely felt doubt. A highly competent missionary, Mrs Sinclair Stevenson, who has written an exhaustive and accurate account of the rites of the twice-born, based on her investigations in Gujarat, has quoted in her book[1] what a pundit said to her when supplying her with information.

> 'Mem Sahib', he remarked, 'these are our sacred things that we are telling you, and we are willing to tell you personally of them, but will the people who read the books also study them with reverence?'

This kind of scruple may still survive.

But there still remains another resource — personal observation of the rites, devotions, and festivals without seeking explanations from the participants. Naturally, it will not be easy for a foreigner to get opportunities to observe, and in any case he will have difficulty in interpreting what he is seeing by himself. But a Hindu can observe his religion in this way both in the cities and in the rural areas. Certainly, even in the villages what is found today are attenuated survivals, but they are also authentic features, so far as they survive. What they show is a structure which is damaged but not wholly in ruins.

If, however, a person has been able to see Hinduism as practised before 1920, when the unsettling effect of the recent social changes was not fully in evidence and, even better, if he has seen it in the first decade of this century as I have done, he will be on firmer ground. Thus, comparing my personal knowledge of the practices of Hinduism with what I have read in the best European writers, I have found that the two generally agreed. Furthermore, with the help of my experience I have been able to bring to life what I have found in these books as well as in the texts which are still used for worship.

All these sources taken together and utilized with discrimination, will enable a writer to present a picture of Hinduism which

[1] Mrs Sinclair Stevenson, *The Rites of the Twice-born.* This book is in the series, 'Religious Quest of India', edited by J. N. Farquhar and H. D. Griswold.

will be reasonably full as well as dependable. That is what is being attempted in the description which follows. Formally it will, of course, be an account of Hinduism as it was in the nineteenth century. There is no reason, however, to think that in the preceding centuries Hinduism was different. To make my description correspond more closely to the traditional form I have excluded from it all the features which the reforming movements brought into the religion under the influence of Western ideas. This involves no sacrifice of accuracy, for the new movements were like man-made canals taken out from a broad natural river and though connected with it they ran in a parallel and far less broad course.

But the question still remains whether Hinduism as it was in the nineteenth century, the only age in its history which provides sufficient material for a more or less full description, was the religion at its best. By that time, as is generally accepted, Hinduism had been in existence for nearly three thousand years, and was certainly the oldest among the living religions of the day. So it can be asked whether at the end of that long history it had not passed its prime and was in decay, or at best was in a static, devitalized condition.

Decadence and Corruption

Some European observers of Hinduism in the nineteenth century, and following them the Hindu reformers of the age, definitely took that view. The Europeans were even discussing, as many of them are also doing today, whether it was not actually dying. Friedrich Max Müller, the most influential, sympathetic, and at the same time the most level-headed and scholarly expounder of the religion and civilization of the Hindus in the latter half of that century, suggested the possibility. Speaking on the Christian missions in Westminster Abbey in 1873 he declared that in spite of the fact that Hinduism was still professed by at least 110 million souls (a census figure which he thought might be far short of the real number) he did not shrink from saying that their religion was dying or dead because it belonged to a stratum of thought which was long buried beneath the feet of modern man.

The worship of Siva, Vishnu, and other popular deities, he continued, was of the same and in many cases of a more degraded and savage character than the worship of Jupiter, Apollo or Minerva. 'A religion', he said, 'may linger on for a long time, it may be accepted by large masses of the people, because it is there, and there is nothing better. But when a religion has ceased to produce defenders of the faith, prophets, champions, martyrs, it has ceased to live, in the true sense of the word; and in that sense the old orthodox Brahmanism has ceased to live for more than a thousand years.'

Sir Monier Monier-Williams, who held the Boden Professorship of Sanskrit at Oxford from 1860 to 1899, and who had a very wide knowledge of the Hinduism of his day, was even more emphatic. In his book *Hinduism*, first published in 1877, he wrote: 'The ancient fortress of Hinduism, with its four sides, Monotheism, Pantheism, Dualism, and Polytheism, is everywhere tottering and ready to fall.'

Both Max Müller and Monier-Williams raised the question of the future. The former observed: 'How long this living death of a national religion in India may last, no one can tell: for our purposes, however, for gaining an idea of the issue of the great religious struggle of the future, that religion too is dead and gone.' According to Müller, the only three religions which were living and 'between which the decisive battle for the dominion of the world will have to be fought', were Buddhism, Muhammadanism, and Christianity.

Monier-Williams wrote: 'What then is to become of the masses of the people when their ancient faith sinks from beneath their feet? Only two other homes are before them—a cold theism and a heart-stirring Christianity. They are both already established in the soil of India. But Christianity is spreading its boundaries more widely, and strikings its foundations more deeply. It appeals directly to the heart. It is exactly suited to the need of the masses of the people of India. Christianity is their true home.'

The idea that Hinduism was in decay was accompanied by another notion which had a greater moral and spiritual force behind it. According to it, Hinduism as seen contemporaneously was a corrupt form of the religion, which in some undetermined past was a very pure religion. This notion was first formulated by the Western Orientalists, who lived in a religious age and could not keep out qualitative judgements from their scientific study of Hinduism, and it was a deduction from their knowledge of the early religious texts of the Hindus, e.g. the Vedas, the Upanishads, and certain other works.

For instance, in 1869, Max Müller wrote to the Duke of Argyll, who was then the Secretary of State for India: 'It is certainly true that the religion of the Hindus, as far as we can gather it from their sacred hymns in the Veda, is free from everything that strikes us as degrading in the present state of their religion and morality in India.' He thought that between the ancient religion of India and religious worship of the Hindus of his times there had been several falls and several rises. Traditional Hindus were not, however, conscious of any corruption. But the reformers, as has been pointed out, took over this historical view.[1]

The Real State

All these connected ideas of decadence, corruption, and restoration of the original pure form of Hinduism really beg the question. It has been shown in a previous chapter that all the historical evidence that we have shows Hinduism to have been in the classical age of Hindu civilization almost what it was in the eighteenth and nineteenth centuries.

In any case Max Müller's contention that in his time Hinduism was dying or already dead did not pass unchallenged. The objector was Sir Alfred Lyall, one of the most distinguished English civil servants in India, as well as a scholar and acute observer of Indian life at first hand. In an article published in the July 1874 issue of the *Fortnightly Review*, then edited by John Morley, he said that it was worthwhile to enlarge on what he described as the very premature interment of Hinduism. He wrote:

> What I want to say is, that to an eye-witness this religion is not dead, nor dying, nor even dangerously ill; and, moreover, that so far from being a non-missionary religion in the sense of a religion that makes no proselytes, one might safely aver that more persons in India become every year Brahmanists than all the converts to all the other religions in India put together.

He pointed out that Brahmanism was kept expanding by the

[1] The Hindu reformer Ram Mohun Roy put forward this view at the beginning of the nineteenth century, but it became popular in India only in the last quarter of the century.

gradual but steady absorption of the primitive peoples of the backward regions into it. He explained that 'Brahmanism is all over India a necessary first stage for the outlying tribes towards Indian civilization, or admission to the citizenship of the great Hindu community.' Internally, according to Lyall, Brahmanism was kept growing by the 'working of the devotees and spiritual leaders who found new sects and set up new lights in divine matters.' He summed up the position in a clear-cut statement on the state of the religion. He also gave the reasons for its being in that state:

Brahmanism still lives and is propagated in India faster than any other religion, for these three principal reasons, namely—

That it is indigenous, the produce of the soil and of an environment that still exists.

That it is a social system, and a very elastic one; while the people of India as a body still need a religion which, like Brahmanism, provides them with social rules, with laws of custom as well as of conduct.

That it encourages and is nourished by a constant miraculous agency working at full pressure, by relays of divine embodiments; while in the present intellectual state of the population in India no religion will be widely embraced without miraculous credentials.

Lyall anticipated that these three characteristics were likely to keep Brahmanism alive for several generations to come. His article was published with a lengthy comment by Max Müller who felt most anxious that it should be published in England as the work of a man who saw with his own eyes and thought with his own brain, though it was directed against himself.

Lyall was wholly right in regarding Hinduism as a living religion in his time and in writing: 'There is nothing in the structure or present state of Brahmanism which need bring final dissolution upon this religion more rapidly than upon others, or that need prevent its undergoing the same modifications, mystifications, and spiritual quickening which have preserved other Asiatic religions.' This was truer of Hinduism at the beginning of the nineteenth century than towards its end when Lyall saw it, for at that time it had not felt the impact of European culture at all. All the evidence we have of the structure and functioning of Hinduism at the end of the eighteenth century or beginning of the nineteenth shows it to be a living phenomenon.

The concept of Hinduism as a stagnant lagoon of religious beliefs and practices in which the Hindus live like its fauna is, of course, an extension of the old and widespread idea of an unchanging East. It is responsible for many unrealistic anticipations regarding the future of Hinduism even now. It has led European observers wholly to exaggerate the importance of any changes they have noticed in the religious life of the Hindus, due either to ideological or economic influences, and to forecast a collapse of Hinduism. In the nineteenth century such a dissolution was expected from the cultural impact of the West, today it is predicted from industrialization. The same kind of uncritical thinking is seen in contemporary European writing on the caste system and the joint family. Of Hinduism it has to be said that the more it changes the more it remains the same thing. So, it creates the impression of staticity, and perhaps even of stagnancy.

But there is living and living. A state of becoming and a state of being are both living states. Besides, nothing can remain in a state of being without perpetual renovation, whose extent and tempo may vary according to circumstances. It is impossible to establish historically when Hinduism was in a state of becoming as distinct from being. But even in its state of being about which we have historical evidence over something like fifteen hundred years, it has been a living current like the great rivers of the northern plains. For instance, we do not know when the Ganges came into existence as a river, but we know that it has changed its course, and when one channel has been silted up it has flowed through other channels.

The living quality of Hinduism is demonstrated by the loyalty it has commanded from its followers. The faith which the Hindus had in their religion never wavered even in its worst days. It has had waxings and wanings which have kept the balance even. Though the religion was inherited and imposed by custom, faith in it was not passive, but always fervent. There was even fanaticism behind it. Within Hindu society any positive disregard of the Hindu way of life was suppressed inexorably by means of social coercion of the most inhuman type. The Hindus, too, had their Inquisition, but it was administered by a whole society. Against attacks, fancied or real, from the outside there was revolt. Privately, many may not have believed what they accepted publicly, but the volume of such disbelief was far less in the Hindu order than disbelief in Christianity among Europeans in the eighteenth or even the nineteenth century. The staunchness of the collective faith of the Hindus made private or individual irreligiosity of no significance, because what Hinduism enforced was public obedience. It took no account of private opinion.

The Question of Vitality

A religious system which has shown such aggressiveness and which can command such submission can never be regarded as devitalized. So, in writing about Hinduism in recent times the idea of decadence and corruption had better be given up altogether. Besides, it is very difficult to find out what is not decay in a religion by the standards adopted in the West for judging the quality of religious life. By that sort of standard the decay of Hinduism could be dated back almost to the Vedic age. Therefore, those who have played for safety in writing about Hinduism have almost reduced it to an airy nothing, serving out abstractions which baffle understanding. Unfortunately, in the West, Hinduism has attracted minds which rise to an ineffable ecstasy by feeding on emptiness or merely on words.

Lastly, in judging the vitality of Hinduism the point should be emphasized that it has maintained itself through the ages and enforced obedience to itself without support from any kind of organization, secular or spiritual. It has created an overall conformity by its own psychological hold, and this shows that there can be a kind of authority over men which is in no way less coercive than that of the State, though it is intangible. This coercive power of Hinduism was so absolute even in the nineteenth century that any idea of disregarding its injunctions even in such matters as wearing clothes or cutting the hair would have evoked horror as well as terror. Hinduism has shown that anarchy can be as authoritarian as any totalitarian state.

Chapter Two

REGIONAL AND SOCIAL
DIVERSITY

TO offer a systematic description of Hinduism without bringing into relief its immense diversities at the same time, would be to mislead the reader. But to emphasize them, which is unavoidable, would be to give the impression that there is no system at all. The diversities in Hinduism are of many kinds. They may, however, be grouped under three broad categories. There are the variations in beliefs, cults, and rituals which make Hinduism appear like a conglomeration of religions. After that there are differences which are due to geographical distribution. Last of all, the attitudes and practices vary according to class affiliations. In this chapter I shall consider the last two kinds of variations, that is to say, those connected with the environment. The intrinsic differences will be dealt with in the next.

No European writer who has described Hinduism at first hand has been so careless as to do so without indicating the region to which his account applies. This was done by the earliest writers, Lord, Roger, and Baldaeus. The Abbé Dubois made it clear that his description was confined virtually to what he saw in south India. 'There is no place in India,' he wrote, 'which does not possess certain customs and practices of its own, and it would be impossible to give descriptions of them all.' Moreover, even in respect of south India he gave the caution that too general a meaning should not be given to what he was saying. He pointed out that there were such differences between the linguistic groups in south India itself that 'careful observers would see less resemblance between a Tamil and a Canarese, between a Telugu and a Mahratta, than between a Frenchman and an Englishman, an Italian and a German.'

Seventy years later W. J. Wilkins of the London Missionary Society had to make it clear that he was giving 'an account of religion and life of the Hindus in northern India.' He pointed out the risk any writer on Hinduism ran when describing it from his own knowledge:

It should be remembered also that descriptions absolutely true of certain classes or certain districts may not be strictly correct of other classes or other districts; and also that some classes are grossly ignorant of the customs of other classes, and the residents of one district, while familiar with the practices common there, are totally ignorant of what prevails in other parts of the country.

Therefore Wilkins thought it necessary to warn readers about too ready and impulsive a disbelief in statements made about the religion. 'When, therefore,' he wrote, 'hearing or reading of certain things being believed or done by Hindus, we are inclined to deny the accuracy of these statements, it is well to inquire whether it is not our limited knowledge that is at fault rather than the accuracy of the writer or speaker.'

I give one example to show how a Hindu showed this impulsive disbelief. This man was the Bengali Christian to whose book I referred in the previous chapter.[1] In it he vehemently denied that small children were ever thrown by their mothers into the mouth of the Ganges in Bengal in fulfilment of certain vows. He even added an appendix to his book to contradict the report, and in it he wrote:

Ever since my arrival in America I have heard with great surprise the statement, received on the authority of missionaries, that the Hindoo mothers throw their infants into the river Ganges. Almost every man, woman, boy, or girl in the United States knows it, and has seen illustrations of it in various books. During my tour over some sixteen States and the Canadas, I noticed that the Hindoo mother, her baby, and the alligator, were the subjects of constant inquiry. The story of the infants being thrown into the Ganges by their heartless mistaken mothers, is believed by the people of this country to be either a custom or a religious institution of the Hindoos.

He declared that he could not 'suffer a groundless and strange story to run so freely through the Christian community, and bring upon the poor innocent women of India such undeserved reproach', and he asserted that he had not heard of it even as a grandmother's story. He wrote: 'I will confess that, although a Brahmin, a native of India, I never saw a child thrown alive into the Ganges, nor heard of such stories until I came to America.'

[1] See p. 109.

In saying this he was not consciously untruthful, but he was amazingly ignorant. The man was born and brought up near Calcutta, on the very river at whose mouth the children were thrown into water. Besides, everybody (including myself as a child) knew it as fact. And what is absolutely decisive, the practice was prohibited by a legislative order of the Governor-General (Regulation VI of 1802), which made the throwing of children into the Ganges equivalent to murder.

So, when describing Hinduism with every intention to be truthful and making every effort to be accurate, a writer should never ignore the possibility that he might not be believed by some of his readers. On the other hand, it is also very difficult to detect a deliberately false statement. So the writer should clearly state what he is describing, and anyone who is too ready to disbelieve should check his own knowledge of the custom or practice described.[1]

Regional Types

It is easy to define the broad regional types and to account for their emergence as distinct forms. These are seen in a number of distinct blocs of beliefs and practices, each in a region which shows not only a physiographical unity, but also homogeneity in social and cultural life. These regions are the following: the great north Indian plain from the Punjab to Bihar, including the western portion of central India formerly known as Malwa: south India where the four civilized Dravidian languages are spoken; Bengal and Assam, including Orissa; Rajputana; the sub-Himalayan regions. There are two more recognizable blocs, the Maharashtra country and Gujarat, that is to say, the whole area of the British Indian province of Bombay; but the Hinduism of the Maharashtra country is akin to that of the south, and that of Gujarat to that in the Gangetic plain. There are, of course, variations within some of these regions. But all the other differences are pushed into a secondary place by the very large contrast between two types, namely, that which exists between the Hinduism

[1] Even when writing this book I myself contradicted a modern Tamil young woman, who I thought knew nothing about Hinduism, when she said that the god Kartikeya had a wife. On checking up I found that in south India the god was given a wife, whereas in Bengal he was regarded as a confirmed bachelor.

of the northern plain on the one hand, and on the other of all the other regional blocs mentioned above.

The original and natural cause of the geographical variations of Hinduism is easy to find. It is the same which has created the diversity of Indian languages and dialects. It was natural that Hinduism, whose centre of diffusion in India was the plain between the Sutlej and Jumna, would show an immense range of regional variations as it spread over the rest of the country towards the east, south, west, and north, a process which may have taken centuries.

But this natural and regular evolution does not explain the starkest contrast: that which is seen between the Hinduism of the northern plain and that of the rest of the country, particularly the south. Most observers have been struck by the contrast, and its awareness has created a notion which is fairly widespread, that south India had a cultural individuality of its own, and that in religion as in culture that part of the Indian peninsula had a course of development independent of the north. All kinds of explanations have been given for the contrast, to which the regional sentiment created by the Dravidian languages has given a political expression. But though the contrast is undeniable, the explanations for it are untenable. It was not due to any natural evolution of Hindu life and culture in a special geographical, ethnic, and cultural environment, but was created by political history—to be specific, by the Muslim conquest of northern India and its destructive effect.

Effect of the Muslim Conquest

This can be most conclusively demonstrated by taking the very thing which creates the impression that the south is different from the north. Those who see the two regions exclaim: 'Oh, the south is the land of great temples!' But the simple historical explanation of this fact is that in the south the temples have survived, and in the north they have not. Over seven centuries from the eleventh to the end of the seventeenth all the great cities of northern India dating from Hindu times were sacked by the Muslim invaders and conquerors of India. All the temples there and in all other centres of Hinduism were systematically destroyed. None were left standing at Ujjain, Ajmere, Delhi, Mathura, Brindaban, Kanauj, Prayag, or Benares — which were the centres of the political, cultural, and religious life of the Hindus. In most of these places mosques were built on the sites of the temples, and in some with pillars taken from them. This religious vandalism also worked its fury on the Buddhist centres. Moreover, it was not simply that the great temples in the cities were destroyed; so were the village temples. For most of the period of Muslim rule, there was a ban on building new temples and rebuilding the old in the regions the Muslims controlled.

The ban was lifted by Akbar, but this was a short respite. It was then that one of the most original and beautiful temples of northern India was built. It was that of Govindaji at Brindaban. It could not be finished, but like the Unfinished Symphony of Schubert it remains a great work of art. The ban on temples was re-imposed, and a period of iconoclastic fury was witnessed under Shah Jahan (himself the son of a Hindu princess) and Aurangzeb, when even the rebuilt temples were again razed. It was only with the rise of Maratha power in the latter half of the eighteenth century that the destruction ceased and rebuilding began. The Marathas rebuilt Benares. The new temple of Visvanath — the old having been converted into a mosque by Aurangzeb — was built by the Maratha princess Ahilya Bai of the Holkar family, and the famous waterfront of Benares was the creation of other Maratha princes and one Rajput prince.

So it is impossible to judge what Hindu temple architecture was like in its homeland in the greatest age of Hindu civilization. We can only guess from scattered references in secular Sanskrit literature. One Sanskrit epic written at the end of the twelfth century laments the destruction of the temples at Ajmere. It was meant to celebrate the victory of Prithviraj, the Chauhan king, over Muhammad of Ghur in the first battle of Tarain, but the next year this king was defeated and killed, and so the poem was not finished. But it was given a prologue in which the burning of the temples and crashing of their steeples are described.

During all those centuries, all over northern India only ruins of the temples were to be seen. But the Hindus did not forget the houses of their gods. When at the beginning of the eighteenth century the Jesuit priest and mathematician Tiffenthaler travelled from the west coast of India to Malwa he saw in the evenings the flickering lights of the earthen lamps placed in these ruins by the villagers at some risk to themselves. It was only in the regions where Muslim power could not penetrate on account of their inaccessibility that the temples escaped destruction, and two of the most notable groups which have survived are those at Khajuraho and Mahoba in Bundelkhand and at Bhuvaneswar, Puri, and Konarak in Orissa. Both the regions were protected by hills and jungles. Even so Orissa suffered a short spell of vandalism in the sixteenth century.

Thus temple architecture in northern India is represented by examples which are provincial and for the most part late. Yet even these examples are so impressive that they are included among the greatest temples to be found in India. The temples at the centres of Hindu political power in the Gangetic plain and in Malwa must have been more numerous and splendid. But they have disappeared, and those which are now seen in these areas are not only smaller but also in a style considerably influenced by Islamic architecture. All this has induced modern observers to give pre-eminence to the south as the land of temples at the expense of the Aryavarta—the home of Hindu culture.

What happened to the temples in northern India happened also to the Hindu princely order and the aristocracy. A majority of them were just exterminated, and the rest fled to the Himalayan foothills. The social and cultural vacuum thus created was filled up by Turkish, Persian, and Afghan colonists and a Muslim aristocracy, and in northern India that substitution was a disaster for every expression of Hindu culture, including religion. The dominant culture in the Gangetic plain became Islamic, and the Hindus became a cultural proletariat. They never recovered their old cultural status during the whole of British rule, and have not done so even today.

Nothing illustrates the transformation of Hindu life in the northern plain better than the change in the economic status and manner of living of the two upper castes, the Brahmins and the Kshatriyas, i.e. the priestley and the fighting castes. They were necessarily dependent on the Hindu kings for providing them with livelihood as priests and soldiers, their caste vocations. Deprived of the patronage, both the castes largely adopted agriculture as their main source of living and became peasants. The establishment of British power in India gave both of them a military function, and a majority of the sepoys of the Bengal Army, i.e. the north Indian army of the East India Company, came from these two castes. It was they who rose in rebellion against the British at an imagined threat to their religion, and the ruthless suppression of that rising gave a further blow to the higher expression of Hinduism in Hindustan. This new name of *Hindustan* for the Gangetic plain is significant in itself. In Sanskrit this plain, the homeland of Brahmanism, was called the Aryavarta, i.e. the land of the Aryas or Aryans. The new name was Persian.

Thus the course of political history in northern India reduced both Hindu culture and religion to the level of a folk culture and folk religion by depriving it of its élite. Both lost their sophistication and pride. Sanskrit learning virtually disappeared from the region, and orthodoxy in the *mores* became less rigorous. The festivals became more and more democratic, although patronized by the wealthy.

Under Muslim rule there remained in northern India only one social order which still carried on the tradition of a high social and religious culture, and that was the wealthy Bania or commercial class. The Muslims could not do without this class, and by means of its wealth it continued a kind of Hinduism which, though not at the old level, was higher than the Hinduism of the common people of the region.

Nevertheless, an overall denudation could not be avoided. This is comparable to the geographical change that has come over the Gangetic basin through deforestation and denudation of the soil. The forests of that region have become scrub; so have culture and religion in a figurative sense. Thus Hindu culture here wears an appearance of poverty which was not its old condition. It is the religious expression of this culture, which is the 'popular Hinduism' of English writers. In reality it was only the remnant, the detritus of the old Hinduism.

Comparison of this kind of survival with a higher kind in the south created an impression of the superiority of the latter. The contrast was noticed even by the earliest writers on India. They were led to think that in northern India Hinduism hardly existed, because they had made their first acquaintance with it in the more elaborate form it had in the south. Robert Orme, the first historian of British India, noted in the first volume of his history published in 1763 that 'the northern nations of India, although idolaters, having scarce a religion, when compared with the multitudes of superstitions and ceremonies which characterize the inhabitants of southern countries, were easily induced to embrace Mahomedanism'. In saying this Orme was really mistaking the effect for the cause. The Hindus of northern India did not embrace Islam because they had no religion; their religion was reduced to its lowest denominator owing to the Muslim conquest.

It should, however, be kept in mind that within these two very large blocs of Hinduism created in north and south India by history, there were differences which created smaller blocs. In the south the Tamil-speaking Hindus constituted the most important and typical group, while those who spoke Telugu, Canarese and Malayalam were associated groups, not minor in themselves, but less assertive and with less prestige derived from the places of pilgrimage and temples than the Tamil area.

In the north, on the other hand, the Hindus of the Punjab had a form of religion which was simpler even than that of the Gangetic plain. In their manners and external ways they were very largely Islamized, and most of them till recently read even their own religious books in Urdu translations, because they could not read the Deva Nagari script. But so far as writing was concerned, it must be remembered that the north-west of India had the right-to-left style of writing from very ancient times. Under Muslim rule, and also with competition facing them from both Islam and Sikhism, the Hindu content of their faith became very elementary.

To sum up the matter, the Muslim conquest pulverized Hinduism in the northern plain, but left it as an old and yet inhabited building in the south. There is no reason to assume that before the Muslim conquest Hindu culture and religion were in any significant way different in the two regions. It must not be forgotten that the most famous commentator of the Vedas, Sayana, and the greatest exponent of philosophic Brahmanism, Saṃkara, came from the south.

Peripheral Hinduism of Northern India

This conclusion is supported by all the features of Hinduism as it is in the peripheral regions of northern India, namely, Bengal taken with Orissa and Assam, Nepal and the sub-Himalayan regions, Gujarat, and Rajasthan. The Maharashtra country may be added to these. The forms of Hinduism in these areas, when taken as a whole, are closer to the form in the south than to that of the Gangetic plain, and besides they exhibit greater similarities among themselves even when separated by large intervening regions, than to the areas adjacent to them on the Gangetic plain. For instance, the cult of the Mother Goddess is virtually absent in the Ganges basin, but is found in Rajputana, Nepal, and Bengal. Also, the paintings of the hill Rajput schools show that the Krishna cult in the sub-Himalayan regions of the north-west is the same as in Bengal. In fact, the paintings most often illustrate the themes found in the *Gita-Govinda*, a famous poem of the Krishna cult written in Bengal.

In none of these regions was the continuity of the highest Hindu traditions ever broken, and both learning and orthodoxy stood behind the practice of the religion. Therefore the Hinduism of the peripheral regions must be taken as the true surviving form of the Hinduism of the north as it was before the Muslim conquest. Furthermore, these, together with the forms in the south, have to be taken as the most sophisticated expression of the religion to come down to modern times.

But there was a difference of attitudes between the north and the south even when the forms were similar, and this too was due to political history. This is best illustrated by comparing the Hindu spirit in Bengal with that in the south. For the greater part of their rule in India the Muslims never penetrated the deep south, and though they ruled in the Deccan and also in the Carnatic, their domination was merely political. They did not establish colonies except in Hyderabad and a few other cities under the rule of the Nizam of the Deccan. What was more important, no extensive conversion of the lower classes of the Hindus took place at all. Even the political domination of the Muslims was a loose military suzerainty, which left local government in the hands of the smaller chiefs, some of whom were called Polygars. The social and religious life of the Hindus was left unaffected by Muslim rule.

Thus control of the social, cultural, and religious life of the Hindus of the south, more especially in the Tamil country, remained in the hands of the Brahmins, who maintained it undisputed till the beginning of this century. The power of the Brahmins also meant the hold of the older and higher form of Hinduism, because of their knowledge of Sanskrit. Though the spoken and written mother tongue of the Brahmins was Tamil or some other language of the so-called Dravidian family, they had a knowledge of Sanskrit which was not surpassed in the north, and was often deeper. Secular life of the region remained wholly within the framework set by Hinduism.

Hinduism in Bengal was different due to the political history of the province. It was conquered by the Muslims at the same time as northern India, and they ruled the province till the coming of the British. Political power became so closely associated with Islam that even a Hindu who had asserted independence and became a king embraced the religion. Moreover, during the centuries of Muslim rule a very large number of low-caste Hindus were converted to Islam. Thus in Bengal there was Muslim domination at the top, and a heavy Muslim ballast at the bottom.

None the less, the social, cultural, and religious life of high-caste Bengalis was left untouched. The reason was that the rule of the Muslims in Bengal was purely military with a very loose administrative organization. With the exception of a small number of Turks, Persians, and Afghans at the top there was no colonization by any large body of Muslims of non-Indian origins. Furthermore, for more than half the period of Muslim rule the Muslim kings of the province were independent of the centre in Delhi. So these rulers had to work with the local aristocracy and gentry, instead of dispossessing them. Actually, in the eighteenth century Hindus held very high positions in the top ranks of the administration, and the lower ranks of the revenue collectors were composed almost entirely of Hindus from the upper castes. Thus the higher administration in Bengal could not afford to be anti-Hindu.

On the other hand, the Bengali converts to Islam who came from the lower castes did not acquire the convert's fanaticism. They had become used to a subordinate position, and did not aspire to a dominant one even though they had adopted the religion of the ruling order. Besides, their Islamization was very imperfect. They joined the Hindu religious festivals and even ceremonies, and furnished musicians for them. Some Muslims even wrote Bengali poetry, and some of it on mythological subjects. So Hinduism was not only spared in Bengal, but actually flourished at a level not seen in the Gangetic plain. Bengal even sent pundits to Benares and Brindaban and kept up the tradition of Hindu learning in upper India.

Through this kind of survival Hinduism in Bengal remained at the same level of sophistication as it had in the south. But there was a qualitative difference between the conservatism of Bengal and of the Tamil country. In the latter the existence of Hindu culture and religion had not been threatened, and therefore the Brahmins and the upper castes were internally stable, self-confident, and unaggressive in their traditionalism. They exercised repression only in respect of the old enemy of Brahmanism in the south, the non-Aryan local population, who were represented by the untouchable castes and classes. Their treatment of the Untouchables, though a very cruel form of apartheid, was accepted without protest.

In Bengal, on the contrary, the presence of the Muslims, both as rulers and as a large internal proletariat, was a continuing threat, not so much from any kind of Islamic zeal which they might have, as from the temptations held out to the Hindus. Muslim rule had brought about an internal dichotomy in the life of high-cast Hindus. For the sake of livelihood and also to rise to a high worldly position very large numbers of them had to be in the employment of the Muslim rulers. In these posts, especially the higher ones, they had to put on Muslim clothes, adopt Muslim manners, speak and write the Persian language. The landowners when they were of the highest rank, also affected the clothes of the Muslim nobility and spoke Persian. In doing all these they could easily overstep the permissible limits and disregard the rules of Hindu private life. So sanctions had to be imposed against such transgression.

Thus strict observance of all Hindu rules of conduct was enforced with very great rigour, and the old taboos against non-Hindu ways were made even more compulsory than before. Brahmanic conservatism in Bengal added a sharp edge to the old rigidity, and became something like Catholicism after the Counter-Reformation. The pundits not only remained the guardians and exponents of the ancient sacred law known as *Smriti*, but also promulgated a new and very elaborate *Smriti* themselves. A new and rigorous code of sacred law promulgated by the most famous of the Bengali authorities on it, the Smarta Raghunandana, regulated every aspect of Hindu personal conduct in Bengal, and was obeyed by all. The gentry co-operated with the pundits in ensuring this conformity. Thus in Bengal, at the beginning of the nineteenth century, owing to the ever-present threat from the Muslims, Hinduism had become intolerant and dour in its attitude. It had developed a fanaticism of which all Bengalis with nonconformist inclinations were afraid.

Aboriginal Areas of Central India

There is one more important geographical and ethnic bloc of Hinduism to be considered. It is quite another world even in the fantastic world of Hinduism. It is contained within the hilly regions of central India, and its Hinduism is that of the primitive tribes who had moved into the perimeter of the religion in ancient times or were doing so in the nineteenth century. Hardly anything was known about it before the latter half of that century when English anthropologists and other investigators began to record the life and institutions of the aboriginals. In giving an account of it I shall depend on the authority of one who knew it at first hand and left descriptions of it. He was Sir Alfred Lyall, who saw and studied this form of Hinduism in one of the backward regions of India, Berar in central India. His account is to be found in the gazeteer of this province and in an article published in the *Fortnightly Review* (February 1872). Though this part of the aboriginal region was more Hinduized than others and there were perceptible differences in the degree of permeation by Hindu influences among the aboriginals, Berar provided a typical illustration of the manner in which they took over Hinduism. There is no better way of describing it than in the words of Lyall. He wrote:

> The cultus of the elder or classic Hindu pantheon is only a portion of the popular religion of the country. Here in India, more than in any other part of the world, do men worship most what they understand least. Not only do they adore all strange phenomena and incomprehensible forces—being driven by incessant awe of the invisible powers to propitiate every unusual shape or striking natural object—but their pantheistic piety leads them to invest with a mysterious potentiality the animals which are most useful to man, and even the implements of a profitable trade.

In his article Lyall described the character of the Hinduism of the people of this province in these words: 'Now just as the word Hindu is no national or even geographical denomination, but signifies vaguely a fortuitous conglomeration of sects, tribes, races, hereditary professions, and pure castes, so the religion of this population of Hindus is at first sight a heterogeneous confusion.' He gave a list of the objects of worship:

1. The worship of mere stocks and stones, and of local configurations, which are unusual or grotesque in size, shape, or pŏsition.
2. The worship of things inanimate, which are gifted with mysterious motion.
3. The worship of animals which are feared.
4. The worship of visible things animate or inanimate, which are directly or indirectly useful and profitable, or which possess any incomprehensible function or property.
5. The worship of Deo, or spirit, a thing without form and void—the vague impersonation of the uncanny sensation that comes over one at certain places.
6. The worship of dead relatives, and other deceased persons known in their life-time to the worshippers.
7. The worship at shrines of persons who had a great reputation during life, or who died in some strange or notorious way.
8. The worship in temples of persons belonging to the foregoing class, as demigods or subordinate deities.
9. The worship of the manifold local incarnations of the elder deities and of their symbols.
10. The worship of departmental deities.
11. The worship of the supreme gods of Hinduism, and of their ancient incarnations and personifications, handed down by the Brahmanic scriptures.

Lyall explains that these divisions in no way denote separate bodies of votaries, nor do they correspond even with any parallel steps of civilized intelligence or social position. This is an acute and profound observation, for nothing in Hinduism is exclusive of anything else, nor is the normal cultural and educational level of a Hindu any indication of the level or levels at which he might believe. So Lyall observed: 'The average middle-class Hindu might be brought by one part or another of his everyday religious practice within any or many of these classes.' Thus it would be a mistake to regard the type of Hinduism found among the aboriginals as their exclusive possession, and it would be equally a mistake to think that only primitive beliefs and practices were their sole religious experience.

Significance of the Geographical Diversities

It has been considered necessary to give a schematic view of the large geographical blocs of Hinduism because otherwise there would be either an abstraction from the reality or its falsification. In writing about Hinduism there is every temptation to avoid trouble by representing one form as the sole form or a complete expression of the whole religious complex. There is a greater chance of overlooking the important fact that the political history of each region has given to its Hinduism a special character, so that the form seen in it cannot be said to have been brought into existence by a self-contained religious evolution. In particular, the distinction between popular Hinduism and the higher Hinduism is seen to be the product of political history. Last of all, a bird's-eye-view of Hinduism *in situ*, so to speak, is indispensable to correct the worst misrepresentation of all—that is, a reconstruction from the sacred texts.

None the less, the geographical diversities should not be over-emphasized. They have not created any exclusive loyalty to a particular regional form. A group of Hindus might live in a particular region, and normally confine their religious life to the practices found there. But they would never show any exclusiveness in doing so, far less any hostility to the beliefs and practices of other localities. No south Indian will think that Benares or the Ganges is less sacred to him than Madura or the Cauveri, and in exactly the same way no north Indian will undervalue the sacred places or rivers of the south. Actually, it is in regard to the geographical diversity of their religion that the Hindus are most ecumenical. The last of the five obligatory duties of Islam, which are called its pillars, is to complete a Muslim's adherence to it by going to the place of its origin and centre of diffusion, Mecca. In contrast, the Hindu seeks to do so by visiting the farthest places his religion has reached in the course of its expansion. Therefore, he thinks he has not arrived at the fullness of his religious life unless he has made his pilgrimage to Amarnath, Badrinath, or Pashupatinath in the Himalayan fastnesses; Somnath on the Arabian Sea; Puri on the Bay of Bengal; Rameshwaram or

Kanyakumari on the Indian Ocean; Jwalamukhi in the Punjab hills; or Kamrup in Assam.

As to deities, no Hindu will withhold his faith in or devotion to any Hindu deity, whoever might be his particular local, personal deity. Kali in Calcutta, Siva at Benares, Krishna at Mathura or Brindaban are gods for all Hindus.

Over and above, the Hindus wherever they might live, have a uniform and coherent outlook on religion. This similarity is seen in the religious position taken by them and not in the identity of cults and rituals. While Hindu religious beliefs and practices are multiform, the Hindu religious outlook is very unitary. Wherever they come from, the Hindus will hold the same view of the deity, express the same views about religious life, and put forward the same apologia for their religion. It is in this that the true unity of Hinduism is to be seen. It is more a particular religious outlook than a particular religion.

The existence of this unity is all the more marvellous because it has not been created by propaganda or intercommunication. On the contrary, the intercommunication has been created by it. Of course, it has its agencies and instruments. The unity has been maintained by the priestly class, the Brahmins, whose mode of life all over India remains the least affected by social changes; by the prevalence of the Sanskrit language, which has maintained the unity of ideology in the Hindu order as effectually as Arabic has done in the Islamic world; and by the corpus of standard religious texts collectively known as the Sastras. But, above all, there has been a subtle exhalation which has created a single atmosphere. Owing to all this there is a general loyalty to the religion which nothing can shake.

Class Differences: Priests and the Aristocracy

The final category of differences in the spirit and practice of Hinduism is the product of social stratifications in Hindu society. These are seen even within a region which is linguistically and culturally homogeneous, because this homogeneity has not prevented Hinduism from being different in complexion in the various classes. At the top of the superimposed varieties is the Hinduism of the priestly class, the landed aristocracy, and the commercial class.

To take the priestly class first, among them Hinduism was seen in a form which has undergone hardly any modification since ancient times, that is, with all the routine of rituals and observances laid down in the sacred texts, including the Vedic. A majority of the Brahmins who followed the profession of priests knew these texts, especially the liturgical, only by rote, and performed the rites and ceremonies more or less mechanically for the sake of a living. But among the Brahmins there was also a *corps d'élite*, the pundits, who were deep students of Hindu sacred law and philosophy, though at times they also took part in the rites of marriage and funerals *(Sradh)*. Their normal occupation was performance of all the rites, initiation and supervision of their spiritual clients as Gurus, the study of sacred text, and teaching young students. In fact, only these men performed the function of the Brahmin caste as laid down in the Sastras. They held the conscience of all lay Hindus, who in all matters of orthodoxy and correctness appealed to them. They enjoyed great authority and respect, and exercised the function of spiritual directors both as individuals with a reputation for learning, and as members of a family with hereditary spiritual clients, even though without learning. It was by them again that Hindu philosophy of different schools was studied and the continuity of the philosophical tradition maintained. Along with these, they were also the custodians of secular Sanskrit literature and the grammar of the language. Personally, these pundits were extremely strict and scrupulous in adhering to the old Hindu way down to the smallest details of daily life, and they always depended on the authority of the sacred texts in their preaching as well as practice. Not even the Pharisees were more rigorous about their Law.

Thus at this level Hindu religious life presented a very austere, self-confident, and arrogant form with a hidebound system of rituals and observances as its content. But the outlook and habits of the pundits, though almost fossilized, showed an intense vitality in the aggressive dogmatism of the whole class. These men were the defenders of the Hindu way of life, to which, as has been pointed out, an ever-present threat was created by the presence of Islam in India. The Muslims were proselytizers by principle, and showed themselves active in this. They brought about massive defections from the Hindu order. But even within that order they were insidiously dangerous, for they tempted the Hindus sorely and often successfully to be lax in maintaining the Hindu *mores*, not only in regard to religion strictly so-called, but also in such things as clothing, eating, care of the person, and toilet. The Brahmin priests and pundits kept such irregularities in check, by punishing transgressions when they passed the permissible limit. They could do so because they had to be obeyed. No Hindu could perform any of the numerous rites, or conduct the worship of the gods, on which their temporal as well as spiritual welfare depended without them. Hindu excommunication was to put a man outside the caste and this power belonged to the Brahmins.

But the class expression of Hinduism had also a more human and easy aspect, which had nothing of the cold aloofness of the religious life of the priestly Brahmins. This was seen in the observances of those who had a high worldly position, namely, the Hindu princes where they existed, the Hindu landed aristocracy, and also the commercial aristocracy. The princes and the landowners could belong to any caste, from the highest to the lowest as defined in the Sastras, and they did. The commercial aristocracy was overwhelmingly of the Vaisya or trading class, though men of other castes including even Brahmins could belong to it. The unity of these classes lay in their wealth and social position, and thus their religious life, too, had great worldly splendour.

Privately, the twice-born in the upper social classes observed the routine of daily life which was laid down in the sacred books or was customary in the class, but the observance was less rigorous and elaborate than among the Brahmin pundits. Their life was in the world, and the typical expression of their religiosity was also worldly. It was to be seen mainly in temple worship and seasonal festivals, both of which were performed with a good deal of pomp. It was in the Hinduism of these men that its full social functioning could be seen, and in it the social and the religious elements were so intermingled that the two could hardly be separated.

These classes played a very important role in the preservation of Hinduism. They were, figuratively speaking, the patrons of the gods in the world, for the gods owed their temples to them. The wealthy landed and commercial families built and endowed temples and created religious trusts from which the worship of the gods was maintained.

These classes were, of course, the economic patrons of the priests and pundits. The relations between them and the sacred order were very close. In one aspect of their religious role the

upper classes constituted the secular arm of Hinduism, reproduc-
ing in a devolved form the relationship which existed in ancient
times between the king and the priest. In another aspect they
provided financial support for the priestly class. They made gifts
of money and goods to the priests on all ceremonial occasions,
bestowed rent-free land on them, and also provided regular
salaried employment to the lower priests for the performance of
all routine worship and rites in their homes.

They were in a figurative sense the owners of the religion, which
the Brahmins were not. Just as in Hindu law all land belonged to
the king and was only usufructuary to all others — which was the
principle behind the land revenue system — the religion, too,
belonged to the ruler as its protector. When and where the Muslims and after them the British ruled in India, only the right in
land passed to them as the new sovereign order, not the right over
the religion. It remained with the Hindu princes where they
existed, but elsewhere was taken over and exercised by the Hindu
landed and commercial aristocracy. To give two examples, in the
second half of the eighteenth century the temple of Visvanath at
Benares was rebuilt by the Maratha princess Ahilya Bai of the
House of Holkar, but the new temples to Krishna at Mathura
and Brindaban were built by the great Seths of Mathura.

These patrons of Hinduism did not make use of their connection
with it for profit, except when they created religious trusts out of
their own properties for the regular worship in perpetuity of a
particular deity in a temple built by them. In that case, they took
for themselves whatever was left after the service of the gods.[1] In
the exercise of their ownership of the religion they were, however,
more trustees than beneficiaries. All the monetary gains from
Hinduism, which though immense were diffused, were for the
Brahmin priests. The secular patrons of the religion regarded it as
a heritage and trust which they had to preserve even if they could
not augment it. The religious function of this class was thus somewhat akin to the political function of a feudal aristocracy.

The true character of their patronage of religion was seen even
more clearly in the way the aristocracy allowed the common
people to join in and see the worship and festivities, and also to

---

[1] To give a small personal example, my great-great-grandfather built a temple
to Kali and endowed it with a part of our property, and down to my young
days we used to get some money from the surplus.

bring in their offerings as outsiders, though the services were performed at the cost of the owners and were meant in the first instance for their own spiritual benefit. As the entrepreneurs of the festivals these classes never thought of reserving them for their private enjoyment. The common people of the village or town came and took part in them as if in the religious sphere too, they were what they were in regard to the land which they tilled for the owners, namely, cultivating tenants. The temples which the upper classes owned were all open to the general public. In this way the aristocracy maintained the hold of the highest existing form of Hinduism over the common people, in which these latter would have had no share if they had stood on their own.

Mass Expression

However, the common people had a Hinduism of their own, which was not only practised by them, but was also kept in a living state as a folk religious culture by means of a process which might be called spontaneous regeneration or replenishment. This was the form called 'Popular Hinduism' by British writers, and they saw that it was in many ways very different from the Hinduism of the scriptures and tradition. L. S. S. O'Malley, who has written a book on this form of Hinduism, giving to it the sub-title, 'The Religion of the Masses', wrote in his preface: 'India has been described as a land of contrasts, but in nothing are the contrasts more marked than in Hinduism, in which the differences between the beliefs and practices of the cultured classes and those of the masses, mostly unlettered villagers, are so great that they almost seem to be differences of kind rather than degree.'

In this Hinduism the hieratic character was subordinate, and the conscious historical tradition was absent. It existed in a perpetual *now*, though certainly it had come down from the past, and perhaps bore the same relation to the higher Hinduism as the dialects of the countryside in India bear to the literary language, or the relationship which sand and mud have to the sedimentary strata of stone in the same sea-bed. Looked at from the point of cultural anthropology, it was a folk culture and not a civilized culture. It was therefore more self-supporting and less dependent than higher Hinduism on conscious transmission for its perpetuation.

But even popular Hinduism had different layers and was not all one. It had a very characteristic expression among the small tradesmen, craftsmen, and prosperous agriculturists. The religion of these classes was nourished not only by the spoken word, but also by the written word, embodied in vernacular renderings of the old Hindu myths, legends, and spiritual teaching. It was more especially under the sway of the popular prophets, who preached wholly within the mode of *Bhakti* or love, and therefore it was more emotional. Again, it was from these classes that the popular preachers and minor prophets mostly emerged. The peasantry took part in the religious life of all the classes in a very simple and loose way. What they received from this religion was what they were capable by their mental development of receiving. No upper class put any religious pressure on them.

Nomadic Expression

The three expressions of Hinduism described so far, namely, the priestly, the aristocractic, and the popular, were all contained within the settled and sedentary social life of the Hindus. In addition to these, there was also an unsocial if not anti-social expression of the religion. This was to be found among men who had left the world to lead a life devoted to religion either as individuals or as members of groups organized in mendicant orders. The individual holy men lived as hermits in forests or mountains by themselves, subsisting largely on voluntary charities from nearby villages. They also travelled a good deal and in some cases settled temporarily or permanently in places of pilgrimage like Benares, and lived on gifts from the pilgrims. Some of them became not only famous but even legendary.

Men in the world tried to exploit their holiness sometimes from a religious motive, that is, for the sake of spiritual guidance, but most often to profit in the worldly way by means of the supernatural powers with which they were credited. But as a rule the individual holy men remained aloof from society, and were thoroughly egoistic. They had broken completely with their social origins and family ties, and so could not disclose their origins. From very ancient times these men presented themselves as the typical representatives of Hinduism, especially to foreigners. By the eighteenth century they had become timeless, though continuing a very ancient institution of Hinduism, whose existence is historically proved.

But the great majority of the nomadic followers of Hinduism were predatory. That is to say, they were not simply benign parasites on society like the recluses, but lived on it by extorting their living from lay Hindus either through a spontaneous submission or by actual robbery and plunder. Their normal life was one of wandering in groups large or small. They came to the great religious gatherings like the Kumbha Mela in very large numbers, each sect or order with its distinctive insignia, regimented and drilled; and at times they fought with the other orders for precedence. They were very truculent and carried tongs, tridents, staves, and brass pots, all of which they used as weapons when occasion arose. All of them were addicts of cannabis and other drugs. If their relationship with society could be regarded as any kind of symbiosis it was like the relation the prowling leopards have with human habitations. These animals usually kill game or stray cattle, but when short of food also raid the village byres.

The ascetics were also capable of organized raids and plunder. At the beginning of British rule they looted villages in north Bengal on their way to Jagannath in Orissa. Warren Hastings reported to the Court of Directors of the East India Company that they were in the habit of making incursions annually into Bengal, which was the Company's territory, from the north-west. In 1772 and 1773 they became very aggressive and came in bands varying in strength from 1,000 to 10,000 Sanyasis (ascetics). They actually succeeded in destroying two detachments of the Company's troops under Captains Thomas and Edwards and killing both of them. In 1773 five battalions of regular sepoys had to be deployed to drive them out of Bengal.

Warren Hastings wrote that their appearances were very sudden: 'for in spite of the strictest orders issued and the severest penalties threatened to the inhabitants, in case they fail in giving intelligence of the approaches of the Senassies, they are so infatuated by superstition, as to be backward in giving the information, so that the banditti are sometimes advanced into the very heart of our provinces, before we know anything of their motions; as if they dropt from heaven to punish the inhabitants for their folly.' Usually, they avoided engagements, and retreated before the troops could catch up with them. This was regretted by

Hastings, and he hoped that some of the Company's detachments might fall in with the parties and punish them in an exemplary manner for their audacity.

It was believed that the so-called Sanyasis were not all members of the well-known orders, but poor peasants turned into ascetics for a share of the plunder. But even now the bands of these ascetics are very large when seen at the great festivals, and it was quite possible that many of the raiding gangs belonged to the well-known orders. What they did during the Governor-Generalship of Hastings was a repetition in miniature of the raids of the Marathas thirty years before, and an anticipation of the depredations of the Pindaris fifty years later. In fact, these wandering Sadhus were the spiritual wing of the secular robber bands of India.

Even in more quiet times and more settled regions they created troubles for the villagers. The Abbé Dubois in his book wrote that, when going on their pilgrimages, they travelled in bands numbering at times even up to a thousand, and they collected food by begging in the villages through which they passed. 'Their manner when demanding alms', Dubois wrote, 'is most insolent and audacious, and often threatening.' 'If their demands are not instantly complied with,' he added, 'they will noisily repeat their request, striking their gongs and producing the most deafening sounds from their *sangus* (conch shells) all the time. If such methods are not successful, they have been known to force their way into a house, break all household utensils, and damage everything they can find.'

They also accompanied their begging with dancing and singing. Of this performance Dubois wrote: 'Their songs are a species of hymns in honour of their deities; and they very often sing indecent ballads. The more freely the latter are interlarded with obscenities, the better are they calculated to attract offerings from the public.'

Nowadays the Sadhus are seen individually and in small parties when they come to the towns and villages to collect money or food, and in large bands formed by the orders only on the occasions when there are great bathing festivals. But, whatever the manner of their appearance, they pursue a profession as well as a vocation.

Chapter Three

INTRINSIC DIVERSITY

WHAT has been written in the previous chapter will have given some idea of the diversity of Hinduism when seen in its geographical, social, and political setting. This alone makes the task of describing the religion difficult enough. But with time and labour it is possible to compile a full account of all its regional variants, and such an encyclopaedia will be far less voluminous than even one of the series on Christianity published by the Abbé Migne, namely, the *Encyclopédie théologique* in 171 volumes. A *catalogue raisonné* of all the beliefs, practices, and sects of the Hindus would require far fewer volumes. And such an account will no more baffle the mind than a tropical forest will overwhelm a trained ecologist.

But it is altogether a different matter with the intrinsic character of Hinduism. A confrontation with its multitudinous features will reveal a mental world which will have a shattering effect on the intellectual faculties, for nothing in it will seem to conform to any logic. The more one studies the details of the religion the more bewildering does it seem. It is not simply that one cannot form a clear-cut intellectual idea of the whole complex, it is not possible even to come away with a coherent emotional reaction. This is the case even with a short text like the *Katha Upanishad*. After reading it with the utmost concentration a reader who does not impose his own fancies on it and supply a connecting thread out of his own head, will find that his eyes have been dazzled by a number of flashes in the dark, but that he has not been in an illuminated room. To read the older Upanishads like the *Chandogya* or the *Brihadaranyaka* is still more puzzling. Even to read the *Gita*, which has a distinct and powerful religious message of its own, leaves an impression of inconsistency in thought and feeling because it has so many other things which do not harmonize with the central theme.

Students of Hinduism soon become like wanderers in a forest who can no longer find the notches they made on the trees to guide them. They become imbued with its *Deo*, formless spirit, which haunts the jungle. They rave about the spiritual mysteries of Hinduism, not realizing that the impression of mystery and awe arises from the paralysing blow which its amorphousness gives to those who cannot bring their intellect to bear on it. Even those who do not lose their head cannot help feeling its eeriness. It would seem that Hinduism, whose inmost core is a persistent animism, has created an animism of its own which takes possession of those who come in contact with it without intellectual inoculation. Then it becomes impossible to perceive the concreteness of the religion, which has been so emphasized in the introduction.

Another intellectual failure is to seek any kind of unity in Hinduism. Yet that is precisely what many Europeans have sought to do. This inclination is due to the rational cast of the European mind which makes this mind almost irrational in dealing with Hinduism. As Lyall put it, the European mind has 'the inveterate modern habit of assuming all great historical names to represent something definite, symmetrical, and organized, as if Asiatic institutions were capable of being circumscribed by rules and formal definitions.' To ask for a definition of Hinduism has become a habit even with the Westernized Hindus of today.

But English writers who have written about Hinduism from direct observation have never committed the mistake of regarding it as a unity. Actually, they were almost reduced to despair in writing about it. For instance, Monier-Williams, who wrote his book on Hinduism from his knowledge of the Sanskrit texts as well as from information derived from the Hindu pundits and reformers, asked the question: 'If such all-comprehensive breadth and diversity are essential features of Hinduism, is it possible to give a concise description of it which shall be intelligible and satisfactory?' His description of the diversity in Hinduism considered as a religion in the European sense was very vivid and, of course, correct. He wrote:

It is all tolerant, all compliant, all comprehensive, all-absorbing. It has its spiritual and its material aspect, its esoteric and exoteric, its subjective and objective, its rational and its irrational, its pure and its impure. It may be compared to a huge polygon, or irregular multilateral figure. It has one side for the practical, another for the severely moral, another for the devotional and imaginative, another for the sensuous and sensual, and another for the philosophical and speculative. Those who rest in ceremonial observances find it all-sufficient; those who deny the efficacy of works, and make faith the one requisite, need not wander from its pale; those who are addicted to sensual objects may have their tastes gratified; those who delight in meditating on the nature of God and Man, the relation of matter and spirit, the mystery of separate existence, and the origin of evil, may here indulge their love of speculation. And this capacity for almost endless expansion causes almost endless sectarian divisions even among the followers of any particular line of doctrine.

Considered as a whole, Hinduism suggests certain images from the world of plants, where vegetation relentlessly proliferates and expands. Monier-Williams wrote that Hinduism was like 'the sacred fig-tree of India (the banyan—*ficus bengalensis*), which from a single stem sends out numerous branches destined to send roots to the ground and become trees themselves, till the parent stock is lost in a dense forest of its own offshoots.' Lyall also wrote: 'Nowhere but in India can we now survey with our eyes an indigenous polytheism in full growth, flourishing like a secular green bay-tree among a people of ancient culture.'

One might also apply to Hinduism some notions of Hindu philosophy and logic. Of the Universal Soul *(Atman)* Hindu philosophy says that to every description or classification only one reply is possible: *Neti, Neti,* Not this, not this. So to every definition of Hinduism one is compelled to say that it does not apply. Hindu logic has the parable of the elephant and the blind men—*andha-hasti-nyaya.* It describes how a group of blind men wanted to form an idea of the shape of an elephant by touching its different limbs. Touching the trunk one of them said that it was like a pipe, touching the leg another said that it was like a pillar, touching the tail a third said that it was like a rope, and so on. Most descriptions of Hinduism tend to be like this. In any case, in them there is always an emphasis on a part at the expense of the whole. Unfortunately, there is no means of wholly avoiding this kind of misrepresentation in a short book on Hinduism.

Another temptation is to omit those features of Hinduism which offend certain modern susceptibilities. This was particularly strong in the nineteenth century. Today the temptation is rather to dwell on those very features. In an objective description of this religion the impression it is likely to produce is better disregarded. On the whole, Hinduism can afford to reveal itself honestly.

Diversities Left by History

Among the internal diversities in the beliefs and practices of Hinduism those created by its evolution must be described first. In its existence at any point of time, today or two hundred years ago, there can be seen an intermingling of beliefs, practices, and experiences coming down from all the known stages of its growth. That is to say, the features of the religion which can be found side by side and simultaneously now, would illustrate almost completely the whole course of evolution it has undergone, just as geological strata illustrate the history of the earth. Sometimes they are present as fully functional features and at others as vestigial.

No feature which is known from the oldest texts to have formed part of Hinduism has been totally lost as has been the pre-Zoroastrian polytheism in Persia. In some cases they have been substantially transformed. None the less, the line of descent remains clear. Thus it happens that, in order to become a coherent and logical system, Hinduism has not shed any of its features in the course of its evolution. For this reason current Hinduism may also be seen as a museum of its entire history. However, it is also a museum of the history of religion all over the world. If the study of Sanskrit gave rise to the science of Comparative Philology, Hinduism gave the initial stimulus to the comparative study of religions. Anthropologists took the study of religion further, but, if they did so by the study of religion among the primitive peoples, they could easily have found the same sort of data in Hinduism. A book like Frazer's *Golden Bough* could be written on the basis of the beliefs and practices of the Hindus alone. All the features of primitive religions, animism, animatism, magic, fetishism, shamanism, etc., may be found in their undisguised forms in the current religious life of the Hindus. Rising from these foundations Hinduism in its superstructure rises to heights at which it is not simply mystical, but succeeds in converting religion into philosophy. And too often this philosophy is regarded as the true Hindu religion, which it is not.

Diversity of Belief

A religion which has been deposited in this manner by its own evolution could have no creed or kerygma, and Hinduism never had any. A Hindu is under no compulsion to subscribe to any dogma or profess faith in a particular thing. So, among the Hindus, heresy is not a matter of belief. There is a Sanskrit word, *pashanda*, which is translated into English as 'heretic', but it only means a person who is un-Hindu in his conduct and behaviour, who neglects Hindu observances, and disregards Hindu taboos. It is not possible to find doctrinal heresy in Hinduism because Hinduism has no fixed doctrine.

This is the basis of the much-advertised Hindu religious tolerance. Since a Hindu has not arrived at any exclusive belief in one God or many gods, it is natural for him to regard any kind of belief as true. With a whole range of beliefs which he accepts as equally true, or at all events true for the person who holds it, he can hardly deny the truth of any other religion. Thus modern Hindus have always considered the Christian denial of salvation to those who do not put faith in the Christian kerygma to be a monstrous perversion of religion. A Hindu's exclusiveness is social: it is created, in the first instance, by his birth which makes him one individual among a chosen people by divine right, and after that by his *mores*, which he regards as superior to everybody else's.

Thus it is as difficult to say what exactly a Hindu believes as it is to discover what he does not. In regard to the very wide choice of cults and observances open to him within the framework of his religion he would follow the motto: Preferences or a preference, but no exclusions whatever. He might even extend his faith to a number of dogmas which are utterly inconsistent with one another without any awareness of the inconsistencies. He is capable of reconciling and uniting them with the help of his faith. Thus the unity of Hinduism lies in the Hindu's unlimited capacity for faith, and not on the oneness of the object of his faith.

But though the objects are many they are all distinguishable. At the same time, they stand at different levels of consciousness, and can therefore be divided into groups. In the foreground stands one object of faith for all Hindus. It is a genuine, monotheistic, personal God. It is impossible to determine when the presence of this God came to be felt by them. He is certainly not derived from the impersonal and abstract one God—*Brahman* or *Atman* (Oversoul) of Upanishadic mysticism or later philosophy. Though in certain parts of India this one God is referred to as

Paramatma (Supreme Soul), the affiliation is simply verbal. For all practical purposes, the abstract God has no place in Hindu worship. For many centuries discussion about him has not been religious even, but only philosophical.

The one God to which I am referring here is a Hindu form of the Christian and Islamic God. The most common name under which he is referred to is Bhagavan. Though he is a personal God, he is never thought of or spoken about as an anthropomorphic God in a physical form. Actually, no physical form is ever assigned to him, though he is a full anthropomorphic psychic entity. He is omniscient, omnipotent, and omnipresent. He is personified compassion and justice at the same time.

The Hindus always turn to him when they are in trouble, in all their sorrows and suffering, but never when prosperous. They would say to others: God will show you mercy, God will judge your actions, or God will not allow this. No particular, individualized, anthropomorphic god of the old Hindu pantheon ever fulfilled this role with any Hindu. To the other gods of Hinduism, even when thought of as a supreme god, the Hindus looked with some confidence based on his right to ask for divine help, since through worship he was performing his part of the contract and giving the god his *quid pro quo*. But to this God, Bhagavan, he appealed when he was wholly without any resource, yet he did so with complete faith in his mercy.

Nevertheless, this Bhagavan has never been worshipped, nor has he even been an object of regular prayer. St Paul said to the Athenians that He whom they worshipped as the Unknown God was being proclaimed to them by him. To the Hindus this Unknown God was fully known, but never worshipped. In the whole religious literature of the Hindus there is no discussion of the nature of this God. Yet in one sense this undiscussed God is the only real God of Hindu faith.

Below this God there was the specific world of the Hindu gods, who are to be found in Hindu mythology and theogony, but whose nature and functions Hindu scriptures have made as difficult as possible to understand. If it had not been for Hindu practice no one would have succeeded in placing them in Hindu religious life. These gods belong to Hindu polytheism, but the three most important divinities stand in a sphere where there is complete coalescence of monotheism and polytheism. In Hinduism, as in Greek and Roman religions, monotheism never excluded polytheism, and *vice versa*. But Hinduism is unique in this respect, that out of its polytheism it has not created a simple monotheism, but one which is polymorphous because it is one monotheism with three gods.

This aspect of Hindu monotheism has not been sufficiently emphasized, and the greatest obstacle has been the conventional doctrine of the Hindu Trinity of Brahma, Vishnu, and Siva (Mahesvara)—the first being particularized as the Creator, the second as Preserver, and the third as the Destroyer. But outside mythology, i.e. in actual ritual and devotion, these functions have never been distinguished. In recent times the worship of Brahma has been exceptional, perhaps for the reason that, his work having been finished, there was not much occasion to take notice of him. The worship of Vishnu and Siva has continued, but it has nothing to do with their specific aspects as Preserver and Destroyer. They are worshipped as a general supreme God with all the attributes and functions of such a god.

It is in the case of Siva that one can see the best illustration of the fact that no god of the so-called Hindu Trinity is worshipped on account of the function which is doctrinally assigned to him. Siva is a complete supreme god in himself. So the most common names assigned to him were Isvara or Mahesvara (the Lord or the Great Lord).

This aspect of the basic monotheism is illustrated just as strikingly in the cult of the Great Mother Goddess of the Hindus, known under many names, but most commonly as Kali and Durga. In both forms, both in mythology and liturgy, she is the destroyer of the demons (Asuras), and in iconography she is always shown as such, though Kali has a fierce and Durga a benign aspect. But neither mythology, nor liturgy, nor iconography ever made Kali or Durga anything other than a complete God in a feminine form.

Since the cults of these gods will be dealt with in the third part of the book nothing further will be said about them here. The point which has to be made at this stage is that all three are thought of and worshipped exactly as a monotheistic divinity would be, but a Hindu can choose any of these three as his particular monotheistic deity, without denying his allegiance to the two others. At some unknown time these distinct gods of the old

Hindu polytheism appear to have undergone a process of conceptual syncretism, which made their particularity irrelevant to devotion, without doing away with that in liturgy and iconography. To this monotheism I would give the name of polymorphous monotheism, because in it one God has three forms. To it can be applied the motto *e pluribus unum*, because it has established a unity of the Godhead without destroying the plurality.

The true Hindu polytheism exists below the special kind of monotheism created by this triad. But it is not the polytheism of the *Rig-Veda*. At first sight the old polytheism would appear to have grown enormously, for the 33 gods of the Vedas had increased to the 330 million of the Puranas or Hindu traditions. The reality was, however, the opposite of the appearance. In Vedic times the polytheistic deities occupied the foreground; in later ages, so far as worship was concerned, they receded to the background. By the end of the eighteenth century a large number of them were no longer worshipped, but it is not possible to say when their worship ceased. Those who survived were minor gods and goddesses. Some of them were still functional, but some were only vestigial. The most important of the polytheistic deities who survived were the following three; Lakshmi, the goddess of wealth and prosperity; Ganesa, the god of worldly and especially commercial success; and Saraswati, the goddess of learning. Certain gods remained locally important, e.g. the war god Kartikeya, who was worshipped in the south and in Ceylon by the Tamils settled there. Hanuman, the monkey god, was important in the Gangetic basin.

Moreover, at the end of the eighteenth century a secondary and crude form of polytheism could be seen practised even by those Hindus who otherwise had a more sophisticated religious life. Again, it is not possible to say when this lower and parallel form of polytheism appeared. Its gods and goddesses may have existed always without being referred to in the older religious texts. This lower polytheism comprised a large variety of gods and goddesses of a utilitarian character, and the more important ones in Bengal were Sashthi, the goddess of childbirth, Manasa, the goddess of snakes, Sitala, the goddess of smallpox, Ghetu, the god of skin diseases. There were gods of this kind all over India, sometimes bearing different names. Nobody thought of denying the power of these gods and goddesses.

Ideas about After-life

Since death is the pivot round which religious thinking invariably revolves all religions offer a coherent view of human destiny after the cessation of earthly life. The view may change *pari passu* with the development of a religion, as it did, for example, with Judaism, but at every stage there is a coherent view. This is precisely what Hinduism has never offered, and strangely enough the Hindus themselves have never felt its absence. They have been given and have been happy with wholly inconsistent views about what happens after death, and they will express any view which suits them in the context of an argument.

The Hindu rites about the dead, which are obligatory and which every Hindu performs, are based on the most archaic view, that of the Vedic religion. According to it, the departed spirits lived in a shadowy world comparable to the abode of Hades of the Greeks, or that of Pluto of the Romans, and Sheol of the Jews. This was called *Pitri-loka* (world of the ancestors) or the *Preta-loka* (world of the spirits).

Hindu mortuary rites are meant to secure their entry into that world and after that to provide for their sustenance there. They could get no food and drink, which they needed like any mortal, unless their descendants in the world offered them in periodic oblations — called *tarpana* (satisfaction) with balls of flour or gram *(pinda)* and water. So these were offered at certain fixed times. The first rites were performed from ten days to a month after death, according to the caste of the family, and another at the end of a year. These were called *Srāddha* (literally, reverence or *pietas*).

Even after a year all departed ancestors had to be offered food and water at regular intervals, among the very scrupulous every fortnight, and also at every ceremony in the family like a wedding, expiation, etc. In fact, the physical needs of the ancestors could never be overlooked by their living descendants. That was why a male issue was such a vital question for all Hindus, for except in unavoidable circumstances only male descendants could offer oblations. The idea of *pinda-lopa* (cessation of oblations) horrified all Hindus.

This rite has continued down to this day without reference to the doctrine of rebirth or salvation. No Hindu ever considers the question of how an ancestor of his who, after rebirth, is leading a mundane life somewhere, could stand in need of food and water from him. In social controversies in the nineteenth century the idea of *Pitri-loka* (the world of the *Manes*) was used as a sanction behind many taboos, and also in favour of child marriage. It was held that unless a girl was married before her first menstruation, the menstrual blood would go into the mouths of the departed ancestors.

But this early concept of after-life remained throughout ritualistic, and never intruded into the living beliefs about the dead. These were the following: (1) the dead if very virtuous obtained *moksha* or salvation, which was liberation from earthly existence and absorption in the Oversoul; (2) they were reborn in the world; (3) they ascended to heaven or descended to hell; (4) they existed as ghosts. Of these, it may be repeated, the notion of salvation was wholly unreal, a matter merely of theorizing. The view of after-life to which the Hindus clung with the greatest fervour was of rebirth in another household.

It is curious that though the Hindus shed their fear of death by implicitly believing that they would all remain in the world they so loved and be united again to those whom they loved, their scriptures did not give that guarantee. These laid down that the actual animal form in which men would be reborn depended on what they had done in one birth. The *Manu Samhita*, the most authoritative book of sacred law of the Hindus, gives a long list of the transmigrations according to the nature of stumbling. According to it, a man could be born again as a rat for stealing grain, and as a partridge for stealing cloth. Distinction is even made for different kinds of cloth: for stealing cotton cloth the thief would become an ordinary or chukar partridge, but for stealing silk he would become a francolin partridge. However, in their actual thinking no Hindu ever took the possibility of becoming anything but a human being seriously.

But another complexity was introduced by the notion of heaven or hell according to merit or demerit. This notion is also very firmly established, and no reconciliation has been sought with the doctrine of rebirth. The Hindu hells are even more elaborately classified and vividly described than the Christian hells, and the Hindu heaven is more like the Islamic paradise than the Christian heaven, for there are in it the Hindu version of the houris.

Over and above, there is unshaken belief in ghosts. In theory, it is asserted that the ghostly existence is an intermezzo between death and the performance of the *Sradh*, but in actual fact the Hindus believe in the ghostly existence as a permanent state after death for certain persons. There is also a caste system among the ghosts. The ghosts of Brahmins are called *Brahma Daitya*, and are believed to live in the sacred peepul or banyan tree.

There has not been any attempt to reconcile all these notions, and Hindus believe in them all at one time or another according to the mood of the hour.

Diversity of Practice

The religious practices of the Hindus are even more varied than their beliefs. This does not solely mean that there are sects and denominations among them and that their rituals and worship differ. The sects of the Hindus are indeed numerous and new sects have always been springing up. Each sect has its particular practices, but Hindu sectarianism, as will be explained later, is not exclusive. In any case, the speciality of a sect is only a minor addition to the general practices of Hinduism, to which the sects also adhere.

The really bewildering diversity lies in the general practices. They have so many aspects that they give rise to the impression that they belong to many religions. In point of fact, one family or one individual might have observances which are as different from one another as they are from those of Christianity or Islam. Nevertheless, no Hindu is perplexed by this fact, and is not even conscious of the incongruities.

A Hindu's religious life is lived on different planes, and his practices call for different degrees and kinds of participation according to his position in society. In the first place, the practices of the Hindus who remain in the world are generally very different from those who have left the world. Again, among the Hindus in the world, these would differ according to caste, sex, and age. A person who is not twice-born, or is a woman, or a child, has no obligation to perform any rite or worship in any way, except in respect of the dead or for sanctifying marriage and other worldly events.

The obligatory religious duties of the twice-born are limited, though usually he takes up of his own will a large number of them, and these latter may be both personal and social. Again, the religious obligations may be discharged, even by a Brahmin, by proxy, i.e. through the agency of a priest who receives a fixed monthly salary or is paid a fee for each occasion. Finally, a large number of religious observances have no devotional character and are only formal rites.

The obligatory rites for the twice-born and especially the Brahmins are those which have come down from the oldest or Vedic stage of the religion, the other features of which have become wholly obsolete. It is compulsory for the Brahmin to perform his three daily rites personally. These are utterances of the famous *mantra* of the *Gayatri* with accompaniments like ablutions, gestures, etc. Now, this *mantra* consists of three lines from the *Rig-Veda* (II. 62. x), namely,

> (Om, bhur-bhuvah-svar)
> Tat Savitur- varenyam
> bhargo-devasya dhimahi
> dhiyo yo nah prachodayāt.
> (Om.)

This has been variously translated, but its general meaning is clear enough, and is given by Max Müller as follows: 'Let us obtain (or according to Hindu tradition, let us meditate on) the adorable splendour of Savitri (sun); may he arouse our minds.' All the Hindu sacred books of later times proclaim these to be the most holy lines of the Vedas. For example, the *Manu Samhita*, the most authoritative of the books on sacred law *(Dharma Sastra)*, says:

> Prajapati also milked out of the three Vedas the letters *a, u,* and *ma,* together with the words *bhuh, bhuvah, svar.* The same supreme Prajapati also milked from each of the three Vedas one of the portions of the text called *savitri,* beginning with the word *tat.* . . . The three great imperishable particles preceded by *Om,* and the *gayatri* of three lines, are to be regarded as the mouth of Brahma.

It is impossible to discover why out of over one thousand hymns and 10,500 verses of the *Rig-Veda* these cryptic lines should have been selected as the supreme credo and prayer for a Brahmin. On the face of it, the *Gayatri* is connected with the worship of the sun, a minor deity in Hinduism, and so far as it can be called a prayer it is only a wish for the mind to be alert. Such an utterance cannot be put by the side of the Christian credo or the Lord's Prayer nor by the side of the Islamic confession of faith and the prayer known as *Fatiha*. Yet it has been uttered for thousands of years as the formula on which Hinduism stands, and which no Sudra can utter. When the Brahmin says his *Gayatri* three times a day he does not have the least religious feeling. But it is said with the utmost gravity and reverence, with what in Sanskrit is expressed by the word *sraddhā*. There is also in the attitude and expression of the performer an air of something awe-inspiring and mysterious which forbids any kind of profanity. But the performance, if it had any mental state behind it, had long ago become purely behavioural, a sort of conditioned reflex of the sacred.

With the recital of the *Gayatri* also went a number of household rites, including sacrifices for counteracting the sin of killing insects and other small creatures unknowingly in the course of household work like sweeping and cooking, and also including offerings to gods who were unknown but in widest commonalty spread and had to be placated collectively. Up to recent times even a worldly Hindu's worship and rites might take two or three hours, and he never grudged the trouble, for his worldly welfare depended on them.

After that came a whole series of rituals and worship which were meant for all Hindus irrespective of caste. They were not enjoined as obligatory, but when taken up voluntarily were performed with the same strictness and regularity as was seen in the case of the compulsory duties. These began with a special initiation, which was sought generally by an elderly man or woman. All Hindu families had hereditary Gurus whom they regarded as spiritual teachers. These Gurus visited the houses of their *Yajamanas* (disciples) from time to time, and were received with great honour and pomp. Even if a young son of the Guru came, say a boy of twelve (called *Guru-kumara*), an old Kayastha gentleman of sixty and his wife would touch his foot and take the dust *(pada-dhuli)* from it on the head. Sometimes they also drank the water in which the Guru dipped his big toe called *Charanamrita* (or nectar from the feet).

These Gurus, if requested, gave a special mantra to the disciple and instructions about his devotions. This was the formal and personal initiation of those who were not twice-born. This worship was not the more or less formal and abstract *tri-sandhya* (three repetitions of the *Gayatri*) of the Brahmin, but was directed towards one or other of the principal anthropomorphic gods. The worshipper could choose the god according to his inclination, and the deity could be Krishna (usually Krishna and Radha) of the Vaishnavas, Siva of the Saiva cult, or Durga or Kali of the Sakta cult. This worship did not require an image, but the worshipper had to invoke in his imagination the features of the deity while reciting the standardized description and also chant a hymn. There was no expression of personal devotion in this worship, and thus it resembled the Brahmin's utterance of the *Gayatri* as a formal rite. But with some Hindus this formal worship developed into a devout personal worship with complete emotional involvement. The motives for this were varied. This amplification could develop within the Vaishnava as well as the Sakta cult, and in the latter case, also in its Tantric form.

Another form of personal worship was seen in the *Vratas* or rites performed annually in obedience to a vow. These had an infinite variety, and were taken up by women only. Generally, a woman would perform them regularly for twelve years, at the end of which the vow to perform a *Vrata* would be completed ceremonially with great pomp. This was consolidation of the merit acquired by observing the vow.

These rites virtually comprised and still comprise all the personal and private forms of religious practice of the Hindus. Beyond these lies the immense and not less varied field of collective and public practice. This is the most familiar aspect of Hinduism, for image worship in temples belongs to the public sphere. In it is to be found the full expression of the polytheistic and anthropomorphic side of Hinduism.

But if this practice is called public it is not to be understood that it is publicly organized or owned. There is no such thing as a centralized or hierarchical organization in Hinduism. It is quite spontaneously coherent in practice, and self-driven. Even the old Hindu state or rather the king who embodied the state in one person, never controlled the practice of religion, though the princes both built and endowed the temples; in fact, the great temples of India were almost all built by them. But the endless clusters of temples that were to be seen all over India like parish churches, were built by the landed gentry and also by the merchants.

But the rituals and worship in these temples were public, that is to say, anyone could come and witness the rites and bring his offerings. There was a very great variety of shrines and temples. On the lowest plane, was the family shrine. Every well-to-do family had its own household shrine, which was either a small building or a room specially set apart within the mansion. The special family god's image was put in it, and, according to the sect or denomination of the family, it could either be an image of Krishna (invariably with Radha) or less commonly the Mother Goddess. But overwhelmingly the deity was Krishna, irrespective of the family's sectarian affiliation. In the same shrine was placed the material symbol of Vishnu as Narayan, which was the fossil ammonite. The worship of this shell was basic in Hinduism. It had to be placed in its cradle, whenever any religious ceremony was performed.

In addition, the more wealthy families had temples by the side of the family mansion, or in the market or again in the burning ghat. They were devoted either to Siva in the form of *linga* (or phallic symbol) or Kali. Very wealthy families would have as many as twelve Siva temples in a row by the side of a river or tank. There were also independent temples to Krishna, but in Bengal at all events they were not as common as the detached temples to Siva or Kali.

Neither in the family shrines nor in the temples of the family did the owners perform any religious rite. For that salaried priests were always engaged, but the members of the family, usually the womenfolk, at times attended the rites. The great temples, irrespective of who was the patron, were in charge of hereditary families of priests, who were responsible for the service of the gods and appropriated the surplus money. All those who went to the temples left money, in addition to their offerings in kind.

Last of all, it has to be noted that the images are of two kinds, permanent and made *ad hoc*. The permanent ones are placed in the temples, and these are of stone or brass, but also at times of gold or silver. Once established, they remained in place for generations.

But there were other images of clay, made for special occasions. After the days of worship these were normally cast into water, either a river or a large tank. These were the images for the religious festivals all round the year. Certain potters made a special trade of them. The most important festival with the most elaborate image was that of Durga in Bengal. For the worship of these images a special hall was set apart in every house that held these festivals. This hall had an open front, with a courtyard in front, where the sacrifice took place and the visitors stood.

In addition to these principal deities, the women had special ones of their own, whose worship took place in the home on certain days of the week. The first in status in this class was the goddess of prosperity, Lakshmi, worshipped weekly on Thursdays. She had an opposite number, a god who was always malevolent and brought misfortune or ruin on the unwary. His name was Sani (Saturn). He was regularly worshipped on Saturdays to appease his malevolence. Over and above, the women gave special attention to the goddess of births, Sasthi. She was worshipped under a banyan tree.

At first sight such a range of observances, in which all Hindus participated with a catholicity unrestricted by any sectarian affiliation, would seem to be a crushing burden. Yet there was no feeling of being burdened. On the contrary, all the rituals were gone through with strict attention to all the details. In their religious practices the Hindus never showed the casualness which marked their activities in worldly life. Here alone was unfailing alertness and efficiency, and even attention to the aesthetic side of life, so absent in everything else. The Hindus, who never serve food with any aesthetic sensibility at their worldly banquets, arranged the food platter of the gods and goddesses in a manner which was beautiful to see.

Pilgrimage

Pilgrimage to holy places is not an obligatory duty for a Hindu as the pilgrimage to Mecca is for a Muslim. But in practice the Hindus are more given to going on frequent and long pilgrimages than the followers of other religions. Hindu pilgrimage is the Muslim's *Haj* multiplied a hundredfold.

But this pilgrimage is different from the Muslim pilgrimage. It is different even from that of the Buddhists. The places of pilgrimage of other major religions are connected with their origin and subsequent history. All those spots have personal associations with either the founder or some notable follower. Among the few places which are holy for such a reason among the Hindus, are

Mathura and Brindaban, which are sacred on account of the connection with Krishna's life. This association is, however, only mythical. Moreover, visits to these two places are not considered as pilgrimages in the strict sense.

The real Hindu pilgrimage is connected with water, especially the river. The Sanskrit word for a place of pilgrimage is *tirtha*, a ford, a bathing place, in its primary meaning. But from very early times, not possible to determine exactly, the word acquired a religious significance, and, in undertaking pilgrimages with a very comprehensive itinerary, even women underwent fatigue and faced dangers, a hundredth part of which no Hindu man will contemplate for any other purpose.

Naturally, among the rivers, the Ganges was the first in holiness, or rather it was the first river to be regarded as holy, and had its sacredness extended to the other rivers of India with the extension of Aryan colonization. The whole course of the river was holy, and in Bengal relatives would carry a body twenty miles to cremate it on the banks of the Ganges. Some spots in its course, however, acquired special importance. These were the following: the traditional source, Gangotri, in the Gahrwal Himalayas; Hardwar where the river entered the plain; Gahr-Mukteswar further down; the great confluence with the Jumna at Allahabad: and Benares.

The other big rivers of northern and southern India—Jumna, Nerbudda, Tapti, Godavari, Krishna, and Cauvery—were raised to a sacred status in course of time, and in different ways. They constituted, so to say, a pantheon of rivers.

In contrast, the sea provided only four notable places of pilgrimage. These were Puri on the Bay of Bengal in Orissa, Rameshwaram on the Indian side of the Palk Straits, Kanyakumari at the extreme tip of south India, and Dwarka on the Arabian Sea at the extreme end of the Kathiawar peninsula. But these places were sacred, not on account of the sea, but for their association with the myths and cults of Rama and Krishna. India has very few lakes. But Lake Pushkar near Ajmer is specially holy, and Manas Sarovar in Tibet also has that status.

All these spots occupied a very important place in the Hindu religious consciousness. They are praised in all the literatures of India in all languages, whether religious or secular. An example might be given from a collection of folk tales—*Vikrama's Adven-*

tures or the *Thirty-two Tales of the Throne*. In one of the stories in it is to be found the following eulogy:

> There is no greater purification than bathing in a sacred place. When a man does not get salvation by asceticism, celibacy, sacrifices, nor indeed by charity, he will obtain it by worshipping the Ganges. Those who, being able, do not see the Ganges, the destroyer of sin, are like people born blind, and they are comparable to cattle and beasts.

Many of the places of pilgrimage on the great rivers also had temples of one or other of the great deities, often Siva or Vishnu (or in the alternative form of Krishna), but also of the Mother Goddess under her various names. This is specially true of Benares. Even when people go there only to bathe in the Ganges on specially holy days, they do not omit to worship at the temple of Siva, who is known as Visvanath, or Lord of the Universe.

It is certain, however, that the places of pilgrimage got their sacred status at first as bathing places only, and the gods were installed there when image worship and temple cults were introduced to give them additional prestige. However, there are certain places not on any important river which became sacred for the temples alone and their particular gods, e.g. Conjevram, Tanjore, and Madura in the south. But these acquired their status late. In northern India no place of pilgrimage stands anywhere except on a river.

Why the rivers were given a sacred status and why certain spots on them became specially holy cannot be explained. There are, of course, stories in Hindu mythology to account for it. For instance, the sacredness of the Ganges has been explained by the legend that it was a heavenly river which was brought down to earth to resurrect the sons of Sagar who had been burnt to ashes by the wrath of a sage, and also that she was received, upon her falling on earth, on the head of Siva. But such stories must have been invented after the river had been regarded as holy for a long time.[1]

As to the spots, some had mythological associations, and some became sacred after being made the seat of a great deity by a king or queen in a political capital. In regard to Benares, I am inclined

---

[1] For a personal, and perhaps over-imaginative explanation of the sacred status given to the great rivers of India, see my *Continent of Circe* (1965), pp. 161–8.

to think that its sacred status for the Hindus is an inheritance from Buddhism. A spot near the present site of Benares was where Buddha first preached his religion, and it is still a place of pilgrimage for Buddhists. The Hindus may have appropriated this sacred status for their own religion.

Hindu Festivals and Fairs

The cycle of Hindu festivals belongs to the same category of celebrations as those of the Greeks and Romans. As they have existed in India for many centuries they are special occasions of worship supplementary to the regular daily worship, but far surpassing them in pomp and splendour. These two bear the same relation to each other as the daily meals do to the special banquets in Hindu households.

The festivals are arranged round the year, and the actual dates seem to have been fixed for varied reasons. Some of them are connected with the seasons. For instance, the most tumultuous of the festivals, the Holi, was certainly a spring festival to begin with. It soon became a Saturnalia with a good deal of sensuality and even obscenity marking its celebration. It became identified with or was by itself a festival of the god of love. Now it is associated with Krishna and his sports with the Gopis or milkmaids. The worship of the Ganges in June is intended to celebrate the onset of the rainy season. Another very important seasonal festival is the Dussera in autumn. It marked the commencement of military campaigns after the cessation of rains. It retains that character in northern India, though in Bengal it is associated with the Mother Goddess Durga. But in this festival she is herself a goddess of war.

Lastly, some festivals, especially those of bathing ceremonially in the great rivers are connected with the conjunction of stars and planets, and other astronomical phenomena like eclipses. Some of these conjunctions are regarded as especially holy.

It is impossible to give a description of the festivals. They are so many and so varied that a book could be written about them alone. A brief enumeration would become only a list, which will convey nothing of the spirit of these occasions. Something will be said later about the joy they bring to Hindu life.

The fairs are the economic complements to the festivals, which enable merchants to sell their goods and give those who come to them the pleasure of being in a crowd. So they always had and have not only temporary shops and stalls, but also all kinds of amusements. I saw the circus for the first time in my life in the fair for the swinging festival of Krishna in my birthplace. To extend the amusement, they were even very considerately provided with brothels. Some fairs were held for special merchandise. For instance, at the junction of the Ganges and the Sone near Patna a great fair is held for the sale of cattle, horses, camels, and elephants. In my home town in East Bengal, hundreds of miles away, I have seen horses bought at this fair. The fairs are, however, too numerous to be mentioned individually.

Chapter Four

PRIESTHOOD AND SECTS

IN Hindu society the Brahmin caste is theoretically the priestly order. But in practice the caste and the profession are not to be treated as one. All Brahmins need not be priests. In fact, a majority of them are not. They can follow any profession or means of livelihood, and have been kings, soldiers, shopkeepers, or peasants. Brahmins who are wealthy or hold good social positions do not perform the religious ceremonies even in their own homes. On the other hand, no one except a Brahmin can be a priest. Thus, in respect of priesthood, the caste system is permissive in giving the Brahmins the freedom not to adopt the priestly vocation, but restrictive in not allowing anyone but a Brahmin to become a priest.

But the Brahmin priests do not have full freedom to perform religious rites for all castes. In some past time the performance of these in the house of a Sudra was considered degrading. But this prejudice disappeared long ago. Nevertheless, the castes which were considered untouchable, i.e. from whom water could not be accepted, were avoided by good Brahmins. But for the sake of money some Brahmins performed religious rites in their houses, and were put in a special category of the caste. On the other hand, many low-caste people made their own Brahmins. It also seems probable that in the past the priests of many of the invading foreign tribes became Brahmins when these were absorbed into the Hindu society. In recent times no distinction has been made between Brahmin and Brahmin, and all of them can perform religious rites somewhere or other.

Priesthood as a Profession

Priesthood was and is a profession among the Hindus, and perhaps it was and is the profession with the largest number of practitioners. But there were and are distinctions of status within the profession. At the top were the spiritual directors, teachers of Hindu philosophy, and consultants on points of sacred law, who also at times performed or at least supervised the important religious rites in the houses of their clients. After them came those who performed the seasonal worship for fees which were more or less standardized. If the first class were consultants, these priests could be described on the analogy of the medical profession as the general practitioners. Lowest in the hierarchy were the salaried priests who performed the daily rites in the houses of the wealthy. These were regarded as superior members of the domestic staff.

But Brahmins could also make a living by giving expositions of mythology or reciting both the religious texts and the epics, combining that with their comments. Some of these men acquired a great reputation as reciters or expositors and were specially invited to the houses of the wealthy to preach on ceremonial occasions.

Another source of income for the priests who were learned in philosophy and logic was provided by the custom of inviting them to hold debates and discussions for the edification of the public. At the funeral ceremonies these discussions were as much expected as were music and dance in other ceremonies. These pundits received large fees and presents on these occasions, and when the patrons were wealthy the presents included silver vessels of all kinds.

The learned men had a dais covered with a clean white sheet, on which they squatted and held debates on points of logic and philosophy. There were neither fixed times nor regular audiences for them. The pundits talked when they felt like it, or simply looked on, taking snuff all the time. The members of the house or the guests came in, stayed, and went out as they pleased like the members of the House of Commons. The arguments at times became acrimonious. Very few listeners could understand the points made by the debaters, but, as they often lost their temper, the exhibition was relished by all.

These exhibitions of learning were regarded as adjuncts of wealth and position, and no great landowner would pass over the pundits any more than they would other kinds of professional entertainers. The listeners to the debates, too, would not look upon the disputes as anything but entertainment, because unless they were pundits themselves, they could not understand the extremely recondite and technical points raised, whereas their loss of temper would be obvious and enjoyable.

To give an illustration of the spirit in which these debates were carried on I would quote from a Bengali novel—*Alaler Gharer Dulal* by Pyari Chand Mitra—published in the middle of the nineteenth century, which described them as they were.

> The professors are taking snuff and discussing the *shastras* [the sacred books] among themselves. But their nature is such that if they get together, it becomes difficult for them to talk coolly. One kind of row or other is bound to arise as a matter of course . . . Such a discussion being on, it seemed blows would soon follow back-talk. Uncle Thug [the Muslim bailiff of the estate] thought it would be better to stop the trouble in time, and walked up warily to the learned men and said: 'I say, sirs, why are you fighting over the question of a jug and a lamp? I'll give you two jugs.' [This was the imagery in a quibble of Hindu logic.]
>
> There was a *smarta* Brahmin [expert on sacred law] among the pundits, who got up and shouted: 'Who is this fellow? Why does a Yavana [Muslim] poke his nose into the *sradh* of a Hindu? Is he the will-o'-the-wisp manager at the funeral of a ghoul?'
>
> Then the abuse turned into fisticuffs, and pushing and cuffing into cudgelling. The master of the house came running and cried out: 'If you spoil the *sradh* I shall lodge a suit for damages at the High Court.'

This was, of course, satire, but no more than a permissible caricature of a reality known to all. One wrong idea has to be given up in considering the standing of Hindu philosophy, and it is that Hindus in recent centuries have had any respect for philosophy and philosophers. The high standing of Hindu philosophy was inculcated upon modern Hindus by European and more particularly German scholars, of whom Max Müller was the most eminent and influential.

The professional priests always had a working knowledge of Sanskrit, and at times were familiar with the Sastras or sacred literature in their way. But what they always had to acquire was a thorough knowledge of the liturgy of worship of all the different gods and goddesses as well as for the rites connected with daily life. In addition, they also had to possess some knowledge of Hindu astrology. All this they learned in their family and never by formal study.

The rites were elaborate, and the incantations long. But it was not necessary to memorize them. The priests always took with them the appropriate text for each ceremony, and it was not considered improper to keep the books open before them while performing the rites, or to pause to consult them. It was considered absolutely essential, however, that the words should be uttered correctly and the gestures be appropriate. If a mistake was made in reciting the incantations it was not enough to repeat the mispronounced word correctly; the whole incantation had to be recited from the beginning or its efficacy would be lost.

In any case, the old ladies of the family saw to it that the priest committed no mistake. Seeing the rites performed year after year, they became so familiar with the procedures that no lapse could escape their eye. They corrected the priests severely, and if the latter wanted to keep their jobs they had also to retain the good opinion of the matrons, who never spoilt the priests as they did their grandchildren. The boys of priestly families learned the liturgies from childhood by watching their elders, and also served as understudies if for any reason these elders were unable to go to the houses of their clients (*Yajamanas*).

The priests had no responsibility whatever for the spiritual or moral welfare of those for whom they performed the rites. The concept of a cure of souls was wholly unknown to Hinduism. Nor did the priests exercise any philanthropic role such as the care of the poor, the destitute, or the sick.

On the contrary, the priests themselves were dependent on what might be regarded as unorganized social service. But neither the givers nor the receivers ever regarded the money and goods given to the priests as charity, for the relations between the two were like the relations between any non-professional member of a society and persons exercising a special function, such as lawyers, doctors, business agents, mechanics, etc. The priests were in charge of the household's relations with its gods because the members of the family could not manage them on account of their extremely technical character. The money earned by the priests was not very large individually, but it was large in its total distribution, so that if it could not be classed as professional income it had to be regarded as social dole.

If the gifts did not seem good enough to the priests, they grumbled and spread stories of the miserliness of the particular householder. Since all Hindus are in abject fear of the unfavourable opinions of their neighbours and relatives, the priests had adequate sanctions behind their demands or expectations in their tongues. Priests with a higher standing, e.g. the Gurus, collected their dues almost like the feared tax-collectors of the Muslim state. Abbé Dubois gave the following account of their method of collecting money from his experience in south India. He wrote:

> From time to time *gurus* make tours of inspection in those districts where their followers are most numerous. They sometimes go as much as a hundred miles from their habitual residence. The chief, if not the only, object of this expedition is to collect money . . . they are merciless in extorting tribute money from their followers, which often greatly exceeds their means. They call this method of obtaining money *dakshina* and *pada-kanikai*, and no one, however poor he may be, is exempt from paying it. There is no insult or indignity that *gurus* will not inflict upon any one who either cannot or will not submit to this tax. Deaf to all entreaties, they cause the defaulter to appear before them in an ignominious and humiliating attitude, publicly overwhelm him with insults and reproaches, and order that mud or cow-dung shall be thrown in his face. If these means do not succeed, they force him to give up one of his children, who is obliged to work without wages until the tribute money is paid. Indeed they have been known to take away a man's wife as compensation. Finally, as a last and infallible resource, they threaten him with their malediction.

There is no reason whatever to doubt the statements of Dubois. In south India the Brahmins generally were much more arrogant and assertive than in the north, because they were the highest caste of the colonial Aryans. The fierce anti-Brahmin movement in the south of today is the natural reaction to the old Brahmin domination.

One particular claim which the priests, and in fact even lay Brahmins, had on Hindu society at large was to be fed sumptuously on every ceremonial occasion. *Brahmana-Bhojana* or feeding Brahmins was a socio-spiritual obligation; so wealthy families had standing arrangements for feeding a fixed number of Brahmins on certain auspicious occasions as well as at the festivals. In the early part of the nineteenth century a wealthy man of Calcutta left a large sum of money with the British authorities to feed a minimum number of Brahmins regularly out of the proceeds of this fund. After some years the number of persons who came to eat fell off, and the money was utilized for other charities.

All over Bengal there was a class of Brahmins who roamed over many adjoining districts in order to eat at all the banquets given in the area in connection with various rites, especially funerals. As these feasts went on from before noon to dusk and everybody who came was fed without question of invitation, these Brahmins and also ordinary people, who were always half-starved, returned at times to eat again. In my young days, when the expense of the ceremonies had begun to pinch, this lavish hospitality of old times was felt to be a nuisance. So precautions were taken to prevent double-feasting. At the funeral of a very wealthy relative of mine at the beginning of this century, a very bureaucratic expedient was adopted to prevent repeated eating by the same person, which was to stamp the palm of a person who had eaten once with indelible ink. One of my brothers, who was present on this occasion, assisted at this procedure with great glee. Finally, it was normal to ask again and again for a particular dish or dishes, especially sweetmeats, and then tie up the leftovers in a towel and take them home for the wife and children.

Not only were the priests not expected to be the guardians of morality, they did not have a high reputation for virtue. The officiating priests in the houses of the wealthy, who were regarded as domestics, were not expected to have any traits of character different from those of the other servants. The priests were not celibate. Indeed, they had a bad reputation generally as to their sexual morals. In Bengal the lower ranks of the performing priests were supposed to have liaisons with the maidservants, and sometimes even with the matrons or widows of the family. This was also the case more or less all over India.

The bad reputation extended to the whole of the Brahmin order, even when they were not priests. After the establishment of British rule the Brahmins went into the professions and the civil service, and thereby not only acquired great respect for their intelligence and competence, but also became a very important class socially and economically. In south India they became the most influential caste.

But before that, and in south India more especially, and also when they were in the priesthood, they had a very low reputation for morals. The Abbé Dubois, who had mixed with them freely, set down his view of them as they were at the end of the eighteenth and beginning of the nineteenth century. He wrote:

But are the Brahmins, who are so easily shocked at the sins and vices of others—are they themselves exempt from all human weaknesses? Are their morals irreproachable? Oh, far from it! My pen would refuse to describe all their wrong-doings; . . . I think that we may take as their greatest vices the untrustworthiness, deceit, and double-dealing . . . It is quite impossible to fathom their minds and discover what they really mean; more impossible, indeed, than with any other race. He would indeed be a fool who relied on their promises, protestations, or oaths, if it were to their interest to break them.

Dubois went on to say:

Intense selfishness is also a common characteristic of a Brahmin. Brought up in the idea that nothing is too good for him, and that he owes nothing in return to any one, he models the whole of his life on this principle. He would unhesitatingly sacrifice the public good, or his country itself, if it promoted his own welfare.

The Brahmin, Dubois also points out, has an overweening sense of self-importance and therefore arrogance. 'He makes it a point of duty not only to hold himself aloof from all other human beings, but also to despise and hate from the bottom of his heart everyone who happens not to be born of the same caste as himself.' Further, the Brahmin thinks himself absolved from any feelings of gratitude, pity, or consideration towards them.

Another failing of the Brahmin was his gluttony. Dubois writes that at the feasts some Brahmins eat so much that they are unable to rise from their squatting position after the meal.[1] Last of all, Dubois singles out the sensuality of the Brahmins. It seemed to him as if most of the religious institutions of the Hindus were designed for the purpose of rousing sexual passions, and he mentions the mythological stories which describe the licentious orgies of the gods, the erotic sculpture on the temples, and dancers and prostitutes attached to the temples. He further refers to the erotic treatises which they possessed and read.

As to practice, Dubois says, so long as irregular sexual relations

---

[1] In my boyhood I heard many satirical stories about this Brahmin failing. One of them was this. A Brahmin had been to a feast and eaten so much that he could not walk back to his village. But as it was on the bank of the same river on which the house of his host stood, he was just put into the stream to be carried back home. While floating down, he collided against the carcass of a dead cow. Stroking it with an outstretched arm, the Brahmin exclaimed, 'Were you too at the feast?'

are kept secret they are thought to be of very small importance. He points out that the presence of young widows is a temptation to debauchery and seduction. As he puts it:

> Look at the crowds of widows in the prime of life who are forbidden to remarry, and who are only too ready to yield to the temptations by which they are assailed. Modesty and virtue place no restrictions on them; their only fear is that their misconduct may be found out. Consequently, abortion is their invariable resource to prevent such a contingency, and they practise it without the slightest scruple or remorse. There is not a woman amongst them who does not know how to bring it about. This odious crime, so revolting to all natural feelings, is of no importance in the eyes of the Hindus.

H. K. Beauchamp, who translated and edited Dubois' final French text and published it for the first time with his annotations in 1897, and who also had first-hand knowledge of social conditions in the province of Madras, made the observation: 'It must be admitted that the Abbé paints the Brahmins in darker colours than, as a body, they deserve.' But Beauchamp overlooked the unquestionable fact that one hundred years of Western education and familiarity with Western moral principles had brought about a revolutionary change among the Brahmins as among all other social classes in India. Where these influences had not penetrated the vices and failings noted by Dubois were to be found among the Brahmins to a greater or lesser degree all over India. It must not be forgotten that the Brahmins were the highest caste in India and that by the end of the eighteenth century they exhibited, as a class, both the fossilization and the degeneracy of a privileged order.

Sects in Hinduism and their Character

It is not only impossible to enumerate all the sects that have existed in Hindu society, it is not easy even to define what precisely a sect is in Hinduism. Horace Hayman Wilson, who gave the most reliable and exhaustive information about the Hindu sects in English in the volumes of the *Asiatic Researches* in 1828 and 1832, had to say that the description he offered was necessarily superficial. He added that he had got most of his information from two works written, strangely enough, in the Persian language, though by two Hindus, and from another work in a very difficult dialect of Hindi. But he was also able to supplement these accounts from his own observation and from oral reports given to him.

There was one place in India where almost all the Hindu sects could be observed. It was Benares, the holiest of all places of pilgrimage of the Hindus, which for that very reason was also the resort of all the religious vagabonds of India. Wilson quoted a Sanskrit couplet on this, and the following is an English translation:

> For those who are ignorant of the revealed scriptures and the sacred traditions, who have abandoned purity and proper conduct, and for those who have nowhere else to go, for them Benares is the refuge.[1]

On the strength of his sources of information, Wilson adopted the traditional classification of the Hindu sects into three large groups, viz., the worshippers of Vishnu (the Vaishnavas), the worshippers of Siva (the Saivas), and the worshippers of the Mother Goddess (the Saktas). But he also found that the subject was much more complex than this broad classification would suggest, and he thought it necessary to set down some reservations:

> The worshippers of Vishnu, Siva, and Sakti, who are the objects of the following description, are not to be confounded with the orthodox adorers of those divinities: few Brahmins of learning, if they have any religion at all, will acknowledge themselves to belong to any of the popular divisions of the Hindu faith, although as a matter of simple preference, they more especially worship some individual deity, as their chosen or *Ishta Devata*: they refer also to the *Vedas*, the books of law, and *Tantras*, as the only rituals they recognize, and regard all practices not derived from those sources as irregular and profane: on the other hand, many sects seem to have originated, in a great measure, out of opposition to the Brahminical order: teachers and disciples are chosen from any class, and the distinction of caste is, in a great measure, sunk in the new one, of similarity of schism: the ascetics and mendicants, also in many instances, affect to treat the Brahmins with particular contempt, and this is generally repaid with interest by the Brahmins.

[1] Śruti-smriti-vihīnānāṃ, ye śauchāchāra-vivarjitāḥ,
Yeṣām kvāpi gatirnasti, tesām Vārānasi gatiḥ.

This would seem to take the sects of the Hindus out of the folds of true Hinduism, and indeed Wilson introduces his list of sects with the following words: 'Excluding, therefore, those who may be regarded as the regular worshipper of regular gods, we have the following enumeration of the several species of each class.'

From one point of view this would be correct, from another not. Wilson himself said that a portion of the populace was still attached to orthodox Brahmanic Hinduism and also paid deference to the Brahmins. The true character of the sectarian differences, which are not all of the same kind, can be fully understood only in the light of their history and by bearing in mind that they were created by three parallel lines of development.

There was, first, the general evolution of the religion by means of which all Hindu beliefs and practices became separated and reduced to three major cults, i.e. those of Vishnu, Siva, and Sakti. So all the sects of orthodox Brahmanism remained affiliated to these cults.

Secondly, special sects were created by the religious innovators, reformers, and popular prophets. These may be called the dissident or non-conformist sects of Hinduism.

Lastly, the sects were also related to the position of a group of people in Hindu society. So, many sects can be classified according to their social affiliations or disaffiliations. The broadest distinction among the sects is that which is seen between the laity, i.e. the Hindus who are in the world, and the ascetics, hermits, mendicants, —i.e. all those who have renounced the world. The sects of the latter are like the monastic orders in Europe, but their members do not have fixed habitations. These sects or orders are either Vaishnava or Saiva.

The sects of the Hindus who have remained in the world have a close connection with the caste system: there are, first, the sects of the upper castes, which are affiliated with the orthodox cults of Vishnu, Siva, or Sakti; in an altogether different category are the sects of the populace, the merchants, peasants, artisans, and the servile classes, both touchable and untouchable. The sects of this second genus are the most specialized, and their connection with Brahmanic Hinduism is both loose and vague.

Before going on to consider the particular sects it is necessary to form a clear idea of the degree of mutual tolerance or intolerance between the sects. In this respect theory, practice, and opinions differed widely. If the sectarian devotional books are referred to, there will be found in them denunciation of other sects by the preachers of a particular sect, and also eulogies of the sect. There are even disparaging comparisons between the main deities like Siva or Vishnu. On the other hand, an equal number of passages will be found which proclaim the validity of each sect for its worshippers, and dwell, on the greatness of all the gods, and even speak of their oneness. In their opinions on religious matters, the Hindus are very catholic and they readily assert that there should be no discrimination between the gods or between their worshippers.

I shall illustrate the overlapping and tolerance between the sects by taking the sectarian differences in Bengal, of which naturally I have more knowledge than about the other regions of India. Here all the upper castes belong formally either to the Vaishnava or the Sakta cult, and an overwhelming majority adhere to the latter. The Saiva sect is virtually absent among the laity. The worship of Vishnu in the form of Krishna (taken with Radha) and that of Durga or Kali have strong sectarian affiliations and there is also a pronounced affectation of antagonism between the two. This corresponds to social stratification: the Saktas are overwhelmingly of the landed gentry, while the Vaishnavas are to be found mainly in the mercantile classes. Since in Bengal the former are definitely the superior social order, they air a good deal of contempt for the Vaishnavas, and make fun of them. The extravagant emotionalism of the Vaishnavas is derided and their devotion to non-violence and their profession of love for all living creatures are dismissed as hypocritical. For example, the Vaishnava formula in Bengali—*Namé ruchi, jivé daya* (taste for the Name, and compassion for animals)—is inverted into—*Jivé ruchi* (taste for animals) and *namé daya* (compassion for the Name.) In Bengal the meat normally eaten is that of the he-goat, and so the Vaishnavas were regarded as the Yama (god of death) of tender kids.

But this chaffing would give a wholly wrong idea of what sectarian loyalty and conduct really are. Even in families which were for generations Sakta, the deity in the family's shrine could be and would be Krishna and Radha. For instance, my family was traditionally Sakta, even aggressively so. Thus an uncle who towards the end of the last century showed leanings towards the monotheism of the Brahmos was brought home from college and bathed in the blood of the buffalo sacrificed before the goddess Durga—and, in fact, he was effectively cured of monotheism by that purification. Nevertheless, our family deities were Krishna and Radha united in a close embrace. Each family gave a particular name to Krishna and Radha, and our couple was called Gopinath (Lord of the Milkmaid) and Gopiniji (Lady Milkmaid).

To illustrate the eclecticism further I might say that in addition to one temple in ruins, our family had another temple, not within the boundaries of the homestead, but a little distance away, by the side of a tank—a brick-built temple—in which there was the usual *linga* of Siva, which was worshipped with proper rituals every day. Every house would also have in addition the Salagram Sila, the fossil ammonite, which was the symbol of Vishnu. In fact, this was the most venerated and sacred religious object in the house. To make matters more complex, any member of a house could have a special initiation into a cult and adopt this particular mode of devotion.

Among the ascetics and the lower castes, the sectarian adherence was more strict. The wandering sadhus always followed the rules of their orders, and could be distinguished by their marks, clothes or absence of clothes, and the sticks or tongs or brass vessels they carried. At the great festivals of bathing, e.g. Kumbha Mela, the orders at times quarrelled and even fought for precedence. But as a rule they exhibited a wide tolerance of each other like the many species of wild animals in a forest.

The popular sects were the most exclusive in regard to religious observances, but they were in no way aggressive to others. When these were sects created by the popular prophets their adherents were normally indifferent to the higher Hindu rites, and worshipped in their own way. This did not, however, exclude going to the temples if they wished to do so.

The Vaishnava Sects

In describing some of the principal sects the sectarian adherence of the general body of lay Hindus will be ignored, and only those sects will be described which have a specialized character, either lay or coenobitic. Even their number is large, and each important sect has given rise to sub-sects whose affiliation to the parent sect is at times very exiguous. The description is intended to be an illustration of the permissiveness of Hinduism considered as a catholic religious system, so that the doctrines and practices of these sects might be regarded as variations on the normal themes of Hinduism in very distant keys.

In offering this description I shall depend mainly on Wilson because his account was based on his knowledge and observation of the sects when they had not come under the extraneous influences emanating from British rule.

In his essay Wilson gave the following list of the Vaishnava sects: (1) Sri Sampradaya or the followers of Ramanuja; (2) Ramanandis; (3) Kabir Panthis; (4) Maluk Dasis; (5) Khakis; (6) Dadu Panthis; (7) Raya Dasis; (8) Senais Panthis; (9) Vallabhacharya Sampradaya; (10) Mira Bais; (11) Madhvacharis; (12) Nimavats; (13) The Vaishnavas of Bengal or the followers of Chaitanya; (14) Radha Vallabhis; (15) The Sakhi Bhavas; (16) Charan Dasis; (17) Harischandis; (18) Sadhna Panthis; (19) Madhvis; (20) Sannyasis, Vairagis, and Nagas.

Though all these sects are worshippers of Vishnu in one form or another they are not all of one kind. For instance, the followers of Ramanuja, Madhva, or Chaitanya fall within the fold of orthodox Brahmanism, whereas the followers of Kabir or Dadu are definitely dissident. Again, the doctrines or dogmas of certain of the Brahmanical sects, e.g. the Ramanuja sect, or the Madhva sect, or the Chaitanya sect are more philosophical than religious. But the devotions and observances of some of these are on the religious plane. The sects created by the popular prophets are not concerned deeply or at all with dogmatic or metaphysical positions, they offer a particular path of devotion together with simple moral teaching.

It has also to be pointed out that the worship of Vishnu as Vishnu is exceptional in the Vaishnava sects. Most of them worship Krishna either singly or in combination with Radha, but Vishnu is also worshipped in the form of Rama, the seventh incarnation.

Followers of Ramanuja. This selective list of the Vaishnava sects should begin with the one founded by Ramanuja, the great south Indian teacher of philosophy and religion who lived in the twelfth century, because it was the oldest among those which existed at the end of the eighteenth century. The members of this sect are mostly to be found in the south. The Ramanujites worshipped Vishnu in his own form together with his consort Lakshmi, as well as the two incarnations of Rama and Krishna. The tenets of the sect were philosophical rather than religious, and are to be found in the commentaries of the founder on the original *Sutra* of the Vedanta, on the *Gita*, and certain other texts. In philosophical terms these are described as *Visishta-advaita* or 'particularized monism'. That is to say, Ramanuja taught that the Supreme Spirit could have attributes.

What made his followers a sect was not this doctrine, but their special rule of life, and externally, too, they were recognized by distinguishing marks. Their daily life was very strictly regulated and the strictest rules were about eating. They had to cook their own food, and eat it in great privacy. If anybody saw them eating the food had to be thrown away at once and buried in the ground. Also, they could not eat in cotton garments, but had to wear those made of silk or wool.

Their distinguishing marks were not only elaborate, but the main substance for making them had to be procured with great care. This was a white calcareous clay, which had to be of the greatest purity like the clay for the best china. The purest came from Dwaraka, a place of pilgrimage on the coast of the Kathiawar peninsula, from a well in which the *gopis* or milkmaids who loved Krishna were believed to have drowned themselves after his death. This clay was called *gopi-chandana* (sandal paste of the gopis). The most important mark made with this white clay was on the forehead, where two perpendicular lines were drawn from the root of the hair above the forehead to the inner ends of the eyebrows below, and connected by a transverse line at the bottom. Between these two lines there had to be a red line made with a mixture of turmeric and lime. The marks on the arms and chest were, however, made only with the white clay. These gave them a spotted appearance, and the marks were supposed to be the four objects which Vishnu held in his four hands and by which he was distinguished. These were the conch shell, wheel, mace, and lotus. Those who wanted verisimilitude in the emblems had stamps of these objects made of wood and then had themselves stamped with the clay. Though this was condemned formally, some even stamped these emblems on their body with a red-hot iron.

Their religious observance was five-fold: cleaning and purifying temples, images, etc.; providing flowers and perfumes for religious rites; presentation of such offerings; counting the rosary and repeating the name; and, lastly, meditation to unite with the deity. The reward of these observances was elevation to Vaikuntha or Vishnu's heavenly abode.

Followers of Ramananda. The founder of this sect was Ramananda, traditionally associated with Ramanuja, as a direct disciple or in apostolic succession. His date is uncertain, but most probably he preached in the fifteenth century. He was a north Indian and taught at Benares. The followers of this sect are to be found mainly in the Gangetic plain. Ramananda's teaching was devotional, and the devotion was directed towards Rama, as the incarnation of Vishnu, and as the manifested God. It is only in the Gangetic plain that Rama is regarded as God. It may be mentioned incidentally that Mahatma Gandhi, when shot, died with the words 'Ram, Ram' on his lips. The name of Rama is also uttered to drive off evil spirits, and in northern India a dead body is taken to the burning ghat to the accompaniment of the cry *Ram nam satya hai* ('The name of Ram is true'). But though he has become an object of devotion there is no cult associated with Rama nor temples to him. The picture of Rama accompanied by his wife Sita, both shown seated like a king and a queen, and attended by Rama's brother Lakshmana as well as the holy langur Hanuman in a prostrate posture, is a sacred emblem. The most fervent expression of the devotion to Rama as God is to be found in the life of Rama written by the great Hindi poet Tulsidas.

The Ramanandis or Ramavats, as the members of this sect were called, were the opposite of the Ramanujites in respect of rules of conduct. They had no rule of life, and even deprecated caste distinctions. Among the disciples of Ramananda were men of even untouchable castes and one who was probably a Muslim.

Followers of Kabir. With this sect Hindu sectarian evolution branched off into what might be called a foreign epiphytic growth, and the affiliation with Hindu religiosity is very exiguous. One of the twelve disciples of Ramananda was Kabir, generally accepted to have been a Muslim. But he became the most famous of the people's prophets of northern India. His life and deeds are embodied in many legends, and he is even supposed to have lived for 120 years. The date of his death is, however, known with relative certainty to have been 1518.

Though he and his sect are included among the Vaishnavites, the connection is nominal, and his religious teaching is very general and eclectic. Its doctrinal side is obscure, and it is also very heterodox. It most strikingly illustrates the almost unlimited scope given to religious teachers in India to become non-conformist. Kabir denounced both Hindu and Muslim formalism with equal severity, and proclaimed his contempt for the Hindu priest and the Muslim mulla alike. His doctrine was one of simple and straightforward personal surrender to God, irrespective of any particular name, and his moral teaching, though very fervent, was of a very simple kind. He characterized his teaching as *Sahaja Yoga*, or 'easy union' or 'easy discipline'. He rejected idolatry and rituals, and said that those who sought God should flee from temple and mosque and try to find him in the fields, in the artisan's workshop, and the happy household. Not surprisingly, he rejected the caste system.

A few of Kabir's sayings might be quoted in order to illustrate his conception of his own prophetic role as well as the complexion of his religious message. About himself he said: 'My word is of the word; hear it, go not astray; if man wishes to know the truth, let him investigate the word . . . My word is from the first; meditate on it every moment; you will flourish in the end like the Jowar plant, which externally shows but beards and leaves . . . Without hearing the word, it is utter darkness; say, whither shall one go; without finding the gateway of the word, man will ever be astray.' But he seems also to have his doubts. One saying has this: 'I have wept for mankind, but no one has wept with me; *he* will join in my tears, who comprehends the word. All have exclaimed, master, master, but to me this doubt arises: how can they sit down with the master, whom they do not know.'

Kabir did indeed propound a doctrine, but it was nothing else than a very simple form of the amorphous Hindu catholicity. The real strength of his teaching lay in its emphasis on sincere faith in God and devotion to him, and equally in his simple moral teaching. One typical pronouncement might be quoted:

To Ali and Rama we owe our existence, and should, therefore, show similar tenderness to all that live: of what avail is it to shave your head, prostrate yourself on the ground, or immerse your body in the stream; whilst you shed blood you call yourself pure, and boast of virtues that you never display; of what benefit is cleaning your mouth, counting your beads, performing ablutions and bowing in temples, when, whilst you mutter your prayers, or journey to Mecca and Medina, deceitfulness is in your heart . . . If God dwells in tabernacles, whose residence is the universe? . . . Behold but one in all things, it is the second that leads you astray. Every man and woman that has been born is of the same nature as yourself. He, whose is the world, and whose are the children of Ali and Rama, He is my Guru, He is my Pir.

Basically, Kabir wanted to make men religious by lessening the burden of religion—an aim all popular religious prophets have had in India.

Followers of Vallabhacharya. The aim of lessening the burden of strict Brahmanism was realized within the orthodox Hindu framework, though in different ways, by the two Vishnuite sects to be described next. These were also the most important and influential Vaishnava sects in northern India at the beginning of the nineteenth century, and both had a large following in their respective regions. One of the sects obeyed the teaching of Vallabhacharya and the other of Chaitanya. The followers of the former were to be found mostly in western India, and of the latter in Bengal. However, on account of the mythological association of Krishna with Mathura and Brindaban, the formal centres of both the sects were in Brindaban.

To begin with the Vallabhacharya sect. It was founded by a teacher named Vallabha, about whom many miraculous tales are current. It is, however, a fact that he was a Telugu Brahmin and taught during the first decades of the sixteenth century. According to tradition, he left behind him eighty-four disciples who were commissioned to preach his message in different regions. But his real successor was his son, and the leadership of his sect became dynastic and apostolic at the same time. This son's many sons succeeded to and divided up the leadership and established branches in different cities. These leaders were all called Maharajas (Great Kings) like secular rulers. They were actually like very wealthy landlords, and had immense wealth. They did not live an ascetic life, and not even a simple one dedicated to religion in the Western sense.

The life of the heads of the sect as well as of its members was based on one part of the original teaching of Vallabhacharya. He preached that in order to worship God a man did not have to turn his back on the world, fast, practise self-mortification, or abstain from good living. He taught positively that satisfaction of the natural desires was legitimate; in fact, according to him they were intended to be satisfied. And in fact they were satisfied to the utmost point of sensual enjoyment by the Gurus, as well as the disciples who were mostly wealthy merchants. Until the middle of the nineteenth century, and even later, the religious feasts and festivals of the sect as well as the tours of the Gurus were marked by gross profligacy, and there is no doubt that every liberty was permitted by the women of the sect to the Maharajas. There was a sensational case in 1862 in Bombay High Court in which the licentiousness was exposed.

A sort of counter-reformation of this expression of Vaishnavism was undertaken by a man who was at first affiliated to this school. His name was Swami Narayan. During the first decades of the nineteenth century he carried on an energetic campaign against the loose life of the followers of Vallabhacharya. Through the example of his own life and the appeal of his religious and moral teaching he gained a large number of followers, and so the orthodox and the wealthy Vallabhites tried to persecute him. This, however, secured more and very militant followers for him.

As it happened, Reginald Heber, Bishop of Calcutta and Metropolitan of India, in the course of his journeys met him in 1825, and found him escorted by two hundred fully armed horsemen. The Bishop's bodyguard consisted of only fifty sepoys, who were met by the Guru's bodyguard with the clash of shields and tramp of horses. Heber wrote in his journal: 'I could not help smiling, though my sensations were in some degree painful and humiliating, at the idea of two religious teachers meeting at the head of little armies.' The Bishop added that the followers of Swami Narayan were ready to fight to the last drop of blood rather than suffer a fringe of his garment to be handled roughly.

This militancy, which was of a kind analogous to that of political leaders, persisted, and it was witnessed by Monier-Williams, then

Boden Professor of Sanskrit at Oxford, when he visited the shrines of the Swami Narayan sect at Ahmedabad about fifty years later. The leaders of this sect had also become known as Maharajas by that time, and there was great rivalry between two of them. So, to show his importance, the more powerful Maharaja took Monier-Williams through a crowd of nearly ten thousand of his followers. Though accompanied by the English magistrate of the district, Monier-Williams was a little cowed by the spectacle. He wrote: 'The vast concourse swayed to and fro like the waves of a troubled sea, each man vociferating to his neighbours in a manner quite appalling. I could not help thinking of our apparent helplessness in the surging crowd, and asking myself how two solitary Europeans would be likely to fare, if, from some accidental circumstance, the religious fanaticism of a myriad of excited Hindus were to break loose and vent itself upon us.'

Followers of Chaitanya. This Vaishnava sect in its practices and devotional life presented an antithesis to that of Vallabhacharya, though doctrinally the two were not very different. The followers of Chaitanya were quietists, and they had to be wholly non-violent, humble, and unostentatious. However, a very important part of the devotions of the sect was to sing and dance to the accompaniment of an earthen drum either in assemblies or processions. This exerted an irresistible emotional power on the populace, and lately the appeal has spread to the West. I have seen the exhibitionism of British and American converts to the sect, and seen it not only in Oxford Street in London, but also in Texas, the home of the cowboys, and at Vancouver in Canada. The devotional aspect of this school will be considered later.

In its social aspect Chaitanya's teaching was both humanitarian and egalitarian. So it was to be expected that he would reject the caste system. One saying attributed to him was this: 'God's mercy does not regard caste or birth.' Another saying is that even a Chandala (a man of the untouchable caste) is to be honoured if he has faith, whereas an unbelieving performer of Vedic rites is not to be. In fact, Chaitanya is said to have converted many Muslims, even some ferocious Pathans, and one of his principal followers was a Muslim. In any case, the social aspect of Chaitanya's teaching, in addition to the character of his religious teaching, made him immensely popular with the common people. The majority of the members of his sect came from the trading and other lowly castes.

But in Hindu society it is not possible to override the principle of heredity and to abandon caste. As in the Vallabhacharya's sect so too in Chaitanya's, the leadership became dynastic, and in the membership of the sect the caste system was both maintained and extended.

Chaitanya relegated the leadership of his sect to two collaborators, both Brahmin. They were Advaita and Nityananda, who with him formed a triad of Maha-Prabhus (Great Masters) of the sect. Their descendants still exercise the leadership in Bengal. Six other followers were known as Gosvamis or Gosains (literally meaning 'master of cattle') and they settled at Brindaban. In addition, there were other families of leaders.

But the sect was not homogeneous in its membership, for it was divided into classes distinguished by their relationship to society. Some were vagrants or mendicants, wandering or living individually. They were called Vairagis. The second class was constituted by those who live a coenobitic life in *maths* and *akharas*, which were like the monasteries of the West. There were men as well as women in these groups, and each community was under a *mohant*, the equivalent of an abbot. The men and women were not segregated as in the West, but lived in the same monastery. The relationship between the Vaishnavas and the Vaishnavis was supposed to be brotherly and sisterly, but certainly in practice it was not so. The Vaishnavis were believed to have promiscuous sexual relations with the *mohant* or other Vaishnavas and this was generally regarded as normal.

To make matters more complicated, individual Vaishnavas often lived with a Vaishnavi who became his married wife by means of a very simple rite, and besides there was a Vaishnava caste, who lived the life of normal householders. The men and women from the *maths*, as well as the Vaishnava householders, often formed parties of professional singers, and went from place to place singing the ballads of Krishna, and making a living out of this.

The monastic Vaishnavas as well as the Vaishnava householders of the lower castes wore distinctive marks, insignia, and clothes. The two marks and signs by which they could be recognized were the sandal mark on the forehead and the necklace of beads made from the tulsi plant round the neck. They also wore saffron-coloured loin-clothes, but without the back-tuck. The coenobitic and vagrant Vaishnavas were also buried, not cremated like other Hindus.

Since this account of the sects is meant only to give a general idea of the character of sectarian differences, and not to describe them exhaustively, the other Vaishnava sects will not be described. For the same reason, an enumeration of the Saiva and Sakta sects will also be omitted. In their social aspect the Saiva sects were similar to the Vaishnava sects, especially the vagrant ones, while the Sakta sects were distinguished by their modes of devotion and rites, not by their organization.

Coenobitism and Vagrancy in the Sects

In recent centuries those Hindus who adopted religion as their sole vocation and profession have either wandered about the country individually but also in parties, taking up only temporary residence here and there, or lived in small or large permanent establishments like monasteries under a superior. The establishments were called *maths, akharas,* or *asthals,* and were scattered all over the country. Some of these were very wealthy and highly regarded, as the five *maths* attributed to Samkaracharya. The heads of such *maths* had immense prestige, and might be called princes of the Hindu church. As to the rest, there was an immense range in importance and wealth. Their income was derived partly from landed property and partly from gifts from the lay public who came to them as visitors or pilgrims. In addition, the inmates of the *maths* also collected food and money by begging.

The actual buildings might be mere huts or sumptuous palaces. They had quarters for the superior and his family when they were married, for the *chelas* or disciples, and also for servants of both sexes. Outsiders could come and visit the shrines, and accommodation was always provided for them in separate rooms. No one could be forbidden entry into these establishments. The shrine was dedicated to the particular deity of the sect, and his daily service was exactly like the service and rites in the temples. Devotional life properly so-called was a private concern of each inmate. Normally no such life existed.

The head of the establishment was called *mohant.* He was either hereditary or elected from among the disciples. Often, the election was by the simple nomination by the previous *mohant*. At times during British rule, the question of succession was taken to the courts. As a whole, considered socially, these establishments might be regarded as the religious wing of secular landlordism.

Vagrancy has already been described as the predatory expression of Hindu religious life. The wandering sadhus represented the most numerous element of those who followed religion professionally. When organized in orders they obtained recruits continuously. Two special groups might be singled out.

The first of them is constituted by the Aghor Panthis or Aghorias, who originally practised both human sacrifice and cannibalism, but in recent times only the latter. Their rites had disappeared from open practice even under Muslim rule, but there is reason to believe that some of these continued secretly even under British rule. These men ate even carrion and filth. Normally, they ate dead bodies, stealing them from funeral pyres. It is recorded that during the Mutiny these ascetics followed the troops and dined off the soldiers who were killed. A friend of mine has related that they stole a corpse in a village near Calcutta during his childhood. They also smeared their body with human excreta. They are not known to exist now.

The other group of ascetics are the Nagas or naked sadhus. They could be both Saiva or Vaishnavite, though the majority of them belonged to the first sect. There was no furtiveness about them, and they flaunted their nudity without any self-consciousness. Immense numbers of them formed corps according to the orders to which they belonged. They can still be seen at the bathing festivals, especially during the Kumbha Mela.

It is these vagrant sadhus who had the most warlike habits. Though completely naked they, especially the Vaishnava Nagas, always carried weapons. They were also given to extreme aggressiveness in asserting their precedence at the festivals. Before the establishment of British rule in upper India there was a bloody riot at Hardwar between two sects of the Nagas in which it was reported that 18,000 sadhus were killed. Such things were, of course, exceptional, and an extreme manifestation of Hindu sectarianism. But in its own way this extremism was also typical; it illustrated the wide compass and endless variety of Hindu religiosity.

Chapter Five

RELIGIOUS CONTROL
OF HINDU LIFE

IN the introduction it has been shown that for the Hindus their religion was a means of living in the world and making their lives successful, happy, and even sanctified, that is to say, living under the Hindu form of grace. It followed from this that their religion exercised a rigorous control over their lives in every aspect and in every activity. So no account of Hinduism can be complete without a description of these manifold controls. To omit that and confine oneself only to those features of Hinduism which are religious from the Western point of view, will be not only giving a partial account, but also seriously misrepresenting it. And to hold forth only on the Upanishads and the Vedanta philosophy with ineffable woolliness would be falsification. Unfortunately, this kind of falsification has become not only common, but even deliberate. Obedience to the inhibitions and taboos which this side of Hinduism has created is as much a part of the Way of Works *(Karma Marga)* of the Hindus as is the scrupulous performance of the rites of the religion.

Submission to Taboos

If a Hindu did not observe these taboos he was subjected to the most cruel social coercion. In extreme cases, he would be subjected to what is Hindu excommunication, and that, so long as it could be imposed, was very concrete. When excommunicated, which, actually, was being boycotted, nobody would visit him, eat with him, or give help in cremation by carrying the dead body to the burning ghat. Even the village barber would not cut his hair or shave him, nor the washerman wash his clothes. The fear of losing caste in this way was the most efficient sanction behind all the restrictive customs of Hinduism.

I shall cite three examples of this. The first was given by Tagore from his own experience. One great Calcutta grandee had gone to visit another grandee, who was a graduate of Calcutta University. When after the visit the first Raja was getting into his landau the host Raja pulled him by his coat, and said: 'You are chewing *pan* (betel)!' Now, when a Hindu is eating anything he cannot be in any kind of contact with another man who is not of his caste, and to be in contact with a Mussulman was the worst pollution. All coachmen in Calcutta were Muslims. The visiting Raja had to spit out what still remained in his mouth of the *pan* which his host had given him.

The next example is from my experience. In November 1927 I was travelling by train from my native town in eastern Bengal to Calcutta, and in the compartment were two Muslim gentlemen. Feeling thirsty, I took out an orange and began to eat it. I knew, of course, that I could not eat cooked food or drink water when a Muslim was under the same roof (even of a railway carriage), but I was not aware that I could not eat even fruit. So I was very much surprised when a fellow Hindu began to wink at me, looking significantly at the Muslims. He said nothing as long as they were in the carriage. But when at the nearest station, where the stoppage was long, they got down to stretch their legs, he asked me in an aggrieved tone why I had eaten the orange with Muslims in the compartment. I replied that I did not mind, upon which he asked me where I came from. I mentioned my village, and he again asked me whether I was a Chaudhuri of Banagram. When I said that I was, he remarked with great asperity: 'If a man from such a family as yours sets such an example what will *not* the common people do?'

Last of all, I shall give an example of the cruelty of the social boycott, the story of which was told me by my father, who became concerned with it as a lawyer. A certain man in a village near my birthplace had been boycotted, and when his grown-up son died, no one would come to help him to carry the body to the burning place or bring firewood for the cremation. He carried the body alone, and was cutting down some trees to obtain the faggots. The village people who had put him on the blacklist collected at a short distance and began to jeer at him. Enraged beyond endurance, he struck one of them with his axe. Of course he was prosecuted for grievous assault, and no lawyer would undertake his defence. My father did.

Of course, this case was very exceptional. But such exceptions made the taboos obeyed. Apart from it most Hindus were so conditioned psychologically that they would submit willingly. They obeyed all the injunctions just as people in civilized countries obey an elaborate criminal law, especially one like the English Common Law. In the course of their daily life, the Hindus learned and observed these rules as people learn and observe social and table manners. In fact, it may be pointed out that when such restraints, however irrational, are felt to be burdensome it is to be assumed that the way of life to which they belong has become decadent.

The Political Reason

From the very beginning of Hindu culture there was a socio-political reason behind such controls. At the end of the eighteenth century these had become even more stringent because of Muslim domination, and British rule, being equally foreign, was an equal threat to the Hindu way of life. I give the history of the growth of the taboos from the earliest times to the nineteenth century briefly.

As foreign colonists in India the Aryans found their way of life threatened from the first by a native population. So, adherence without questioning and in its entirety to the customs and practices which they had brought with them, i.e. an unwavering loyalty to the *mos majorum*, became the basic principle of their life in India, for they were not ready to give up their group identity and culture. This accounts for the attitude to the Vedas as the religious basis of all their way of life and as the fundamental charter of their existence in India, though they did not practise the religion found in them, nor even understood them wholly. This sense of duty to the Aryan heritage must also have been felt in respect of minor customs. No feature at all of the original way of life was to be abandoned.

The rigidity increased through the ages as the danger to the identity continued and grew. The first threat was from the non-Aryan aboriginals, and it was dealt with by introducing a system of apartheid which was applied in one way to the free aboriginals and in another to the servile aboriginals. The first were left in geographical isolation in their jungles and hills, the second in social isolation through untouchability. Thus a pattern of coexistence was created.

Then came a new threat from the external non-Aryan bar-barians—the nomadic and semi-nomadic people who invaded India from the first century B.C. to the third century A.D. and again in the fifth century. The last horde of invaders, the Huns, created as great a terror in India as they did in Europe. Their invasion must have fixed the notion of *Mlechchha*, unclean foreigners, which henceforth stood for the external enemies of the Hindu order. In addition, it must also have created the image of Kalki, the tenth incarnation of Vishnu and the destroyer of the *Mlechchhas*, who rode on a war-horse and wielded a sword as flaming as a comet. From this time, *Anarya* (the non-Aryan) yielded place to the *Mlechchha* (the unclean foreigner) as the enemy of the Hindus.

These invaders were absorbed, but no sooner was the process completed than a new and far more dangerous enemy appeared who could never be absorbed. This enemy was the Muslim, who threatened the Hindu way of life in a manner never seen before. The Muslims asserted the superiority of their own way of life, and began an active onslaught on Hinduism. Therefore the old loyalty to the Hindu way became fanatical, and all the tried means of protection were refurbished both internally and externally. Henceforth there could be no question of abandoning any feature of the religion, rational or irrational.

At the next stage the English created a new threat, and the notion of *Mlechchha*, together with the developed system of defence against Islam, was extended to the new rulers. However, in the exercise of their political power the English did not show themselves as the enemy of Hinduism. On the contrary, they were extremely careful not to give offence to Hindu suscepti-bilities. Even when they had to stop inhuman practices like infanti-cide or the burning of widows, they took these steps with extreme reluctance and dilatoriness. However, the Hindus were not dis-armed in their fears, for they felt that a new danger was arising from within. The impact of Western culture through education in English was inducing the Hindus themselves to question their religion as it was and to change their outlook and habits of living. The Muslims had used force, the English held out temptations, and that was a greater peril.

At first the old Hindu order could not resist the influence of their Western education, and many Hindus started an active movement of religious reform. But the same education and the writings of the European Orientalists enabled other Hindus to create a new and powerful conservatism. It is the arguments of these conservatives which enable us to get a retrospective insight into the Hindu mind as it worked in earlier times to make the entire body of beliefs and practices a single block, impervious to changes.

The Hindu conservatives of the nineteenth century saw the enemy, not in the Englishman, but in their own reformers, and told them that the so-called superstitions of the Hindus had very good reasons behind them and were not to be abandoned thoughtlessly. This campaign was noted even by the English administrators. Sir Henry Maine as Vice-Chancellor of Calcutta University told the students at a convocation in 1866 that they were committing a mistake by calling in ingenious analogies and subtle explanations to justify usages which they did not venture to defend directly, and then observed: 'There is no greater delusion than to suppose that you weaken an error by giving it a colour of truth. On the contrary, you give it pertinacity and vitality, and greater power for evil.'

But as nationalism grew under British rule, so did the religious conservatism. The movement of the Hindu mind in this direction was bound to find its way into imaginative literature. So, in a famous novel by Tagore—*Gora*—which was published in 1910 but depicted the religious controversies of the last decades of the nineteenth century, a young neo-Hindu is made to say to a Hindu reformer: 'It is only by learning by rote from English books that you are calling these customs evil. You will have the right to speak in this way only when you have acquired the capacity to speak about the evil customs of the English in exactly the same manner.' He defined his position by saying: 'My point is that our understanding of the real aims of our society can become limpid only when we have accepted it wholly in all its aspects. To quarrel with it, is not simply to obstruct it, but also to misunderstand it.' This total obedience was the demand of the Hindu conservatives even under British rule. Though the arguments they employed cannot be traced back to any previous age, there can be no doubt it was thinking on such lines that induced Hindus of older times to defend their religious and social heritage in its entirety, even when it was irrational. A closed society does not change willingly, and when it survives in the face of attacks on it, it becomes all the more incapable of giving up anything. Thus it may be said that from the ancient Aryan self-consciousness to the recent Hindu self-consciousness there is an unbroken line of descent.

Control of Daily Life

The actual control of personal and social life of the Hindu by his religion has now to be described. It is quite impossible to describe all the injunctions and taboos, and so only a sampling will be offered. To a Hindu exponent of the sacred law of old times this account will appear to be sadly attenuated, but to a non-Hindu it will seem, even from the relatively small selection I am giving by way of illustration, that in his daily life a Hindu is bound hand and foot in regard to all his actions.

The ultimate source of all the rules is the sacred law, or *Dharma Sastra*, in the ancient texts like the *Manu Samhita* and the *Parasara Samhita*. These texts are also called *Smriti* (Traditions) collectively, and when British rule was established in India there were Brahmins who had specialized in it, as they had specialized in philosophy or grammar. When any question of what was permissible or not permissible arose it was referred to one or a number of these authorities, and they gave their opinion. But the opinion had always to be supported by a definite text.

For the greater part, the rules were so well established that they had become custom, so that even when no authority for a practice could be found in any text it was binding if it had been customary for a long time. In the early nineteenth century the two regions of India in which the injunctions and prohibitions were most rigorously enforced were Bengal and the Tamil country. I do not, however, have any first-hand knowledge of Tamil practices, nor do I know the texts which were followed in that region. So the account given here is of the practices in Bengal, of which I have fairly full knowledge. In Bengal the rules of the *Dharma Sastras* had been summarized and codified by a great authority on *Smriti*, Raghunandana, whose version of them was regarded as binding. Only in the case of very difficult points was any reference to the ancient texts made, though every pundit knew the most important of them almost by heart. Of the rules I am enumerating I can say that even down to the end of the nineteenth century no

Bengali Hindu would have dared to disobey any. On the contrary, it was a matter of pride for all Hindus to be unfailing in doing what was enjoined and in refraining from all that was forbidden. This they described as having *achara* (observance, good conduct) and *vichara* (discriminating between actions). The Muslims and the British were held in contempt as people who had neither *achara* nor *vichara*.

A further general observation has to be made about the permissibility and non-permissibility of actions of every kind. Even when a certain thing was permitted it could become forbidden for certain persons, in certain conditions, and at certain times. For instance, a particular food which was universally eaten could become impure and therefore uneatable, and again it could not be eaten on certain days and at certain times. These special restrictions will be dealt with in the sections 'Pure and Impure States' and 'Astral Control of Actions', which follow. In this section only general permissibility and non-permissibility is being set down.

Food and Drink. There is sufficient historical evidence for thinking that the food habits of the Hindus in ancient times were different from what they became later. Meat was certainly eaten, at least by the warrior caste, which included the entire princely order and the aristocracy. There are references to this in the *Mahabharata*. In one of his inscriptions the Emperor Asoka set down that, before his mind had turned to Dharma (Buddhism), thousands of animals were slaughtered for the royal kitchen, but that at the date of the inscription this had been brought down to one peacock and one gazelle. The medical treatise attributed to Charaka, which is placed among the scriptures (*Sastra*), definitely says that for nutrition no food can surpass meat. Furthermore, the old Sanskrit word for a cook is *Supakara* (maker of broth or soup), and it must not be forgotten that both the Sanskrit word *supa* and the English-French 'soup' are derived from the Indo-European root *seu*.

But the date at which vegetarianism became established among the twice-born castes cannot be determined. Nevertheless, by the eighteenth century it had become binding on all high-caste Hindus except in Bengal, as it is also today. The strength of the taboo will be understood from the following facts: modern Hindu women, who both in India and in England get drunk on strong spirituous liquors and have no scruples about sexual intercourse, will yet not eat meat; I have also seen Hindu men in Delhi who have been educated abroad, sniffing at the snacks taken round in diplomatic cocktail parties to detect if they contain meat.

But there were exceptions. Lower castes generally ate meat. In the Punjab, generally, the men would eat it but not the women. In Bengal all castes and classes took and take animal food, i.e. fish and meat, although some refrain for the sake of holiness or self-restraint. Widows, of course, cannot eat any animal food. Hindus also cannot eat certain vegetables like onions and garlic.

Beef is the supreme taboo for all Hindus, and observance of this taboo is for all practical purposes the only infallible religious test for them. This is an extension of the worship of the cow and abstention from cow-killing, which was the most common reason behind Hindu-Muslim riots before politics came into this feud. But here, too, there is indisputable historical evidence that in ancient times the Hindus could eat beef. In fact, it was considered to be the best food which could be offered to a *Rishi* (Sage) or a very distinguished guest.

As to other meats, in Bengal there was and is no bar against that of goats (male but not female), sheep, deer, pigeons, and ducks. Chicken, however, was taboo. Normally, traditional Hindus did not slaughter goats for the undisguised purpose of eating. So if they wanted to eat meat they would send a goat or two as a sacrificial offering to Kali, which was easy because every Hindu village in Bengal had a temple of the goddess. After the sacrifice the head was taken by the goddess (i.e. by the priest as her proxy) and the carcass brought away by the sacrificer to be cooked and eaten. In my young days in Calcutta there was a meat shop which attracted Hindu customers by slaughtering the goats before a large clay image of Kali.[1]

Fish was the common animal food in Bengal, and all classes of Bengalis ate it. But it was not only not eaten, but loathed in northern India. Actually, eating of fish was the greatest religious offence which Bengali Hindus gave to other Hindus. The objection to eating fish was on mythological grounds. A fish was the

---

[1] I myself as a boy many times bought meat from this shop.

first incarnation of Vishnu, and so eating fish amounted to eating Vishnu in all his forms, including Krishna. A very large number of Bengalis were Vaishnavite, i.e. worshippers of Vishnu as Krishna, and they were also very devout. But north Indian Hindus mocked at their claim to worship Krishna. I one day heard a Hindustani sadhu who was smeared with ashes shouting at all the Bengalis passing before him: 'Oh, Bengalis, you worship Krishna? Krishna goes out by your arse.' In Delhi, the pundit who taught Sanskrit to my sons spat on the ground when he saw my wife buying fish at the door.

To drink alcohol is a major sin in Hindu sacred law, while murder, unless it is the murder of a Brahmin, is not. The expiation for drinking it is to drink boiling alcohol and die. Even association with a drinker is a sin. In India anyone who sells spirituous drinks becomes untouchable, and there are castes of wine-sellers as of merchants of other commodities. Nevertheless, there is historical evidence that various kinds of wines were drunk throughout India by the princes and warriors, and even by the womenfolk of these classes. It would seem that the prohibition of alcohol in Hindu sacred law was like the prohibition in Islamic sacred law, *Sharia*. Among the Muslims, too, the princes and the nobles drank habitually, while the priests and learned men did not.

A not less binding control in connection with food and drink was that which concerned commensality, or, to be more accurate, acceptance of food and drink from other people. No Hindu could eat with anybody who did not belong to his caste. It was not simply that a Brahmin could not be in bodily contact with or sit alongside a man of another caste, he could not even eat with him under the same roof, sitting at a distance. So, at banquets the different castes, even though all socially high, would be seated in different halls or in wholly separated areas in an open courtyard.

All this did not imply the slightest social disrespect for anybody. A Kayastha would not mind if a poor Brahmin whom he employed as priest, agent, or even cook, did not eat with him. This was giving to God things which were God's, forgetting Caesar for the time being. Nor did it follow that a Hindu could not entertain his Muslim friends or a Muslim his Hindu friends. At weddings friends of both communities could be asked, but separate arrangements would be made for each under the management of Muslims for Muslims and Brahmins for Hindus, and under separate marquees.[1]

It should be added that in well-to-do families in which the women did not cook, only Brahmin cooks would be employed, and neither the men nor the women, even if they were not twice-born, would take food cooked by servants of the Sudra caste. As a matter of fact, cooking became the sole profession of poor Brahmins who were not educated enough to be priests and of Brahmin women who were destitute.

All these restrictions applied to cooked food, and to the acceptance of cooked food. Raw foodstuffs could be accepted from anybody. But acceptance of water was more complicated. It could not be drunk if a Muslim or an untouchable was under the same roof, and it could be taken only from the hands of a man who was of a caste which was 'water-permissible'. All Hindus had to know which castes were so and which were not. All water in a room had to be thrown away if a man from whom it was not permissible to take water came into it. But milk could be taken from anybody if it was *not boiled*. Boiling destroyed its immunity from ritualistic pollution.

Clothing and Adornment. Rules in respect of clothing were only slightly less rigorous than those for food and drink. In ancient times, it would seem they were stricter, or rather there could be no question of any departure from Hindu usages. But the Muslim conquest and rule brought into India a wholly different family of clothing, and that made adjustments necessary. These were, however, kept to the minimum, and no departures from the Hindu costume were permitted in private and religious life.

The first requirement in all Hindu clothing was that it could not be sewn: the Hindu could wear only unsewn clothing which had to be draped round the body. Normally, both for men and women, there had to be two pieces of cloth, one worn round the waist to cover the lower limbs, and the other thrown round the

[1] Till my young days, a Kayastha could not invite a Brahmin directly to a feast, but had to employ a Brahmin as an intermediary. So, when in 1916 I went to invite Brahmin families to the feast at my sister's wedding, a Brahmin accompanied me. He pointed to me and said that he was speaking on my behalf.

torso. But the full dress for women would consist of three pieces, the third piece being a girdle like the Roman *zona*.

But this was not enough. To distinguish himself from the non-Aryans the Aryan had to wear his lower piece with two tucks (*kaccha* in Sanskrit), one end going through the legs and tucked at the back in the middle of the waist, and the other gathered and worn in a flounce tucked above or below the navel in front. For normal occasions these two tucks would be sufficient, but for religious rites a third was necessary. The end of the flounce had to be taken up and tucked at the left side of the waist. Women also had the tucks. In south and western India the women had these till very recent times, and even now the orthodox wear their sari in this way.

When the Muslims came to India they would not tolerate this dress in the Hindus whom they employed, because among them it was indecent to keep the body bare. So the Hindus who served them had to wear the Muslim dress, and henceforth they kept it for all ceremonial and public appearance. This was permitted, but with a very important reservation. These sewn garments could not be taken into the inner apartments of any house, far less into the family shrines. The wearers had to put them off in a dressing-room in the outer house, put on the Hindu dress, purify themselves by sprinkling themselves with Ganges water, and then go into the women's rooms. This rule was extended to European clothing when the British came. In my young days in Calcutta I saw the master's European clothes hanging in a dressing room by the side of the outer sitting-room.

When the restrictions became less rigorous and both men and women began to wear a sewn upper garment, they had nevertheless to put that off for religious ceremonies, including weddings. The religious part of the ceremony could not be gone through with sewn clothing on, though a most elaborate crown, in the shape of that seen on the heads of the princes in the paintings of the Ajanta caves and made of pith and tinsel, had to be worn by the bridegroom. Another important restriction was that no clothes made from cotton could be worn for any religious ceremony. The participators had to be dressed in silk.

The rule about the permissibility of certain kinds of clothing and the manner of wearing it had as its converse another rule which forbade the use of clothing which was obligatory for religious ceremonies or even in daily wear, for impure actions, such as defecating and urinating. The clothes in which a Hindu did the former could not be kept on afterwards, and had to be put off and washed. So to go to a closet men and women simply wrapped a towel round the waist. In my young days I myself saw both men and women throw away either the dhoti or the sari as they slipped into the closet like a rabbit going into its hole.

Again, the tucks being a quasi-religious feature of Hindu clothing, the back tuck could not be kept on when urinating, though its removal was not necessary for the act. So all strict Hindus squatted and removed the back tuck, keeping its upper end in his left hand during the act. The failure to do so made him subject to a religious sanction; for if the tuck was kept the urine went into the mouth of the departed ancestors if its flow was to the left, and into the mouths of the gods if it was to the right.

As to ornaments, most of them were of solid gold, precious stones not being very highly regarded. But gold, being a noble metal, could not be worn below the belt. So the ankle and toe ornaments were in silver. But the hips being very highly prized among feminine charms, the hip girdle furnished with jingles and slung across the widest and highest part, could be of gold. Widows could not wear any ornaments, and in Bengal, as soon as the body of the dead husband was taken to the burning ghat, all ornaments were ceremonially removed from the limbs of the widowed woman, and if she had glass bangles they were taken off and broken. A widow who wore ornaments was regarded as loose. Here it might be mentioned that the widows could not wear saris with a coloured border, but only a white sheet. *Per contra*, a married woman in Bengal had always to wear an iron bangle (plated in gold in well-to-do families), for otherwise the husband was likely to come to harm. In other provinces these insignia were different; for instance, in upper India married Hindu women wore a silver toe ring.

As to make-up, widows could not wear vermilion, whereas vermilion at the hair-parting was obligatory for a married woman with her husband living. Unmarried girls could not have vermilion there, but they could wear it on the forehead as decoration.

The question of cutting hair was a far more serious matter. To cut it for certain purposes and not to cut it otherwise were religious obligations for a man. Married women had to wear their hair long, but widows very short. For them it was cut at the same time as the ornaments were removed.

For the men a *sikha* (tuft of hair) at the top of the head or at its back was necessary for performing the daily devotions of the twice-born. Therefore it had to be kept. On the other hand, hair could not be cut for the sake of appearance. There were only nine legitimate occasions for cutting hair, e.g. pilgrimage, death of father, mother, and preceptor, conception, purification, etc. Now, the great Hindu reformer Rammohun Roy, who habitually affected the Muslim costume, also cut his hair regularly. He was ferociously attacked by the pundits for this.

Guilt and Atonement

The basic feature of Hinduism is that in it the notion of sin is not confined to matters which the West regards as religious or moral (showing, as the Hindu thinks, a narrowness of outlook on life), but covers almost everything that can befall a householder or be done by him, e.g. the accidental death of a cow, being bitten by a dog, or sexual intercourse during the day. All conceivable transgressions from the murder of a Brahmin, incest, or robbery to those just referred to are classified in order of gravity, with due regard to justice and the degree of responsibility. In doing so the treatises on sacred law *(Dharma Sastras* or *Smriti)* display that relentless logic which makes all Hindu reasoning the height of irrationality.

In this section nothing will be said about the offences which are religious or moral in the modern sense, but only a small selection will be given from those which arise from normal worldly life. Hindu sacred law classifies offences as *Ati-pataka* (sins beyond classification), *Maha-pataka* (great sins), *Anu-pataka* (minor sins which are equivalent to mortal sins), and *Upa-pataka* (venial sins).

1. If a man has sexual intercourse during the day-time, bathes naked, or looks upon a naked woman *who is another man's wife and not his own*, he must expiate for the offence by fasting for a day.

2. If a man will *not* have sexual intercourse with his wife at the end of her menstruation, provided it is not a festival day, he will have to make a penance.

3. If a man has repeated sexual intercourse on a festival day he must make the same penance.

4. If a man eats after massaging oil on his body but without bathing first he must bathe and recite the *Gayatri mantra* 1,008 times.

5. If a man or a woman eats while wearing blue cloth he must fast for three nights if he did so accidentally, but for six nights if it was done deliberately.

6. If a man is bitten by a jackal, beast of prey, horse, mule, boar, monkey, crow, or unchaste woman, he has to go through a penance, which varies according to whether he is bitten above or below the navel, on his trunk or in the head, and whether the wound is superficial or deep. If there is a deep bite above the navel he must bathe either in the sea or a river and fast a hundred times.

For most of these offences the penance is *Prajapatya*, which lasts 12 days, during which meals have to be regulated as follows—for the first 3 days, only at night and restricted to 22 mouthfuls; for the next 3 days both day and night but restricted to 26 mouthfuls; for 3 days following only to take food which is given unasked, restricted to 28 mouthfuls; and finally 3 days' complete fast. There are other penances equally elaborate.

The most serious offence in this category of *Upa-pataka* (venial sins) is, of course, the death, intentional or unintentional, of a cow. A householder is responsible even if a cow dies from cold, fire, strangling by a rope when straining for food, drowning, falling in a pit, or is killed by a tiger. Penance is prescribed even if a horn, bone, the tail, or an ear is injured. Castration of a bull calf has to be expiated. However, no penance is called for if an ox dies in the following circumstances: having been previously diseased and after being yoked to a plough or cart it falls down when beaten, but gets up, walks at least seven paces, takes grass and water, and dies only after that.

But expiations for these bovine deaths are graded by the castes as well, and they are categorized as follows: deliberate killing of a Brahmin's cow by a Brahmin, a Kshatriya, or Vaisya, or unintentional killing in the same caste group; deliberate killing by a Sudra of a cow belonging to a Brahmin, a Kshatriya, or Vaisya, and similar unintentional killing. In this manner all the possible combinations of the four castes are worked out. There is necessarily a difference of responsibility and expiation for culpable bovicide amounting to murder, and non-culpable bovicide. The killing of cows in calf is a greater offence.

For the death of a cow or ox there are Sastric penances, but there is also a popular penance, which is to go from door to door with a rope round the neck and grass in the mouth, beg food by bellowing, and eat only the grains so obtained.

On the other hand, if anyone falsely accuses a man of causing the death of a cow he is also subject to a severe penance. This is treated as a very serious libel.

There is only one other transgression which has to be mentioned, one that made its appearance in the nineteenth century and was dealt with in the established manner. It was to travel to England for professional education or on business. At some unknown date sea voyages had become taboo for the Hindus, and those who came to England were further suspected of eating beef. Therefore when they went back to India they were made to go through an elaborate expiation ceremony, after which alone were they restored to their place in their caste. Otherwise, they became outcaste. This practice remained in force even down to 1920.

In the last century the penance was uniformly required, and many men remained outside the pale even after that, and could not marry among the orthodox. Max Müller has related a very interesting anecdote about Dwarkanath Tagore, a very wealthy Bengali landowner and grandfather of the poet Tagore, who was living in Paris in great style. Young Max Müller asked him if he would have to perform penance after his return to India. He laughed and replied: 'No, I am all this time feeding a large number of Brahmins at home, and that is quite penance enough.' Part of the rite of penance for crossing the 'black waters' was to swallow five products of the cow called *pancha gavya*, namely, milk, ghee, curds, urine, and dung. There was one very important part of the expiation, and that was the bestowing of gifts to Brahmins according to one's capacity. Also, for social transgressions which were analogous to these taboos a family had to pay a social fine to the leading families of the village, which shared it, and this was called *Samajik* in Bengal. It may even be said that there was hardly any sin in Hinduism which could not be remitted by money. In ancient times it was gift of cattle, and later it became hard cash.

Astral Control

The Hindus always were, and in their overwhelming majority still are, firm in their conviction that everything in their mundane existence is determined and controlled by the planets and stars. The stars were not, of course, all those which were visible to the naked eye, but only 27 or 28, i.e. those which were in the stages of the moon. Even today nothing is undertaken without finding out whether the hour is propitious, and to deny the influence of stars is to provoke derisive contempt. In my young days stories were told of mythical Englishmen who did not believe in the influence of the stars, but who became converted through experience.

Usually, the Brahmin priests, who were also the astrologers, were consulted as to the suitable hour. But the more common actions could have their times determined by an elderly house-holder, who decided with the help of the almanac. It gave all the information needed under each date and day, and more than any Hindu scripture it was the family Bible. Even today all families except the very westernized have the annual almanac, and large impressions are printed of the more established ones.

I shall give a random example of the entries on one day: the first day of the Bengali year 1376 (1 Vaisakha = 14 April 1969). They begin with a mention of the phase of the moon and the position of the stars. Then the influence of the stars and planets is described, and also the class to which a person born on that day will belong (see below). After that the auspicious and inauspicious periods of the day are specified. Lastly, come specific prohibitions and permissions: aubergines cannot be eaten till 11 hours, 43 minutes, and 2 seconds at night; after that a particular kind of pulse cannot be eaten, nor can women, oil, fish, meat, etc., be enjoyed; penances cannot be undertaken. As to travelling, it is on the whole permissible, but not towards the east or south; after 4.48.58 only east is forbidden, but after 8.7.2 south is again forbidden. Paddy can be cut during the whole day, but journeys by boat, commercial transactions, the making of idols of the gods, preparing and taking of medicines, sowing seeds, planting trees, taking and giving loans must be done before 4.48.58 in the afternoon. Women, oil, fish, and meat are always grouped together for specifying the times permissible for their enjoyment.

Time of birth. Though all other acts could be performed at a chosen time, the time of birth was beyond control, and therefore it was the fixed datum for finding out what an individual's life would be, what he would be capable of doing, and what his aptitudes would be. And not only that, from this date and hour even particular events of a person's life could be calculated.

The time would be given to the family's *jyotishi* or astrologer, and he would prepare the horoscope of the child, indicating not only the general trends—that is to say, whether he or she will be happy and prosperous and at what periods—but also specific events at certain ages, and more especially dangers to his life or career. With the help of this information both the parents and the person concerned would remain confident or reconciled on the one hand, and on the other would be able to take preventive measures against the evils predicted. These were propitiatory or magical ceremonies.

In a Hindu, faith in his horoscope was far stronger than his faith in any god or goddess or even God, and this faith was evinced in every act of his life. If a particular prediction in a horoscope came untrue that made no difference, for it could always be explained away by assuming an error in giving the exact time of birth.

Marriage. Success and happiness in the married state was assumed to be completely under astral control, and therefore the main use of the horoscope for a practical end was in connection with marriages. Even if both the parties in a match were otherwise highly eligible from worldly considerations a marriage proposal could be rejected if the horoscope indicated any incompatibility of nature between the bridegroom and the bride. The agreement was called *Yotaka*, and the best agreement was described as *Raja Yotaka*.

But its determination was complicated. By one calculation all persons belonged to one or other of three orders according to the day of their birth; the order of the divinities, of the humans, and of the demons. Marriages within each other were sought, because in that case the nature of husband and wife would agree. Marriages between the gods and the demons resulted in conflicts because in Hindu mythology these two were always at war, but marriage between a human and a demon was bound to result in the death of the person of the human order.

A far more complicated agreement was determined by means of the zodiacal signs and the stars. Persons born under one or other of these fell into eight categories. Permutations and combinations among these created an immense range of desirability or undesirability in marriages. This may be illustrated by taking only two of the categories: the category of dominance and the category of species. The first depended on the zodiacal signs. Thus a person born under Leo would dominate persons born under all the rest, but, among the latter, persons born under the biped zodiacal signs dominated those born under quadruped signs. For example, one born under the Gemini dominated one born under Capricornus. It was desirable that the groom should belong to the dominant sign.

On the other hand, the species category was determined by the star under which a person was born. To mention two pairs of species: a person born under Spica belonged to the tiger species, whereas one born under Alpherat belonged to the cow species; again, one born under Pollux was a cat while one born under Regulus was a rat. It would be obvious that such persons could not marry one another. In this manner the agreement had to be worked out over all the eight categories. It was no wonder therefore that in the case of specially desirable matches false horoscopes were often furnished.

A different kind of astral control of marriages was about the days and hours of the wedding. Weddings could not take place at all in certain months. In Bengal three months were wholly forbidden, and these were Bhadra, Paus, and Chaitra. The day and the hour were given by the priest. No Hindu wedding could take place at day-time. But it could at any time between dusk and dawn, according to astrological calculations.

Other Activities. These necessarily included everything besides those already mentioned. Nothing is excluded, and for everything that can be done, certain days and hours are propitious, while others are not. Even now no application for a job or nomination for a parliamentary election is submitted without consulting an astrologer.

All religious festivals have their days predetermined round the year, and for them, though the season remains constant, the particular days vary wihtin a month. Religious ceremonies which concern individuals have on the contrary to be fixed *ad hoc*, and there are options in respect of months and days. If for any reason a month is inconvenient for a householder he can choose another month. However, the ceremonies must be performed not only on days free from objection, but on days and at times which are particularly favourable so that they may be fully effective.

The whole system is so complex, with checks from so many different data, that it is impossible to say on what general principle it is based. But whatever the theory, every malign astral influence must be avoided and every benign influence ensured. For instance, the position of a star (or what the Hindus regard as a star) may be the deciding factor, but a day of the week by itself may be propitious or unpropitious. Thus, leaving out the stars, Mondays, Wednesdays, Thursdays, and Fridays are auspicious for all actions; Sundays, Tuesdays, and Saturdays for certain actions only.

There is no doubt that the discrimination between days has come down from very ancient times, i.e. from the age in which the Hindus had political independence. So it was laid down in the almanacs published during British rule that Sunday was suitable for coronation, for beginning a military campaign, while Tuesday was suitable for taking up military commands, for training in the use of weapons, and for hunting. The almanac for 1969 which I am using for giving all this information also lays down that Tuesdays are propitious for theft; that for riding an elephant or a horse for the first time Saturdays are auspicious. But again certain hours of the day, otherwise good, may have certain times when action is harmful. This is particularly true of the afternoon of Thursday.

In recent times it was in respect of journeys that the question of the auspicious hour became most important, for going on a journey at an inauspicious hour could result in death. It was natural therefore that the injunctions regarding journeys should be very elaborate. The favourable and unfavourable combinations were so many that reconciling all of them was never easy, and various loopholes were provided to make journeys possible when they became absolutely necessary. For instance, if a man had to go on a certain day or a certain hour and that was inauspicious he could leave his bedroom at an auspicious hour before the starting time, and wait in another room.

Though this has nothing to do with stars, it might be mentioned in this context that certain omens are good for journeys. A man will be successful in the object of his journey if, when he sets out, he sees a king, a Brahmin, a prostitute, a cow with a calf, flames which are twirling on the right side, a banner, or fresh meat.

It is particularly dangerous to go towards certain directions on certain days, because on these days the direction in question is 'spiked' or 'speared'. The west is spiked on Sunday and Friday, north on Tuesday and Wednesday, east on Monday and Saturday, and south on Wednesday and Thursday. If a man goes in these directions when they are spiked he will die even if he is as powerful as the god Indra. In my young days I could see what terror the idea of going in a 'spiked' direction caused to my fellow Hindus.

Pure and Impure States

A Hindu's concept of life was dominated by the notion of impurity. All material things, including the human body, could become horribly impure, and some were intrinsically and irredeemably impure. This idea was as obsessive as the idea of the innate sinfulness of man has been to many Christians. To the Hindu Pharisees of this description (and they were mostly women) *all* things were naturally unclean and had to be purified. The purification was the Hindu counterpart of Christian regeneration. But while the Christian could become regenerate only through the grace of God, a Hindu could always employ a rational and material means of purification, for example, water or cow dung. The latter was obligatory to purify the cooking oven.

To begin with the material universe. During both solar and lunar eclipses the whole atmosphere and earth became impure, and no Hindu could take food, urinate, or defecate as long as they lasted. Next, Mother Earth herself became impure for three days every year during the rainy season, when she, like a woman, was supposed to menstruate. At that time widows would not take food or even water.

For understandable reasons roads and paths were regarded as generally impure. So, after a journey or walk, men and women would always wash their feet, hands, and face, as well as change clothes. This certainly originated with the idea of dirt in a physical sense, but developed into impurity in a religious sense, so that it was not enough to have a simple wash: men and women had also to touch Ganges water or *tulsi* (basil) leaves, both of which were holy, in order to be restored to purity. The failure to do so was made a charge against Westernized young women in a Bengali satire published at the end of the last century. After a walk in the village the young lady asked her servant to take off her boots and gave him her cap. The impertinent fellow remarked: 'Does putting off things worn at the two ends make away with the sin of walking on the roads in this village? In mine they have to change altogether, wash the feet, and put Ganges water on the head.'

In Bengal elderly women became maniacs for this kind of purity. They never took a step without sprinkling the path before them with Ganges water if it was to be had, or a solution of cow-dung and water from a pot which they carried in their left hand and from which they scooped out the liquid with the right. Cow-dung, it must be explained, purified everything, while buffalo or horse dung did not, though they were herbivorous. The excreta of flesh-eating animals were abominably impure, and that of the omnivorous humans even more so. Even the faeces of strict vegetarians were regarded as impure. In south India a twice-born person became contaminated if he trod on the shadow of an untouchable in the streets. When one of the latter walked along, he kept shouting: 'I am an untouchable, I am an untouchable', so that the twice-born might not come too near him.

A house or a room became impure in a wide variety of circumstances. To mention one contingency, which must have been rare, if a dog died in a room—most likely to be the kitchen where it might go to steal food and be beaten to death—all the utensils had to be taken out, scrubbed with cow dung, sniffed at by a goat, and then washed with water sanctified by *mantras*, and with some gold and kusha grass in it. (This is taken from Smarta Raghunandana's *Vyavastharnava, Ocean of Directions*.)

Next, a room became impure if death of a human being took place in it. If a man of the Sudra caste died in a Brahmin's room it could become pure again only after a month; if a dog died, after ten nights; if a man who had lost his caste died, after two months; if a Mlechchha (unclean foreigner, e.g. an Englishman) died, after four months. But if a Chandala (untouchable) died the house or hut had to be abandoned. A room was made impure by any death. When a room was contaminated by a corpse, all earthenware and cooked food in it had to be thrown away. Therefore all dying persons were removed from any roofed-in place and taken out in the open to die.[1]

Rooms also became impure if childbirth took place in them, and anyone who went into such a room had to put off his clothes and take a bath before he could go to other rooms or touch another person. No wonder that a temporary shed was often built for childbirth. Equally impure was the period of menstruation, and a woman in her monthly periods had to go to a shed at one end of the courtyard, and sit and sleep on a mat until she was clean again. In consequence most Hindu women suffered from all sorts of puerperal infections.

The human body and clothes were, of course, more susceptible to impurity than anything else. After taking food, as was and still is customary, with the *right* hand, a person had to wash that hand thoroughly. After excreting, both the orifices had to be washed, and the anus very thoroughly with the *left* hand. For decontaminating that hand it had to be rubbed many times on the ground or with mud, and then washed. Even so it was never used for eating anything.[2] The mouth was the most sensitive part of the body in regard to contamination. It both communicated impurity and became impure easily. It was impure *per se*, and remained so despite any washing. Therefore kissing was a very risky exhibition of love. A high-caste woman who would allow a low-caste paramour (normally the manservant) to have sexual intercourse with her, would not allow him to kiss her.

Touching any kind of cooked food made one contaminated, but uncooked foodstuffs did not, nor did anything cooked in ghee. Clothes, earthen vessels, including china, and glass were conductors of impurity. So if anyone drank anything from such a vessel, the hand in which it was held became contaminated and had to be washed. Clothing of all kinds, particularly if made of cotton, became very easily impure. Especially, those worn in bed had (and still have) to be put off by the women before they could go into the kitchen to cook or supervise cooking. They had also to

[1] One of my great-aunts was taken out under a mistaken impression that she was dead, and when she made a sound in the yard, everybody was shocked and wanted to take her back. She firmly resisted, and died after a few days.

[2] The Abbé Dubois sets down twenty-three rules which have to be observed by a Hindu when answering calls of nature. Dubois (1897), pp. 239–42.

take a bath. Many strict women washed even the quilts they used in the cold season every morning.

It has to be pointed out that the notion of impurity had a special connection with the liquid state of material bodies. The gaseous and solid states were not so contaminating. Dust and sand were even considered as cleansing mediums when no water was available. But among all the liquids bodily secretions like saliva, semen, urine, or faeces (which are necessarily viscous in India) were specially impure. So was blood, more particularly menstrual blood. The main reason which made overnight clothing taboo (but of which the women were not conscious) was of course marital relations at night. Even unmarried girls and grown-up women who were away from their husbands had to change because they might have had lascivious dreams and emitted secretions.

Certain periods and times also became impure for other than celestial reasons. For example, both after birth and death a house and a whole family remained impure for specified periods, and no one outside the family ate or drank at the houses. If anyone did he also became impure. The period varied according to caste, the longest spells of impurity being for the lowest castes.

So, in fixing dates for weddings, which could not take place during the period of impurity for birth as well as death among relatives within seven degrees of consanguinity, special care was taken. Deaths could not be anticipated of course, but note was taken of all the pregnancies of women among those of seven degrees of consanguinity. Such a taboo necessarily resulted in subterfuges. It was assumed that no wrong was done if the parties remained ignorant of a birth or a death. Therefore relatives living at a distance never gave news of birth or death to another relative who was going to have a wedding in the family.

Events of Life

A people who had brought religion into its day-to-day life in this manner could not possibly leave the most important events of a man or woman's life free from its control and sanction, uninvested with its consecration. Thus they made all these events, e.g. conception, birth, coming of age, marriage, and death, as well as many other occasions which other societies look upon as purely secular, subject to religion.

The rituals concerned with these began with conception, from which the Hindus reckoned their age. For religious purposes age was counted from the assumed date for it; that is to say, the whole period of pregnancy of the mother (conventionally given as ten lunar months and ten days) was added to the age from the date of birth.

In recent times the conception ceremony was performed only after the first menstruation of the girl. As long as child marriage was the universal custom this took place, of course, years after the wedding. But when due to economic reasons marriage of the girls began to be delayed till after puberty, the first menstruation after marriage was politely regarded as the first one. Sometimes, to save appearances, a few periods were even allowed to be overlooked.

In old times the ceremony was an occasion of considerable pomp and publicity, and as in all religious worship it was accompanied by music of the usual noisy kind, i.e. beating of drums and gongs, clanging of cymbals, and blowing of pipes. There was a strictly religious part of the ceremony which was conducted with great solemnity by the priest. Incantations were uttered, and the young man's genitals were touched to give them potency. But this was done very decorously, as a matter of mere form, and since nobody understood what was being said in Sanskrit there was no embarrassment.

But the ritual had also a non-religious festive side under the management of the women in which there was no pretence at reserve. The Hindu code of social behaviour enjoins the utmost modesty on women but also wisely makes an exception by saying that *lajja* (modesty, shame, bashfulness) is no adornment in sexual behaviour. Therefore the women treated the occasion of a conception ceremony, which was called *garbhadhana* (bringing about pregnancy), as one in which sexual behaviour could be exhibited vicariously, and so they indulged in a good deal of ribaldry and horseplay, throwing mud at each other. There was so much of it that the ceremony could be regarded as a saturnalia for the women.[1]

---

[1] In 1964 or thereabouts my wife and I, and about one hundred other guests, attended the ceremony of first menstruation of the daughter of an Indian member of the French Embassy in Delhi. It was performed in the grounds of the Embassy itself. The father was a Tamil Roman Catholic Christian. But whatever his religion in the strict sense he had not shaken off the control of worldly life by Hinduism.

During the period of pregnancy there were four formal ceremonies which had to be performed in the third, fifth, sixth or
eighth, and ninth month. The special desires of the woman,
especially in regard to food, were attended to. The last ceremony
was even called the 'fulfilment of wishes', at which rice-pudding
was ceremonially given to the expectant mother. I myself have
seen a grown-up married son with children of his own, holding
this ceremony for his mother. This was possible in the days of
child marriage when a woman could become a grandmother on
the daughter's side before she was thirty.

The birth of a child was the occasion for other religious ceremonies, both for the mother and the child, and both purificatory
and propitiatory. The first of these was held on the sixth day after
birth, when a name was provisionally given to the child. The
mother came out of the confinement room to be purified on the
next day, and a more elaborate ceremony for ending the period of
impurity was held later, the day being determined by the caste
of the family.

Then followed, year by year, the rituals connected with the
male child's progress towards manhood. The first of these, the
ceremony of taking solid food for the first time, was also for the
little girls. Before it was performed no child could take anything
but milk, and the time for it could be any month from the fifth
till the ninth according to convenience. Since Hindu children
were kept at the breast till they were even two years old the first
taste of solid food was only a permissive rite. In the ceremony
there was a banquet for the relatives and gifts for the child, which
were mostly gold ornaments. Both boys and girls wore them, and
I myself had both bangles and a necklace of gold and wore them
till I was about five years old, and afterwards took them out of
my mother's jewel box and looked at them for my satisfaction for
some years. The child was given another and his final name at
this ceremony. The real name of the child was always kept secret,
for fear of being used by enemies for harming him by black magic.

Teething was not a religious ceremony. But it was watched as
an omen. If a boy was born with teeth, both the parents were
bound to die. If the teeth came out in the first month the father
only was to die, in the second the mother, and in the third the
brother. After that good and bad alternated, but if the teeth came
out in the tenth month the child itself died. The harmful results of

teething could be counteracted by appropriate rites, and by feeding Brahmins and making gifts of money to them according to capacity.

The twice-born had to get their ears pierced, and have a formal tying of the tuft of hair at appropriate months. Starting to read or write was also the occasion for a religious ceremony. The initiation was a very important and obligatory ceremony for the twice-born. Strictly, it had to be in the eighth year for the Brahmin boy, in the eleventh for the Kshatriya, in the twelfth for the Vaisya. However, in recent times these ages have not been strictly adhered to. The ceremony is very arduous, and in my young days my Brahmin playfellows looked forward to it with terror as well as pride. It is performed in strict accordance with the procedure laid down in the sacred scriptures for the stage of life called *Brahmacharya*. The boys had their head shaved, put on the correct clothes, carried a staff, and ate only the permitted food. For some reason or other if there was any rumble of clouds during the ceremony it was spoilt, and had to be done over again. Marriage was a sacrament and had very solemn rites, and the funeral rites were equally solemn. They are so elaborate that a whole chapter could be written about them, all to themselves alone.

As explained, I have given the rules for worldly life very largely as they were and still are in Bengal. But in their broad features they are the same all over India, though every region has its special customs which are regarded as valid in spite of the absence of scriptural authority.

The details I have given in this chapter are likely to raise a smile among Western readers, even among those who treat the absurdities of Tantra and even its obscenities with a more-than-absurd solemnity. Hinduism is, however, indivisible, and in its requirements for salvation it expects its injunctions about all actions to be taken as seriously as the directions about sexual intercourse with one's mother, as is to be found in Tantra. The Western idiot who seeks salvation *à la hindoue* has no right to be disrespectful towards the rules for defecating and urinating *à la hindoue*.

PART THREE

ANALYTICAL

Chapter One

SOME SPECIAL FEATURES
OF HINDUISM

IN this part of the book I am going to offer a detailed treatment of a number of important features of the Hindu religion which were dealt with in a general way or only referred to in the previous parts. My aim in the first instance is to make the reader more fully acquainted with the content of the religion, at all events with the most widely practised parts of it. But no less is it my intention to imbue the reader with its spirit, so that he might realize that Hinduism is as peculiar in the emotions it evokes or satisfies as it is in its beliefs and rites. The reader should be made to feel its presence in flesh and blood, so to speak. Thus this part of the book will give an account of the three great cults of Siva, the Mother-Goddess (Durga-Kali), and Vishnu-Krishna as fully as the scale of the book will permit, and it will also describe what the Hindus get from their religion.

But before that can be done, it is necessary to consider three special features found in Hinduism. This is necessary for a proper understanding of what follows, and besides even these will illustrate its peculiar spirit. Much of the existing misunderstanding of the religion has been due to the fact that these features have not been given due weight.

I have to give another explanation about what will be found in this and two of the chapters which follow. In discussing the topics contained in them I have been compelled to be very frank. This compulsion comes from the simple claim of truth. Hinduism has been the victim of both moral and intellectual dishonesty. On the one hand, there have been people who have gone to Hinduism from certain motives, but have never had the courage to avow them. They have camouflaged their motives in rigmarole. This is specially true of the present age. On the other hand, there have been others who have suppressed these very aspects, always refusing to take them for what they really are. Both groups have offered explanations for them which if they are not due to ignorance, can only be set down to hypocrisy.

Now, the difficulty in meeting this hypocrisy lies in the scruples many scholarly writers on Hinduism feel to set forth without bowdlerizing the evidence provided by the basic texts or commentaries, on the score of what would be regarded as indecency. Unfortunately, those who are hypocritical about Hinduism have always reckoned on the decency of honest writers, which, they have felt, would prevent their exposure by citing the more outspoken passages bearing on the points. I have not given them this advantage by embarrassing myself with this false delicacy.

The Hindu Word

The first of the three features which have to be considered in this chapter is the nature of the Hindu word about the religion. All scholars make use of the Hindu basic and exegetical texts without considering how far they can be utilized to give a rational view of Hindu religious beliefs and practices.

The very first difficulty arises from the nature of the Sanskrit language. There is an impression among those who want to learn the language that its grammar is difficult, both in accidence and syntax. It is not, and anyone with a good memory can learn the elaborate declensions and conjugations in six months. Sanskrit syntax is also for the most part a matter of arbitrary rules, and can be memorized. The real difficulty in Sanskrit is over the meaning of words. Ancient Sanskrit lexicography was never good, and the modern is also very unsatisfactory. So one can never be sure what a word means in a particular context.

This was perceived even before the eleventh century by the great Muslim scholar Alberuni, who had learnt the language. Thus he said in his famous book *Indica*, in which he gave an account of the religious and philosophical ideas of the Hindus:

> The language (Sanskrit) is of an enormous range, both in words and in inflexions, something like the Arabic, calling one and the same thing by various names, both original and derived, and using one and the same word for a variety of subjects, which in order to be properly understood, must be distinguished from each other by various qualifying epithets. For nobody could distinguish between the various meanings of a word unless he understood the context in which it occurred, and its relation both to the following and preceding parts of the sentence.

Modern lexicographers of Sanskrit, both Indian and Western,

have not as yet produced any dictionary which can be considered to be adequate, especially in regard to religious texts. There is besides a special defect of the modern dictionaries due to the fact that a very large number of words in classical Sanskrit are to be found in all modern Indian Sanskritic languages, in which they are wholly unaltered in form. But these words are often used in meanings which are different from the ancient, and they also have different meanings in different modern Indian languages. All modern Sanskrit dictionaries are coloured by local or provincial usages, and one can never be sure that these correspond to ancient usage and meaning.

Next, difficulty springs from the fact that most of the texts are in verse, and for the sake of metre different words have to be used for the same meaning, and also many superfluous words or particles have to be introduced. This was also referred to by Alberuni. After explaining that verse was employed by the Hindus to facilitate memorizing, he observed: 'Now it is well known that in all metrical compositions there is much misty and constrained phraseology merely intended to fill up the metre and serving as a kind of patchwork, and this necessitates a certain amount of verbosity.'

But besides this linguistic difficulty in the way of interpreting any religious text in Sanskrit, there is the whole Hindu attitude to language. From the very beginning of their speculations the Hindus exhibited a deep reverence for the Word *per se*. This was certainly descended from the original wonder of man at the dawn of his mental awakening when he considered the phenomenon of language. Among the Greeks this created the doctrine of the *Logos*. The Hindus equally had their doctrine of the Word. In the *Satapatha Brahmana*, one of the ritualistic treatises considered to be revealed, it is stated: 'The Word is imperishable, the first-born of the cosmic order, mother of the Vedas, and the centre of the deathless condition.' But for the Hindus the Word is not the *Logos* of the Greeks, Romans, and Christians, who identified *Logos* with the reason immanent in the cosmos. With them it is just word, speech as uttered or embodied in writing. This led the Hindus to create a world of words parallel to and co-existent with the world in which they lived and carried on their activities. Thus for them the universe became a space-time-word continuum, instead of being only a space-time continuum.

This peculiar disposition to speak and write without any relation to what existed objectively in the world and what could influence their actions is seen even in the practical treatises of the Hindus. All of them are padded with theoretical and even fanciful notions which have no relation to the practical instructions given, and, besides, they indulge in a systematization which is thorough to the point of absurdity. But those who went to these treatises for practical purposes could always separate the theories from the directions. On the other hand, even some of the authors of the treatises had the good sense to recognize that practice could be different from their injunctions. For instance, the author of the *Kama Sutra*, who indulges in a grotesque systematization of every activity connected with sexual intercourse and also lays down a rigid order of execution, nevertheless observed: 'The directions of the Sastras [scriptures] apply only so long as sexual excitement remains weak in men and women. When once the cycle of sexual intercourse has begun there is neither Sastra nor sequence.' Of course, this good sense was only the recognition of the obvious, which is the last thing a Hindu theorist will voluntarily do.

But theorizing without any regard for what existed or was done could be wholly merciless in those spheres of human activity which existed in the mind. Thus Hindu philosophy, Sanskrit literature, and the Hindu religion, all were seized by the Hindu theorists as the subjects on which to practise their hair-splitting and systematization. In philosophy, however, this did very little harm, for it permitted a wide gamut of discussion varying from stimulating thought to arid word-mongering. It had, however, a disastrous effect on Sanskrit literature. The Hindu literary theorists virtually killed it.

Sanskrit rhetoric and poetics — *Alamkara* or *Rasa Sastra* as these were called — were as pretentious as they were arid. They divided the heroes and heroines of literary works into types in an elaborate taxonomy, and reduced their states of amorousness to ridiculous abstractions. If the rules laid down in these treatises had existed in the early and creative age of Sanskrit literature, neither Kalidasa nor Bhavabhuti could have written anything. The only service that these rhetoricians and analysts rendered to Sanskrit literature was by preserving as illustrations to their categories some gems of lyric poetry, which otherwise might have been lost. Their writings gave Sanskrit literature a bad name as a collection of mere artificial prettinesses and far-fetched conceits.

In religion the theorizing and the practice remained largely independent, and religious life had enough vitality not to be petrified by the empty metaphysics or theology of the Hindu pundits. In recent times the learned men who concerned themselves with theoretical discussions carried on their analysis and interpretation with the object of asserting their professional eminence and asserting their superiority over other exegetists. The commentators as a body hold only a subsidiary place in the literature of Hinduism.

Naturally, Hindu religious literature has an immense volume. Once a species has been created in it, it goes on proliferating itself by means of variations which are not less extensive than those found in the animal world. Only the Vedas remained confined to four, but that probably was due to the fact that they were regarded as inherited heirlooms, and so had to be necessarily limited and kept apart from the acquired wealth in India. In any case, their small number was compensated for by the doctrine that they contained everything that followed. Even at the next stage of the revealed scriptures, Brahmana followed Brahmana, Aranyaka followed Aranyaka, Upanishad followed Upanishad until there was even an *Allah Upanishad*. The Hindus never discriminated among these, and it is only Western scholars who have considered ten, eleven, or thirteen Upanishads to be authentic and the rest spurious. Furthermore, when an eponymous author has been found for an original work, those which follow in the same genre or even other genres must have the same name. For example, Veda Vyasa is the compiler or arranger of the Vedas, and he is also the writer of the *Mahabharata* and of many Puranas. The proliferation in the non-Vedic literature is far greater.

Hindu religious literature falls into groups whose value for a student of Hinduism varies. In the first group are the scriptures considered as revealed. A number of books in this class are products of religious feeling and even exultation, while the others are concerned with rituals. What intellectual discussion these contain is extremely crude, being founded on false physics and false biology. It is futile to seek any rational meaning in it. But as expressions of the religious feeling of the Hindus these have to be read.

The largest part of the Hindu religious literature is taken up with mythology, and the most important works in this class are the Puranas, or treatises on old times. These are composed in Sanskrit verse, but possess no poetic merit. For that one has to go to Sanskrit literature in its truly literary genres, to which many Puranic stories furnish the themes. The Puranas are as entertaining as the *Arabian Nights* in their mythological stories. If, however, anyone tries to extract a consistent account of the gods and of their character and activities from them he will be baffled at every point by their inconsistencies and exuberance.

The third group of Hindu religious literature is constituted by the devotional books of which the *Gita* is the most outstanding. They shed full light on the character of Hindu religious sentiment. Many of them also contain a greater or lesser amount of meta-physical and theological discussion. In that aspect the devotional books should be classed with the next category.

This group contains the exegetical literature properly so-called, and the books in it are mostly commentaries on well-known texts of an older epoch. These commentaries offer quasi-philosophical and quasi-theological interpretations of the cults and beliefs, and as a rule are either pedestrian or meaningless. In connection with the erotic elements in the religious life of the Hindus they hold forth some very unpleasant rigmarole, about which more will be said later. These are of no use in discovering the exact nature of the Hindu religious ideas, because any interpretation might be put upon them. To try to analyse the statements of the commen-tators and determine their meaning would be a futile attempt to make what is basically irrational, rationally intelligible.

Therefore I have not drawn on the commentators to offer my interpretation of the religious ideas of the Hindus. But their statements can be put to use for a different purpose, that is to say, for illustrating the working of the Hindu mind when it has con-sidered religion intellectually. One cannot describe Hinduism scientifically from the Hindu word about it. The exegesis pursues a course of its own in a world of mere words. It is a prolix exercise in word-mongering.

Mythology, Cults, and Devotion

The second feature which has to be considered is Hindu mytho-logy. Even at the risk of being considered paradoxical and even eccentric, I must say that Hindu mythology has been the most serious obstacle in the way of understanding Hinduism as a religion. It has become a fixed habit even with modern Hindus to equate their mythology with their religion, and thus present those who want to attack it with a very vulnerable target. This is due to the fact that Hindu mythology is even worse than the Greek and Roman in respect of the morals of the gods and goddesses, and therefore the critics have been able to point to their doings and say that a religion which prescribes the worship of such gods must be very degraded.

The mythology of Siva and Durga is not as well known as the legends of Krishna, and so those who wanted to demonstrate the immorality of Hinduism, drew upon the stories of Krishna's affairs with the gopis (milkmaids, or rather, the wives of the milkmen). Nowadays, in the West, these very stories have become the main attraction of Hinduism to a certain class of people. But both the attitudes are wrong, because Hindu mythology and Hindu religion are essentially different things.

The relationship between Hindu mythology, cults, and devotion is extremely complex. At times they seem to coincide, but most often they do not, and remain independent of one another. That is to say, the cults do not follow the mythology, and the devotion disregards both mythology and cult.

The fact has to be faced that appearances are all against such a separation of the three. There is first the iconography which exhibits the violent traits of the deities and to a lesser extent also the erotic. Next, at the seasonal festivals the mythological books are always read, and their stories expounded. Thirdly, the celebrations exhibit not only extravagant emotionalism, but also orgiastic behaviour. Very erotic songs are sung, and dancing when it is seen has erotic suggestions. At the same time these violent and erotic features make no pretence to be symbolic. They have simply to be taken for what they undisguisedly are. All this makes it extremely difficult for any outside observer to perceive that the true religious sentiment of the Hindus is independent of mythology, and that it remains a thing apart from the violence or eroticism of the mythology. This has to be brought out clearly.

To begin with, it should be pointed out that the separation of religious feeling from mythology is not exclusive to Hinduism. It was a feature of all Indo-European religions, and more especially of Greek and Roman religions. To illustrate this I shall give only one example, that of Zeus. It is unnecessary to list all his amorous adventures. One of these alone, his seduction of Leda in the form of a swan, became one of the stock erotic themes in classical as well as Renaissance art.

Nevertheless, the Zeus of mythology is not the Zeus of the cult, whether at Olympia or elsewhere. He is not the Zeus of even the poets, of Aeschylus, Sophocles, or Euripides. And he is not the Zeus of the philosophers. The difference can be best judged from the famous hymn to Zeus composed by the Stoic philosopher, Cleanthes (*c.* 331–232 B.C.). He begins his hymn by addressing Zeus as 'The most glorious of Immortals, under a thousand names Omnipotent for ever, O Zeus, Lord of Nature, who governs all things in accordance with law', and closes the hymn with the following prayer:

O Zeus, universal benefactor, god of dark clouds, the Thunderer! Save men from their fatal ignorance. Dispel it, O Father, far from their heart; and grant it that they arrive at the thought which guides Thee to govern all with justice, so that honoured by you we render honour to you, singing of your works without ceasing, as is proper in a mortal, because neither for men nor for gods is there a greater privilege than to sing for ever and ever, in the form of justice, of the Universal Law.

Even Aphrodite, the goddess of sexual love, does not remain the goddess of seduction and rape she is in Homer. She becomes different in the hands of Aeschylus and Euripides. The latter connects her with wisdom. Even in the age of decadence of Greek literature, the idyllic joy in her cult is given expression in the fifteenth idyll of Theocritus.

Thus, in keeping mythology and religion separate, the Hindus were keeping company with the Greeks and the Romans. But the manner in which they did so was very individual, because they made their devotion more passionate and their mythology more sensual. Not less individual is the persistent intrusion of mythology into worship, and the insulation of devotion from its sensuality. The extremely complex relationship between Hindu mythology, cults, and devotion in connection with the worship of Siva, Krishna, and Durga has to be described. Here I take up only the worship of Siva.

The relationship of mythology and devotion, with its twofold aspect of association and dissociation, can be illustrated by quoting many hymns to Siva, which are of the type of the hymn to Zeus of Cleanthes, and setting them against the stories as they are related in the Puranas. But I think the best way to bring out the strangeness of the phenomenon is to take a writer who shows devotion to the monotheistic Siva and at the same time writes at length about the mythological Siva. As it happens, such a writer is present in the person of Kalidasa, the greatest poet of ancient India. He was a Saiva, and therefore invoked the god in the prologues to his works. I shall quote two of them, from the epic poem *Raghuvamsa*, and the play *Sakuntala*.

In the first he prays to Siva and Parvati in the following words: 'I bow to the parents of the world, Parvati and Paramesvara (Great Lord), who are as united with each other as is the word with its meaning, so that I may achieve meaning for my words.'

In *Sakuntala*, he says: 'May that Lord protect us who is made perceptible to the senses by means of eight tangible manifestations: (1) water which is the first creation of the Creator; (2) the sacrifice and (3) the sacrificer; (4) the sun and (5) the moon who determine time; (6) the ether which pervades the universe as the carrier of sound; (7) the earth which generates seeds; and (8) the air by which all creatures live.'

But Kalidasa also composed a long epic poem in which he gave literary expression to the mythological story of the marriage of Siva and Parvati and of the birth of their son Kartikeya, the war god of the Hindu pantheon. Its title is *Kumara-Sambhava*.

In it the story unfolds as follows: the gods headed by Indra are greatly troubled by their enemies, the demons, and they will be saved if only Siva will marry and procreate a son to fight the demons. Yet after the death of his first wife, Sati, the daughter of Daksha Prajapati, he has fallen into meditation on the Himalayas and will not be roused from it. In the meanwhile, Parvati or Uma,[1] the daughter of the Himalaya Mountain, has fallen in love with him and wishes him to be her husband. The gods think that if she presents herself to him in all her beauty and with all her adornments he will abandon his meditation. To break it, they

---

[1] Siva's second wife was the daughter of the personified Himalayas, and was therefore given the name of Parvati, i.e. the daughter of *Parvata* or Mountain. But her personal name as a maiden was Uma. The exact meaning of the name is not known and even Kalidasa gave a fanciful explanation.

send the god of love, Madana, with Uma, to shoot his arrow into Siva. As Uma stands before Siva, he does so. Awakened by the shaft, Siva feels a strange excitement which he cannot explain. Then he sees Madana, and in his wrath shoots out a flame from the third eye on his forehead, and reduces him to ashes.

Uma goes back in deep mortification, with a sense of intolerable humiliation. She resolves to abandon her bodily appeal and womanly blandishments and undergo severe self-mortification as a penance and thus make herself deserving of Siva. She puts off her robes and ornaments and goes into a garment of tree-barks in order to carry on her penance under rain and snow. After she had done so for a long time, Siva himself comes to her in the disguise of a hermit to dissuade her from it. This dialogue is one of the most moving in Sanskrit literature. But Uma remains steadfast, and at last Siva is pleased with her, and he shows himself ready to marry her.

Up to this point, Kalidasa deals with the mythological story of Siva and Parvati in a spirit which is indeed different from that which he shows in his invocations, but which can be said to have represented the whole episode as a triumph of Aphrodite Urania over Aphrodite Pandemos. But after describing how devotion and austerities brought about the marriage of Siva and Parvati and thus achieved what the arrows of Cupid could not, Kalidasa makes a staggering *volte face*, and in the eighth canto of the poem describes their sexual enjoyments with a frankness and gusto which is not surpassed even by Casanova. If one has to understand Hinduism such acrobatics of the mind have to be faced squarely. I shall give the details because without them the distance that separates Hindu mythology from Hindu devotion cannot be correctly measured, and to omit them would be to imitate the deplorable habit of suppressing the truth which the modern expositors of Hinduism have acquired.

During the first month after the wedding Siva leads Parvati step by step and with extreme patience into a whole-hearted enjoyment of sexual intercourse and makes her skilled in it. The description is elaborate and leisurely:

At first Parvati would not reply when spoken to, would wish to go away even when held by her sari, and when in bed would keep her face turned away. Yet Siva was pleased with her. He pretended to be asleep and out of curiosity Parvati looked at his face, but when he opened his eyes and smiled, she shut her own eyes as if dazzled by lightning.

When Siva placed his hand in the region of her navel she pushed it away with her trembling hand, but her sari slipped off and her girdle got loose, both of themselves. Though told by her companions to serve Siva in private without fear, when face to face with him, she forgot their instructions in her flurry.

When robbed of her sari, she covered the eyes of Siva with her two hands, but he could see everything with the third eye on his forehead, and this failure chagrined her.

Siva felt disappointed that he could not bite her lips when kissing, or could not squeeze her breasts but had to embrace her gently; even so, frustrated though he was in his desire, he was pleased with a bride's coitus with its unavoidable inadequacies. Parvati, too, learned to tolerate coitus by her kind beloved, which was free of biting and scratching.

Though she could not tell the story of the night to her companions out of bashfulness she felt eager in her heart to do so. She made many gestures of bashfulness when she saw herself in the mirror with the signs which enjoyment had left on her face. Her mother too felt happy to see the youth of her daughter enjoyed by Siva.

After some days of coitus with Siva Parvati slowly learned to take pleasure in it, and abandoned her fear of it. So she embraced her beloved when he wanted to be pressed to the breast, did not deprive him of her mouth, and when he lovingly put his hand on her girdle did not check him firmly.

At last she gave back to Siva, as fees to a teacher, all the skills befitting a young woman which she had learnt by receiving lessons on coitus from him in private by becoming his pupil.[1]

After this Siva took her away on a honeymoon to many beauty spots, and took up his sojourn on the hills of Gandhamadana in the south. He stayed there for a long time, and one day he made Parvati drunk with wine. He felt very pleased to find her faltering in speech, rolling her eyes, and free from bashfulness. So he carried her into the bedroom, and placed her on a bed covered with a sheet which was as white as the plumage of a swan.

[1] Cf. Casanova's remark about Hedvige and Hélène: 'Mes leçons avaient fructifié, et mes deux élèves étaient passées maîtresses dans l'art de goûter et de communiquer le bonheur.'

There she had coitus with him of such violence, accompanied by such defiance and scratching, that her coiffure came loose, the sandal paste on her breasts was rubbed off, and the girdle torn. Still Siva was not satiated with her coitus. Only when the stars were sinking below the horizon, out of sheer pity for her, he clasped her to his breast, and deigned to close his eyes. But soon the couple were awakened by the morning song of the minstrel. At that moment Siva's eyes were so charmed by the rows of nail marks on her groins that he forbade Parvati to put on her slackened sari. He was roused and pleased by looking at the face of his beloved, with the eyes reddened by loss of sleep, lips wounded by deep bites, hair all dishevelled, and the vermilion mark on the forehead rubbed off. So he would not leave the bed marked by the red paint on Parvati's feet, with her girdle lying on it in a coil and the bedsheet tumbled.[1] Yet it was day. Thus he stayed on the Gandhamadana hills for a hundred days in continuous coitus with Parvati, and they seemed but one night to him. Still, his desire blazed like fire under the sea.

In the meanwhile, the gods had become very anxious at the delay in procreating their war god. They waited anxiously outside and sent messages through Parvati's handmaiden Vijaya, but Siva would not listen. At last in their desperation, they decided to send in one of themselves, Agni, the Fire God, to remind him of what was expected of him. Agni dared not go in his own form for fear of provoking the wrath of Siva by interrupting his coitus, and took the form of a pigeon. He danced round them bowing, and imitating Parvati's murmurs of pleasure with his cooing.

However, Siva recognized him and flew into a rage, at which Agni resumed his own form, gave his message, and implored forgiveness. Mollified but embarrassed, Siva withdrew his member

---

[1] In such matters Kalidasa does not make any distinction between gods and men, nor does any other Sanskrit poet. What is said here by him about Siva is paralleled in the nineteenth canto of *Raghuvamsa* in the descriptions of the sexual orgies of King Agnivarna. Kalidasa says in Verse 25 that the various objects and stains (all of which are named) indicated the variety of coitus of the luxurious King. The commentators are more explicit. They identify each object and each stain with a particular posture. For instance, a torn girdle shows that the woman had played the man, and the red stain on the sheet from the dye of lac on her feet, that she had either taken the pose of a beast or been on top of the man. The acumen shown in such detective work is unsurpassed. More examples of it will be given.

and the imminent orgasm took place outside. Siva dropped the semen on the body of Agni himself. Parvati on her part, infuriated by the interruption of her pleasure at its climax, cursed Agni, and said that he would for ever carry black smoke about him, and appear like a man disfigured by leprosy.

Now, all this is related by Kalidasa in the most natural manner without any awareness that there were unresolvable contradictions in his various attitudes to Siva. No rational person can reconcile them. I think that is beyond the capacity for intellectual dishonesty even of the pedlars of Hindu spirituality, Indian or Western.[1]

I shall give a second illustration of the antithesis between the Siva of devotion and Siva of mythology from a Bengali poem written in the middle of the eighteenth century by Bharata Chandra Ray. Here the Siva of devotion is not an abstraction as with Kalidasa, but has become a personal god of love, while Siva of mythology has become a rustic clown. The theme is again the marriage of Siva and Parvati.

The poet Bharata Chandra prays to Siva for himself, preceding the prayer with his praise of the god:

O creatures! Utter the name of Siva if you would have the happiness of going to the abode of Siva.

---

[1] At this point it might be mentioned that later profane poetry in Sanskrit introduced erotic imagery even in the invocations or praise of the deities. I give two typical examples from the well-known collection *Arya-Saptasati* by Govardhanacharya, which concern the divine couples, Vishnu and Lakshmi and Siva and Parvati:

(1) Pratibimbita-priyā-tanu sakaustubham jayati Madhubhidc vakṣaḥ,
Puruṣāyitam'abhyasati Lakṣmīr'yadvīkṣya mukuram'iva.

(Victory to the chest of the destroyer of Madhu [Viṣnu] [adorned] with [the gem] Kaustubha, in which the figure of his beloved [Lakṣmi] is reflected, seeing which as in a mirror Lakṣmi practises coitus in the posture of man.) *Arya*: 12

(2) Unnāla-nabhi-pamke-ruha iva yenāvabhāti Śambhur'api,
Jayati puruṣāyitāyās'tadānanam Śaila-kanyāyāh.

(Victory to the face of the Daughter of the Mountain [Parvati], who is engaged in coitus in man's posture, on account of which Śambhu [Siva] too appears like Viṣnu with a lotus and its stalk rising from his navel.) *Arya*: 19. The commentator takes the trouble to explain that this simile emphasizes not only the beauty of Parvati's face, but also the slimness of her figure when engaged in this particular action sitting on the waist of Siva.

Many such instances can be given, and in Jayadeva this becomes a mannerism.

I shall utter his name, pass through all sorrows, and overrule death
with ease.
How can I praise Siva, to whom shall I compare him?
He who says 'Siva, Siva', becomes *siva* [pure and auspicious]
in his body, and Siva gives him the refuge of his feet.
Show mercy, O Siva, on those who are sorrowful, take away their
sins and their sufferings, and make me, Bharata, steadfast in your
worship.

Nevertheless, in dealing with the god of mythology, the same
Bharata Chandra makes Siva the bridegroom a grotesque fakir
attended by unclean and malicious spectres. He has matted locks,
his body is smeared with ashes, he wears only a stinking tiger skin
kept in place by the snakes coiled round his body. The spirits who
accompany him jump about, clap their hands, utter guffaws,
indulge in wild horseplay, and piss (the Bengali word — *muté* — is
the exact colloquial equivalent of the English word) in the wedding pavilion. All the women beat their forehead when they see
such a groom for their young and beautiful Parvati.

Worse follows when Siva goes into the inner apartments to be
received in due form by Parvati's mother, Menaka, and her
women. Vishnu, represented as a mischievous young man, takes
it into his head to play a practical joke of a very rustic kind. He
calls his mount Garuda, half man and half bird of prey and the
eternal enemy of all snakes, into the room. At the sight of him all
the snakes on Siva's body uncoil themselves and disappear into
corners, and Siva's tiger skin falls down on the floor. Seeing her
son-in-law stark naked, Menaka puts out the light and runs away.
The women begin to shriek. None the less, they start quarrelling
in a very significant manner. One woman says to another: 'As
soon as the old fellow became naked you stared at him.' The other
replies in kind. Vishnu is hugely amused. Siva smiles, and even
Parvati smirks.

The description of the married life of Siva and Parvati which
follows has no eroticism. The two live as a poor Bengali couple,
on the whole very happy but at times quarrelling with outrageous
crudity of behaviour and language. Yet if he had wanted, Bharata
Chandra could have given the story an erotic colouring, because
he was the author of the most famous erotic poem in the Bengali
language, and the book is not crude. Here, too, there is no awareness of any contradiction.

SOME SPECIAL FEATURES OF HINDUISM

I have now to illustrate the separation between cult and devotion so far as it exists in the worship of Siva. Iconographically, this is a phallic cult, for the god is now worshipped almost universally in his *linga* (representation of the penis), and not in anthropomorphic images. But his anthropomorphic representation, both in stone and metal, is one of the glories of Hindu sculpture. These seem to have been solely illustrations of the Siva mythology.

Now, the phallus, as it is made today in stone and can be bought in Benares, has no ambiguity whatever. It has the form of the male member very magnified, and it stands on a platform which is ritualistically called the *gauri-patta* (slab of Gauri or Parvati) but is actually a stylized representation of the vulva, and is also quite recognizable as such. Thus the combination is unnatural, for it shows the penis coming out of the vagina. This made a Bengali Freudian, a friend of mine, take the image as a symbol of infantile sexuality as it had to be before birth. To put it simply, the *linga* showed the child in the womb having sexual intercourse with his mother from the wrong side, and therefore protruding the member outside the vagina. When Freudians get hold of Hinduism they can run amuck, and of course Hinduism can be condemned, so to speak, out of its own mouth.

But not less foolish is the palaver about the fertility cult. Everybody knows that both animal and plant fertility was a concern of primitive religion, and the Hindus are not the only people to have images of the male member. In fact, compared with the enormous phalluses on the island of Delos the Hindu phallus is a puny childish thing. But whatever the survivals of the worship of the phallus found in living and civilized religions, to connect them with the fertility cult has no justification whatever. One might as well say that the Allah of Islam is the cubic black stone at Mecca. Such objects are only vestigial survivals.

Even the ancient Hindu perceived the obsolete character of such things. Rites of fertility and procreation are found in the Vedic ritualistic treatises called the Brahmanas. I give an example from the *Aitareya Brahmana*, in which the following directions for a fire sacrifice are prescribed. If in reciting the four lines of a Vedic stanza, the first two are uttered with a pause between the lines, that signifies the opening of her thighs by a woman for intercourse; and when the next two are recited in a sequence, this indicates that she has closed the thighs for the movements. Next, if in reciting the verses the sacrificer *(Hotṛ)* lowers his voice that means the ejaculation of semen. Again, when the principal sacrificer *(Hotṛ)* utters a verse, his second *(Adhvaryu)* goes on all fours and turns his posterior to the sacrificer, indicating that a four-footed animal is copulating and ejaculating semen; in the second movement, he stands and faces the sacrificer indicating that a biped is ejaculating semen.[1] This ensures fertility among men as well as cattle. After these gestures a woman is brought into the sacred sacrificial field and the *Hotṛ* has sexual intercourse with her publicly, so that he might recover the virility which he has lost in a year of continence for the rite. But even by the time the *Srauta Sutras* (the treatises for public sacrifices not regarded as revealed but wholly authoritative as codifications of traditions or *smriti*) were composed this kind of rite was forbidden. As the *Sankhayana Srauta Sutra* wrote: 'This is a thing belonging to ancient times, which has gone out of usage, and is not to be performed.' *(Tad etat purāṇam, utsannam, na kāryam.)*

When the ancient Hindu had himself rejected the fertility cult, it is strange that it should be dragged in for interpreting historic Hinduism. The reality of the worship of the Siva *linga* is wholly different. I have seen it from my childhood. My ancestors built a temple of Siva with three *lingas*. It came down in the great earthquake of 1897 and was in ruins in my boyhood, with the three *lingas* still in place. Every year after the immersion of the image of Durga the whole clan went in a procession to bow down before the *lingas*, though daily worship was no longer provided for them there. I have seen my aunts and other elderly women relatives make the *linga* themselves with clay for the daily worship at home, and worship it with a devotion unconnected with the image. They never thought of its material character, though they always used the word *linga*. The prayers they uttered before it were also always solemn.

Young girls in Bengal also worshipped Siva in his *linga*, so that they might deserve to have husbands who would be like Siva. In the mind of the women Siva was the ideal husband, loving and generous, and yet reverential to his wife, who gave lessons to Parvati about religion and at the same time treated her as his

[1] Parāñcam catuṣpadyāsīnam abhyāhvayate tasmāt parāñco bhūtvā catuṣpādo retaḥ siñcanti samyaṅ dvipād bhavati tasmāt samyañco bhūtvā dvipādo retaḥ siñcanti. *(Aitareya Brahmana, 10. 6. 1–6.)*

equal. The old blessing for a good young girl was: 'May you have a husband like Siva!' In the worship of the young girls there was certainly the memory of the penance of Uma, but no knowledge whatever of the eighth canto of *Kumara-Sambhava*.

Eroticism in Religious Art

It is common knowledge that there are strong erotic elements in Hinduism as it is found in the texts. Erotic details occur even in the *Rig-Veda*, and some of them are very crude. But the eroticism is of one kind in the mythological books, and of another when found in the texts on cults. As to actual practice, it is very difficult to discover how much of it was or is actually prevalent, for the only cult which has made sexual relations between men and women part of its ritual is the Tantric form of the worship of the Mother Goddess, but no Tantric openly acknowledges his practice of them. In the Krishna cult, so far as it is devotional, certainly there is no eroticism, but in the reading and expositions of the legends of Krishna and in the festivals there is always a substratum of erotic feeling. These questions will be dealt with in the chapters devoted to the two cults. In this chapter only the significance of the erotic sculptures in the temples will be discussed. The artistic expression of the erotic element in the cults of Krishna and the Mother Goddess is part of the cults, and need not be discussed separately.

Although, generally speaking, discussion of Hinduism is not marked by a very strict regard for intellectual honesty, as I cannot emphasize enough, on no other subject connected with it is it less in evidence than about the erotic sculptures on the temples. Everybody knows that the recent interest in it is pornographic, but in writing about it, no one faces that fact and offers explanations which would be called balderdash if the innocence of the writers were above question. This is an insult to these sculptures for they are as good examples of the particular genre as any that have been produced all over the world, since the palaeolithic age. Such things are found in Greek, Roman, Chinese, and Japanese art, to mention only four national expressions, and there is no reason why they should not exist for their own sake in India among the Hindus.

They are no more startling in their frankness than are the descriptions in Sanskrit literature I have quoted, and I shall quote more. Anyone who has read a line of Sanskrit cannot place Hindu erotic sculpture and the erotic descriptions in literature in separate categories or assign different motives for them. The objection would be that they are found on temples. But that sort of argument would apply to literature as well, for the literary descriptions are also of the doings of the gods. Actually, the fact that they are found on temples does not give them any religious significance at all, for the simple reason that from the truly Hindu point of view, a temple is not a religious structure but the abode of a divine king, as has been already explained.

In order to understand these sculptures one should begin with the idea behind them. There is a Sanskrit treatise entitled *Vishnu Dharmottara Purana* which deals with the arts and crafts. In it there is one chapter, the forty-third, which is devoted to painting. After laying down the rules for composition and execution, the writer considers the subjects and their suitability for various rooms. Obviously, he is thinking of frescoes. In respect of the choice of subjects he shows that he considers literature and painting to be parallel artistic creations, which give expression to the same moods and emotions in their different mediums.

Now, in Sanskrit literature the whole gamut of emotions and moods which can be expressed in literature is contained within a series fixed by the Sanskrit rhetoricians. These are called *rasas*, and there are nine of them, beginning with the *adi* (the first) or *sringara rasa* (the erotic mood), and forming a series with the humorous, peaceful, affectionate, heroic, terrifying, pathetic, bewildered, and so on. All of them are legitimate in painting also, but not legitimate in all places. According to the Purana, only such pictures as give expression to the erotic, humorous, and peaceful moods are suitable for an ordinary home. But pictures expressing *all* the moods can be painted both in the royal palaces and the temples. The palaces and the temples are thus placed in one class in respect of the subjects, which, of course, implies that the temples are only considered to be palaces of a different kind.

Domestic erotic painting or sculpture in India has not survived from ancient times. But there is definite evidence of their existence in houses and palaces in Sanskrit literature. I give only one. In the *Uttara Naishadha Charita* of Sri Harsha there is an elaborate description of the palace of King Nala. In it are to be found references to two erotic representations, one a series of paintings and

the other reliefs in sculpture. The poet says that on a wall of the
inner apartments of the palace the story of Brahma's incestuous
sexual intercourse with his own daughter *(Padmasamvabha-sutā-*
ramsutā) was painted in all its sequences (Canto 18, v. 20). On
another wall the gorgeousness of Indra's adultery *(pāradārika-*
vilāsa-vaibhavam) with Ahalya, the wife of the sage Gautama, was
carved with chisel (v. 21). The commentator explained that the
intention was to excite lust *(kāmo-ddiipanārtham)*. It should be
noted that the erotic themes are from Hindu mythology. But
Hindu poets were not satisfied solely with making the inner
apartments like those at Pompeii. They set down other erotic
attractions of the royal palaces. The poet of *Naishadha Kavya* adds
that in the loggias before the bedroom sparrows were always
chirping, and in the pools in the courtyard below ducks and other
waterfowl swam. Thus watching their mating King Nala and
Queen Damayanti could feel excited for sexual intercourse.
Naturally, the description of the sexual enjoyments of the two is
even more elaborate than those in Kalidasa.

The erotic sculptures in temples were only an extension of these
from human residences to divine residences, and since the temples
were public resorts, the artistic representations could also amuse
those who went to them. In sculpture the subjects found in the
temples are rarely mythological, and as a rule the figures are those
of ordinary men and women. Why it has become a convention to
describe the women as the courtesans of the gods *(apsarasah)* I
cannot understand. What then are the men? In mythology these
courtesans can only be the mistresses of the gods, and not a single
male figure has the iconographical features of any god. Whenever
the divinities are introduced in such representations their correct
features are also present. Besides, anyone who knows the physical
types in different parts of India will have no difficulty in recog-
nizing in the sculptures the idealized features of each region. The
faces from Khajuraho are clearly distinguishable from those at
Konarak, and all conform to the local types.

Moreover, the sculptors were capable of satirizing the abuses
of religion in their works. On the basement of the Chhatra-bhoga
Mandapa (the fourth pavilion in a temple built to full specifica-
tions) of the great temple at Puri are to be found friezes showing
Vaishnavas and Vaishnavis engaged in coitus in the most shame-
less manner. These were originally at Konarak and were brought

over from there and fixed to the basement of the pavilion which
was built by the Marathas in the eighteenth century. Probably
they thought these were too amusing to be left unseen in the
wilderness of Konarak. One thing which distinguished the Hindus
before they were corrupted by a certain kind of European hypocrisy was their capacity to face all realities, and wherever possible
derive pleasure from them.

Apart from that ancient Hindu poets did not feel embarrassed
to combine profane erotic descriptions with religious allusions if
that suited their artistic aim. Normally the mood created by one
emotion could not be disturbed by the introduction of a discordant
emotion, e.g.—a pathetic mood could not combine with an erotic
mood or vice versa, the affectionate mood could not mix with the
terrifying, and so on. Thus the lament of a queen on seeing the
severed hand of her killed husband on the battlefield, in which she
cries out: 'There lies the hand which removed my girdle', is condemned. But the poets would also create a clash between emotions
if it were needed either to create an artistic dissonance (as sometimes in musical chords) or if the necessities of a realistic situation
demanded it.

I give a very striking (almost incredible) example of this from
the *Naishadha Charita* to which I have referred before. The poet is
giving a circumstantial description of King Nala's coitus with his
queen, Bhaimi (or Damayanti). He becomes aware from Bhaimi's
appearance that she is nearing the climax before he is ready, and
as that would come in the way of the pleasure from simultaneous
orgasm for both, he checks her by distracting her by pointing to
his own reflection on the polished wall and crying out: 'Who is
there?'

But immediately afterwards he feels that he himself is nearing
the climax while his queen, having been interrupted once, would
necessarily require more time. So, in order to prevent his orgasm
when the queen could not desire it, he contemplates the courses of
the sun and the moon and checks himself. (*Naishadha Charita*,
Canto 18, vv. 115–16). This is not simply a case of checking a
physiological process by an intellectual exercise, but is also a
religious manipulation, for the courses of the sun and the moon
have a religious significance. Indeed, the commentator Narayana
says that Nala could not have delayed his orgasm unless he had
practised *yoga*—(*etena bhangyā Nalasya yogābhyaso'pi sūcitah; anyena*

tathā kartum'aśakyatvāt—by this manipulation Nala's practice of *yoga* is indicated, because such a result was not likely to be obtained by any other means).

One further illustration might be given of the readiness of the Hindus to bring erotic suggestions into their idea of temples. It comes from an inscription of A.D. 437 which records the building of a temple to the Sun god by a guild of silk weavers of Dasapura. The builders did not think it enough to give the date simply as the thirteenth day of the bright fortnight of the month of *Sahasya* (Paus = December–January), but embroidered on it in the manner of Sanskrit poetry, by saying that it was built—

> In that season which unites young men with their lovely mistresses; in which the sun becomes mild and the fish lie low in water; in which the light of the moon cannot be enjoyed on the roofs, nor sandal paste used as perfume; . . . in which young men obeying erotic desire, closely embrace the immense, plump, and beautiful thighs, breasts, and *mons veneris* of their beloved mistresses and are able thereby to deride frost and cold.[1]

Perhaps it would be difficult even for the most mendacious of the symbolist interpreters of Hinduism to connect such erotic leanings with the mysticism of the Upanishads. Nor is it easier on the testimony of the Hindu poets themselves to take the erotic sculptures, which only illustrated what they wrote, back to the primitive fertility cult.

These sculptures can be taken literally for what they appear to be. In them there was only the expression of a psychological preoccupation of the Hindus. Ancient Hindus did not stand in need of subterfuges. But the next step, i.e. the idea of giving material expression to the mental imagery and the acquisition of the craftsmanship for this purpose, calls for explanation. In giving it, the history of the entire material expression of Hindu culture has to be kept in mind. I have already said that this expression was the result of the impact of foreign influences and models, primarily Persian and Greek influences. The erotic sculpture with other important things takes its place among the borrowings from the Greeks. I have no doubt whatever that the idea of such a genre

[1] The appropriateness of this statement lies in the fact that in mild seasons the Hindus slept in the open on the flat roofs, and opportunities for intimate relations were offered only by the cold season. The princes and the aristocracy had separate and high roofs. But this inscription was by silk-weavers.

of sculpture was taken from them, and it was also from them that the craftsmanship was learnt.

In the first place, Greek erotic art is much older than anything in this line produced in India. Next, the Greeks were on the borders of India and must have possessed portable works of erotic art which were common in the Hellenistic world. Bowls and other objects with mythological designs like the pursuit of Daphne by Apollo or the rape of Europa have been found in Afghanistan, and there is no improbability that vases, bowls, lecythi, terracotta figures, toilet trays, mirrors, and lamps with erotic designs were also to be seen among these Greeks.

As the Hindus have always shown an extreme readiness to adopt arts and crafts from foreigners, they must have taken over these things as well. Some fairly old terracotta erotic figures have been found in India which can bridge the gap between the disappearance of the Greeks from the Indian region and the first dated erotic sculpture in India. In any case, there is no improbability in assuming the derivation. In deciding questions of cultural borrowings, I proceed on the assumption that if close similarity can be seen between two sets of cultural products and the existence of contact can be established, the older set has to be accepted as the model of the later. In respect of the relationship between Greek erotic art and the Hindu there can be no doubt about which is earlier.[1]

---

[1] I shall give two examples from my early experiences to show that the addition of erotic features to religious iconography was not even noticed. Our family had the chariot of Krishna (the car of Juggernaut), which was taken out during the festival of the chariot journey (*Ratha Yatra*). Our family idols of Radha and Krishna were put on it fully dressed. Krishna also had a charioteer, Uddhava, who was placed in front like a coachman. We had his image as well, and it was kept in one of the rooms of our house. It was made of wood, and was of the size of a boy of seven or eight. He was, of course, dressed for the occasion in the correct Bengali clothes. But the naked image quite needlessly was given human genitals, and not only that, also an immense erect penis. We often handled the image, but no one ever tittered. Such was also the case with the lion on which the Mother Goddess Durga stood fighting the demon Mahishasura. The lion very properly showed its teeth and was given the posture of attack. But it was also given genitals, and with surprising ignorance of feline anatomy it was given, not the organs of the lion, which would not have been seen, but those of a dog which are under the belly. It was *de rigueur* to show the penis protruding out of the sheath and to paint it bright scarlet. I never found anybody drawing attention to it, but there is a facetious story about it.

Chapter Two

THE CULTS OF SIVA AND DURGA-KALI

SIVA, the Mother Goddess who is his consort and goes under the names of Parvati, Durga, Kali and many others, and Krishna are the most important objects of the religious devotion of the Hindus. In comparison with them the other gods of their polytheistic pantheon are minor. The worship of these three deities is also the most important feature of Hinduism as organized in cults. Furthermore, the cults of these three constitute the expression in three forms of what I have called the polymorphous monotheism of the Hindus, which in its turn, is the most important development in Hinduism in its transition from the prehistoric to the historic age.

As to the process of evolution of these cults, what happened in the case of Krishna can be related more or less fully, although the reasons for the very surprising transformations of his divine personality, which will be described in the next chapter, cannot be given except as conjectures. That even an account of the transformations can be given is due to the fact that the cult of Krishna originated and reached its full development in India, and the most significant part of the development took place in the historic period. But the origins and early history of the cults of Siva and Durga-Kali are very obscure. All the historic evidence which has been found in India about their existence shows them as more or less fully developed. After that no change in the conception and worship of Siva is seen, and the cult of the Mother Goddess had only one feature added to it. But that did not alter the main character of the cult. The addition remained an isolated feature.

Early History of the Cults

I shall set down only what may be conjectured about the early history of the two cults. In Hindu worship and mythology Siva and Parvati (who is worshipped both as Durga and Kali) are always associated as husband and wife, though they are worshipped separately. In this connected relationship both the deities certainly go back to the pre-Indian existence of the Indo-Aryans. On this point there is definite historical evidence whose significance has never been pointed out in the previous accounts of Hinduism.

As in the case of the major gods of the Vedic religion, the earliest evidence for the existence of this divine couple has been found in Asia Minor, and in the same locality, namely, the environs of Boghazköy. In fact, the evidence is more decisive, and is found in actual iconography, and not simply epigraphic mention. At Yazilikaya near Boghazköy there is a rock-cut sanctuary, in which a long procession of gods and goddesses was carved in bas-relief. This relief contains the figures of sixty-six gods and goddesses, facing each other. At the centre of the relief stand a god and goddess facing each other, and they are obviously the most important deities. Both hold in their hands special weapons and symbols. The figures are almost life-size. The god is the Hittite Storm or Weather God, and the goddess his consort. Their names as given in inscriptions are Teshub for the god and Hepat (or Hebat) for the goddess. These are not Hittite names, that is to say, the linguistic form of the names is not Indo-European. These are really Hurrian. But the deities had been fully adopted by the Hittites, and may have been Hittite gods in spite of their Hurrian names.[1]

Certainly, the prototypes of Siva and Parvati are to be seen in this Hittite divine couple. The most decisive argument in favour of this conclusion is the identity between the mounts of the Hittite god and goddess and those of Siva and Durga. Teshub stands on bulls and Hepat on a lioness, as do Siva and Durga. It is impossible that it can be mere chance coincidence that two supreme deities of two pantheons should be both husband and wife and stand on the same animals in Asia Minor and India. Besides this there are two other analogies. The Hittite deities are connected like Siva and Parvati with mountains, and Teshub stands on some minor gods of mountains. Next, the couple have a son named Sharruma, who is shown standing behind his mother on a lion and is apparently a god of war like Kartikeya. These figures date from the thirteenth century B.C., when the Mitannians were still in upper Mesopotamia.

[1] K. Bittel, R. Neumann, H. Otto, *Yazilikaya, Architektur, Felsbilder, Inschriften und Kleinfunde* (1941), in *Wissenschaftliche Veröffentlichungen der Deutschen Orient Gesellschaft*, no. 61; also Bittel, *Hattusha* (1970), pp. 95–100.

It would not be unreasonable, therefore, to suppose that the Hittite divine couple travelled from Mesopotamia to India with the Aryans in their eastward migration, and then became Siva and Durga. But how that happened is wholly unknown.

Siva as Supreme God

The line of descent none the less was not wholly obscured. In respect of Rudra of the Vedic pantheon, with whom the Siva of the later cult is certainly connected, it can be said that he bears resemblances to the Hittite Storm God. For one thing, Rudra is described as the father of the wind gods. There is also an analogy ni character. As indicated by their names, both the gods are functionally dynamic if not destructive, but both are expressly described as benign to men in their attitudes. But in explaining the emergence of the cult of Siva as a supreme god of the monotheistic type, his distant origins in Asia Minor and his existence as Rudra in the Vedic pantheon are only of formal importance, in as much as the prototypes furnished divine figures on whom the attributes of a new Siva and new Mother Goddess could be imposed.

The new Siva does not belong to the Vedic pantheon except by his formal descent. He is a new god created in India, and the mythology relating to him and his consort was created after a definite event in the history of the Aryans, namely, the rupture of relations between the Aryans who remained in Iran and those who became Indo-Aryans. An important part of the mythology of Siva and Durga rests on this conflict. The Vedic pantheon certainly existed substantially in the same form as a common pantheon of all the Aryans in Persia before the emergence of Ahura-Mazda as a monotheistic god put an end to polytheism in that country. Therefore the Vedas contain no allusions to any conflict between these two sections of the Aryans. But later mythology has as one of its main themes the story of a cyclical war between the Asuras or Danavas and the Devas, which can only be a mythological transformation of a historic conflict.

Both Siva and Durga are key figures in this conflict. But there is a difference between the roles of the two. Durga-Kali has no friendly relations with the Asuras, and is simply their killer and destroyer. In contrast, Siva plays an ambivalent part. There are clear suggestions in the epics and the mythological literature of the Hindus that he is in some unexplained way also a god of the Asuras and Danavas and their patron. At the same time he is also made the killer of certain Asuras, especially of one formidable Asura, Tripura. Moreover, in Hindu mythology he is the father of the warrior god of the Hindu pantheon, Kartikeya, whose exclusive function is to kill the demons.

But in this awareness of a conflict between themselves and the Persians, the Indo-Aryans must also have become familiar with the supreme monotheistic god of the Persians, and been influenced by the conception of that god. Siva as a god of the monotheistic type is obviously derived from Ahura-Mazda. This is suggested in the first instance by certain modes of referring to Siva as the supreme god. He is the only god in the polymorphous monotheism of the Hindus who is given the title of the Lord (Isvara) *par excellence*. He is given a higher status by being called Great Lord (Mahesvara). This position is not given to Vishnu-Krishna.

Now, it should be noted that whenever the Hindus added such adjectives as 'great', 'supreme', etc., to any substantive of status, that was under the influence of the Persians. For instance, a Hindu king was simply a Raja, a tribal chief, so that in recent times even a village chief was called a Raja. In fact, the common Hindu surname Ray(a), held normally by landowners, is its derivative. It should also be pointed out that Asoka, although an all-India ruler, styled himself 'Raja' and nothing else. But in imitation of the Persians great Hindu kings began to call themselves Maharaja (Great King) or Rajadhiraja (King of Kings), echoing or translating the Persian 'Kshayatiya Vajraka' and 'Kshayatiya Kshayatiyanam'. It is also significant that those who did this first and most emphatically were the kings of foreign origin who reigned over the regions bordering on Persia, e.g. the Kushans. They gave themselves the titles of Maharaja, Rajatiraja, Shahanushahi, Shaon Shao, Basileius Basileieon, Basileious Megaus, etc. In the same way, Siva came to be designated as Isvara, Mahesvara, Paramesvara, or Maha-Deva.

But there are facts of deeper significance to establish the Persian affiliation of Siva as a monotheistic god. As an object of devotion, he is not identical with Rudra of the Vedic mythology, nor with the Siva of the Puranic tradition. Furthermore, he is not the god of destruction of the Hindu trinity, nor the leader of all sorts of low demigods living in squalor. He is a high and complete god with attributes which were never given to any anthropomorphic Hindu god before him, and hardly even afterwards. The *Mahabharata* describes these attributes. In reply to a question by Yudisthira, Bhisma says:

> I am incapable of enunciating the attributes of the wise Mahadeva, who is ubiquitous but nowhere visible; who is the creator of Brahma, Vishnu, and Indra and their lord as well; whom all the deities from Brahma to the Pisachas worship; who transcends all natural phenomena *(Prakriti)* as well the Absolute Spirit *(Purusha)*; whom the Rishis who practise discipline and have arrived at truth contemplate; who is indestructible, supreme, the Brahman himself; who does not exist and yet exists (and so on).

This Siva is identical with the Siva whom Kalidasa invoked. In this form he is almost identical with the *Atman* of the Way of Knowledge, and yet he is a personal and anthropomorphic god. A god like him never existed before in Hinduism. The character of the devotion to him also remained exceptional. It never assimilated itself to any form of human love. It remained on the plane of divine love. In northern India the fervour in the worship of Siva declined, probably due to the rise of the competing cult of Krishna. Nevertheless, he continued to be worshipped as the god of sanctified welfare. This was the reason why the mythology and legends of Siva, as well as the popular worship of Siva based on the mythology, remained separate from the cult of Siva, the supreme god. The original character of the monotheistic devotion to him was seen in a substantially unimpaired form in the Saivism of the south.

This peculiar character of the cult makes it permissible to infer that Siva was probably the first and only god of the monotheistic Hinduism which replaced Vedic polytheism as the highest expression of the religious sentiment of the Hindus. That is to say, originally the monotheism was unitary. In fact, even in recent times the Saivas of the south maintained that Siva was the *only* supreme deity. This monotheism became polymorphous only when the idea of Siva as a monotheistic god was extended to other deities. Through that process both Vishnu-Krishna and Durga-Kali became supreme deities in their turn. Their cults were extensions of the Saiva cult. This would be perfectly consistent with the eclectic and latitudinarian inclinations of the Hindu mind.

The Mother Goddess

Siva's consort Parvatí, known in her cults either as Durga or Kali, as well as by alternative names, has been referred to by me as the Hindu Mother Goddess, because the divine *persona* behind both the forms is one, and it is awkward to give two names in every context. But she is not a Mother Goddess of the Semitic type worshipped in Western Asia. Her character is wholly different. As the Hindu Mother Goddess, she is not a hieratic divinity, but a goddess of rulers and warriors. Re-created in Hindu mythology out of the original Hittite goddess on account of the Indo-Iranian conflict, she remained the goddess of war throughout. Beginning as the goddess who fought and killed the Asura enemies of the Devas or Hindu gods, she remained the patron goddess of conquests. It is significant that the worship of Durga with its accompanying animal sacrifices has survived only in those parts of India where Hindu rulers and the Hindu aristocracy have also survived, notably, in Rajputana, Nepal, and Bengal. Even in Bengal where many other associations gathered round the worship of Durga, it never lost its military character. As I myself saw it, the worship had as one of its final features a ceremonial presentation of weapons. As we sat on the ground, the priest came up to each of us, marked our forehead with vermilion, and touched it with one of the scimitars.[1]

It has only to be added that the idea held by some historians of Hinduism and popularized by them that the cult of the Hindu Mother Goddess was taken over from the aboriginals of India may be dismissed not only as improbable but as absurd. The reasons for which no Hindu religious belief or worship could be borrowed from the non-Aryans has already been discussed. Nor is there any evidence for such borrowings except that some aboriginals do worship the Mother Goddess. But that is a case of borrowing by them from the Hindus and bringing the cult down to their crude level. It should also be remembered as an uncontestable fact of cultural history that a basically crude or degenerate cult cannot be raised to a higher level, though a simple one can be.

[1] Having gone through it year after year, I am familiar with the spirit of the worship of Durga in all its shades in Bengal. I have described it fully in my *Autobiography*, pp. 63–73.

The cult of the Mother Goddess in its fully developed form is found in the *Markandeya Purana*, and those parts of this Purana which describe her deeds are known popularly in Bengal as the Chandi (The Terrible One). These accounts are read regularly as a part of her worship. But the date of the book is not known. The point which should, however, be noted is that in the case of Durga-Kali, the ritual of her worship has remained in agreement with her function and activities as described in her mythology.

The historical evidence as to the emergence of the cult has been summarized in Chapter 2 of Part I. The most impressive artistic representation of Durga at a fairly early date is to be found in a splendid relief at Mahaballipuram near Madras. In it she is shown as engaged in a fight with the demon Mahisha (Buffalo), who is given the head and horns of the animal. These sculptures have been assigned to the seventh or eighth century. They show her cult to be virtually the same as I knew it in my boyhood. The sculpture of an early date at Aihole also confirms that by the eighth century the cult of Durga was fully established.

Beyond this nothing more definite can be said about the origin and development of the cult of the Mother Goddess. But once established, it has remained unchanged, and has not undergone any transformation like that which was seen in the cult of Krishna. The only addition which was made to it was the Tantric mode of worship. But this has to be regarded as a side-shoot, with no organic relationship to the open cult of the goddess, and though some Tantric mumbo-jumbo is found in the liturgy of her worship, this has nothing of the esoteric in it. This offshoot will be dealt with in its proper place.

Worship and Ritual

The Mother Goddess is one. In her divine personality no distinction is made between Durga and Kali. But the iconography and mode of worship are different. To deal with the physical appearance first, the figure of Durga, though shown as fighting with ten weapons or emblems in her ten hands and even driving her spear into the chest of the demon Mahisha, has a wholly benign expression and her face is lit up with a smile. The facial type is of the images of northern Buddhism and even as made today the face is given eyes with a pronounced slant, which makes it somewhat Mongoloid.[1] Her complexion as given, is also golden yellow. In addition, she is gorgeously dressed. In her *dhyana* or contemplation she is described as follows:

> *Om!* I meditate on her in the form in which she is described: she has braided hair, three eyes, and a face like the full moon; her complexion has the colour of molten gold; her eyes are beautiful; she is in her fresh youth, with beautifully set and sharp teeth, and swelling and high breasts.

Kali, on the other hand is described in these words:

> *Om!* I recall her whose complexion is that of the *bandhuka* flower, who stands on Siva the five-headed, in whose crown the moon shines like a jewel, who has a garland of human heads, who has three eyes, whose apparel is red, whose breasts are high and full like bowls, and who has her hands raised in the gesture of giving and reassuring. I bow to Kali, the beloved of Siva, whose feet are adorned with bejewelled anklets, whose hips have a bejewelled girdle, who has a pike and a thousand weapons, whose breasts are high and have sharp points, and whose crown has jewels which shower nectar.

It would be seen that the ancient Hindus were incapable of loving or worshipping any woman, divine or human, unless she not only had beautiful features but also ample feminine charms. Besides, she had to be gorgeous with splendid dresses and ornaments. Her jewellery had to jingle as much in fighting, as it did in sexual intercourse, as described in mythological stories. Even the actual appearance of Kali in her image, fierce and frowning as it was, had an extraordinary beauty, on which as a boy I often looked with fascination.

The manner of worshipping the two forms was also different. Durga was worshipped once a year in the autumn (with a duplication in the spring) in an image made for the occasion only. After the festival of worship this image was thrown into water. Her temples were very exceptional, and, so far as I know, at present there is only one at Benares. On the contrary, Kali was normally worshipped only in permanent temples, of which the

---

[1] As a boy I was given the mould from which the face of Durga was made by the potter who made our image, and I often made one myself in clay. The fineness of the features showed that the original of the mould was first made many centuries ago.

most holy and important is that at Kalighat in Calcutta, and an equally holy one at Kamrup in Assam. In Bengal every village and every town has a Kali temple, and wherever the Bengalis go they build a temple to the goddess. There are two in Delhi. But Kali is also worshipped by the Bengalis once a year in a clay image made for a special occasion; her worship falls on the day of the new moon following the worship of Durga. This image is also thrown into water.

I shall describe here how her image is infused with life. The ceremony begins with the recital of the famous *Purusha Sukta* of the tenth Mandala of the *Rig-Veda*, to the accompaniment of which the image is bathed. This is a very elaborate affair, though symbolic rather than literal. Then she is given eyesight. Lamp-black paste is taken at the end of a blade of grass and it is put on the lids of the image. After that the image is given life. Grass and flowers are taken by the priest in his right hand, which is placed on the head of the image, then he has to utter the basic incantation *(mula-mantra)* one hundred and eight times, touch other limbs and last of all place his thumb on the heart of the image and utter a Vedic incantation so that life may come into her and remain in the image. Again, he has to place his hand on her heart and utter a Vedic *mantra*, which ends thus: '*Om,* may Vishnu endow you with genitals, Tvasta carve the form, Prajapati inject semen, and Dhata make you pregnant.' All this is wound up with the recitation of the most holy formula in the Vedas, the Gayatri *mantra*.

Devotion to Durga and Kali

Personal devotion to both Durga and Kali, however, had no relation to their mythology or ritual, and its aspect must now be considered. As to the image of Durga no attention was paid to her warlike posture and role, and only her beauty and splendour were admired. Even the naked image of Kali raised no feeling which was not reverential. A devout old gentleman would stand before her image with folded hands and say, 'O unclad Mother mine!' I myself used to sing two songs of devotion which referred to her nakedness. The first ran like this: 'O Kali, why do you roam about naked?' The second song was more elaborate:

I

O Mother mine, Daughter of the Mountain![1]

Why are you clad like this?
You have put your feet on the body of a god,
and you have no trace of shame,
you have placed your feet on Hara,
you are naked and wear no covering,
your tongue is lolling out and flicking,
your long hair is flowing loose.

But, O terrible wife of Siva, you are chewing the flesh
in your hand for the sake of saving this world . . .

As to Durga, even after looking on that blood sacrifice we sat
down and sang songs of devotion of a different kind altogether. As
I have written in my autobiography:

When about an hour after the sacrifice we sat down to chant the
praise of the goddess in chorus the mood had miraculously changed.
My old uncle gave the word: 'The world is pain . . .' and we began
gravely and slowly:

> The world is pain,
> Its load all bearing past;
> Never pine I, never thirst,
> For its kingdom vain.
>
> Rosy are her feet,
> A shelter free of fear;
> Death may whisper *I am near;*
> He and I shall smiling meet.

Then followed song after song, song of mortals to the Immortal, of
the helpless and weak to the Strong, of the weary and heavyladen
to the Comforter. There were even songs voicing perplexity at the
destructive fury of the Great Mother.

In fact, the worshippers of Durga or Kali never considered
them in any light except as a divine mother, as omnipotent in
power as she was without reserve in her love and mercy. A famous
devotee of hers named Ramprasad has left a whole series of songs
called after his name, which sing her praise. There is an edificatory

[1] *Giri-kumari* = Parvati.

tale which tells of his reward. He was one day working on a partition of matting for his house, and had no assistant to hand him the ribbon of cane from the other side to fix the mat to the strips of bamboo. Suddenly, he found someone who was invisible behind the mat, pushing forward the cane from the other side. When the work was finished a little girl ran away from that side. She was Kali herself.

I shall add to this hagiographical but significant story an illustration of the spirit in which Durga-Kali was worshipped from actual life. It comes from the autobiography of a noted leader of the monotheistic Brahmo movement of the nineteenth century, Sivanath Sastri, who wholly rejected polytheism and idolatry. When he was a small boy his great-grandfather was living. He was ninety-five years old and both blind and deaf. Still the old man devoted an hour and a half every day to perform his usual rituals of a Brahmin's life. After that he used to pray personally for half an hour, bowing again and again at the feet of the family deity, Kali the Mother Goddess. In doing so the sightless man struck the floor so many times that at last a tumour was formed on his forehead. I quote from the autobiography what Sivanath wrote about the conclusion of the prayer.

One day my mother heard him praying extempore in Bengali for my father who was working away from home: 'O merciful Mother! he is away among strangers, preserve him. He does not listen to anyone, give him virtuous inclinations.' Then he stood up and began to dance, clapping his hands. He also called for me. I was then a child and used to go about naked. My mother dragged me out of the room in which I was playing, and putting my hands into his hands asked me to dance. And we danced together forthwith. On all the three hundred and sixty-five days of the year he sang the same song. I remember only two lines of it:

> 'Durga, Durga, balo bhai,
> Durga bai are gati nai.' (In Bengali)
> 'O brethren, take the name of Durga,
> There is no refuge except in her.'

I think this disposes of all that one hears about the violent and horror-inspiring character of the worship of Kali or Durga.

As Durga, the Mother Goddess is not only the giver of prosperity, but also the dispenser of food to mankind, and in that role

her name is Annapurna — 'She who is full of food'. If she turns
away her face, there will be famine and starvation. But that never
happens, and cannot happen. However, she cannot endure un-
happy homes, which are made so by the quarrelsome disposition
of its members, especially the wife. So, another Bengali poet of
the same age as Ramprasad wrote that one day she was running
away from such a home and going to another household as a
village woman. She came to a river bank and asked the ferry-
woman to row her across. As the boat was going to the other bank
of the river (it was the Hooghly River near Calcutta) the boatwoman asked her name, and she gave it in very equivocal words,
so that the woman concluded that she was the wife of a Brahmin.
But she saw an extraordinary thing. Her passenger was trailing
her feet in the water over the gunwale. She said: 'My lady, do
not do that. This river is full of crocodiles, they might drag you
down.' The passenger drew in her legs and, to avoid getting wet
in the water which had leaked into the boat, she placed her feet
on the wooden scooper with which boatmen drain a leaking boat.
At first the boatwoman had noticed that lotuses had begun to
bloom suddenly in the river, and when the passenger got out she
saw with greater astonishment that her wooden scooper had
turned into gold. At last, realizing who her passenger was, she fell
at her feet. The Great Mother smiled and said: 'Ask a boon of me.
What do you want?' And the woman asked that gift which is in
the Lord's Prayer: 'May my children know not the fear of starvation and always have milk and rice.'

In addition, the worship of the goddess was joyous. This joy
was seen at its most exuberant in the evening of the worship,
when the priest danced before the image with a five-branched
candelabrum in hand. I have described this too in my autobiography. I shall only quote the opening lines of that description:
'The evening which followed had no suggestion of what we had
seen in the morning, nor of what we had sung at midday. It was
neither orgiastic nor devotional, but gay and heartfree, with
lights blazing, a whole crowd laughing and jostling, and the wild
music more self-abandoned and noisy than ever.'

The Erotic Element

The sexual obsession of the Hindus did not leave even such a cult

248

free from eroticism, and this aspect must be looked straight in the face. As it happens, it is only in the cult of Durga or Kali that sexual intercourse became a part of ritual, and not merely a mythological adjunct. This element is found only in that part of the cult which is known as Tantra, and the contemporary Western interest in it is even more degraded than the recourse to Yoga.

As a subject of religious history, Tantra has to be put in its place. The first point to emphasize is that it was and is confined to a very limited number of adherents and is not general. Secondly, it-is esoteric, and not like nine-tenths of Hinduism wholly open. The third and the most important thing to note is that Tantricism has three aspects, and what is being presented to the contemporary West is only one aspect, with a dubious reputation even among the Hindus.

These three aspects are the following. The first and the most widespread and openly practised Tantric devotion has nothing to do with sexual intercourse. It is a course of esoteric self-mortification and gymnastics accompanied by the worship of Kali, based on the most absurd physiological and psychological notions. These Tantric practices can be regarded as being of the same type as Yoga, with an affiliation to the cult of Durga or Kali.

The second and the third forms have sexual intercourse as part of its practice. The second is particularly cruel and cold-blooded. It was practised by the devotees of Kali known as Kapalikas, or men who worshipped with human skulls. They performed their austerities sitting on the corpse of a man whom they had sacrificed. To complete their course of devotion they raped a virgin and then sacrificed her. This form of Tantricism may have lasted till the middle of the nineteenth century. But it has disappeared wholly.

It is the third form of Tantricism which has continued and is most widespread and insidious, because it is sensual indulgence under the guise of religion. This practice is called *Vamachara* — the left-handed or perverse way — and consists in ritualistically indulging in five M's (*Pancha Makaras* in Sanskrit), namely, *madya* (alcohol), *mamsa* (meat), *matsya* (fish) and *mudra* (gestures with the hands), and *maithun* (coitus). It should be pointed out that drinking alcohol is a major sin in Hindu sacred law, and that in recent centuries orthodox Brahmins have not eaten meat or fish. That all this, and more especially coitus, could be indulged in by way of religious practice should not surprise anybody who has read what I have described and shall describe of the doings of the Hindus in the name of religion.

What is more relevant to the discussion of Tantra is to find out what the Hindus themselves have thought of Tantra. The Kapalikas when they existed were both hated and feared. Even in a Sanskrit play a Kapalika who wanted to sacrifice a maiden was killed by her lover, and nobody sympathized with him.[1] Bankim Chandra Chatterji, whom I have often mentioned in this book, has written a novel on this subject, and it is one of the most beautiful in the Bengali language.[2]

The Tantric practitioners of asceticism were regarded as cranks or faddists, but their sincerity was not questioned. However, for the Tantricists of the third school, i.e. the *Vamacharis*, the Hindu community had nothing but contempt and ridicule as hypocrites who wanted to satisfy their evil propensities under the pretext of religion. The Tantrics of this class have themselves shown that they are conscious of this by never acknowledging openly that they are *Vamacharis*.Those who practise the five M's secretly are spotted and pointed at with a good deal of malicious amusement. Even the modern Hindu reformer, Rammohun Roy, who drank in moderation and was a Tantric scholar, had the Tantra cast in his teeth. The orthodox pundits who attacked him said that in drinking alcohol he was only obeying the Tantric precept— '*Pitva, Pitva* . . . Drinking, and drinking, and drinking again, rolling on the ground, rising and yet drinking, a man saves himself from rebirth.'

The women who satisfied these devotees were even more perverted than the men. In fact, they were sexual maniacs. I shall relate an incident about which I was told by a friend in Calcutta in 1923. He was walking along a deserted lane late one evening in the Kalighat quarter of Calcutta. Suddenly, in the light of a street lamp, he saw through an open french window, a powerful, bearded man in red loin cloth and with a red mark on his forehead, standing before a full-limbed stark naked woman. He was so startled by this sight that he jumped backwards, and the woman sent a peal of laughter at him. As he walked forward again with a bowed head he heard more satirical, tingling laughter.

[1] *Malati-Madhava* by Bhavabhuti.
[2] *Kapala-Kundala,* published in 1867.

What Tantric esotericism meant for the Hindus in general I shall illustrate with reference to the form of Kali known as the Chhinnamasta, i.e. 'she who is beheaded'. She is one of the ten Mahavidyas, or manifestations of Kali. The iconography shows her holding her severed head in her hand and drinking the blood which is cascading out of her neck into the mouth of the head. At the same time she is shown standing on Kama, the god of love, and Rati, his wife, who are engaged in reversed coitus under her feet. Old pictures showed even the junction of the genitalia, though the modern ones show the couple discreetly covered to the shoulders by a sheet.

As it happened, I heard a song about this manifestation of Kali in a village in Bengal in 1918. The singer was a professional, in fact a local maestro, and a Muslim at that. With staccato bowings of the violin on which he was accompanying himself he sang, 'Maddened by lust Kama and Rati are having reversed coitus' (in Bengali, *Kama Rati kamé mati, viparita karé rati*). And he even stabbed the air with his bow to demonstrate the energy of the movements of the couple. I was young then, and got rather angry. But the audience was listening spellbound.

Similarly, when I was ten or eleven years old I was told by a schoolfellow of the same age that there were pictures showing Kali sitting on Mahadeva with all her weapons and having sexual intercourse with him. Such pictures were painted in Calcutta, and I have seen them since then. But this information made no difference to my feeling for Kali. Every day before going to school I stood before the Kali temple which was near it, and with folded hands uttered my prayer. In the same way, all Hindus knew about the sexual associations of some of the Tantric religious rites, and did not think any the worse of their religion for these, any more than they thought that their society was not worth living in because there were prostitutes, adultery, or sexual crimes in it.

But the rehabilitation of Tantra for modern educated Hindus was the work of an Englishman, Sir John Woodroffe, who was a Judge of the High Court of Calcutta. From 1918 he began to expound Tantra in a series of books, some of which he wrote under the pseudonym of Arthur Avalon. I myself watched his activities with interest, but I did not regard it as anything but the hobby of an eccentric. His writings had no religious significance or influence whatever. Not one Hindu capable of reading his books was likely to be converted to Tantric practice by them. But he appealed to them, among whom were also the barristers of Calcutta High Court, for a wholly different reason. He appealed to their nationalism. By 1918 not only Tantricism but even the highest spiritual message in Hinduism, as in the Upanishads, had ceased to be an influence in the life of modern Hindus, and so far as they did not practise religion from superstition, it was a part of their nationalism. The spectacle of an English judge of the High Court speaking for a form of Hinduism which had always been deprecated by themselves, tickled their national vanity, and they began to think much of Woodroffe and his work on Tantra. The men who would now defend Tantricism in theory would be the last men to adopt any Tantric practice, and those who would adopt it would be too well aware of their motives to speak about it.

Origin of Tantric Eroticism

There remains only one question about Tantricism. How and from where did sexual intercourse enter the cult of the Hindu Mother Goddess? The Tantric texts cannot be dated, and they are certainly all late, not composed before the eighth century at the earliest. This, however, proves nothing. Some scholars have suggested an ultimate source for Tantra in the sexual aspect of the Vedic religion. But the ancient sexuality of the Hindus had become obsolete. The new sexuality of the Krishna cult was of a quite different nature. It was honest sexual passion, not masquerading under a false name, although brought into religion. Tantric sexuality was particularly repulsive on account of its pretentiousness, cynicism, and hard-boiled licentiousness in the men and women alike. Its source has to be sought in something nearer its time of origin.

Other scholars have suggested that it came into Hinduism from Buddhistic Tantricism. The two are certainly analogous, but for that reason it is not necessary to assume that the Hindu form of Tantricism was derived from the Buddhistic. It is more likely that both were derived from the same source. There can be no doubt that Tantricism in both forms has come from the north, and from that side the only possible source for the sexual aspect of Tantricism can be Taoism.

The facts which are indisputable are these: first, Taoism is older than any form of Tantricism known in India; secondly, Taoism has the same kind of anatomical and physiological fantasy oriented towards erotic feeling; lastly, Taoism has a cold-blooded theory of the profit to be derived from sexual intercourse by making it a part of religious and moral life.

There is in the forefront the Taoist rigmarole about *Yin* and *Yang*. These are complementary forces which stand behind the whole cosmos, *Yin* being the female principle and *Yang* the male. Their coming together is necessary in order not only to maintain the cosmic order, but also to ensure immortality for an individual. Sexual intercourse is therefore made the central activity in the cult of Taoism, which certainly dates from the Han period (*c.* 200 B.C. to A.D. 220). But in this activity the *yang* or the male side must always cheat and gain at the expense of *yin*, the female side. Therefore the male should withhold orgasm, so as not to lose vitality, and by inducing it in the woman make her give up part of her vitality to the man. It was assumed by Taoist doctrine that a man shortened his life by being unable to control his passion and having emission in intercourse. So he was to practise such a measure of self-control as to have full pleasure from the activity without losing his strength by orgasms. Taoists laid down four principles for sexual intercourse: 1. maximum contact; 2. minimum emission; 3. frequent change of the woman; 4. intercourse with virgins.

The last principle was very logical. If the man was to gain vitality by draining it from the woman, an experienced woman was the last person to be exploited. All this theory is expressed in quite straightforward language: 'When coupling you should consider your opponent as a cheap claypot, whereas you are a precious piece. When you feel the seed is near withdraw. Sleeping with a woman is like riding a galloping horse with rotten reins, like walking on the edge of a deep precipice with swords and being frightened of falling. Spare your seed, and lengthen your life.' So a series of prescriptions are laid-down which will enable a man to have the utmost out of sexual intercourse without losing anything himself.

But if the Hindus were to take over such things from the Chinese they were not likely to do so in the Chinese spirit, for to a Hindu the idea of surrender to a woman in intercourse is the height of happiness. Moreover, the Hindu outlook on life and the Chinese differed fundamentally, for the Hindu sought power and the Chinese tranquillity. The same distinction was to be seen in the conception of religion, which for a Hindu was a means of attaining power. So, the incorporation of sexual intercourse in Tantricism was accomplished in a different manner and to a different end. It was to be a concerted affair between the man and the woman and the more experienced a woman was, the greater was the satisfaction and profit likely to be. With this adaptation of the aim of sexual intercourse in religion there was no obstacle to the adoption of the practice of Taoism by the Hindus. Both Tantricism and Taoism were equally cynical, but in different ways. On the Tantric side the cynicism was as much in the woman as in the man, on the Taoist side it was only in the man. After all, the Hindu was Indo-European, and he refused to make the woman merely his slave, instead of a companion.

Chapter Three

THE CULT OF KRISHNA

AMONG the three major cults of Siva, Krishna, and the Mother Goddess, that of Krishna is the most important. It is very popular in the sense that people are attracted to it for its human quality, and in northern India certainly it has the largest number of adherents, which does not mean, of course, that those who make Krishna their personal supreme deity ever withhold their worship from the other two.

The Krishna cult is also the most joyous over the whole of India, though in Bengal the cult of the Mother Goddess Durga is not less so. It has four very happy festivals directly connected with the life and doings of Krishna, namely, the festival of his birth, and the festivals of his outing in the car (the car of Juggernaut of the West), swinging with the so-called milkmaids, and dancing with them. In addition, the most tumultuous and colourful festival of the Hindus, the Holi, which is both a festival of the spring season and a saturnalia, has become associated with Krishna.

The cult is distinguished from the two others in a number of ways. First, it cannot be traced back to the Vedic religion, i.e. to the Aryan religious heritage except indirectly. It is also unconnected with the two ways of religion known as the *Jnana Marga* (Way of Knowledge) and *Karma Marga* (Way of Works, or more correctly, of rituals), which evolved out of the Vedic religion as the standard forms of Brahmanic Hinduism.

Secondly, it is not the worship of a god of the Hindu pantheon as himself, but of his incarnation in a human form, i.e. as Krishna. He is a god because he is the human form of Vishnu, who is a Vedic god, though not a major one. But he is not an incarnation in the Hindu sense, that is, a god born into the world for a specific purpose, and therefore he is not included among the ten incarnations of Vishnu of Hindu mythology, viz. the Fish, Tortoise, Boar, Man-Lion, Dwarf, Parasurama, Rama, Balarama, Buddha, and Kalki. Krishna as an incarnation is God himself, full God and full man, thus showing a close similarity to Jesus of Christian theology. As such he has virtually supplanted Vishnu as an object of worship.

Thirdly, except through Vishnu, his cult is not founded on Indo-Aryan mythology, but on Indo-Aryan legends, that is to say, on the sub-historical memories of the early existence of the Aryans in India. Thus it is a wholly Indian development within the framework of the Indo-European religion.

Lastly, and this is the most important feature of the Krishna cult, it inaugurated a wholly new form of religious sentiment among the Hindus, and communicated this particular feeling to the other cults, in which it was not originally present. But the most typical and intense form of the new sentiment is to be found in the Krishna cult.

This has come to be known as *bhakti*, which signifies the self-surrender of human beings to a personal god of love, who is also to be worshipped with love and adoration. But neither *bhakti* nor the cult of Krishna founded on that sentiment has remained the same through their later evolution. Both have undergone strange and inexplicable transformations which are not paralleled even in the drastic metamorphoses in the insect world.

The feature common to all the phases is a strong emotionalism. But this, too, has changed from a concentrated and self-contained passion rather like the motive power of a ship or aeroplane driving these on a purposive course, to a maudlin exhibition of emotionalism bordering on hysteria. This last has been noticeable particularly in the cult of Krishna as practised in Bengal. There choral singing has become a form of worship, almost a ritual. Sometimes processions go out with drums and cymbals, and those who join it not only sing but dance wildly. At other times, there are sessions of singing at home, and these continue in a marathon of singing for twenty-four hours. But even after listening to the singing for half an hour men begin to cry and roll on the floor. This mode of worship has caught on in the West, but there the exhibition is not quite as exuberant as the home product.

Origin of Bhakti

The origin of this form of devotion known as *bhakti* certainly raises the most difficult question in the historical study of Hinduism, and unfortunately it has become involved in Hindu nationalism. On account of this theories have been put forward which cannot lay any claim to scholarship. In addition to the carelessness, amounting almost to unscrupulousness, which has been shown in considering the historical evidence, there has also been seen a total absence of psychological insight in discriminating between *bhakti* and *bhakti*, for there are surprisingly different forms of it in the Krishna cult itself.

The source of all this stumbling is the controversy about the origin of the specific kind of *bhakti* or devotion which is found in the *Gita*. This book is not only the earliest text of this kind of devotion, but also that in which a very clear-cut and coherent conception of *bhakti* is presented. In reading the *Gita* no one can form a wrong notion of what *bhakti* means in it, and the exposition is driven home in emphatic words all through the book.

Now, the *bhakti* of the *Gita* has a very close resemblance to the Christian notion of the love of God embodied in the Greek word *agape*. The similarity between many ideas of the *Gita* and the doctrines of Christianity was noticed by Warren Hastings, who set down that opinion in his introduction to the Wilkins's translation of the book. Later, at the end of the nineteenth century, a German scholar, Dr. F. Lorinser, in his translation of the *Gita* into German drew attention to a number of passages in it which bore a close analogy to many passages in the New Testament, and thought that the doctrine of love in the *Gita* might have been arrived at under the influence of Christianity.[1]

Trouble started at once. The Hindus had by that time acquired the notion of historical scholarship and also nationalistic sentiment from the West, and they were not prepared to accept a Christian origin of the concept of *bhakti*, which was the most popular form of their religious sentiment. The most obvious way to reject any Christian influence on the *Gita* was to date it back to the pre-Christian era. That was done, as has been seen, without a scrap of historical evidence. Then attempts were made to push back the idea of *bhakti* to the very beginnings of Hinduism, that is, to the Vedic religion. By means of a grotesque misinterpretation of verses, 2, 4, and 5 of the 125th sukta of the tenth Mandala of the *Rig-Veda* the idea of self-surrender to a personal deity was sought

[1] *Die Bhagavad Gita übersetzt und erläutert*, by Dr F. Lorinser (Breslau, 1869). The appendix in which Lorinser showed the similarity was published in English translation in the *Indian Antiquary* (October 1873).

to be taken to the Vedic age. Actually, in these verses the personified goddess of speech, *Vak*, only says that she will confer wealth, food and drink, and strength on those who sacrifice to her with devotion. The word *bhakti* is not used here, and the idea expressed has no resemblance whatever to the idea of self-surrender to God as presented in the *Gita*.

At the next stage the evidence for an early origin of the idea of *bhakti* has been sought in the occurrence of the word in old texts. That is to say, wherever the word *bhakti* has been found, it has been assumed that the notion behind it is that of *bhakti* of the *Gita*. The word *bhakti* does not occur in Vedic literature, but the word *bhakta* (meaning, one who has *bhakti*) occurs in the *Rig-Veda* together with the word *abhakta* (who has not *bhakti*) in verse 5 of the 127th sukta of the first Mandala. The word *bhakta* singly occurs in one of the Khila suktas. In neither of these contexts do the words mean the devotion of the *Gita*. Sayana interprets them as *sevamana* and *asevamana*, those who serve and those who do not.

Not to speak of the texts which can be presumed to have existed before the *Gita*, even those which came later and which undoubtedly preach the *bhakti* of Vaishnavism do not mean by *bhakti* what the *Gita* means. This will be demonstrated at some length in this chapter. It might be pointed out here that the mere occurrence of a word in books dating from different times does not prove that the meaning was the same in all ages. By assuming such a continuity of meaning, the notion of love in the New Testament as preached by St Paul can be taken back to Homer, for the word *agape* occurs in his writings. Even the great Attic dramatists did not use the word to mean what the Bible expressed.

In the Sanskrit language any argument about the existence of an idea based on the incidence of a word is more fallacious still, owing to the difficulty of determining the exact meaning of most words in Sanskrit, which I have already discussed.[1] Here I am illustrating the difficulty with reference to the word *bhakti* itself. As given in a good modern Sanskrit dictionary by a competent Hindu scholar, it means (1) separation, partition, division; (2) a division or part; (3) devotion, attachment, loyalty, faithfulness; (4) reverence, service, worship, homage; (5) texture; (6) decoration, ornament, embellishment; (7) an attribute; (8) being a part.

[1] See p. 216.

Another common word in religious texts, which is also derived from the same root as *bhakti*, has a variety of meanings. It is the word *bhaga*, which combined with the suffix *van* (or *vat*), i.e. as *Bhagavan*, gives the most common name for God. Now, this word in the masculine gender (it is used also in the feminine) has at least twenty different meanings, of which the most important are the following: (1) final beatitude; (2) omnipotence; (3) morality; (4) love, affection, etc.; (5) supernatural power to become small and light; (6) name of one of the Vedic Adityas; (7) prosperity; (8) desire and also absence of desire and (9) the female organ. And just as the word *Bhagavan* is the most common name of God in religious literature and speech, the word *bhaga* and not *yoni* is the most common name for the female genital organ in the erotic texts. Therefore the word *Bhagavati*, which is the name of Durga but literally means a woman who has *bhaga*, might be very differently interpreted out of its context.[1]

Therefore the attempt to find the notion of *bhakti* as it is expounded in the *Gita* in all other contexts in which the word occurs in Sanskrit is futile, and its absurdity would have been realized if the intelligence of modern Hindus had not been paralysed by a fanatical nationalism. The exact nature of the feeling intended to be conveyed must be discovered only by taking full account not only of the immediate context but also of the character and tone of the book in question as a whole. The application of this method will lead to very startling results, as will be seen in this chapter. It will show that *bhakti* is not the same thing even in all the Vaishnava texts and that it has undergone as drastic changes as the cult of Krishna itself. In fact, the evolution of the two runs along parallel lines, but every phase in the history of the cult corresponds to every phase in the history of the sentiment. It is this history which will now be briefly summarized.

From the Epic Krishna to Krishna the God

There can be no doubt that Krishna as he is depicted in the *Mahabharata* is the earliest Krishna. In it he is an epic hero, and no god, far less God. It will perhaps be objected that the epic has

[1] In ancient India a man when he wished to show the highest respect to a lady addressed her as *Bhagavati* and not simply as *Devi* (= *Domina*). What did he mean?

many passages which refer to Krishna as God or as an incarnation of Vishnu. But the *Mahabharata* in its present form is a compendium of mythological, legendary, and religious information of every kind, which was current when it was put in its final shape. Thus two treatises of the Krishna cult whose contents in no way agree with the epic's depiction of Krishna in its narrative parts are also incorporated in it. These are the *Gita*, which makes its teaching an episode before the beginning of a battle in total disregard of common sense; and the *Harivamsa*, an early treatise of the Vaishnava cult in which Krishna's voluptuous sports with the gopis or the so-called milkmaids are described. The epic itself does not say a word about the gopis, though it refers to Krishna's early upbringing among the cowherds. The incidental references to the godhood of Krishna in the epic have also to be regarded as interpolations in the main narrative.

If these references are not taken into account, the personality of Krishna as he is seen in the narrative portions of the *Mahabharata*, stands out clearly as a man of the heroic age. The book leaves no doubt about what he is and what he does. He is the first cousin of the Pandavas, their adviser, helper, and friend. He is also the brother-in-law, besides being a cousin, of Arjuna, the third Pandava. He acts as the charioteer of Arjuna in the battle of Kurukshetra, and saves the Pandavas from many critical situations either by his wisdom or by his cunning. The *Mahabharata* has even an abusive tirade against him from another cousin of his. Taking all these activities and traits of character into consideration, the great Bengali writer, Bankim Chandra Chatterji, depicted the Krishna of the *Mahabharata* as the ideal man and hero.[1]

At this point note has to be taken of a recent theory about the *Mahabharata*. Georges Dumézil, following the adumbration of the idea by the Swedish Sanskritist Stig Wikander, has demonstrated in his very important and massive work *Myth et Epopée* that the story of the Pandavas is a transposition into the epic form of the mythology of the Vedic Aryans, which presents a tripartite pantheon. This forms part of Dumézil's specific contribution to the study of the mythology and religion of all the Indo-European peoples.

[1] Bankim Chandra Chatterji, *Krishna Charitra* (The Personality of Krishna), written in Bengali and published in 1892.

But even if the mythological interpretation of the *Mahabharata* was to be admitted as valid it would make no difference to the character and spirit of the book as a compendium of the early legends of the Indo-Aryans. In its narratives and descriptions it embodies the features and atmosphere of a particular society very realistically, and this is not found in any other work in Sanskrit. For reconstructing the spirit of the first few centuries of the Aryan settlement in India the epic remains the most dependable source.

But the Krishna of the *Mahabharata* underwent a revolutionary transformation which became clearly perceptible by the beginning of the Christian era. It must have taken place a century or two earlier. Through it Krishna became the personal supreme deity of a monotheistic cult by becoming identified with Vishnu, and this Vishnu was not the Vedic Vishnu, but the Vishnu of the triad of Brahma, Vishnu, and Siva, which had grown out of the Vedic religion. The Vishnu-Krishna personal god came to be generally called Vāsudeva.

This combination is so surprising that some modern scholars have put forward the idea that the Krishna of this compound personality is not the Krishna of the *Mahabharata*, but a second Krishna. This duplication is wholly gratuitous, for the references to the new Krishna do not leave any doubt that he is the Krishna of the epic. Many inscriptions not only testify to this identification, but even assign the mythological wife of Vishnu to Krishna, and the legendary wives of Krishna to Vishnu.

Obviously, the Greek Heliodorus who became a worshipper of Vāsudeva, was a convert to this new cult. But we have no testimony whatever as to the character of the devotion which this deity evoked. I have already suggested that this Vishnu-Krishna cult was probably an imitation of the monotheistic cult of Siva. Both were part of the post-Vedic movement which brought into existence what I have called the polymorphous monotheism of the Hindus.

Krishna and Bhakti in the Gita

The mists that envelop the origin and early existence of the Vishnu-Krishna cult lift all of a sudden with the appearance of one book, the *Bhagavad-Gita*, and a new Krishna appears in it as the real, the supreme, and the only God. He also proclaims himself with an overpowering verve and resonance of tone which recalls the words in the Revelation of St John the Divine: 'I am Alpha and Omega, the beginning and the end, the first and the last.' For the first time in any Hindu text the nature of *bhakti* is also fully communicated, both intellectually and emotionally. The words *bhakti* and *bhakta* are employed, but they are never explained formally. It seems to be assumed that the meanings are known to all. The manner of employing these words are similar to that with which the word *agape* and its corresponding verb are employed in the New Testament. But no doubt is left as to the nature of the devotion which is expected, and what the devotees are expected to be.

It is impossible to determine the date of the work. But the fact that it is written in good classical Sanskrit[1] and employs the two most common classic metres would justify the conclusion that it could not have been written before the second century A.D., but may have been written a century or two later. It cannot be much later, because it contains no allusion to image worship in temples which became established and widespread by the fifth century. The *Gita* refers with lofty disdain to Vedic rituals and the florid tales of those who advocate them, and with its particular conception of devotion it could not have had more respect for the temple cult.

But whenever it was written, it established itself once and for all upon its appearance. This was all the more remarkable because it rejected the Vedic ritualistic religion. In spite of that, it captured the Hindu heart. The reason was that it offered something which no previous Hindu theory or practice had done. Thus, despite its revolt against *Sruti* (revealed scriptures, i.e. the Vedas), it was raised almost to the status of *Sruti*.

The status of the *Gita* has continued through the ages among the Hindus, though the devotion which was special to it passed out of their religion after creating a successor in whom the message was transformed. In recent times the *Gita* has been put to political use. But that exploitation, too, has become obsolete.

---

[1] I cannot understand why the Sanskrit of the *Gita* has been called archaic by some scholars, unless it is to prove the pre-Christian date of the book. Its style and diction are as simple as that of the *Mahabharata* and the *Ramayana*. The style of classical Sanskrit poetry is infinitely more difficult.

When it appeared, its teaching obviously appealed to the mind of the Hindus by the novelty of religious sentiment and experience it offered. But the book was not all new. There was a good deal in it of the traditional Hinduism of its age. Therefore, taken as a whole, it creates an impression of heterogeneity, and owing to this some scholars have supposed that it is a composite work, which certainly it is not. The impression of disunity in it is created by the fact that the old and new elements in it do not naturally cohere. It had two old elements and two new elements.

The first old element in it was its version of the *Jnana Yoga* or the discipline of knowledge, which it calls *Samkhya* without meaning the systematic philosophy which bears that name. The doctrine of this part of the *Gita* is in no way different from that of the Upanishads, with which it has many passages in common. Had this philosophical message been its only feature, it would simply have been regarded as another Upanishad. The second old element in it is Hindu self-discipline minus Hindu asceticism and self-mortification. This, the *Gita* calls *Yoga*, but this, again, is not the *Yoga* of the Yoga school of philosophy. It simply stood for that state of the mind in which a man is neither upset by sorrow nor elated by success. A man in this state is called *sthita-prajna*, i.e. a man of stabilized mentality. He is likened in a striking simile to a tortoise which withdraws its limbs into its shell. In the same way, the man of 'stabilized understanding' withdraws his senses from the objects of sense.

But the two new elements in the *Gita* were not part of the established Hindu traditions. The first of these was the doctrine of disinterested action, or *niskama karma*. According to it, a man could remain in the world and do everything which had to be done in it without any sacrifice of his religious aspirations. Indeed, no renunciation was expected from him. But the condition was that he must not expect any profit from his worldly actions and efforts. This is emphasized again and again, and a couplet which defines it has become a proverb among the Hindus. It says:

> Karmany evā 'dhikāras te
> mā phalesu kadācana.

> Thou art entitled to work,
> but never to its result.

(II. 47)

Now, such a doctrine is opposed to the natural inclinations of the human mind generally, and even more opposed to the inclinations of the Hindu mind, for a Hindu does not even worship his gods without the motive of gain. None the less, it appealed to choice spirits among the Hindus as Stoicism appealed to the Greeks and Romans. In fact, in India the attraction was greater for reflective minds. The Indian environment engendered, on the one hand, wild desires unrelated to ability and beyond all possibility of realization, and, on the other, put infinite difficulties in the way of gaining even the most reasonable objects of desire, thus creating an intolerable feeling of frustration and sorrow. This was not mere disillusionment, which cried *vanitas vanitatum, omnia vanitas*, but an open festering sore rankling day and night. The whole of Hindu philosophy was an attempt to rescue men from this mire of sorrow.[1] But the remedy it prescribed was inhuman: Be incorruptible stone or remain corruptible flesh. The *Gita* did not urge this severance of all links with the objects of the senses or with the world. Its doctrines of disinterestedness in action was easily intelligible and also emotionally satisfying. It brought into the mind peace and reconciliation with the world from a sense of having done one's duty, and it offered freedom from both sorrow and wild desires.

But the second new thing the *Gita* offered was infinitely higher, something which was not merely an armour but an adequate and positive prop of life, a great love. And the object of this love was to be a God who would never disappoint the devotee who loved him. This God was totally different from any god the Hindus had known before.

I. He was a God who was above men and not dependent on them for his functioning as the old Hindu gods were. He sought no gain from men, nor exacted any material tribute. In worshipping Him the Hindus could feel that they were not dealing with the senior partner of a business concern. The idea of contract between gods and men was wholly rejected in the new message of the *Gita*, though strangely enough it was retained in the book's exposition of orthodox doctrine.

II. This God was omnipotent, omniscient, all-pervading, and yet not an abstraction. He was personal and even more than that: he was full God as well as full man.

[1] See Chaudhuri, *The Continent of Circe* (1965), pp. 144 ff.

The way of worshipping Him was also new and easy, if only men had the mental capacity and readiness. The heavy burden of performing endless rites was taken off their shoulder. He wanted only one thing—total self-surrender and love. Yet this personal God was affiliated with the most ancient and deep-seated religious sentiment of the Hindus, which was also their Indo-European heritage, namely, pantheism. Next, as man He was one of the most beloved figures of the early Hindu legends, Krishna.

But in assessing this part of the message of the *Gita* it must not be forgotten that it was neither a dogmatic nor a philosophical treatise, but a work of devotional poetry. It follows from this that the grandeur of its message cannot be felt fully unless it is read in the original, where by the combined power of its diction, sound, and rhythm, all of which transmit an intense passion, even an unbeliever is swept off his feet. I can give only a few examples which will convey nothing better than an ideological reduction of the whole message. The ring and the intensity will be lost. It should be noted that in the *Gita* Krishna speaks as God in his own person, as Allah does in the Quran or Jesus in the Bible.

I. *Declaration of the Nature of Krishna as God.*

I am the father of this world, its mother, its nurse, its grandmother. I am the object of knowledge, the purifier, the syllable *Om*. I am *Rik, Sama, Yajus* (i.e. the three Vedas) as well. (IX. 17)

I am the goal, the supporter, the master, the witness, the abode, refuge, and friend. I am the origin, preservation, and destruction. (IX. 18)

I am the soul which abides at the heart of all things. I am the beginning, the middle, and the end. I am the letter A of the alphabet. (X. 20; X.33)

I am the foundation of the immortal and imperishable Brahman, as well as eternal righteousness and bliss. (XIV. 27)

II. *What He Demands and What He Promises*

Abandon all the ways of religion and take refuge in Me alone, and I shall emancipate thee from all evil, and be not afraid. (XVIII. 66)

Let me be all in all in thy mind, be my devotee, sacrifice to me, bow down to me, and to me alone thou shalt come. (IX. 34)

Men who have no faith in this Truth do not attain me. They will travel round the circuit of life and death. Fools despise me because they know not my status as the Lord of all beings. (IX, 3; IX. 11)

If a man offers me a leaf, a flower, a fruit, or only water with devotion, that offering of devotion I accept from him. (IX. 26)
Even if an evil-doer worships me with single-minded devotion he must be regarded as righteous in spite of all, because he has the right inclination. (IX. 30)
If those who are of base origin, such as women, Vaisyas, and Sudras, take refuge in me, even they attain the highest end. (IX. 32)
How much more would the virtuous Brahmin and the devout prince gain![1] (IX. 33)

After having proclaimed his Godhood in such words, Krishna revealed himself to Arjuna as the whole universe, and Arjuna uttered his famous hymn to Krishna as the embodiment of all phenomena. Krishna then declared that this vision could not be seen by the study of the Vedas, nor by charities, nor by performing rites, nor by severe self-mortification. This form of Krishna as the universal, infinite, and primal God was shown to Arjuna as an act of grace.

At the same time this God is also a God of righteousness, of wrath, and of retribution. Thus one finds in the *Gita* the assurance which has sustained the Hindus in all their secular tribulations:

> Whenever there is any decline of righteousness
> and an upsurge of unrighteousness,
> then do I create myself
> to destroy the unrighteous
> and to save the righteous,
> and thus re-establish righteousness
> from age to age.
> (IV. 7–8)

It has to be pointed out that this is not the orthodox Hindu doctrine of the incarnations of Vishnu. Those incarnations were meant to be special acts of intervention of the god to save the Aryan order from specific crises. And the last incarnation, Kalki, traditionally still to come, is to destroy all the unclean foreigners who have oppressed the Hindus. The incarnations which Krishna promises will come in order to save mankind from unrighteousness. Such a voice was never before heard in Hinduism, and was

[1] In its social doctrine, the *Gita* was not egalitarian, but staunchly attached to the caste system, and to it only the Brahmin and the Kshatriya were noble by birth.

not heard again after the *Gita*. But it was heard, as related in Acts of the Apostles, at Athens, where the Parthenon gleamed above the speaker: 'He hath appointed a day, in which he will judge the world by righteousness by *that* man whom he hath ordained; whereof he hath given assurance unto all *men*, in that he hath raised him from the dead.'

The question where the two new elements of the *Gita* came from has now to be considered. One thing is certain, neither existed in Hinduism before the book was written. It can be set down briefly that the doctrine of disinterestedness in action came from Stoicism, and the God of the *Gita* from Christianity. It is equally certain that both the notions were present in the Graeco-Roman world in a fully elaborated form when the *Gita* was written. These facts are so decisive that an attempt has been made to evade them by postulating that the God of the *Gita*, or at all events a prototype, existed in a popular form of Hinduism whose existence is not recorded in the old and orthodox texts. This is quite characteristic of those who deal with Indian history or Hinduism. Whenever they cannot find any evidence for anything in which they believe *a priori*, they assert that the evidence has disappeared. To deny that which exists, and to explain with prolixity what does not, has become such an integral feature of the methodology of those who deal with India and Hinduism that its queerness is not even noticed.

I shall dispose of the question of the derivation of disinterestedness in action briefly. No such thing existed before and even though preached by the *Gita* it has not taken root.[1] On the other hand, it may be assumed that the Hindus had some information about Greek philosophy. Even in the Greek translations which Asoka provided for his inscriptions familiarity with Greek philosophical vocabulary is seen.

But the question of the derivation of the God of the *Gita* from Christianity has to be taken up at greater length. The view was first put forward in a scholarly form by the great German Sanskritist, Albrecht Weber, and Lorinser was one of his students. Two lines of argument were at once advanced against the theory. First, it was pointed out that the parallel passages were analogous rather than exact reproductions, and, secondly, that the *Gita* does

[1] In Delhi I had a small roof-garden. Watching the amount of trouble I took to keep it up, all my neighbours assumed that I was a nurseryman.

not contain the Christian *kerygma,* or the developed theology. Anything more naïve can hardly be imagined. If the book contained the Christian doctrine verbatim then the Hindus would have been Christian themselves. Secondly, there was no reason for the *Gita* to be a translation of the New Testament.

The question of derivation should be decided, not by comparing the so-called parallel passages, but by the general cast of the feelings and thoughts. I would call that taking note of the typology of thought and feeling. No one reading the *Gita* without preconception can help feeling that its teaching has a remarkable similarity to that of the New Testament, so far as its notion of God and idea of devotion to him are concerned. In cultural history independent creation of ideas which closely tally with each other is very rare.

A parallel instance of derivation can be given from the cultural evolution of India in the nineteenth century. There is no doubt that the monotheistic movement in Hinduism of the late nineteenth century known as the Brahmo movement was inspired by Christianity. But the formal dogmas of this monotheism were all referred back to the Upanishads. And the Brahmos themselves were very unwilling to acknowledge their debt to Christianity. Sikhism, too, had behind it the monotheism of Islam. But Guru Nanak cited the Upanishads in his credo.

The only question which has to be considered is whether the Hindus could have any knowledge of Christianity in the age of the *Gita.* Weber assumed that there might have been Christian colonies on the borders of India to the north-west. There is no evidence for it, but it is not inherently improbable. Apart from that, there is the legend of St Thomas in India. He is supposed to have preached Christianity in south India. But knowledge of Christianity could have existed in India just as some knowledge of Hindu philosophy was present in the Graeco-Roman world.

I would, however, lay particular emphasis on the fact that neither the concept of a God of love nor the kind of devotion for him which is found in the *Gita* took root in India. Both were so exotic that they were transformed into wholly new things. The God of the book became Krishna of the Vaishnavism of later texts. The love which he demanded in the *Gita* also became a different kind of love. This transformation will now be described.

THE CULT OF KRISHNA

Krishna and the Gopis

The cult of Krishna which is now current among the Hindus and the devotion or *bhakti* on which it takes its stand, are not founded on the *Gita*. Certainly, the book has a firm place in Hindu religious life, but that only makes it like the fossil ammonite which is the symbol of Vishnu in every Hindu household. The living Vaishnavism originated with three texts: the *Vishnu Purana*, the *Harivamsa*, and the *Bhagavata Purana*. Of these, the last is the most authoritative. Doctrinally, it remains the basic book of the Krishna cult.

In the current Krishna cult the gopis or womenfolk of the cowherd clan of Vraja, where according to legend Krishna was brought up as a child, are always associated with him. They are not mentioned in the *Mahabharata*. They make their appearance in the Krishna cult for the first time in these three texts. They not only appear but are also shown engaged in singing and dancing with Krishna, and also having amorous sports collectively. The degree of familiarity varies in the three texts. In one it is not much closer than what is usually seen when young men and women amuse themselves together. Even such association is frowned upon by their elders as immodest. In another text there is a strong display of amorousness, with embracing and kissing. The degree of voluptuousness displayed also varies. But in the *Bhagavata Purana*, the basic text of Vaishnava doctrines and especially of the new Vaishnava *bhakti*, both nudity and sexual intercourse are described. No vagueness is left on this point.

The dates of these books cannot be determined. But they cannot be earlier than the eighth century, for Krishna's sports with the gopis are not mentioned in the works of classical Sanskrit literature considered in the historical part of this book. At first sight, these stories seem to have originated as secular pastoral poetry from the legend of the early life of Krishna among the cowherds. But no such work has been found. The *Vishnu Purana* and the *Harivamsa* are the only early works extant which describe Krishna's amorous adventures. Both the books belong to the class of Puranas, and it is not unusual for them to tell the stories of the gods in more or less human terms. Even those books which are regarded as religious texts at times contain passages which read like secular poetry, and describe love between men and women.

In any case, in respect of Krishna and the gopis, it was the *Bhagavata Purana* which definitely established the norm.

This book contains a good deal of dogmatic and doctrinal exposition in the philosophical style. As has been just said, doctrinally it is regarded as the most authoritative text of Vaishnavism. Anything can be made out from these expositions by a person with a metaphysical turn of mind, or nothing at all. The doctrines are obscure, and the exposition verbose. This style is normal in what might be called Hindu patristic literature.

What is neither obscure nor esoteric in the *Bhagavata Purana* is the illicit character of the relations of the gopis with Krishna as well as its erotic tone. Adultery is both the doctrinal and the practical expression of the cult of *bhakti* in this book, and adultery itself is committed collectively and promiscuously. The whole concept of religious devotion in it is based on adultery, which is given a spiritual value. The doctrinal position is that a person who loves Krishna as God must be ready to sacrifice for that love what the world regards as virtue. To give a stronger colour to this doctrine, it is represented that the sacrifice of virtue must be of the kind which is seen when a woman becomes unfaithful to her husband for the sake of a lover. But an extraordinarily subtle point, intelligible only to a Vaishnava of the Bhagavata school, is made in regard to the quality of the love which the woman must feel for her lover, Krishna. Even though they are being unfaithful to their husbands for his sake, they must not think of him as their paramour *(jāra)*, but as husband *(pati)*, because a woman's purest love is for her husband. Thus, according to the dogmatists, there is no conceptual adultery in the practical adultery.

This doctrine is driven home in parables in the manner of the New Testament. Some Brahmin women come to Krishna and offer themselves to him. But in order to put their devotion to test he upbraids them severely for their unchaste inclinations. Ashamed of themselves, they go back, and thus reveal the shallowness of their *bhakti* and lose their chance of being one with Krishna. On the contrary, some cowherd women, i.e. the gopis, also come. They are also tested in the same manner. But they refuse to be dissuaded from adultery, and are rewarded for their staunchness. Krishna accepts their love and has sexual intercourse with them, accompanied with scratching, biting, etc. These are particularized in the *Bhagavata*.

Modern Hindu commentators dwell on the sublimity and purity of the conception, and pour scorn on those who see only adulterous sexual gratification in these proceedings. They all say that these accounts must be taken allegorically. But nobody explains why such allegories should have been necessary to persuade the Hindus to have *bhakti* for Krishna, and why again, if such allurements were necessary, the *Gita* did not offer them. Even the exponents of *bhakti* of the Bhagavata school admit that the form in which it is presented in that book is the highest.

Yet the new elements which are introduced into the idea of *bhakti* can be accounted for. These elements are the following: first, love for Krishna as God must correspond to sexual love between men and women; secondly, it must be adulterous sexual love; finally, this love must be simple physical satisfaction, accompanied only by that much and that kind of emotion which is always felt when the intercourse is brought about by passion, i.e. when it is not that which is offered by a prostitute.

All three elements are intelligible in terms of life led by the Hindus in India and the psychological compulsions created by that life. First, the notion of love among them was very concrete: it was either love for a woman, wife or not, for the child, and for the mother. They could not conceive of any love which was impersonal and disembodied. Therefore as soon as they acquired the notion that a god could be loved, which was totally absent in their religion before, they began to love the supreme goddess as mother, and Krishna both as a lover and as a child, in the latter form as *Bala Gopala*. Of these two kinds of love, the sexual was bound to be the stronger, and therefore it was made the more common form. Thus in later Vaishnavism love for Krishna as God was transposed from the key of *agape* in which it was given in the *Gita*, to the key of *eros* in obedience to the law of cultural interaction that all influences received from outside are recast in the national mould.

From this to the preference for adulterous love was a short step. If the intensity of *bhakti* was to be equated with the intensity of the sexual passion, both were likely to be enfeebled by confining the latter passion to its humdrum expression in wedlock. This is universally true, in so far as sexual satisfaction is the primary object in the man-woman relationship.

Early marriage, arranged marriage, polygamy, and perpetual

widowhood generated an intense yearning for sexual satisfaction outside wedlock among Hindu women. Of this, there is overwhelming proof in Sanskrit literature, in literature in the modern Indian languages, and also in practice so far as it can be observed. The position was something like what was seen in France when arranged marriages were the rule in that country, and when every married woman actually had or was supposed to have an *amant*. Hindu poets, of course, made the most of it, and I translate a lyric by a witty Bengali poet of the eighteenth century, who makes a woman vehemently reproach Brahma the Creator for a sad failure in creation. She says:

> O cruel Creator, how can I admit thy skill,
> when thou hast failed to meet the wishes and hopes
> of a woman who does not regard the world?
> Thou couldst give two of each,—legs, eyes, and ears,—
> and yet could'st not give two wings to fly.
> Didst thou trick me because I have tested
> the strength of every variety of man in all the fourteen worlds?
> How shall I endure all this sorrow, but how can I blame others,
> when even Thou with thy four faces and regal attributes
> hast miserably failed me?

Of course, this was hyperbolic, but all notes, however high, must have a tonic as the starting point.

Lastly, the whole satisfaction in the sexual relationship is sought in the physical act, however casual. Any occasion, any man, is good enough. Even in the married state, love between husband and wife in Hindu society meant nothing more than pleasure in the sexual act, so far as it was an intimate passion, and not the more social affection.

This reduction of love to its most concrete realization stemmed from the suffering inflicted by the conditions of living in India, especially the climatic. There was only one escape from it, and that was through the swoons induced by sexual intercourse. As I have put it in an earlier book:

There is a passage in Plato, in which he gives an example of release from the sexual desire, that tyrant which is homicidal and suicidal at the same time. Cephalus is reported to have asked Sophocles in old age whether he still sought the pleasure of intercourse and was capable of it. Hush, replied the poet, my greatest joy is to have escaped from that fierce and savage master. No Hindu would have called that joy. In his revulsion from sexual enjoyment he was capable of some very tortured psychological and physiological acrobatics, but to have complete freedom was the last thing he cared for, because to give up lust was for him to turn his back on life itself.[1]

So, the supreme happiness was to continue the forgetfulness from sexual intercourse indefinitely, and if that could not be done practically the oblivion had to be sought in its vicarious creation in literature and religion. This terrible compulsion was bound to transform *bhakti* into sexual enjoyment. The *Bhagavata* only initiated the movement, which was completed in later works. *Bhakti* pursued its Hinduized course.

Krishna and Bhakti in Brahmavaivarta Purana

It is in this Purana that the Krishna cult reached the form in which it is seen today. That is to say, he is seen in it for the first time with Radha, and she as an equal object of worship with him. Krishna's love affairs are no longer with a nameless bevy of gopis. Radha is named in this Purana as the supreme mistress. In it, however, she is his wedded wife. The others remain certainly, but only as mistresses. They are legion.

Radha is wholly unknown in previous literature, and how and why she comes into the Krishna legend cannot be explained. However, after entering it she remains. For many Vaishnavas she is even more important than Krishna, for she represents the worshipper.

Since the date of this Purana is unknown the time at which the Krishna cult received this addition cannot be determined. Two inscriptions of the tenth century refer to her. This would make her cult as old, and there is no inherent improbability that the *Brahmavaivarta Purana* existed in some form in that century. I have found a reference to Radha in the well-known collection of poems in Prakrit which is called *Gatha Saptasati*, in the 89th poem of the first hundred *(sataka)*. This is surprising, for this anthology is generally dated some centuries earlier than the time of the *Brahmavaivarta Purana*. However, there is no reason to accept all the poems in this collection as equally early.

[1] *The Continent of Circe*, p. 203.

There is no doubt that the *Brahmavaivarta Purana* brought about a revolution in the cult of Krishna, and made it substantially different from what it was even in the *Bhagavata Purana*. It not only continued the erotic trend in the cult which had begun with the *Vishnu Purana* and *Harivamsa* and risen to a *forte* in the *Bhagavata* but also made it *fortissimo*. This heightened eroticism was to remain a permanent feature of the cult of Krishna.

Yet the irreconcilable dichotomy between *bhakti* and eroticism is not resolved in this Purana, strong as the latter element is in it. Its doctrinal stand is unexceptionable. Not only is the illicit and adulterous element in the love of Krishna for the gopis in the previous texts removed by making Radha his wife, the relationship is also defined metaphysically. There are some inconsistencies in the statements, but the main position is clearly set down in more than one place. This exposition is put in the mouth of Krishna in speeches to Radha. The following is the translation of one of them in the Chapter 15 of the *Krishna Janma Khanda*, or the fourth part of the book:

> Wherever you are (says Krishna) there also am I, and verily there is no difference. As whiteness is in milk, power to burn in fire, scent in earth, so am I invariably in you. Just as the potter cannot make pots without clay, goldsmiths cannot make ear ornaments without gold, in the same way I cannot create without you. You are the basis of creation by me. I am the imperishable seed . . . I am simple 'Krishna' when without you, but 'Sri (prosperous)—Krishna' with you. You are 'Sri' (prosperity), you are possession, you are like a vessel, and the embodiment of all the power belonging to others and to me. O Radha, you are the woman, I am the man, not even the Vedas can deny that. O imperishable! you are the embodiment of all, I am the same. When I am energy, you are then the embodiment of energy. Since I am not corporeal, you too are incorporeal. O Beauty! when I become the seed of everything through yoga, you become the embodiment of power and assume the form of all women!

This definition of the mutual relations of Krishna and Radha is accompanied in the book by many descriptions of the practical activities of the incorporeal couple. I cannot quote all of them, and so restrict myself to a single description out of many of their coitus, which is to be found in the same chapter from which the definition has been quoted. These narratives and descriptions are put in the mouth of Narayana or Vishnu himself who is explaining the greatness of Krishna to Narada.

Narayana *uvacha* (Thus spake Narayana):
Krishna pulled her (Radha) with both of his arms to his breast and stripped her of her clothes. Then he kissed her in four different ways. In the combat of coitus the bells in Radha's girdle were torn off, the colour on her lips was wiped off by the kisses, the leaves drawn with sandal paste on her breasts were rubbed off, her hair came loose, and the vermilion marks on her forehead disappeared.

Then Radha mounted Krishna and had reversed coitus. The red lac on her feet was rubbed off, she had goose-flesh on her body, and in her swoon could not perceive whether it was night or day. Afterwards, Krishna had coitus with her in eight positions, and tore her body to shreds by biting and scratching. The bells in Radha's girdle and her anklets made sweet sounds, and unable to bear any more Radha ceased from the combat of coitus.

Krishna now felt that in his preoccupation with Radha he was doing injustice to the other gopis, who were equally devoted to him, and so he went out to satisfy them in the park. There were, however, 900,000 of them, and in order to satisfy them Krishna became 900,000 different men. These exact figures are given in the text, and it adds that the park resounded with the coitus of 1,800,000 persons. Then it proceeds to describe the collective sexual orgy.

Narayana *uvacha* (Thus spake Narayana):
Then the supreme Guru of all the Yogis assumed many forms and had intercourse with them in such a manner as would satisfy them. O Narada! from all this coitus arose the charming sound of bells, bangles, and anklets of the women. All of them swooned from pleasure . . . Recovering consciousness Krishna began to bite and scratch them, and they him. Krishna scratched their breasts with his nails, and made marks on their firm buttocks. They were beautiful in their nakedness.

Then Narayana explained to Narada that out of the sixteen modes of coitus prescribed by those who were learned in sexual matters, Krishna executed twelve and besides performed all that was laid down to be done at the beginning of coitus, during it, and after its end. Indeed, Narayana said, Krishna did more.

The most remarkable feature of the book is not that these descriptions are found in it, but that these are accompanied by the denunciation of licentiousness in women in ferocious language, some of which is extremely coarse, e.g. the description of the vulva of a woman as a cesspool and the statement that at the mere sight of a handsome young man their organ becomes moist *(yoni klidyati)*.

Finally, the book closes with the following statement about the profit to be gained from listening to it:

> Whoever *with due control over his passions* and after having avowed the purpose of performing a rite on an auspicious occasion, listens to the fourth part of this Purana from beginning to end is undoubtedly released from the sins committed by him either in childhood, or while attaining the age of puberty, youth, and old age in tens of millions of births. [Italics mine.]

The new dimension given to *bhakti* by the *Brahmavaivarta Purana* was continued by others. But one basic departure from its version was made by them. They completely ignored the status of wife given to Radha by this *Purana* and made her, not only his mistress as the wife of another man, but also his maternal aunt *(Māmi)* as the wife of his foster-mother's brother. Thus there was not only a reversion to the pattern of *bhakti* as adulterous love established by the *Bhagavata Purana*, but also its intensification as incestuous love. The men who followed the *Brahmavaivarta Purana* as continuators of the erotic tradition were poets of considerable merit. They had more psychological insight than the author of that book.

The most famous of them was Jayadeva, who flourished in the twelfth century and is supposed to have been a poet at the court of Vallalasena, the last great Hindu king of Bengal before the Muslim conquest. His version of *bhakti* has now to be considered.

Bhakti in Jayadeva

The *Gita-Govinda* (Songs of Govinda or Krishna) has been accepted since it was composed in the twelfth century as one of the greatest texts of *bhakti* in the Vaishnava cult. Its influence has been immense all over India. Its episodes have been given graphic expression in painting, and the whole poem has been sung, because in form it is a song-cycle like Schubert's *Schöne Müllerin* or *Winterreise*, with precise directions about the melody and time for every aria. At the same time it is lyric poetry of consummate artistry, and so far as erotic feeling is legitimate in literature it expresses the feeling at its most burning.

Jayadeva himself placed it in the hands of wise and learned men with a modest confidence, and wrote that these men who might have derived pleasure from the book would correct its faults, though he had put in it all that was virtuosity in music, meditation in the Vaishnava faith, analysis in the consideration of erotic feeling, and artistry in poetry.

No fault whatever was found in it, and its high status was admitted from the very beginning. A well-known work of hagiography by Chandradatta (probably written in the sixteenth century) contains an account of Jayadeva's life in three chapters and relates a curious story about the test to which the *Gita-Govinda* was put. It says that the king who was his patron became jealous when he heard the poem, and composed another *Gita-Govinda* himself. He ordered that only his poem was to be sung and no other, and threatened severe punishment for those who disobeyed. So Jayadeva's work was neglected. But one day, going to the temple of Jagannath, the king found the poet himself singing it. In great wrath he asked whether he was not aware of his order.

The frightened Jayadeva replied that he certainly knew it, but he was singing his own poem because the Lord preferred it. In order to convince the king of this he suggested the test that both the books might be placed before the image of the god and he asked to indicate by a sign which he liked the better. The king agreed, and taking both the books placed them before the image, saying that the work which was preferred should be placed on top of the other. Then he went out with all the others, and closed the door of the sanctum himself. After a little while he re-opened the door and everybody saw that Jayadeva's *Gita-Govinda* had been placed on top of the king's. In great mortification the king gave up eating and drinking, but Krishna appeared to him in a dream, comforted him, and reconciled him to Jayadeva.

The poem is not long, and as printed in large type it occupies without the commentaries 42 demy-octavo pages. It does not relate the whole story of Radha's relations with Krishna, but only a few incidents occupying one day, thus observing all the unities of time and place. It opens with a scene in which on a cloudy day Radha is seen wandering in sorrow at her separation from Krishna, and closes with a full description of her reunion with him. As it is not possible to include here all that happens on that single day, I shall translate only the opening lament and the description of the last scene. I shall add to the translations the annotations provided by the commentators to only one stanza to show what they made of the poem.

The aria is in the second cycle, and is to be sung in the Gurjari melody. In it, unable to endure her distress any more, Radha asks her friend: 'O *Sakhi*, make Krishna have coitus with me, for I am inflamed with the desire for it', and then she recites in six strophes her anticipation of what will happen to her on the one hand and to Krishna on the other, when he arrives:

I.   I shall feel bashful meeting him after such a long time:
     but he will make me willing by saying a hundred pretty things.
     I shall smile sweetly and speak gently:
     and he will loosen the silk sari on my mons veneris. (Refrain)

II.   I shall be laid on a bed of leaves:
     and he will lie for a long time on my breast.
     I shall embrace him hard and kiss him:
     he will embrace me equally hard and kiss my lower lip. (Refrain)

III.   I shall close my eyes in langour:
     His cheeks will become beautiful with lines of pleasure.
     My body will become wet with the sweat of exertions:
     He will become tremulous with the excitement of supreme lust.
                                   (Refrain)

IV.   I shall coo with the notes of the cuckoo:
     He will surpass the directions given in the erotic books.
     Flowers in my hair will fall, and my chignon will come loose:
     He will mark my heavy and full breasts with his nails. (Refrain)

V.   The bejewelled anklets on my feet will tinkle:
     He will complete the demonstration of coitus.
     My girdle will jingle and become torn:
     He will pull me by the hair and give me kisses. (Refrain)

VI.   I shall become languid from pleasure at the moment of orgasm:
     He will half close his eyes which are like lotuses.
     My creeper-like body will sink, unable to endure any longer:
     and Krishna will be delighted by the satisfaction of his passion.
                              (Refrain: *O Sakhi*, etc.)

One should have thought that the poet was frank enough. But the commentators did not think so. They elaborated every statement circumstantially, explaining what was done and according to which direction of the *Kamasutra*, and they quoted the relevant aphorisms. I have consulted five commentaries, all old, viz. *Rasika-priya* by King Kumbha, *Rasamanjari* by Samkara Misra, *Sanjivani* by Vanamalibhatta, *Padadyotika* by Narayana Pandita, and *Jayanti* by Krishna. I shall cite what they have to say about the fifth strophe translated above.[1]

They identify the postures of coitus, as well as the movements, by the limbs involved and the sounds described. It should be explained that the *Kamasutra* not only prescribes postures *(samvesana* or *bandha* in Sanskrit) but also the movements for friction *(upasripta* in Sanskrit). Thus, with the indications given by Jayadeva, the commentators say that three separate acts of coitus are described in the fifth strophe, the first and the third by Radha in man's posture, and the middle one by Krishna in the normal man's position.

They further say that the ornaments and their sounds indicate particular movements. Thus the tinkling of the anklets on Radha's feet means she was executing the movement known as *bhramaraka* (*Kamasutra*, Bk. 2, ch. 8), in which the woman sits erect on the man with her knees flexed and rotates her hips like a potter's wheel, but only in a semicircle. That would make the anklets rotate in the same manner and the small bells on them tinkle. Then Krishna goes on top, because this particular movement was very tiring and Radha had to rest. The commentator puts that in the mouth of Radha as an explanation: 'Finding me tired by the *bhramaraka* [posture], Krishna himself would continue the coitus *(bhramaraka-bandhena śrāṃtām viditvā svayam api mām ramayishyati).*' Then Radha resumes her position on Krishna and the sounds made by her girdle with its little bells and the additional fact that its string is broken indicate, three commentators say, that she is executing the movement known in the *Kamasutra* as *prenkholita*, in which the woman waves her hips forwards and backwards and from side to side.

To conclude the description of Jayadeva's *bhakti* I shall only translate the essential verses of Radha's reunion with Krishna from the twelfth cycle:

At last Krishna comes, and they quarrel a little. But she is reconciled and, in order to punish him, she defiantly begins her coitus in the posture of a man. The poet writes:

[1] For these see *Gita-Govinda*, edited by M. R. Telang (1899); and the same work edited by A. Sharma, K. Deshpande, and Sundara Sharma (1969).

Even though tightly clasped by her arms, pressed by her heavy breasts, scratched by her nails, bitten in the lower lip by her teeth, pounded by her buttocks, pulled by the hair, and intoxicated by the honey of her lips, the Beloved felt only a partial satisfaction— O how crooked is the way of desire!

She had impetuously mounted above, resolved to win a victory over her beloved with confidence in her dexterity in the combat of coitus: but how long can man's airs be assumed successfully by a woman? The region of her mons veneris became numb, her arms and her thighs slackened, her breast throbbed, and her eyes closed.

The episode ends with Radha imploring her beloved to restore her clothes and adornments, and Krishna contemplating her body with ecstasy. Jayadeva concludes: 'May Krishna, with his eyes fixed on the breasts of Radha, purify us!'

I have already explained why in writing this book I had decided not to fight shy of plain speaking. I quote all these elaborate explanations of Jayadeva because of the stand taken up by modern Hindus. They fanatically maintain that these descriptions only illustrate in allegories man's union with God. I quote two such opinions. The author of the most exhaustive work on Hindu philosophy, the late Professor Surendra Nath Das-Gupta, C.I.E., M.A., Ph.D. (Cal. and Cantab.), D.Litt. (Rome), Fellow of the Royal Society of Literature of the United Kingdom (so he is designated on the title-page of the book), writes on p. 389 of the fourth volume of his *History of Hindu Philosophy*: 'Most of these were mystic songs of love for Krishna in erotic phraseology.'

The second explanation is from a former high official of the Government of India, S. P. A. Ayyar, M.A. (Oxon.), I.C.S., Barrister-at-law, Fellow of the Royal Society of Literature of the United Kingdom (so he also is designated on the title-page of the book from which I am quoting). He actually takes the offensive in the preface to his book *Sri Krishna: The Darling of Humanity* (1952) and declares:

There is nothing wrong in this conception of Krishna as the Husband of all Women, any more than in the conception of God as the Father of all Men. It means only Marriage with Krishna like the Marriage with Christ.

In support of this argument he quotes from the very strophes I have quoted but in a translation by Sir Edwin Arnold so unrecognizably bowdlerized that it raises doubts about the intellectual honesty of Edwin Arnold himself. Then S. P. A. Ayyar quotes St Teresa's declaration of her devotion to Christ, to parallel Radha's to Krishna.

Not all modern exponents of the Krishna cult exhibit such blatant failure of intelligence or alternatively such repulsive hypocrisy. But all of them are infected with an unctuous furtiveness in dealing with the quite open, unabashed, and even defiant eroticism of the cult. They never squarely face the psychological situation presented, which, as has been explained, is easy to see and to account for.

Fortunately, the cult can dispense with these feeble antics of modern Hindus, and the great authorities on the 'philosophy' or 'theology' of Vaishnavism are honourably free from such sophistries. For instance, the six philosophical exponents of Vaishnavism of the sixteenth century — the so-called Goswamis of Brindaban — are quite straightforward about the matter. One of them, Rupa Goswami, so far from trying to represent the eroticism as the symbolic expression of a mystic union of man with God, actually assimilates the sexual intercourse between Radha and Krishna to the absurd systematization of the sexual relationship as found in Sanskrit poetics. His gloss on the coitus between Radha and Krishna as described by Jayadeva in the aria quoted above is most revealing.

He says that the exhaustion of Radha after her strenuous coitus with Krishna in the reversed posture is one of the divergent or transient motifs of the *madhura* (literally 'sweet', but really signifying 'erotic') aspect of Vaishnava *bhakti*. This interpretation is to be found in his famous treatise *Ujjala-Nilamani* (ch. 13, v. 18), and in it he says that Jayadeva's verse embodies only that state of Vaishnava *bhakti* which is seen in the temporary exhaustion *(glani)* produced by violent coitus: i.e. it is an accidental flat in a bright melody in C major.

None of the Vaishnava 'theologians' considered the kind of *bhakti* as manifested through sexual intercourse accompanied by kissing, biting, scratching, squeezing of the breasts, waving of the hips, and orgasm as any kind of lust *(kāma)*. They took the view presented by the *Bhagavata Purana*, and developed it further. They held no truck with symbolism.

Their interpretation is found in its most characteristic form in the famous hagiographical work on the life of Chaitanya written by Krishnadas Kaviraj, a disciple of the Vaishnava philosophers of Brindaban, in the last quarter of the sixteenth century. He says that lust *(kāma)* differs from love *(prema)* as iron differs from gold. 'Lust' is satisfaction for self, whereas 'love' is nothing but satisfaction of Krishna, or in other words, lust is self-indulgence and love is the pleasure of Krishna.

Next to that, self-indulgence *(atma-sukha)* consists in paying regard to social conventions, to the way prescribed by the Vedas, to activities concerned with the body, to the promptings of shame, to the laws of restraint, to bodily pleasure, to the unrelaxed grip of the Aryan path, to the opinion of one's relatives, and to their denunciation and persecution. On the other hand, those who disregard all these and dedicate themselves to Krishna for the sake of giving pleasure to him alone, only surrender to 'love' *(prema)*.

It is this, Kaviraja declares, which is to be regarded as 'firm love' for Krishna. This love is like a laundered piece of cloth on which there is no stain. There is thus a great difference between 'lust' and 'love'—lust is darkness and love is the shining sun. There is not a trace of lust in the love of the gopis for Krishna, all that they do is for the sake of giving pleasure to Krishna.[1]

This is indeed a revolutionary doctrine of surrender to the sexual impulse in the name of religion. The only thing which it does not explain is why Krishna as God should always exact sexual intercourse as the supreme act of surrender to him and also why he would, for preference, play a passive part in the sexual intercourse. But that is Vaishavism in its latest phase. This is the strange climax to the *bhakti* or *agape* of the *Gita*, which was derived from Christianity. The dying Julian had to admit defeat at the hands of Christ, but the Hindu could say: 'Thou hast *not* won, O Galilean!'

Chaitanya and his Vaishnavism

Chaitanya is certainly the most striking figure in the whole history of Vaishnavism, and the way of devotion he preached one of the most astonishing and bizarre phenomena in the history of religion. The historical evidence on his life and activities is very complete and reliable, in spite of the presence in it of many hagiographical stories of miracles. Out of this evidence Chaitanya emerges as a

[1] *(Chaitanya Charitamrita,* Adilila, ch. 4, vv. 164–72.)

figure of history and not of legend as many of the prophets and preachers of Hinduism even of recent times have become. As presented in the two biographies written within fifty years of his death, he appears to have been a character of demoniac passion and Dionysiac frenzy, given to extravagant emotional fits from an early age. He was also a man of impressive appearance, tall and fair, as well as very handsome. The date of his birth is given as 1407 of the Saka era (A.D. 1485) and that of his death as 1455 Saka (A.D. 1533). The forty-eight years of his life are also precisely accounted for. For the first twenty-four years he lived in the world and was married. Even then he was very religious and was often engaged in devotional singing and dancing. At twenty-four he left the world and after that lived the life of a Hindu holy man, mostly at Puri on the Bay of Bengal, the seat of the famous Jagannath (anglicized as Juggernaut). During this period he also travelled for six years, going to south India as well as to upper India as far as Brindaban. He died at Puri.

His physical presence, personality, and behaviour were the real force behind the new form of Vaishnavism he preached. These impressed people so much that they joined his movement in crowds, and increased its momentum by the sheer weight of numbers. He was looked upon as an incarnation of God, and miraculous tales gathered around his life. Three of these might be reproduced here.

He was said to have been born after not less than thirteen months of pregnancy of his mother, and soon the symbols of Vishnu were seen on his feet and hands. He was also born with philosophical knowledge. One day, when he was a toddler, his mother gave him some parched rice and sweets to eat, and went to the kitchen to finish her cooking. When she came to look after him again she found him eating the soil from the mud floor instead of the rice and the sweets. When she scolded him for this he cried and complained of unfair treatment. He said that the rice and sweets were only products of the earth, and so, instead of eating earth at one remove, he was doing that directly. Astonished, his mother cried out: 'Who has taught thee *Jnana Yoga* at this age?' This remark showed what *Jnana Yoga* (the Hindu Way of Knowledge) appeared to be in popular imagination.

With his devotional singing and dancing he tamed and converted wild beasts, even surpassing Orpheus. When going to

Brindaban from Puri he took a short cut through the forests of Orissa instead of going by the well-known roads. Even now this region is infested with wild elephants and tigers. But these and other wild animals always made way for Chaitanya. One day in his absent-mindedness he trod on a tiger which was lying in his path. His companion was terrified. But Chaitanya only asked the tiger to chant the name of Krishna, and the beast stood up on its hind legs and began to sing about Krishna. Shortly afterwards, deer were so charmed by his singing that some does joined and marched with him reciting the name of Krishna. Some tigers also came up, and overwhelmed by the message of love began not only to sing with the does, but also to embrace and kiss them, and the does too returned the caresses.

In later tradition the memory of the true personality of Chaitanya became dim, and he was represented as a very gentle character, who was always preaching love and was also ready to turn the other cheek. But near contemporary biographers show him as a very aggressive man, always ready to go over to the offensive against those who thwarted him. He defied not only the Brahmin pundits who opposed and vilified him, but even the Muslim Qadi who at the instigation of the Brahmins forbade the processions. Chaitanya threatened to kill the judge, and with his followers attacked his house, upon which the Qadi admitted the truth of the new message.

Such a revolutionary character was bound to dominate the populace, and Chaitanya put an irresistible power behind his movement by the sheer abnormality of his goings on. The Brahmins said that his extravagant singing and dancing bouts were due to drunkenness. But besides the impression created by his personality, the religious situation in Bengal in the late fifteenth century also helped his movement.

Chaitanya's movement was one expression of a revival of the Vaishnava cult during the fifteenth century all over northern India. The cult had not only continued to exist after the Muslim conquest of northern India, but was given a more fervent form by a number of popular preachers and writers. Of this, two poets in early Hindi, Suradas and Tulsidas, provide sufficient testimony. On the other hand, the erotic pastoral poetry with a religious colouring, as initiated by Jayadeva in Sanskrit at the end of the twelfth century, was also continued, and by the end of the fifteenth century a large body of poetry of very great excellence had been written in the middle Bengali and Maithili dialects by four poets, namely, Chandidas, Vidyapati, Govindadas, and Jnanadas. It is not known if this poetry was in any way connected with the actual practice of Vaishnavism in Bengal. In any case, the cult itself, even if it existed there, did so in a very weak form, and was not brought to life until Chaitanya revived it. Therefore this poetry of the loves of Radha and Krishna had better be regarded as secular pastoral poetry, despite the religious formulas which were inserted at the end of the pieces to connect them with Krishna.

Chaitanya, however, read them eagerly and continuously, and imbibed all their passion. On the one hand, he brought the strong erotic feeling present in this poetry into the love for Krishna preached by him, and, on the other, made this corpus of lyrics part of the new Vaishnava literary canon. This gave a new dimension to the cult of Krishna. This was a revolution in the religious life of Bengal, for it had reached a stage of dry formality at the higher social level and triviality at the lower. The most recondite form of priestly pursuits was to be found in the study of *Smriti* (Hindu sacred law) and philosophy, more especially logic *(Nyaya)*, in both of which Bengal and Mithila had pre-eminence. But both the pursuits were formal, scholastic, and incapable of touching the heart. On the other hand, practice was confined to the performance of the elaborate rituals of Brahmanism. At a lower level was the worship of the minor deities of the common people like the goddess of birth (Shashthi) and the goddess of snakes (Manasa or Vishahari).

The followers of Chaitanya were perfectly conscious that they were rescuing the people of Bengal from a state of religious decay. Brindaban Das, his first biographer, expressly referred to the state of religion in order to explain the reception of the message of his master by the people. He said that Chaitanya was wholly misunderstood by the orthodox Hindus of his times on account of his ecstatic behaviour. He was given to shouting, roaring, dancing, and crying from religious excitement, and nobody understood that. People at large, he added, only knew the rituals of daily worship. Some worshipped Shashthi, some Manasa, and others Mangal Chandi (a popular form of Durga who confers welfare), and they took great pride in doing all this. Brindaban Das also referred with disgust to yet others who worshipped demons with meat and alcoholic drinks. This was, of course, a reference to Tantric worship. The whole world, Brindaban said, was sunk in darkness *(tamas)*. The aversion of the followers of Chaitanya to the orthodox pundits who specialized in sacred law and philosophy was greater because they were the most determined opponents of their master. They poured scorn on these men as 'sophisters' with Rabelaisian contempt and derision. In fact, argument, according to the school of Chaitanya, was the great enemy of faith.

To this world Chaitanya brought a passion which created not only enthusiasm for religion, but also an exuberance which was orgiastic. In his own religious feeling the strongest element was eroticism, whose precise character as it existed in his mind has to be explained. He felt a love for Krishna which went beyond Radha's adulterous love, because in spite of the keenness which the awareness of adultery gave to it, mere adultery was not sharp enough for him. At first his love for Krishna resembled the per-fervidness of a young girl who had fallen in love with a man but, though erotically excited, had not yet been united with him. Then it sought even greater intensity in a vicarious experience of fornication, that is, in the pleasure found by an unmarried girl in pre-marital sexual intercourse with her lover.

Of this Chaitanya's fondness for a famous lyric in Sanskrit provides striking proof. It runs as follows:

> Yah kaumāra-haraḥ, sa eva hi vara!—
> s 'tā eva Chaitra-kṣapā!—
> S'te ch'onmīlita-mālati-surabhayaḥ
> praudhāh kadambā'nilāh;
> Sā ch'aivāsmi; tathāpi tatra
> surata-vyāpāra-līlā-vidhau,
> Revā-rodhasi, vetasī-taru-tale
> chetaḥ samutkaṇṭhate.

I also reproduce the translation of the piece I have given in my *Continent of Circe:*

> Stole he my maidenhead, and today's husband he!
> Just the same are nights of spring;
> Blossoming málati, cadámba's pollen blown
> Scent the self-same heavy breeze;

I, too, the same, same she!—Still, by Reva narrows,
  'Neath a tree in tangled cane,
Ah! on that very spot, for coitus-fantasies
  wistful, wistful grows the heart![1]

Now, this poem is quite straightforward in its confession of an awareness of the difference in the intensity of passion between permitted and habitual sexual relations within wedlock and their romantic beginnings in secret meetings in wild places before marriage. How and why Chaitanya established an analogy between this feeling and his love for Krishna is most interesting to see.

One day he was going with the car procession of Jagannath at Puri, dancing, and also shouting at the sight of the idol that he was at last meeting Him for whom he had been burning with erotic excitement. At that time he came upon the lyric quoted above and at once realized that his feeling for Krishna was embodied in it. He said to his followers that only he and one of his disciples, Damodar Svarup, knew the real meaning of this lyric.

This would not be understood without a reference to the legends and iconography of the Krishna cult. Though Puri is one of the great centres of Vaishnavism, the image of Krishna in the great temple is not joined with that of Radha, as it is in all later iconography. In the form of Jagannath, Lord of the Universe, he is shown there with his brother Balabhadra and sister Subhadra. That is to say, the image is of the Krishna of the *Mahabharata*. This Krishna did not satisfy Chaitanya, who wanted not only a 'Krishna associated with Radha in a bond of adulterous love, but also a Radha who felt like the young woman of the lyric.

One of the disciples of Chaitanya, Rupa Goswami, was present when Chaitanya found this poem. He at once guessed what was in Chaitanya's mind, and wrote down his interpretation on a piece of palm-leaf. Then he thrust the leaf into the thatch of his own cottage and went off to bathe in the sea. At that time Chaitanya came to see Rupa, and accidentally looking up saw the leaf. He took it down and read what was written on it. He was astonished to find how exactly Rupa had set down his own feelings. He had written a *sloka* (stanza in verse) by way of interpreting the old lyric and put it in the mouth of Radha as a remark to a companion of hers:

[1] See *Continent of Circe*, pp. 142–3.

The Krishna whom I am meeting at Kurukshetra is the
   same beloved.
I am also the same Radha.
The pleasure we get from our union is still the same.
None the less, my heart yearns for the woods on the banks of
   the Jumna,
   made joyous by the sweet treble notes of his flute.

Chaitanya was so delighted that when Rupa came back from
the sea the first thing he did was to fall on him and give him slap
after slap of affection. Then he asked: 'How didst thou guess what
was in my mind?' What it meant was that, as Chaitanya felt,
Krishna could not be loved with the utmost possible intensity
when he was being taken out with pomp and splendour in that
procession at Puri, which was like his being with the Kuru clan
as depicted in the *Mahabharata*; he could be really loved in the
woods of Brindaban where there was Radha and the love was
illicit; and not only that, even that illicit love had to be consum-
mated not in adulterous sexual intercourse alone, but in fornication on the part of a virgin in love, as described in the lyric. There
could be no clearer rejection of the Krishna of the *Mahabharata*
and of the *Gita* than was seen in this attitude.

It was natural that the preachings of Chaitanya which was
marked by such an intensity of passion should make converts
among a people for whom religion had degenerated into mere
ritual or sordid adherence to superstition. The outcome was that
in Bengal the status given to Vaishnavism by Chaitanya has never
been lost. Decisive evidence for the stamp which he left on the
religious life of the Bengali people is to be found in the fact that
in almost every affluent household there is a family shrine with
the images of Radha and Krishna in close embrace. Even the
Saktas, or worshippers of Durga by sectarian affiliation, have this
shrine as a matter of form, though they, being mostly of the aristocracy or the gentry, look down on the Vaishnavism of the professionals and the common people.

But weakening of this Vaishnavism also began quickly, almost
with the death of Chaitanya. For one thing, passion of the type
as seen in Chaitanya who had a very abnormal type of sensibility,
and as preached by him with all the ardour of that abnormality,
could never last indefinitely. Human nature cannot tolerate such
a thing for a long time. But the dogmatic turn that the movement

took immediately after his death diluted the passion and made the love for Krishna as felt and preached by him still weaker. This was a strange paradox, because his disciples took the very path in trying to create a philosophical dogma of Vaishnavism which the movement had vehemently denounced and totally rejected. That was philosophizing about religion.

The basic stand of this school of Vaishnavism was that no one could realize Krishna in his life by means of intellectual effort, *tarka* or argument as the original Vaishnavas called it. According to them Krishna was accessible only to love. Yet some of the most eminent followers of Chaitanya took this very barren path of dogmatizing. In fact, their philosophizing was worse than the expositions of the professors of sacred law and logic, because those forms of mental activity were intellectual and could give scope to a good deal of finespun argumentation. But when applied to a form of devotion like that of Chaitanya, which was wholly emotional, philosophizing made the message fall between two stools. On the one hand, it froze the emotion and even ossified it, and, on the other, it could not create any valid intellectual system. Worse rigmarole than what is to be found in the philosophizing of the Vaishnava dogmatists, especially the three Goswamis, Rupa, Sanatana, and their nephew Jiva, cannot be imagined. It is permissible to assign a motive behind this word-mongering, which was to camouflage the frank eroticism of the Vaishnava cult.

But it was accompanied by something worse, a dogmatic exposition of the eroticism as eroticism, which made it vicarious and therefore unpleasant to the last degree. Lust if red-hot is natural and contagious, but if it becomes frigid it repels. The Vaishnava exegetists brought in this frigidity. The pioneer in this venture was Rupa Goswami, who established analogies between the different amorous states of Radha and the states of sexual feeling as systematized in Sanskrit poetics or *Rasa Sastra*. As applied to secular poetry, this systematization was heartless and absurd enough; by being extended to the religious sphere it became repulsive, and only a pretext for indulging in vicarious sensuality by men who had neither the strength of body nor the strength of passion to satisfy lust in action. The discussion of *Rasa (Rasa-ālāpan)* in private was one of the *menus plaisirs* of the Vaishnavas, especially learned Vaishnavas. Certainly, the discussion of the other *rasas* (emotional states), especially affection for children (*vātsalya*), was also included in these discussions. But for the most part they concentrated on the sexual passion. It was like the facetious recreations of salacious old men. This unpleasant streak of eroticism never disappeared from Vaishnavism.

The next reason for the weakness of Vaishnavism was its institutionalization. A whole hierarchy of the Vaishnava cult as preached by Chaitanya was established. It has been briefly described in a previous chapter. This was also accomplished by the kind of monasticism which Vaishnavism introduced. The *maths* and *akharas* with their *mohants* (abbots) created a social order with vested material interests. Furthermore, there appeared in Bengal a special Vaishnava caste. All that tended to make the living faith of Chaitanya a structural extension of the static Hindu society.

Last of all, the message of Chaitanya, so far as it remained living, gradually acquired a class affiliation in Bengal, which was like a wealthy family's going down in the world. When Chaitanya preached, his followers came from all classes of society. In fact, many of his most distinguished adherents came from the pundit or learned class. But in course of time the emotional devotion of this school of Vaishnavism became the possession of the lower castes, especially those who carried on trade. It was not that the aristocracy or the gentry wholly rejected Vaishnavism, but among them it remained a formal cult, whereas among the common people it was emotional. However, this class affiliation also made the emotion crude. It became maudlin and undignified, so as to draw on it the ridicule of the more sophisticated classes or castes.

Devotion to Krishna in the People

Bewildering in its variety as the Krishna cult has been seen to be so far, that however does not complete the story of the cult. Beyond all its specialized forms it also created a general devotion which constitutes a very attractive part of Hindu religious life, interwoven as it is with the world. If one wants to see how the love of Krishna can exist apart from its more extreme forms and bring a soothing influence on Hindu life he cannot do better than turn to Mirabai, a princess of the sixteenth century, and read her songs of devotion to Krishna.

Her existence is historical, though many legendary details have been added to it. She lost her husband before she was twenty-four, and also her father, father-in-law, and grandfather. These bereavements made her turn to religion in the specific form of Vaishnavism. She became famous for her songs, which are sung all over northern India by those who worship Krishna in a truly religious spirit. Her love of Krishna is so typical of Vaishnava *bhakti* at its most popular that some idea of it has to be given.

Almost all her songs are quotable, for although their keynote is the same they range over a wide gamut of emotions. I can only quote one:

O Shyam[1] I am afflicted with Thy love.
By the Grace of the Teacher, have I found Thee.
So is my folly driven away from me.
Of this body I will make the lamp and of my mind the wick:
With the oil of love will I fill it and tend its flame day and night.
Wisdom shall be the parting of my hair, and understanding its
    ornament.
O dusk-faced One, for Thy sake will I sacrifice my wealth and my
    youth.
Many-coloured is this bed and diverse are the flowers spread over it.
I await the coming of Shyam. To this day He has not come.
The months of *shravan* and *bhadon* have come and with them the
    rainy season has set in.
The brows, like dense clouds gathered in the sky, send down the tear
    drops like rain.
Unto Thy care did my parents entrust me. Thou knowest best what
    is for my good.
No other Master will I dote on excepting Thee.
Thou art the perfect Brahma, O Lord. O let me share Thy seat!
Make Mira Thine own, O Lord: she is bewildered in her separation
    from Thee.[2]

This is a love which is very different from Jayadeva's. None the less, it is not *agape*, but *eros* raised to the spiritual plane, which is also an expression of love recognized both in Greek philosophy and Christian piety. It has marched towards the goal, but not yet made the ascent from human to divine love, of which both the Neo-Platonists and Dante spoke.

This is a kind of love which a woman can feel either for God or

[1] Shyam (meaning Dark) is a name of Krishna.
[2] The translation is by R. C. Tandan in *Songs of Mirabai* (1934). It must be added that Mirabai's language is difficult, and texts differ.

husband when the relationship with the husband rises to the spiritual without taking off its feet from the physical base. A great many women, who have never found love of any kind in life, have thought of both husband and God in this way. To illustrate this, I shall quote two dialogues between two young women in each case from two novels by that very great writer of Bengal, Bankim Chandra Chatterji.

In the first of these dialogues one young woman asks another whether she is married. The other replies:

2nd Girl: Yes, after a sort.

1st Girl: What is 'after a sort'?

2nd Girl: I was married to Krishna.

1st Girl: Is he your husband?

2nd Girl: Yes, because he is my master in every sense. So, he is also my husband.

1st Girl: I don't know. You have not had a husband, and you can say that. If you had you would not have been satisfied with Krishna.

2nd Girl: Every woman can love Krishna, for his beauty is infinite, his youth is infinite, his splendour is infinite, and his virtues are infinite.

1st Girl: I do not understand this.

2nd Girl: Why not? Above everyone else, God is the master of us all. The husband is only a woman's master, but God the master of all. Why two Gods, my dear? What will be left for any of them if we divide the little *bhakti* of our little hearts between two Gods?

1st Girl: Nonsense. There is no limit to a woman's *bhakti*.

2nd Girl: There is no limit to a woman's love. But *bhakti* and love are different things.

1st Girl: I have yet to learn that. Both are new to me.

Saying this she bursts into tears, and the other wipes her tears and says: 'I see that you have suffered much, sister. I had no idea of that love.'

The other dialogue takes place between two young women, one of whom is a *sannyasini*, who has left the world and become a *religieuse*, and the other a woman who has had to leave her husband due to very tragic circumstances. After the second young woman had related why she has taken to the road and is going from one place of pilgrimage to another, the *sannyasini* says: 'It seems you have hardly met your husband. How could you love him so much?'

2nd Young Woman: You love God. Have you seen him?

S.: No, but I think of him day and night.

2nd Young Woman: I too think of my husband day and night, and I have done so since he forsook me when I was a girl. I have worshipped him every day when I have worshipped our god at home. When I have bowed down at his feet I have thought I was bowing to my husband.

There are cases in which human love and divine love come so close to each other that they are not distinguishable, for both partake of divinity as well as humanity. Mira's love for Krishna was of this type, and many women have felt for Krishna like her.

Nevertheless, love for Krishna at every level of Hindu society or with all types of character, has never been the same. One kind of love for him has never been able to shed the old Hindu lust. Thus a substratum of sub-erotic feeling is always lurking in his cult. This sometimes leads women to dangerously ambiguous relationships with their Gurus or spiritual guides.

One thing which should always be kept in mind in dealing with the Krishna cult is that Krishna can be all things to all men. He can give the liar the impudence to utter any lie, the man who serves truth the courage to face the starkest truth, the jester the occasion to exhibit his drollery. But to *l'homme sensuel moyen hindou* he is the most accessible of all his gods. Even an Englishman, who is hated by all modern Hindus as an arrogant imperialist, could write of Krishna in this vein:

There came up from the water a snatch of a love-song such as the boys sing when they watch their cattle in the noon heats of late spring. The Parrot screamed joyously, sidling along his branch with lowered head as the song grew louder, and in a patch of clear moonlight stood revealed the young herd, the darling of the Gopis, the idol of dreaming maids and of mothers ere their children are born— Krishna the Well-Beloved.[1]

---

[1] R. Kipling, 'Bridgebuilders', in *The Day's Work* (1898), p. 33.

Chapter Four

GAIN FROM RELIGION

A PEOPLE who had submitted to the jurisdiction of religion so completely in respect of every activity of theirs in the world had the right to expect religion to offer them an adequate *quid pro quo*. That, the Hindus received in full measure, and it was not simply in the form of material welfare, with which they expected to be rewarded by their gods. With men, the satisfaction of a passion is a far more powerful motive for action than the satisfaction of an interest. So far as anything desired by men can be fully realized, this satisfaction the Hindus obtained from their religion. The two most powerful human desires are for power and for protection, the first being dominant in those whose vitality is above average, and the second in those in whom it is not sufficient for the trials through which they have to pass. The Hindus got all the opportunities for asserting power on the one hand, and, on the other, protection and a sense of security, from their adherence to their religion.

Naturally, the two urges cannot be wholly separated even in one individual, but by and large those who want power and those who look for protection can be found to form distinguishable groups in a society. In ancient times perhaps the Hindus as a community were distinguished more by pride of life and love of power than by inertia and a weak will to live. But in recent centuries the majority has been formed by the weak ones, who yearn after protection and peace of mind and not for power and domination. This division of character was clearly seen in the religious history of the Hindus. Some religious Hindus, who were however a minority, sought power through a religious vocation, but the majority looked only for protection and comfort. The professionals in Hindu religious life, that is to say, those who left the world to devote themselves to religion, were ready to concede that a majority would remain satisfied with protection and peace, but they had a certain condescension for this aspiration, and considered power to be the higher end.

One day this was brought home to me in a casual, but therefore all the more significant, way. I was listening to a conversation between an eminent barrister of Calcutta who was also a well-known political leader, and a learned professor of Sanskrit who belonged to the Guru clan of the barrister. The barrister suddenly looked up and appeared to be meditative. Then he remarked as if to himself: 'There is peace in religion.' The pundit, who had a blazing vermilion mark on his forehead, replied with a smile which seemed to be compassionate, though he was the younger man: 'Also power.' The barrister had completed his education in England, the pundit was the product of traditional Hindu learning.

In describing the gains from religion of these two groups, which were of different kinds, the humble ones should be given precedence because they were more numerous than the proud ones. But these were only the 'Commons', so to speak, in Hindu religious life, whereas the proud ones were the 'Lords'.

Part I—Gains for the Commons in Hinduism

Support in the World. The majority depended on religion for support in going through life for which their animal vitality was not sufficient. In the first instance, this was due to the weakening of the will to live brought about by the decadence of all cultures, but also by the exposure over centuries to the enfeebling climate. The two in combination undermined confidence in dealing with the problems of life rationally and created a sense of the inadequacy of human effort. Thus the Hindus came to feel that without help and succour from the gods their life and welfare would always be in peril.

Political history also made its contribution to the sense of insecurity. Political order and stability have always been exceptional in India, and the longest of these exceptional periods was certainly the two hundred years or so of British rule. But even then ordinary people could expect protection solely from the more flagrant or widespread type of oppression. Petty oppression and economic exploitation were continuous. So, even for security of life, and not simply for prosperity, the Hindus had to turn to religion. They did so, not through the promptings of that religiosity which regards all that comes to or is given to man as gifts from God, but from a conviction of its practical urgency.

The general sense of insecurity also created as its particular product an obsession among the Hindus with the idea of being surrounded by relentless enemies. No one who has lived in India and come in contact with the life of the people can remain unaware of this. Fear of enemies haunts Hindu life. This fear is, of course, descended from the primitive's fear of all strangers, but was extended to an absurd degree. All relatives, neighbours, acquaintances, even wives and sons, were regarded as potential enemies. Often quite unjustifiably, every Hindu regarded some of his acquaintances as his actual enemies and attributed his failures to their machinations. Beyond them were the unknown enemies, like the unknown gods of the Greeks.

In the social outlook of the Hindus the enemies of a person far outnumbered his friends. So one preoccupation in their life was to disappoint the enemies. So, all well-wishers urged a man not to give joy and comfort to his enemies by quarrelling with friends and relatives. In Bengal, for instance, if two brothers quarrelled a well-wisher would ask why they were providing joy for their enemies. Looking at a healthy child a grandmother, mother, or aunt would say: 'May he grow up like this and put ashes in the mouths of our enemies.' One of the satisfactions of doing well in life for a Hindu was not only to be comfortable himself, but also to mortify his enemies. In the villages the news of a woman in labour would not be given for fear that some enemy would utter spells to delay the birth of the child. This fear from fellow-men was, from the practical point of view, greater than the fear from evil spirits, terrifying as that also was.

Comfort for these fear-ridden men and protection from known and unknown enemies and all evils could come only from religion in the last resort. Thus all religious observances and rites had a protective orientation. In addition, there were particular deities and rites to ensure welfare and security. Some of the rites were meant to enlist support from a god or goddess against evil, others to bribe a mischief-making deity. For instance, in Bengal a goddess called Mangal Chandi or Chandi of Welfare (a popular form of the Mother Goddess Kali) was worshipped every Tuesday in order to secure immunity from evil, and every Saturday Sani (Saturn), who in Hindu mythology is the personified Evil Eye, was worshipped to be bribed off from mischief-making.

Consolation. Hindus would fall back on religion in their sorrows and disappointments as if they had heard the message: 'Come unto me, all ye that labour and are heavy laden, and I will give you rest.' This attitude is certainly one of those which came into the original Brahmanic religious consciousness from the outside. So far as the ancient Hindus had recourse to religion for combating their troubles they went to it, not for consolation after accepting defeat, but only to stage a return after being reinforced by the power of religion. Hindu philosophers were even more severe. They did indeed declare that philosophy was intended to deliver men from sorrow, but for this end they propounded systems-of philosophy of such a character that ordinary Hindus thought that the medicine was worse than the disease. But in Hinduism as it has been known for centuries, consolation in sorrow has certainly been one of the most precious gifts from their religion for its followers.

But though the Hindus wanted consolation, they did not want freedom from sorrow, because sorrow was a real emotional enjoyment to them, and even the grief from bereavement they kept alive as long as they could by hanging up a photograph of the lost father, mother, husband, or child, adding it to the collection of tawdry pictures of Krishna or Kali. Men and women, when cheated by relatives of money, went mad, or turned their back on the world to become religious. This also happened in recent times when there was frustration of an idealistic aspiration. In the course of the nationalist movement, some Bengali revolutionaries turned sadhus in the traditional Hindu manner when they were released from imprisonment or detention and had realized the futility of their method of political action.

A woman, when she lost a child, would become a pathetic *dévotée*, not in the spirit of European women of former ages who took refuge in convents, but simply as the same mother who had recovered her child physically in an image of the baby Krishna. The same type of iconolatry would be exhibited by a barren woman or a woman abandoned by her husband. This is also an appeal of Krishna, added to those described in a previous chapter.

Joy of Life. Furthermore, in recent centuries their religion has been for the Hindus the only source of joy in their life. If the consolation derived from religion was its cool and shady side, the joy which they derived from it must be regarded as the bright and sunny aspect. This must be regarded as the most positive and cheerful side of their religious practice.

The general tenor of Hindu life is a dull grind into which a living quality is not infused even by the insatiable avarice which is the strongest secular passion of the Hindus.[1] From this only religion provided a way of escape. The many festivals of the Hindus distributed round the year were interludes of real happiness, breaking the monotonous and dreary course of their worldly life. Without these the Hindus would have died of inanition.

The happiness was of different kinds. At one end was the wild breaking out from fullness in the festival of Holi with its sprinkling of colour, horseplay, and ribaldry, which certainly was a survival from primitive life, in which Saturnalias provided a safety valve. But there were other festivals in which the joy, though rising to exuberance, was as normal and refreshing as the rain during the monsoons. The most important of these festivals were the Durga Puja in Bengal, the Dussera in northern India, the Diwali and the Janmashtami everywhere. All of them brought renovation to life.

Till recently every kind of public entertainment, display, music, dancing, plays, or banqueting, was provided by religion, and was hardly ever seen as purely secular amusement. It is necessary to note that movement and excitement in life did not come to the Hindus through their social intercourse, which was extremely formal and staid. These came from their gregarious associations. Thus gregariousness which makes them spill out of their homes in immense concourses is a very strong emotion, almost a passion, with the Hindus. To satisfy this Hindu society has devised a means, and it now goes under the name of *tamasha*, i.e fun of all kinds. Everyone who has lived in India has noticed the irresistible attraction which being in a crowd and watching some spectacle has for Indians. In recent years even the funerals of great national leaders like Mahatma Gandhi or Nehru have had the character of a *tamasha* for those who lined the streets. In old time all such *tamashas* were part and parcel of religious life, and the idea of purely secular amusement was not present in the Hindu mind. They regarded all sensuous enjoyment not associated with the sacred as sinful, and therefore legitimized it by making it part of religion.

English observers who witnessed the festivals and fairs, with

[1] I have described the sorrowful aspect of Hindu life in Chapter 11 of my book *The Continent of Circe*, see pp. 223–34.

their immense crowds, and the accompanying wildness and complete absence of reverence and self-restraint, were often scandalized, and the missionaries often denounced them as grossly immoral. More especially, the car festival of Jagannath at Puri in Orissa and elsewhere was singled out as an orgy of licentiousness. But an Englishman signing himself 'A.A.' wrote a very sensible article on the subject in *Fraser's Magazine*, then edited by the historian Froude. (See *F.M.*, New Series, Vol. VII, January–June 1873.) He had lived in Calcutta, and himself seen the car festival of Krishna at Serampore near Calcutta, and he wrote:

> The other charge, of obscene and immoral practices, seems even more captious. Of course, in gatherings of such magnitudes as the annual *melas* at Puri, Serampore, and other seats of Jagannath's worship, excess and immorality must to some extent occur; but all reliable evidence has hitherto gone to show that the people are more decent and orderly than any English multitude of the same dimension would be. From a personal observation of three festivals of Jagannath at Serampore, in the vicinity of Calcutta, the second seat of Jagannath's worship, the writer has no hesitation in asserting that, apart from the feeling that the whole ceremonial is essentially idolatrous and barbaric, there is nothing said or done by either priests or worshippers that need offend the taste of the most extreme precisian.

There is, however, one aspect of the matter to keep in mind. Religion among the Hindus was never separated from their general life, and so they saw nothing wrong if provision for sensual enjoyment was made at the fairs and festivals. Just as men went to the religious fairs to sell their goods, so also professional prostitutes moved to them to earn extra money. Everybody knew that, and I have seen that myself. In the town in which I was born and brought up there were on its outskirts licensed houses in which the prostitutes lived permanently. But at the time of the great fair which was held near the town for the swing festival of Krishna they moved to temporary huts on the site of the *mela* or fair. In ancient India, prostitute mothers sent out their daughters properly dressed up to attract rich clients at all festivals.

These large festivals and fairs were very democratic, though many of them were formally held under the patronage of a prince, priestly family, or landowner. Participation in them was spontaneous, and the people who came to them, for entertainment or profit, all made contributions to their success in their different ways. The numbers of people seen in them constituted an important element of their success, because all emotions gain in volume and intensity in proportion to the size of the gatherings.

In addition to such large festivals to which people came from a whole province and in some cases even from all over India, there were smaller local festivals which were privately organized by a local prince, landowner, or well-to-do middle-class family, but which, too, were open to all. These were less tumultuous, but not less joyous for that reason. In fact, the joy and happiness which the participants got out of these smaller festivals or fairs had a different quality. For one thing, the feelings were more personal than collective. Besides, they conveyed a greater sense of hallowedness, and balanced the movement and animation with a weight of fullness.

E. M. Forster has described such a festival as held under the patronage of a minor Indian prince in his *Hill of Devi*, and it is an account of Gokul Ashtami, i.e. the festival of the birth of Krishna. I myself as a boy felt this happiness in my ancestral home, and I have described that in my autobiography. By a subtle association the happiness created, or rather had, a material complement, and would certainly not have been complete without that. In my ancestral home, which was a collection of traditional huts, the joy of the Durga Puja was given a touch of exotic glory by the lighting imported from abroad: the lustre chandeliers, sconces, inverted bell-jars serving as oil lamps, as well as Chinese lanterns of coloured paper. The women put on all their jewellery and finest clothes. 'The women in shining silk and loaded with gold ornaments, stood at the sides of the image of the goddess like two rows of ballerinas, making on the whole a well-composed scene even when in motion.'[1] Yet in all this display there was no motive of showing off, present or perceived. Here at all events the extravagant Hindu adornment became a part of devotion, as if it was only an offering to the gods.

I do not think I can convey the spirit of tacit happiness in these smaller festivals better than by translating from Bengali the description given in a book published at the beginning of this century of the worship of a minor goddess, Shasthi—the goddess of births who is shown as riding a cat, the symbol of prolificness.

[1] *Autobiography of An Unknown Indian* (1951), pp. 68-9.

In the villages she is worshipped outdoors, under a banyan or a
peepul tree. This is the description:

> Most of the women who were there had come in their best make-up
> and adornment, and were gathered under the tree. They had in
> their hands trays laden with incense, lamps, and food offerings.
> The priest had taken his seat, with all the vessels of worship
> arranged about him. The women stood near and watched. The
> low and sweet hum of their talk filled the shrubbery. Some of them
> had nose-pendants, some nose-rings; their bangles tinkled, silk
> saris rustled in the wind; the scent of hair-oil filled the air. The
> foliage above them was so dense that the sun in the sky could not
> see their faces lit up by a peaceful contentment. A little girl in blue
> was leaning against her mother and watching the rite opening her
> large eyes with their lashes shaded with lamp-black even wider. A
> young mother stood with her baby at the breast, looking by turns
> at the worship and her baby, and fanning it with the fringe of her
> sari waved with graceful twists of her bangled wrist.[1]

The life of these women apart from religion was not only trivial,
but also disturbed by rivalries and jealousies, and at best it was
spiced only by petty gossip. It became transformed at the festivals.

Another extraordinary feature of the religious life of latter-day
Hindus was that it was religion alone which kept them in touch
with Nature and its beauties. The Hindus in ancient times were
as sensitive to Nature as any European could be. But with the
centuries they became totally insensitive, in fact so insensitive
that they neither would nor could say like blind Milton: 'Thus
with the year seasons return, but not to me returns day, or the
sweet approach of ev'n or morn, or sight of vernal bloom, or
summer's rose . . .' Yet religion re-established the contact, in the
first instance by making them aware of the cycle of seasons with
their varied beauties and by making it identical with the cycle of
their *fasti*.

The Hindus then responded to the seasons with something like
the response of the plants. Thus it happened that the Durga Puja
in Bengal could never be visualized without the accompaniment
of white fleecy clouds in a lapis-lazuli blue sky, white plumes of
the pampas grass, the changing pink of the hibiscus mutabilis, or
the scent of the night-blooming flower of sadness. In northern

[1] Dinendra Kumar Ray, *Palli Chitra*.

India people say that spring comes in only with the Holi festival, and in Bengal the rainy season begins with the worship of the Ganges.

Furthermore, modern Hindus have no eye for flowers except for worship, for which they are indispensable. At every ritual they have to greet the deity with this phrase among others: *Etena gandha-puspena* — 'with this scented flower . . .' In old times they planted flowering trees or shrubs only for getting blooms for worship. When, with British rule, there came secular gardening the neighbours always stole the flowers, and there could be no protest against that. Once, in an unrealistic fit of temper, I sent a complaint to a police station in Calcutta against some boys who had robbed my flowers, and the police dismissed the complaint as absurd, because by that time stealing flowers from another man's garden for the sake of worship had become almost legalized by custom, and objection to it was looked upon as interfering with religious freedom. In any case, in spite of the dubious method employed for obtaining them, flowers entered Hindu life through Hinduism. Only in the south of India the old Hindu use of flowers for adornment persisted.

Personalization of the Support from Religion. Last of all, a special way of obtaining religious support in order to go through life has to be considered. Those whom I have called the 'Commons of Hinduism', that is, those who need and look for this support, have not remained satisfied with an abstract psychological entity from which they could secure help and protection only by an equally abstract psychological effort on their part. They have created a personal incarnation of religion, so to speak, in order to make the support from religion as concrete as protection from a powerful person in their worldly life.

This religious protector is the spiritual guide and teacher known as a man's Guru. But this personal Guru is not the traditional hereditary Guru of Hindu families. He is a special Guru for a particular individual, chosen by him according to his judgement. He is always a man who has attained to a high religious status in the world by leading a genuinely devout life or practising nothing better than charlatanry. He usually has a permanent station of his own, known as his *asrama* or hermitage, but he also tours large areas and often the whole of India preaching his message and securing followers. These Gurus always come from among those Hindus who have left the world and made religion their vocation or profession, about whom more will be said later. Here the point of view of the followers will only be considered.

Religiously-minded Hindus have always sought a Guru of this type, because it is a Hindu conviction that no right path in religion can be found without instruction, through initiation, by a qualified guide. Therefore when a man or a woman has chosen a Guru he or she also follows his directions without question, surrendering all his or her spiritual and moral freedom and judgement. The extent to which this is done is astonishing, and the subserviency is not paralleled even in the political sphere where the Hindus have always submitted to autocracy. In fact, they become almost slaves of the Gurus. They hang up portraits of the Guru in their homes, and not only worship the Guru as if he was the deity, but also sanctify their food by offering it first to the picture of the Guru. The most remarkable thing about this cult of the Guru is that in recent years it has become more widespread than ever before, though every other aspect of Hinduism is losing its hold. This is particularly true of the class which has received Western education and lost religious awareness in all its most elevated aspects.

But there is no doubt that those who submit to a Guru feel morally and spiritually stronger, and acquire a confidence in facing the problems of life they never had by themselves. The relationship between the Guru and his disciple is very much like that which existed between the liege lord and his vassal in the early age of feudalism. This is another illustration of the tendency in Hinduism to humanize all religious ideas and practices.

Part II – Gains of the 'Lords' in Hindu Religious Life

The Hindus who left the world and adopted a religious life or vocation lost nothing by giving up worldly occupations and cutting themselves adrift from society. On the contrary, they ensured an alternative means of livelihood which was as satisfactory as any in the world and which brought even substantial wealth to many of them, and besides it brought the fulfilment of two desires which drive all men who are endowed with a strong and assertive personality, namely, the desire to possess power and the desire to have freedom. Actually, the aspiration after freedom is also a form of the desire for power. What the Hindu holy men got from religion was the power to dominate over other men, and to be themselves free from domination by others. The two aspirations have to be considered separately.

Enjoyment of Power. In every way the power which came to Hindu holy men through religion resembled the power of those who had it in the political sphere. For this reason these men, taken as a body, could be regarded as the religious counterpart of a secular ruling order, with one important difference. The secular rulers shouldered the responsibility for protecting the life and property of their subjects, whereas the religious rulers had the advantage of keeping all the practical gains from power to themselves, giving nothing more than psychological confidence to the men whose minds they dominated.

However, both the classes acquired power in the same manner. In the latter half of the eighteenth century and the beginning of the nineteenth, all British observers noted with some surprise how easy it was in India for any exceptional man to rise high in life on the strength of his talents alone. Many rose to the status of prince and minister from lowly and even menial stations. In fact, while Hindu society retained its natural functioning, that is, allowed power to find its natural outlets and achieve its natural aims, it could be said that a man who had the necessary aptitude and capacity within himself, carried the sceptre of a king in his *jhula*, i.e. shopping bag.

A parallel career could be pursued through religion. If a man had the strength of character to pursue it with vigour, the same kind of power, prestige, and domination over men could be obtained by him. Actually, it was easier to acquire and keep the power obtained through religion because it was purely psychological, and did not require the collaboration of other men or the maintenance of an army or a body of officials. Besides, when obtained, the position was never lost by any holy man.

Of course, in order to reach such a position of authority, the holy man had also to acquire a reputation for possessing occult power by means of which to work miracles. Stories of such powers in the sadhus is current all over India, and even highly educated people believe them. As a rule, no exalted religious status is admitted in a man who has not an aura of the occult. But the better type of sadhus regard this only as a means to an end and their reputation for working miracles as a secondary instrument of domination. Some holy men even frankly declare that their supernatural tricks are only tools of the trade, to be employed against the ignorant and the *vulgus profanum*. They are intelligent enough to be aware that their power is really the domination of superior minds over common minds, and they relentlessly press this advantage.

Thus these men always have the same collective homage and command the same obedience as the secular rulers. In the case of many, the worldly appanage of power has not been less impressive than that of a prince. Anyone who has seen the processions at the head of which great religious personages enter a city, often on richly caparisoned elephants, will bear testimony to the worldly grandeur of the princes of the Hindu religion. In one respect their power is more complete, for with the power they exercise over the minds of a whole populace they are also comparable to great demagogic political leaders, and with this power they try to control the private life of their followers, both as individuals and in families, and succeed in a manner which the rulers cannot achieve. In fact, their power extends to places beyond the reach of political power. It is perfectly natural, therefore, that the holy men in India are invariably addressed as Maharaj or Great King.

This psychological power is exercised more completely over women, who usually find the holy men irresistible. Whenever anyone goes to see a holy man he will find him surrounded by a crowd of women, mostly young, and many of them will be seen to be ministering to his bodily comfort by massaging his feet or fanning him. There can be no doubt that there is a para-erotic streak in this homage, and at times the relationship goes very much further, and if the holy men choose to be sensual the women do not scruple to surrender their honour and chastity to them. Men also obey them implicitly, and will be guided in their worldly affairs, especially in respect of the marriages of their sons and daughters, by their Gurus. Many of these Gurus have an unlimited pride of power and even arrogance. Normally, however, their power is so undisputed that they feel no need to be aggressive. The wiser holy men usually exercise their power with moderation.

Nevertheless, even when genuinely religious and seeking

religious satisfaction only, these men are never less avid for fame and recognition than other ambitious men. I shall give an example of this. In 1900 there came to Max Müller at Oxford a genuine holy man from India who had a high reputation in his own country, but on coming to England he gave vent to his indignation and disappointment. He said: 'I had come to teach men the subtle enigmas of existence. However, England is like a poisonous fruit, fair and attractive to view, but full of deadly juice.' The poor man had assumed that his fame must have preceded him from his country to England, and he had expected to see big crowds at Victoria Station come to receive him. Instead, he was stranded there with his pots and pans and chela (disciple) until a porter took pity on him, and after ascertaining what he was, sent him with a shrewd hunch to the Society for Psychical Research, which sent him on to Max Müller. This new traffic in 'Light from the East' had begun with Swami Vivekananda's famous speech before the World's Parliament of Religions in Chicago in 1893, and it has now become a regular trade to exploit the gullible and the superstitious in the West.

Thus Hinduism offered to those who had the capacity to use it in this manner, a real alternative to political power, for which all persons with a developed urge for self-assertion yearn, but which they cannot secure owing to a lack of political aptitude. This often kept within the fold of the Hindu religion those very men who could be expected to be repelled by religion on account of their pride of life, lust of the eyes, and lust of the flesh. Thus even in its apparent unworldliness the religious vocation maintained the unbreakable link between the world and religion.

Gift of Freedom. Hinduism also offered a splendid opportunity for leading a life liberated from all the obligations, constraints, and compulsions which weighed on the existence of the Hindus in the world. Its appeal was not likely to be less strong than the attraction of power for those who wanted such freedom, and, as I have said, the desire for power and desire for freedom are very closely connected. Of course, this was very much a matter of temperament. But those who renounced the world to become sadhus, got from religion a very comprehensive freedom. In fact, the freedom they obtained comprised all the four freedoms preached by President F. D. Roosevelt, but were realized more fully by the sadhus through their wandering life than by any secular pursuit of freedom. The sadhus had full freedom of speech and expression, freedom of worship, and, above all, freedom from want and freedom from fear.

First, there was complete freedom from the compulsion to work for food. The sadhus freed themselves from the curse: 'By the sweat of thy brow thou shalt eat bread.' The wandering sadhus could get food everywhere and from everybody. If need arose they could commandeer it. But in practice nobody would think of denying them food. The sedentary sadhus had food brought to their huts by the villagers.

The second freedom was from the bondage to soil which agriculture has imposed on man. They had no need to be tied to land and remain stationary on it. It was not simply that they had recovered the life of the nomads, they were free even from the necessity of keeping and feeding the animals on which they lived. In reality, theirs was the freedom to wander, which was the heritage of the herbivorous wild animals.

After that they were free from the compulsion to find houses and wear clothing. It was no sorrow to them that, though they were sons of man, they had nowhere to lay their heads. They could lay them anywhere. And in regard to clothing their freedom was so complete, and so admitted on all hands, that they could laugh at the Western talk about going back to nature through nudity, regarding such gestures as comically affected and self-conscious. With their nudity they impressed even the Greeks who practised occasional nudity.

Lastly, they had no need to stay anywhere longer than they pleased. They had recovered man's migratory life without the necessity of having a goal for their migrations. Thus the sadhus acquired an insatiable *Wanderlust*. One sadhu, whom Warren Hastings patronized, travelled through Afghanistan and the Caucasus to Moscow, went from Moscow to Peking overland, and then came back to Benares through Tibet.

These freedoms were freedoms from all the elemental compulsions and restraints on human beings. In addition, the sadhus acknowledged no social ties or social obligations. Once they had adopted a sadhu's life, they would not even mention their original social ties or their original names. The breach with society became complete, though society was not free from them. For once society was totally beaten by individualism. If Rousseau had seen the life of our sadhus he would have written: Man is born in chains, but he can be free.

Any sadhu even now can say to a man who remains in the world what a Corsican bandit did to the hero of one of Prosper Mérimée's novels:

> How can you be insensible to the charm of absolute liberty under a fine climate like ours? With this self-preserver (he pointed to his gun) a man is king everywhere. He can command, redress wrongs . . . This is a most moral amusement, and agreeable to boot, which we would not refuse to ourselves by any means. Can there be a finer life than that of a wandering knight, when the man is better armed and more sensible than Don Quixote? Believe me, nothing else is comparable to the life of a bandit.[1]

Actually, the sadhu could claim more. He was not an outlaw, dependent on his gun. His tongs, brass pot, and ashes were enough. What was not less important, and perhaps as alluring as the other rights the sadhu had, he could become free even from the workings of his conscious mind by being wholly unrestricted in his use of cannabis.

There must have been a particular reason to make the natural aspiration for freedom take this special channel in order to satisfy itself. As members of Hindu society, the sadhus wanted to recover freedom not within the social framework but outside it and at the same time to preserve all their claims to social support. The nature of Hindu society drove them to it. It was authoritarian, and the authoritarianism had become self-generating in it. It imposed an inescapable regimentation on its members from one end of India to another, so that Hindu behaviour became uniform all over the country. The most coercive aspect of the regimentation was the rule of life enjoined for a Hindu, which even in regard to the routine of daily life was a jumble of injunctions and taboos. In respect of obedience to the restrictions imposed by the caste system the coercion was even more ruthless.

After that there was the coercion exercised by opinion. No people regulated all their conduct with such abject obedience to the opinion of his neighbours and relatives as the Hindus. Even when they abstained from immoral actions the restraint came more from the fear of neighbours than from moral scruples.

[1] Speech of the bandit Castriconi (the Curé) to Orso in *Colomba*.

GAIN FROM RELIGION

All this virtually crushed the desire for freedom in those Hindus who remained in society, and made their social and personal life in all its major aspects, the life of uncomplaining slaves. The only safety-valve left to them was in the freedom allowed for petty indiscipline and anarchy, which no more affected the rigidity of Hindu society than dust affects the solid structure of the earth's crust. It was on account of the hold of authoritarianism on Hindu society that the more intractable spirits sought freedom by going out of society altogether. They thought that they would not only gain freedom thereby but also make it inviolable by affiliating it with religion.

In creating this affiliation the Hindu sadhus only extended the rule of life prescribed for the Hindus by their sacred law. According to it, the life of a man was divided into four stages: first, that of the devoted student; second, that of the dutiful householder; a third stage of retirement to the woods for moral and religious contemplation; and the last stage in which the man became a wandering sadhu without any tie with anyone, obtaining his food by begging. This last stage is generally regarded by modern interpreters as the stage of renunciation, but in reality it was the stage of release from the crushing burden of Hindu life in the world. The sadhus made this stage their whole adult life and lost nothing by it.

HINDU SPIRITUALITY

AFTER reading the account of Hinduism offered in this book its readers are likely to be so overcome by a sense of its inadequacy that they would perhaps apply to it a well-known cliché, worn out though it is. They would say that it is the play of *Hamlet* without the Prince of Denmark, because the account has left out what everybody nowadays looks upon as the truly religious content of any religion, namely, its spiritual message. Hinduism, more especially, has been credited with an exalted, rarefied, and esoteric spirituality in the West, and it is this Western myth of Hinduism which has attracted to it both sincerely religious people and pedlars of religious charlatanry. I am therefore bound to be accused of leaving out the most important part of the religion.

I have no right to resent this charge, for the omission is deliberate. In the body of the book I have described Hinduism as a means of living in the world with the help of supernatural agencies, and I have also suggested that the Hindus never took any other view of their religion. But the significant point is that Hindu spirituality so far as it has any existence can quite naturally be brought within the worldly framework of the religion. It is this which gives to Hindu spirituality its special quality. In this concluding essay this aspect of Hinduism will be considered.

As a preliminary, however, the notion of spirituality has itself to be defined, and it is not identical in all religions. Just as the current conception of religion is derived from Christianity, so is the current conception of spirituality. In it the notion has reached its full development from the seminal utterances to be found in St Paul in such phrases as 'spiritual gift' (Rom. 1:11), 'Ye which are spiritual restore such a one' (Gal. 6:1), 'spiritual wickedness in high places' (Eph. 6:12), or 'to be spiritually minded is life and peace' (Rom. 8:6). This kind of spirituality is concerned with what is called soul, an entity quite distinct from the body, in which it only sojourns temporarily. Starting from an antithesis between the *carnal* and the *spiritual*, between the *flesh* and the *spirit,* Christian spirituality has travelled a long way. It has a long history behind it as well. The whole process of its evolution has to be examined briefly in order to bring out the true character of Hindu spirituality.

All spirituality, including the Christian, springs from a psychological urge which from the same Christian point of view is the most unregenerate in man. In the language of Christianity, the urge behind all spirituality may be described as a combination of *concupiscentia carnis, concupiscentia oculorum et superbia vitae.* To put it simply, what is now known as spirituality is the product of man's love of life or, as seen from the outside, the product of his unwillingness to submit to the laws of nature and biology. Aware of the limitations on his existence and powers imposed by these, man has persistently refused to submit to them, and has tried to circumvent them by creating a subjective world in which his existence will be eternal and his aspirations unobstructed. Thus, from the point of view of Nature, man is the Revolting Angel, driven by a superb arrogance.

Among the limitations, that which man has resented most and desired most eagerly to overcome is, of course, death, which puts an end to his existence as an individual. As it happens, he remains almost at the animal level in regard to the death of other men, for it does not affect him very deeply or for long. But he is seized with panic at the idea of his own death, and that drives him almost mad. Yet, to all appearance, death is inevitable and inescapable. Haunted by his fear of it, man has tried to get rid of his sense of impermanence and insecurity by creating a double of physical life, or in other words, by conceiving of life as an external indestructible element which enters and leaves the destructible material body. Through this belief he has established the diuturnity of his self, which is a contradiction to biology but not to religion.

This has created that image of life, as bounded by the two earthly events of birth and death, which was evoked by the Northumbrian nobleman who recommended the adoption of Christianity as a means of making it worth living: 'O King,' he said, 'the life of a man is a sparrow's flight through the hall when you are sitting at meat in wintertide. So tarries for a moment the life of a man in our sight, but what is before it, what after it, we know not. If this new teaching tells us aught certainly of these let us follow it.' There can be no doubt that the most powerful attraction of Christianity came from the idea of resurrection and the promise of eternal life.

The idea of a disembodied existence as real as the bodily one, has been derived from the observed facts of breathing when alive and its cessation at death. They have given rise to the notion that something independent of the body comes into it and goes out of it. and that though it is imperceptible to the senses, it has continuity as an individual personality independently of the body. It is significant that the words which stand for this incorporeal personality are in many languages the same as those for breath.[1]

The idea that the self continued to live as a spirit or soul was bound to be applied to all men, though not to animals, and also to lead to the belief that all these disembodied spirits formed a community in an imaginary world which was a double of the material world. A further extension of the idea was seen in the creation of beings of the same incorporeal type but who existed independently and constituted an immortal order with powers similar to those of man but unlimited in their exercise. To them men gave the name of gods. There was one more extension of the notion of incorporeal beings made in the image of man. This was seen in the personification of the forces and phenomena of nature. One cannot, of course, be certain that these different classes of mental creations were a sequence, instead of being simultaneous in appearance. But in any case they are closely connected, and thus they cannot be separated. In their combination they have created a complete supra-mundane and supra-natural order. To remain continuously in contact with this order was spirituality in its most elementary and basic form.

But Christian spirituality rose far above this foundation and even hid it under its superstructure. In this developed form spirituality transformed both the supra-mundane world and man's relations with it. The Christian transcendental world became the repository of all the highest moral ideals of man in their realized form and it was also placed under a divinity, the Christian God, who became the embodiment of a perfection so absolute that it was regarded as unattainable by man, although the ideal itself was man's creation. He could only submit to that perfection in a spirit of humility, devotion, and adoration.

[1] It might be pointed out that the Greek word for 'spiritual' is 'pneumatikon'.

Spiritual life was the mental existence of man placed in perpetual contact with the transcendental world created by his own mind, and also the regulation of his worldly life by the light of that world. To live like that was to be the recipient of grace and to be blessed. Furthermore, in this type of spirituality whatever perfection or strength was within the reach of man was not only attainable solely through a gift of grace, but had also to be accompanied by a conviction of man's inherent weakness (*astheneia* in Greek and *infirmitas* in Latin), so that the idea was established that strength for a Christian had to be made perfect in weakness.

Thus Christian life when lived in the Christian manner naturally generated a revulsion from the world, and also a sense, not only of its transience, but also of its vanity. In those cases in which the psychological contact with the transcendental world was at its closest and most intense, it produced a bodily effect, and this combination of mental and bodily reactions produced that brand of religious sentiment which has come to be known as mysticism. This was the most concentrated form of Christian spirituality.

There can be no doubt that this particular form of spirituality developed from its original starting point of an unresolvable conflict between the spirit and the flesh, has enriched the human mind. It has added a new field of activity to it, which is partly self-contained and partly overlapping with the intellectual and moral fields. It has thus added a new quality to the activities within the latter fields. As a result, there has emerged an ampler human mind which is a triad of intellectual, moral, and spiritual activities incapable of being wholly separated into its constituent elements. The Christian faith has never been based on a rejection of reason, it has taken its stand on a superior reason, a *raison raisonnante*. Pascal's proclamation of a great gulf between the order of reason and the order of charity was due to an extreme position to which he was perhaps driven by his dislike for Cartesianism. But even he admitted the validity of the reason which came from the heart. This type of spirituality has had a profound effect on human behaviour by bringing about a catharsis of his natural impulses.

Hindu religious sentiment never took this line of development, but remained true to the original motivation of spirituality, which was to become free from all the restraints imposed on man by Nature. Thus Hindu spirituality is a pursuit, not of beatitude, but of power. It has to be pointed out that in Sanskrit there is no word for spirituality, nor was there any in any modern Indian language until the notion was introduced through the English language. Then with a grotesque and illogical disregard of its original meaning, a Sanskrit word (*adhyātmik* = concerning the self) was made an equivalent of 'spiritual' in English.

This has never been understood by Occidental writers who have dealt with Hindu spirituality. I might illustrate the failure by referring to a famous story by Kipling, that of the saint Purun Bhagat. The story was based on fact. In it the Prime Minister of an Indian princely state, with an outstanding record of public service, becomes a hermit and devotes himself to religious medi-tation in the Himalayas, living only on the food brought to him by the people of a nearby village. One night he is awakened by the tremors of a landslide and rushing out as a man of action saves the villagers. On this, Kipling's comment was: 'He was no longer the holy man, but Sir Purun Dass, K.C.I.E., Prime Minister of no small State, a man accustomed to command, going out to save life.'

This was all wrong, for in Hinduism the distinction does not exist. In it the minister and man of action Purun Dass, and the saint Purun Bhagat are the same man in two characters and roles, complementary to each other. In the ultimate analysis, Hindu spirituality is interwoven with the cosmos. It is the Old Guard of the world, always held in reserve to be launched into action when a serious crisis arises which cannot be met with any mode of rational action open to man. Or, to vary the metaphor, in his spiritual activities the Hindu is like the dynamo which generates electricity, and in his worldly life the motor which expends it. Hindu spirituality and Hindu phenomenal existence are inseparable. They stand together.

However, a reservation to this general statement has to be made due to the presence in the observable features of Hindu spirituality of a different quality, and that of the kind which is mainly a creation of Christianity. This shade of spirituality is more notice-able in the simple forms of Hinduism preached by the popular prophets. It is, however, an extraneous feature which has re-mained in Hinduism in its standard form for a long time and has been reinforced twice in the recent centuries.

Partly, this spirituality is a survival from the original form of *bhakti*, in which *agape* had not been transformed into *eros*. Partly, it was also revived by the impact of Islam. This type of spirituality is commonly found among those Hindus who remain conscious of the unseen God who is never worshipped formally but still remains the ultimate God of all Hindus. This God remains a person and receives devotion, and yet he is not invested with a human form.

Awareness of this God and devotion to him was powerfully reinforced among the Hindus as a result of the preaching of Christianity by the missionaries. The Hindus, especially those of the upper castes, rejected the religious system of Christianity, but absorbed a good deal of the idea of the Christian God. This amplified the idea of the unworshipped God and strengthened the devotion to Him to such an extent that what the Hindus precisely felt about him before Christianity came to India cannot be recovered from their spiritual life today in so far as it shows a similarity to Christian spirituality. But there is no uncertainty in respect of the religious status given to the men who exhibit this religious attitude by the Hindus in general. They are regarded as pious men, but never as holy men. In order to be endowed with that status all religious Hindus have to be spiritual in the Hindu sense, that is, either seekers or possessors of supernatural powers. This attitude to holiness is so deeply established that even those holy men who deprecate or even despise the supernatural extensions of their religious life often have to keep up the appearance of being workers of miracles for the sake of status or livelihood.

It must also be kept in mind that the Hindu spirituality which is truly Hindu, that is, when it is a pursuit of power, is not of a single type. The most obvious contrast is to be seen between its introvert expression and its extrovert expression. The first is seen in the Way of Knowledge—the *Jnana Marga*, and the second in the Way of Action—the *Karma Marga*. Both are important aspects of Hindu spirituality and have to be examined more closely.

Of these the introvert form, which is the creation of the Way of Knowledge, has to be considered first, because it is this which has given to the Hindus their current reputation for spirituality. This, too, never broke with the original motivation of Hindu spirituality, i.e. the desire to overcome the limits to human existence and to be free from all the limitations on human power imposed by nature. The prayer in one of the oldest of the Upanishads, which

I have already quoted, voices this aspiration: 'Lead me from non-being to being.' In the same Upanishad the wife of a sage declares: 'What should I do with anything which does not make me immortal?' To the Hindus truth is what exists.

But in their quest for immortality and indestructibility through the Way of Knowledge the Hindus did not create a transcendental world in which human beings could have eternal life. They looked for indestructibility, not simply for themselves but for the whole cosmos, and hit upon the idea that behind all the manifested phenomena which were subject to change and therefore also to destruction, there existed, consubstantial with them and yet inaccessible to the senses, an unmanifested, attributeless, unchangeable and all-pervasive element which was eternal and indestructible. They also formulated the corollary that phenomena were only particular parts of a general and absolute reality. This idea, arrived at so early in the history of human civilization, was akin to that which has been discovered by modern physics. By its adoption they avoided the setting up of an unresolvable antithesis and conflict between an absolute and eternal reality and transient cosmic phenomena accessible to the senses. This must be regarded as the highest achievement of the Hindu Way of Knowledge so far as it made true knowledge its aim.

But the concept of an absolute and unmanifested reality as preached by the Hindu Way of Knowledge raises two questions. First, how was it hit upon; and, secondly, how could such an idea, purely intellectual as it might seem to be, contribute to religious experience and evoke religious exultation? The two questions are connected, for the emotional effect which the concept produced must have been due to the manner in which its realization came.

One negative answer to the first question suggests itself at once. It is that the ancient Hindus did not arrive at the notion by means of any intellectual process. Neither the technique of experiment, nor the mathematical capacity to deduce theories from observed facts existed in that age. Besides, the theory thus arrived at could not be proved by application to techniques concerned with doing and acting. It has also to be kept in mind that the Hindu Way of Knowledge did not concern itself with objective information for its own sake or for making things; its main preoccupation was with values, and it wanted to discover what mattered and what did not in conducting our life. Empiric knowledge, it deprecated to such an extent that one Upanishad said that worldly people pique themselves on their intelligence and learning, but remain in the maze of their ignorance, being like blind men led by the blind. True knowledge for the Hindus was a qualitative assessment.

On the other hand, the discovery of an absolute reality could not have been elaborated from the primitive belief in after-life, which was a deduction from the observed fact of breathing. The Hindus had, of course, their own brand of that kind of notion of after-life, but it was not connected with the line of thinking or feeling of the Way of Knowledge. The commonplace notion of an after-life remained in one channel of Hindu religious life, and the notion of an absolute unchanging reality in another.

How was it hit upon then? A rough and ready answer would be that it was arrived at by intuition. There is nothing improbable in that, for some of the most important scientific theories have also originated, not from conscious deduction, but from flashes of intuition. However, intuition in science is a sort of super-reasoning working below or above the level of consciousness. It is a part of the whole process of intellection. In contrast, the intuition to which I am attributing the Hindu discovery must have been more elemental, something akin to instinct in animals. It has to be regarded as a subconsciously operating faculty of perception brought into play by the combination of an extreme acuteness of the senses with an intensely emotional temperament. Phenomena of nature impinging on such a neuro-psychological constitution could have produced in the human mind when it was young sensations of there being some intangible living force behind the tangible world, as there actually is. These sensations in their cumulative effect could have generated a super-animism.

But this super-animism or even the crude animism of primitive peoples might not have been simply one-sided; that is, only a reaction of the human mind. It is usual to think that animism is only the primitive man's attribution to inanimate nature of the living quality of his own existence. I am, however, inclined to think that there is more to it. To be explicit, I am ready to assume that inanimate nature is only seemingly inanimate, but at bottom it is the outward appearance of an active process, which sends out emanations to beat upon the human mind and generate vague perceptions of its real nature. It is logical to assume that the impact would be more powerful before the full development of man's intellectual capacity than afterwards. Expression in speech, however imprecise, was also likely to follow as soon as sufficient linguistic competence was acquired provided that the primitive sensitiveness was not lost with that acquisition. The period of coincidence of the two could not be long. The notions and feelings roused in the human mind at that stage might be described as intimations of immortality granted to mankind in its youth.

That such an interaction can take place even in men living in highly civilized societies with a fully developed intellectual life is seen in the case of Wordsworth. In many of his poems he consciously formulated a theory of the impact of nature on man, and in the well-known lines in his *Tintern Abbey* he described the result of the impact:

> . . . Nor less, I trust
> To them I may have owed another gift,
> Of aspect more sublime; that blessed mood,
> In which the burthen of the mystery,
> In which the heavy and the weary weight
> Of all this unintelligible world,
> Is lightened:—that serene and blessed mood,
> In which the affections gently lead us on,—
> Until, the breath of this corporeal frame
> And even the motion of our human blood
> Almost suspended, we are laid asleep
> In body, and become a living soul:
> While with an eye made quiet by the power
> Of harmony, and the deep power of joy,
> We see into the life of things.

It would be a great mistake to discount or dismiss this statement as mere poetic fancy or conceit. It has to be taken more or less literally as the description of a real experience. With less clearness many others have felt in the same way. Of course, it is not possible to take all the utterances which claim to be intuitive realizations at their face value, because the human mind is an extremely imprecise instrument with colorations of its own, and its responses have a very wide range, some of which project its own prepossessions when under stress. None the less, at times it can register correctly and perceive the existence of something which is not its own creation. Unfortunately, it is very difficult to determine which is the correct response and which is not.

The Hindu Rishis or Seers to whom the perception of the absolute reality is attributed also gave utterance to a wide variety of notions, some of which are extremely crude. These would justify one's regarding them as no higher in knowledge and insight than the medicine men of primitive peoples. But they also set down feelings and ideas which came from a sensibility akin to that of Wordsworth. The expression of these feelings and ideas scintillates like precious stones in a bed of common rock in the writings attributed to them. These utterances are very much like poetry, if they are not a particular kind of poetry in themselves. It should be kept in mind that ancient Hindus did not regard the poet as a *mystique manque*, that is, as a man of religion strayed from the path of truth. On the contrary, in Sanskrit the word *kavi*, which later meant a poet in the usual acceptation, was applied originally to the seers who got revelations of truth, and could communicate what they had received to others in suitable language. The Vedic hymns were regarded as such revelations. The Hindus always remembered the religious affiliation of poetry, and described the pleasure derived from secular poetry as something like religious exultation, or as they put it: joy from poetry is the brother of the joy from the perception of the Brahman.

All this may appear to be very fanciful. But we still do not know enough about the workings of the human mind in relation to its environment to be capable of explaining all its reactions. However, even on the conscious plane we find most sensory perceptions producing emotions of the recognized types, and there is no reason to rule out the possibility of more rarefied effects, of which the aesthetic emotion which natural scenes produce is one. On the same analogy contact with nature might produce an excited state of the human mind which can be described as religious emotion. The early Hindus showed in all their writings an extreme susceptibility to the beauty and grandeur of nature. It is impossible to disassociate this from their religious sentiment.

The explanation that I am hazarding about the origin of the Hindu notion of an eternal and absolute reality immune to change and destruction, which is at the same time manifested to the senses as the changeful cosmos, should also explain why the notion could rouse emotions of a kind which can be described as religious exultation. What the Way of Knowledge evoked by way of emotion or exultation was only a higher form of the religious excitement displayed by the priest-magicians of primitive peoples. As a matter of fact, all religious emotion is partly physiological, and what is known as mysticism certainly most so. Nobody can deny that religiosity is dependent on the physiological make-up of men, and that it is not within the physical potentialities of all men to be religious. Being religious according to the Way of Knowledge could not be an exception to this general rule.

The followers of the Way of Knowledge could feel that they had conquered death by discovering a form of the cosmos which was imperishable and ever-lasting, and derive joy, not only from that conviction but also from the establishment of an intermittent feeling of oneness with it. But we know nothing of the manner in which the Way of Knowledge in its original form was practised by those who preached and followed it.

There is no historical evidence besides the Upanishads themselves to show when or how the ideas embodied in them formed part of Hindu religious life. Even those passages in them which give expression to mystical exultation are embedded in contexts of philosophical and ritualistic arguments. Neither in the Upanishads nor in other Sanskrit texts is there any description of the religious or devotional life of those who followed the Way of Knowledge. The epics, for instance, often describe the daily life of the sages, and also reproduce their discussions. But these are always shown to be concerned with moral questions or mythology. All this suggests that the proper content of the Way of Knowledge passed out of religious life very soon after it came into existence.

But in so far as it provided a psycho-physiological experience it survived, because on the one hand it could be planted on the practice of the well-known later cults, and on the other could be induced by auto-suggestion and special physical exercises. The desire to continue the experience by means of these is intelligible: the experience was too pleasurable to make those who had once had it reconciled to its loss when the capacity for having it naturally was lost. In order to continue the experience even a faked form of it was sought by the taking of drugs, cannabis more especially.

It is not necessary to describe the philosophical pursuit of the concept of reality formulated by the Way of Knowledge, because with that transition it ceased to be part of religious life, though Hindu philosophy too had passion—the passion roused by the sorrows of mankind as its driving power. In later stages it became nothing better than arid exercise of logical analysis. However, the Way of Knowledge survived in Hindu religious life in its modal part, and in this form it continued to be followed till recent times. Its prestige was such that it is still followed, but unfortunately it is also exploited by men who are nothing but charlatans.

In its respectable form, it was followed by men who left the world and lived their life of renunciation as individuals instead of becoming members of the ascetic orders. As a rule, they were not votaries of any of the major cults, but professed to seek knowledge about the ultimate meaning of existence, and remain in a state of joyousness through that knowledge. These men usually assumed or were given honorific titles like Swami (the most common one), Maharshi, Param Hamsa, Mahatma, etc., and lived as recluses, very often in inaccessible places in the hills and mountains. They devoted themselves to contemplation and meditation, and often went into trances or *samadhi*. They claimed to have arrived at true knowledge or ultimate wisdom, and to have found answers to the enigmas of human existence.

But no one has yet been able to find out what their knowledge or enlightenment amounted to, so far as these were spiritual. Normally, they aired almost complete taciturnity, at times giving the reason that what they knew could not be divulged to unworthy persons. If, however, they became vocal at all, their religious ideas could be recognized only as variations on the themes of the Upanishads and similar ancient mystical treatises. It is this reticence of theirs which has created the notion that the deepest Hindu religious message is esoteric.

But when they are social—and they cannot avoid being so altogether because men come to them to receive instruction—they can become loquacious. However, their teaching then is seen to be wholly didactic, and that too in a very commonplace form. Their teaching or preaching consists wholly of the moral ideas which have been current among mankind ever since it became civilized. They are often even trite.

None the less, the value of this moral teaching is not to be underrated. The erosion of moral sensibility is continuous in human societies and it is most so in respect of those simple principles which sustain social life and which seem to be obvious. Therefore these simple principles have to be propagated ceaselessly. This can be compared to modern advertisements urging drinking milk, eating oranges or using soap. When one thinks of these advertisements without taking them as unavoidable accompaniments of contemporary life, one is startled by the thought that civilized human societies should have to be reminded of the necessity for the things they urge on us. But it is so, in regard to hygiene as well as morals. What the cessation of elementary moral teaching can mean is clearly seen in the prevalence of hatred, violence, vice, and dishonesty in the present-day world. Therefore didacticism, even when it is as cloying as advertisements of everyday necessities, is not to be deprecated.

But the practitioners of the Way of Knowledge in Hindu society in recent times could never have exercised so decisive a moral influence if they had not been regarded as men who possessed supernatural powers. All the ascetics and hermits who remained in this Way were credited with such powers, and often they themselves condescended to adopt the tricks of their trade in order to be supported by society, when for themselves they only sought religious experiment. Through its supernatural aspect or coloration, the Way of Knowledge disclosed its links with the spirituality of the Way of Works, which has now to be described.

I have distinguished the spirituality (or rather religiosity) of the Way of Action or Works from that of the Way of Knowledge by characterizing one as introvert and the other as extrovert. The distinction is justified. If the religious life led in the Way of Knowledge is also partly a quest of power, it is so in a passive manner and that power is sought for the inner life of the devotee. That is to say, it gives the devotee the capacity to rise above the termination of selfhood, and the destruction of all things outside the self. In contrast, the spirituality of the Way of Action *(Karma Marga)* is oriented towards action in the form of unobstructed self-assertion. Its object is to acquire the capacity to do things beyond what is within the natural physical and mental powers of man—e.g. the capacity to see into the future, read the minds of other men, control physiological processes, even disregard the laws of gravitation, in short, the capacity to perform miracles.

Spirituality of the Way of Action can therefore be regarded as a specialized and highly intensified form of the general religious practices of the Hindus. While the object of the latter was to ensure security and prosperity in the world to the extent they were attainable by natural means, or at best to obtain these in such a measure as could be expected only from luck or special favours of the deities, the spirituality of the Way of Action sought supernatural powers, to be used or not used as the possessor chose. The main satisfaction was the pride of possession.

Yet there was one extraordinary paradox in the methods of this form of spirituality. Although its obvious descent was from primitive magic, and its object the working of miracles, the methods adopted by it to obtain supernatural powers were wholly human. Except that in some forms of this spiritual pursuit incantations were employed, generally speaking it was held that miraculous powers or gains beyond the reach of human effort could be obtained by special physical and mental exercises, one of which was asceticism and self-mortification. Hindu renunciation, asceticism, and self-mortification were wholly different from what these were in Christianity.

From the Christian point of view, the renunciation and asceticism of the Way of Action might be regarded as a pampering of the very urges which these were meant to repress, namely to satisfy all the desires which are generated by the flesh. The whole of Hindu religious and secular literature leaves no room for doubt as to the motives of Hindu renunciation and asceticism. They are courses of action which can be described in the formula — *reculer pour mieux sauter*. These constitute the method of obtaining more and ever more power over men and nature by showing for some time how little one cared for the prizes and enjoyments offered by the world.

There are many legendary tales in Sanskrit which relate how certain sages performed such feats of self-mortification that Indra, the Lord of Heaven, became alarmed. He thought these men would attain such power that they would be able to usurp his heaven. So he sent his courtesans to tempt them, and they invariably brought about the fall of the sages, none of whom came through the trials like St Antony or Buddha. Sanskrit literature also has stories of defeated kings who practised the same type of self-mortification to recover their kingdoms. The story of Uma's penance to gain Siva as husband, already referred to, also reveals the same orientation of asceticism.

Even in historic times asceticism of this kind has been associated with the acquisition of occult powers of all kinds, including the power of overriding the laws of nature, controlling physiological processes, curing diseases, or foretelling the future. It has never been believed that these powers can be acquired by rational investigation and experimentation, and it has been assumed that they can come only from an esoteric discipline, of which severe self-mortification is a part. As has been shown, this kind of power had as its complement or rather fulfilment, the power to dominate other men. Actually, an appearance of indifference to things that the world has to offer, even without occult powers, has by itself created a moral authority for those who have shown it. As a means of acquiring and exerting power, renunciation has always been so effective among the Hindus that Mahatma Gandhi felt compelled to bring it into politics in order to obtain mass support for the nationalist movement.

This particular kind of religious practice, with its mingling of religious gymnastics and renunciation, has had such a hold on the Hindus, and its observances have been so conspicuous in all their activities, that outsiders have been led by the spectacle to attribute a deep, comprehensive, and esoteric religiosity to them. And this religiosity has been mistakenly associated with the Western conception of spirituality.

It has to be explained at this point that there was also another form of renunciation of worldly life among the Hindus, and that was seen in the Way of Knowledge. However, strictly speaking, that was not renunciation, far less asceticism. It was only living a life of self-restraint away from the distractions of the world. This retired life is extensively described in the epics and other books. These descriptions show that the sages lived normal lives in their families, and did not have to give up even sexual relations. This type of retired life was meant only to help concentration of mind in seeking knowledge.

The distinction between the two kinds of renunciation and their respective purposes is very strikingly illustrated by the story of the enlightenment of Buddha. At one stage of his quest for knowledge he practised severe self-mortification for six years and was reduced by it to a skeleton. But in the end he realized that all this was futile. So, afterwards he led a quiet life of normal regimen and arrived at enlightenment. But in no form of Hindu renunciation is there any trace of the religio-moral idea that man's nature is innately sinful and that it must be repressed by severe and painful methods.

There is another question about the methods of the Way of Action in its search of spirituality which has to be faced, even if it cannot be answered satisfactorily. That human beings can gain occult powers by means of magic is, of course, an idea current in all primitive societies. But the Way of Action sought them through human effort, special psychological and physical exercises, and above all by means of self-mortification. So far as the exercises were concerned, the Hindu ascetics could demonstrate that these gave a control over bodily states or processes which went beyond the natural, and therefore this part of their method was empiric. But how did they entertain the idea that self-mortification could secure occult powers for them, whose validity could never be demonstrated? This appears to have been assumed *a priori*.

But a matter of fact explanation for this, too, may be suggested. In Hindu social and family life, refusal to take food or go out and expose oneself to cold or heat is a recognized method of psychological coercion designed to make relatives, neighbours, creditors, or even debtors, yield to one's wishes or demands. Generally, it succeeded.

Bishop Heber, who visited Benares in 1824, left in his journal an account of the application of this method of coercion against the British administration by the people of that city some years before that date. I quote the whole narrative:

> Government had then, unadvisedly, imposed a house-tax of a very unpopular character, both from its amount and its novelty. To this the natives objected, that they recognised in their British rulers the same rights which had been exercised by the Moguls,—that the land-tax was theirs, and that they could impose duties on commodities going to market, or for exportation: but that their houses were their own,—that they had never been intermeddled with in any but their landed property, and commodities used in traffic,—and that the same power which now imposed a heavy and un-heard of tax on their dwellings, might do the same next year on their children and themselves. These considerations, though backed by strong representations from the magistrates, produced no effect in Calcutta; on which the whole population of Benares and its neighbourhood determined to sit 'dhurna' till their grievances were redressed. To sit 'dhurna' or mourning, is to remain

motionless in that posture, without food, and exposed to the weather, till the person against whom it is employed consents to the request offered; and the Hindoos believe, that whoever dies under such a process becomes a tormenting spirit to haunt and afflict his inflexible antagonist. This is a practice not unfrequent in the intercourse of individuals, to enforce payment of a debt, or forgiveness of one. And among Hindoos it is very prevailing, not only from the apprehended dreadful consequences of the death of the petitioner, but because many are of opinion, that while a person sits dhurna at their door, they must not themselves presume to eat, or undertake any secular business. It is even said that some persons hire Brahmins to sit dhurna for them, the thing being to be done by proxy, and the dhurna of a Brahmin being naturally more aweful in its effects than that of a Soodra could be.

According to this custom, Heber went on to relate, notices were sent out to the people of the city and surrounding villages to come and join such a demonstration. The result was described by Heber:

Above 300,000 persons, as it is said, deserted their houses, shut up their shops, suspended the labour of their farms, forebore to light fires, dress victuals, many of them even to eat, and sate down with folded arms and drooping heads, like so many sheep, on the plain which surrounds Benares. The local Government were exceedingly perplexed. There was the chance that very many of these strange beings would really perish, either from their obstinacy, or the diseases which they would contract in their present situation. There was a probability that famine would ensue from the interruption of agricultural labours at the most critical time of the year. There was a certainty that the revenue would suffer very materially from total cessation of all traffick. And it might even be apprehended that their despair, and the excitement occasioned by such a display of physical force would lead them to far stronger demonstrations of discontent than that of sitting dhurna. On the other hand, the authorities of Benares neither were permitted, nor would it have been expedient, to yield to such a demand, so urged. They conducted themselves with great prudence and good temper. Many of the natives appeared to expect, and the Brahmins perhaps hoped, that they would still further outrage the feelings of the people, by violently suppressing their assemblage. They did no such thing, but coolly reasoned with some of the ringleaders on the impossibility that Government should yield to remonstrances so enforced. They however told them expressly, in answer to their enquiries, that if they chose to sit dhurna, it was their own affair; and that so long as they only injured themselves, and were peaceable in their behaviour to others, Government would not meddle with them.

At last, the demonstrators got tired and dispersed. But the authorities in Calcutta abolished the tax afterwards. This was the real historical precedent of Mahatma Gandi's application of Hindu spirituality to the Indian nationalist movement in order to secure India's political independence. Naturally, Occidentals, put on a wrong track by his professed admiration for the Bible and Tolstoy, never understood what his method really was. It would seem that the practice of extreme self-mortification to obtain supernatural power was an extension of the social method to religious life.

Whether the men who followed this path of Hindu spirituality actually exercised supernatural powers cannot be asserted as a certainty. But the Hindus believe that they did, and even today people tell stories of supernatural deeds with a perfect conviction of their being true. As to the practitioners, whether they actually possessed any such powers or not, they exhibited extreme confidence and through this confidence could always exert their power on other men. Thus the reputation for possessing spiritual power actually gained through the methods of the Way of Action conferred a power which was a variant of political power, as I have already explained. Thus this type of spirituality never disassociated itself from the world, nor failed to gain worldly advantages.

The final result was that Hindu spirituality arising in both its forms from the cosmos, lost itself in the material cosmos. Of these, the brand of spirituality found in the Way of Action could never have avoided its worldly destiny. But the spirituality of the Way of Knowledge perhaps could. It had arrived at a notion of the universe which was a possible alternative to the subjective transcendental world created by all religions, including Hinduism itself in its less abstruse form. That world, intangible as it was to the senses, had real permanence. Starting from this discovery— that is, the realization that non-material existence could be as real as the material, a religion could have been created which would have been immune to the destructive impact which science has had on conventional religions. But the obstacle was that religion is sustained only by passion and never by intellectual concepts. The intuitive adumbration of the real nature of existence at first could arouse religious emotion through bodily responses. When that faculty was lost, the most basic religious discovery of the Hindus passed out of religion and was reduced to philosophy, which was incapable of supporting spiritual life. So Hindu spiritual life became pursuit of power through religion. It is this infatuation with power which has nullified the greatest religious discovery of the Hindus. Perhaps the history of their spiritual effort can be summed up in these lines:

> Heaven lies about us in our infancy!
> Shades of the prison-house begin to close
>   Upon the growing Boy,
> But he beholds the light, and whence it flows,
>   He sees it in his joy;
> The Youth, who daily farther from the east
>   Must travel, still is Nature's Priest,
>   And by the vision splendid
>   Is on his way attended;
> At length the Man perceives it die away,
>   And fade into the light of common day.

BIBLIOGRAPHY

This bibliography is very selective. It is meant only for those who would like to go beyond this book to get a feel of the Hindu religion from some of the texts, and also to compare the description and interpretation given in it with what is to be found in a number of scholarly books which are regarded as standard works.

I. Texts. (Only translations into English are listed. It should be kept in mind that the original texts being in verse and some of great poetic merit, their spirit is substantially lost in the translations.)

The *Rig-Veda*. The only English translation of the whole work is by R. T. H. Griffith. 1896–7.

The Upanishads. *The Thirteen Principal Upanishads,* translated with an introduction by R. E. Hume.

The *Gita*. *The Bhagavad Gita* translated and interpreted by Franklin Edgerton. Two volumes. 1944. There is also a more modern translation by R. C. Zaehner.

A useful selection from the sacred books of the Hindus will be found in *Hindu Scriptures* by R. C. Zaehner in Everyman's Library series. Those who are ambitious might look into *Original Sanskrit Texts* in five volumes collected, translated, and illustrated by J. Muir. A large number of volumes in the series, *The Sacred Books of the East,* edited by F. Max Müller, contain many standard texts in translation.

II.   Works on Hinduism

Bouquet, *Hinduism.* 1948.

Dubois, J. A., The Abbé, *Hindu Manners, Customs, and Ceremonies.* First published in 1817, latest edition 1926.

Farquhar, J. N., *A Primer of Hinduism.* 1912.

Gonda, J. *Les Religions de l'Inde:*

Vol. 1, *Vedisme et Hindouisme Ancien.* 1962.

Vol. 2, *L'Hindouisme Récent.* 1965.

(These two books were originally published in German.)

BIBLIOGRAPHY

Hopkins, E. W., *The Religions of India*. 1895.
Monier Williams, Monier, *Hinduism*. 1877.
Morgan, K. W. (Ed.), *The Religion of the Hindus*. 1953.
O'Malley, L. S. S., *Popular Hinduism*. 1932.
Renou, Louis, *Religion of Ancient India*. 1953.
Walker, Benjamin, *Hindu World*. 1968.
Wilkins, W. J., *Modern Hinduism*. 1887.
Zaehner, R. C., *Hinduism*. 1962.

Many of these books have extended bibliographies.

INDEX

Aboriginals of India
  influence on Hinduism, 96ff; Bengali view, 98; missionary view, 97
  religion of, 133
  untouchability of, 188
Abortion in Hindu society, 171
Action, way of,
  and spirituality, 323ff
Administrative interest in Hinduism, 107
Adultery in Hindu society, 272
After-life, Hindu notion, 9, 152ff
Aghor-panthis, 185
Agni, 72ff
Alberuni
  on monotheism and polytheism, 92
  on Sanskrit, 216
Alcohol, drinking of, 194
Alexander the Great, 3, 94
Andha-hasti-nyaya, 146
Animals, sacrificial, 75
Aphrodite, 222
Arya-Saptasati, 227
Aryan and non-Aryan, 97
Asceticism, Hindu, 324
Asiatic Society of Bengal, 108
Asoka
  slaughter of animals, 192
Asokan inscriptions
  in Greek language, 94, 267
  and Sanskrit language, 37ff
Asramas, 302
Astral control of life, 201ff
Astrologers, 202
Asuras and Devas, 239ff
Atman, 87, 146

Baldacus, P.
  book on Hinduism, 106
Banyan tree as symbol of Hinduism, 146

Barbarians, and Hindu order, 189
Beauchamp, H. K.
  defends Brahmins, 171
Beef, eating, 193
Benares, character of, 172
Bengal
  Hinduism in, 131
  in Chaitanya's age, 285
Benveniste, E., 66
Besnagar pillar inscription, 44
Bhagavata Purana, 269
  Krishna cult in, 270
Bhakti, way of, 95ff
Bhakti
  in *Bhagavata Purana*, 270ff
  in *Brahmavaivarta Purana*, 273ff
  in *Gita*, 264ff
  in Jayadeva, 276ff
  origins, 256
  sexual impulse and, 271
Bharatachandra Ray
  devotion to Siva, 227
  on the mythology of Siva, 228
Birth, time of, 202
Boar incarnation, 51
Boden Professorship at Oxford, 108
Boghazköy inscription, 42
Brahman, notion of, 317
Brahmavaivarta Purana
  and Krishna cult, 273ff
Brahmins
  caste functions, 164
  economic status, 127
  feasts for, 168
  gluttony of, 170
Brahmo monotheism, 268
Breath and soul, 86, 313
Brindaban Das
  describes religious conditions, 285
British rule
  as threat to Hinduism, 189

British Rule *cont.*—
peace in India, 295

Cadenza of Hinduism, 63
Car festival of Krishna, 301
Casanova, 9, 225
Chaitanya, 282ff
and Vaishnava poetry, 285
eroticism in, 286ff
followers of, 182
life of, 283
scene at Puri, 287
successors of, 183
Chatterji, Bankim Chandra
on Bengali landlords, 16
on culture, 12
on Krishna, 260
on Love and *Bhakti*, 292
on worldliness in Hinduism, 11
Chhinnamasta, 251
Children thrown into the Ganges, 123
Christianity and Gita, 257, 267ff, 282
and Hindus, 148, 268, 316
Cicero, 2, 92
Class differences in Hinduism, 136
Classical writers on Hinduism, 3, 53ff
Cleanthes, hymn of, 222
Clement of Alexandria
on image worship, 92
Clothing, religious control of, 195ff
Coenobitism in sects, 184
Colebrooke, H. T., 108
Colomba (novel), 308
Conception ceremony, 209
Consolation in religion, 296ff
Contemporary state of Hinduism, 103
Contractual character of Hinduism, 13, 17
Cosmic order and the gods, 15
Cow, penance for killing, 199

Daily life of Hindus
religious control, 191
Dawn in Vedic literature, 71
Death, man's revolt against, 312
Decadence of Hinduism, 116ff
Describing Hinduism
problem of, 103

Devotional books of Hindus, 220
Dharma Sastras, 34
Dosha, Hindu notion, 20
Dravidian languages, 64
Dubois, the Abbé
knowledge of Hinduism, 111
on Brahmins and priests, 170
on diversities in Hinduism, 122
on Hindu arrogance, 113
on Hindu gods, 15
on Sadhus, 143
work on Hindu manners, 111
Duméezil, G., 44
on the Mahabharata, 260
Tripartite character
of Indo-European Pantheon, 82
Durga
appearance, 243
Bharatchandra's story, 248
cult of, 242ff
devotion to, 245ff
infusion of life, 245
Mahaballipuram image, 243
ritual of worship, 243

Ears, piercing of, 211
Eating, rules for, 192, 201
Enemies, fear of, 296
England, visits to, 200
Entertainment in religion, 298
Eran sculptures, 51
Eroticism in Hinduism, 231ff, 248ff, 269ff, 280ff, 286ff
Erotic descriptions
in *Arya-Saptasati*, 227
in inscriptions, 235
in Jayadeva, 278
in Kalidasa, 224ff
in Naisadha-Charita, 232, 234
Erotic sculptures, 231ff
Greek derivation, 235
European accounts of Hinduism, 104ff
Eusebius of Caesaria
on image worship, 93
Events of life, consecration of, 208
Excretion, rules for, 197, 207

INDEX

Fa-Hien's account, 55ff
Fame and religious life, 306
Fertility rites in Hinduism, 229
Festivals, Hindu, 299
Festivals and fairs, 162
Festival days, 203
Fire—private and public, 78
Fire, worship, 72ff
Fire-god Agni, 73
Fish, eating of, 193
Flowers in worship, 302
Food regulations, 192
Food and impurity, 207
Forster, E. M., 300
Fourth Stage of life
  and Sadhus, 309
Fraser's Magazine
  on Car Festival, 299
Freedom in religion, 306

Ganges, the, 161
Gangetic plain, Hinduism in, 125ff
Gangooly, J. C., 109, 123
Gayatri mantra, 155
Geographical diversities in Hinduism,
  135ff
Girnar inscription, 39
Gita, the, 261ff
  bhakti in, 257, 261, 264, 282
  Christianity and, 257, 267ff
  date of, 32, 262
  devotion in, 264
  four elements in, 263
  Krishna in, 261, 265ff
  nishkama karma, 263, 267
  on sacrifice, 13
  position of, 30
Gita-Govinda, the, 276ff
God in Hinduism, 148
Gods, Indo-European, 81
Gora (navel), 190
Greek accounts of Hinduism, 53
Greek influence in India, 94
Greek religion, 1, 22
Guilt and atonement, 198
Gujarati Hindus, 105
Gunas, 21
Guru cult, 302

Gurus, 156
Gymnosophists, 4

Hair-cutting, 197
Harivamsa, 269
Hastings, Warren
  interest in Hinduism, 107
  on the *Gita*, 5
  on meditation, 5
  on Sannyasi raids, 142
Hearth, Roman and Hindu, 78
Heaven and hell in Hinduism, 153
Heber, Reginald
  Benares incident, 326
  Swami Narayan's sect, 181
Heliodorus, 44, 261
Heresy in Hinduism, 148
Herodotus on Persian religion, 80
Hindus, xi, 24
  writing on Hinduism, 112
  distrust of Western observers, 114
  sexual obsession, 272
Hindustan, name for northern India,
  128
History of Hinduism
  Buddha's date, 32
  comparison of ideas, 33
  Chinese accounts, 55
  conclusions from evidence, 60ff
  conventional chronology, 27, 30
  early inscriptions, 44ff
  epics and Puranas, 58
  epigraphic data, 42ff
  evidence from architecture, 51ff
  evidence from art, 49ff
  foreign accounts, 53ff
  Gupta art, 50
  Hindu attitude, 28
  methodology, 29ff
  Sanskrit literature, 57ff
  sources for, 41
  Western reconstruction, 27ff
Hiuan-tsang, 56
Holiness, notion of, 20
Holwell, J. Z., 106
Human sacrifice, 75
Husband, love for, 292
Huxley, Aldous, 8

INDEX

Image worship, 90ff, 158
  Greek, 92
Immortality, aspiration for, 312
  in the Way of Knowledge, 317
Incarnation, Hindu, 16, 255
Indecencies in Hinduism, 97, 215
Indian nationality and Hinduism, 24
Indo-European, concept of, 65ff
  languages, 66ff
  religion in Greece, Rome, Persia,
    and India, 22ff
  religious concepts, 79
  ritual, 74ff
  temples, 80
  vocabulary, 67ff
I-tsing, 57

Jayadeva, 276ff
Journeys, 204
Joy of life in Hinduism, 297

Kabir, 178
Kali, cult of, 48, 150, 242ff
  devotion to, 245
  physical appearance, 244
  ritual and worship, 245
  songs to, 246
Kalidasa
  date of, 35
  devotion to Siva, 223
  Kumara-Sambhava, 223ff
Kamarupa, 56
Kama-sutra, 218, 279
Kapalikas, 249
Katha Upanishad, 144
Kausitaki Brahmana, 73
Kikkuli's horse treatise, 43
Kipling, R., 76, 293, 315
Knowledge, Way of, 85ff, 316ff
Krishna, cult of, 44, 46, 88, 158, 255ff
  and bhakti, 256ff
  and Gopis, 269ff, 275
  and Mirabai, 291ff
  and Vishnu, 44, 46, 255, 261
  as incarnation, 255, 266
  duplication of, 261
  festivals of, 299ff
  in Bhagavata Purana, 270ff

in Brahmavaivarta Purana, 273ff
  in the Gita, 261ff
  in the Gita-Govinda, 276ff
  in the Harivamsa, 269
  in the Mahabharata, 259ff
  in Vishnu Purana, 269
Krishnadas Kaviraj, 282
Kumara-Sambhava, 223ff

La Grue, Thomas, 4
Landed classes and Hinduism, 138ff
Light, Hindu worship, 68ff
  Sanskrit word for, 69
Linguistic evidence on Hinduism, 64
Liquid states, impurity of, 208
Literature of Hinduism, 219
Lord, Henry, 4, 104, 110
Loyalty to Hinduism, 120
Lust and love in Vaishnavism, 282
Lyall, Sir Alfred, 133ff
  aboriginal religion, 133ff
  European attitude to Hinduism,
    145
  strength of Hinduism, 118ff

Mahabharata, Krishna in, 259
Maharaja, title, 240, 305
Maine, Sir Henry, Hindu orthodoxy,
  190
Manu, on rebirth, 153
Marriage, astral control, 202
Mass expression of Hinduism, 140
Menstruation ritual, 209
Methodology of history, 27ff
Migne, the Abbé, 144
Mirabai, 290ff
Missionaries
  on aboriginals, 98
  on Hinduism, 3, 104ff, 109ff
Mitannian gods, 42
  Horse treatise, 43
  Kings, 63
Mlechchha, notion of, 189
Mohants, 184
Monasteries, Vaishnava, 184
Monier-Williams, Sir M.
  decadence of Hinduism, 117
  diversity of Hinduism, 145
  Swami Narayan sect, 182

INDEX

Monotheism, Hindu, 88ff, 91ff, 148ff
Morality and Hinduism, 15ff
Mother-Goddess, Hindu, 242ff
Müller, F. M., 117ff
Muslim conquest and Hinduism, 100, 125ff, 127
Mythology, cult, and devotion in Hinduism, 220ff
Mythology, exposition of, 165

Naga Sadhus, 185
Naishadha-Charita
  erotic descriptions, 232, 234
Nationalism, 24
  Hindu apologia, 112
  Hindu orthodoxy, 190
  and Tantra, 252
Nature and Hinduism, 301
Night in Vedic literature, 71
Nomadic expression of Hinduism, 141ff
Non-anthropomorphic stage of Hinduism, 85ff

Occult powers, how secured, 325
Orme, Robert, on Hinduism, 128
Orthodoxy in Bengal, 132, 191
Oxford, Hindu Sadhu at, 306

Panini, 36
Pantheon, Indo-European, 81ff
Parvati
  epigraphic reference to, 47
  penance of, 224
  sexual experiences of, 228ff
Penances, 198ff
Personal observation of Hinduism, 113ff
Phallus of Siva, 229ff
Philosophers, Greek accounts of, 54
Philosophical discussion in Hindu society, 165ff
Philosophy and priests, 165
Pilgrimage, 135, 159ff
Place, E. des, 1
Plotinus, 2
Poetry, Hindu view of, 320
Political History

effect on religious outlook, 295
Political and religious power, 304
Political reasons for taboos, 188ff
Polymorphous monotheism, 88ff, 151
Polytheism, Hindu, 151
Popular Hinduism, 128, 140
Power, desire for, 294
  in religion, 304, 329
Practice of Hinduism
  diversity in, 154ff
Pregnancy, ritual of, 210
Prehistory of Hinduism, 62
Priests, Hindu
  character of, 137, 164
  classes of, 164
  Dubois' view of, 169
  extortion by, 168
  knowledge of, 166
  moral and spiritual responsibility of, 167
  supervision by women, 167
Priesthood
  Brahmin monopoly, 164
  Profession of, 164ff
Prostitutes in fairs, 299
Protection from religion, 294
Punjab, Hinduism in, 129
Puranas, 219ff
Puran Bhagat (Story), 315
Pure and impure states, 205ff
Purity mania, 206

Radha
  date of, 273ff
  relationship with Krishna, 274, 276, 288
  theory of, 274
Radha and Krishna
  modern Hindu interpretation, 280
  sexual intercourse between, 275, 278ff
  Vaishnava interpretation, 281
Raghuvamsa, 223, 226
Ramananda sect, 178
Ramanuja sect, 176
Rammohan Roy
  and Tantra, 250
  and Upanishads, 112, 118

INDEX

Ramprasad—devotee of Kali, 246
Rationalizing Hinduism, 145
Reality, absolute, 317ff
Regional diversities in Hinduism, 122ff
Regional types of Hinduism, 124ff
Religio (Latin), 2, 19
Religion and its followers, 17ff
Religion and scruple, 19ff
Religion—meaning of the word, 2
Religious practices of Hindus, 154ff
Renunciation, Hindu, 303ff, 322, 324ff
Rhetoric, Sanskrit, 218
Rig-Veda
  date of, 30ff
  position of, 29
Riots and Sadhus, 185
Rites of Hinduism (obligatory), 63, 154
River worship, 160
Roger, Abraham, 4, 105ff
Roman religion and Hinduism, 74ff
  ancestor worship, 77
  domestic rites, 77
  hearth, 78
Romantic movement and Hinduism, 7
Room
  purification of, 206
Rta (cosmic order), 17
Rudradamanas inscription, 39
Rupa Goswami
  interpretation of lyric, 287
  interpretation of Jayadeva, 281

Sacrifice in Hinduism, 13, 74ff
  public and private, 76
  Roman and Hindu, 75
Sadhus, 5, 141ff, 306ff
  as robber bands, 142
  as teachers of morality, 322
  their wanderings, 307
  their wisdom, 322
  their worldly position, 305
Saiva cult, 60
Sakta orthodoxy, 174
Salvation, Hindu, 10, 153
Samkara, on Atman, 87

Sanctification of worldliness, 20ff
Sannyasi raids, 142
Sanskrit, classical, 36ff, 216ff
  and Asoka inscriptions, 37
  creation of, 39
  epigraphic evidence for, 38ff
  Girnar inscription, 39
  lexicography, 217
  metrical composition in, 217
  in South India, 65
Sanskrit literature
  date of, 35
Sanskrit rhetoric, 218
Schlegel, F., 7
Schweitzer, A., 10
Scruple in religion, 19ff
Sects in Hinduism, 171ff
Shashthi, worship of, 301
Sin in Hinduism, 198
Siva
  cult of, 237ff
  as Lord, 89
  as monotheistic god, 89ff, 239
  in art, 51
  in Asia Minor, 238
  in Indo-Iranian conflict, 239
  in inscriptions, 47
  in *Mahabharata*, 89, 241
  mythological treatment of, 221
  Persian influence on, 240
  phallic worship, 229ff
Siva-Parvati
  Bharatchandra on, 227ff
  Kalidasa on, 223ff
Sivanath Sastri on worship of Durga, 247
Smriti, Hindu sacred law, 191
Social boycott, 187
Social coercion and religious life, 308
Soul, concept of, 86, 311, 313
South India
  contrast with northern India, 128
  role in Hinduism, 99ff
Spirituality, Christian, 311ff
Spirituality, connection with breathing, 313
Spirituality, Hindu, 314ff
  as quest of power, 314, 323, 329

INDEX

Spirituality, Hindu, *cont.*—
  in Way of Action, 323
  in Way of Knowledge, 316
  intrusive elements from Islam and Christianity, 315
  Sanskrit word for, 315
Sraddha (ritual), 152
St Paul on spirituality, 311
Stagnancy in Hinduism, 120
Starting point of Hinduism, 84
State of Hinduism in the 19th century, 116
Stevenson, Mrs S., 115
Stoicism and the *Gita*, 267
Sunlight in India, 72
Supernatural inseparable from natural, 18
Superstition and religion, 19ff
Support for life from religion, 295
Surkh Kotal, temple at, 52
Swami Narayan, 181

Taboos in Hinduism, 186
Tagore, R.
  novel of Hindu orthodoxy, 190
Tamil country
  Hinduism in, 130
Tantra
  character of, 249ff
  Hindu opinion of, 250
  rehabilitation by Woodroffe, 252
Tantric eroticism, origin of, 252
Tantric worship, 249
Tantric worshippers, depravity of, 250
Taoism and Tantra, 252
Teething, significance of, 210
Temples, Hindu
  early structures, 52
  destruction by Muslims, 125ff
  erotic sculptures in 233ff
  origins, 94
  in Sanskrit literature, 59ff
  Surkh Kotal, 52
Temple worship, 90ff, 157ff
Tertullian on *religio*, 2
Theorizing by Hindus, 218
Transmigration, 153

Trinity, Hindu, 150

Udayagiri sculptures, 51
Unity of Hinduism, 135
Upanishads, 144, 219, 321

Vagrancy in sects, 184
Vaishnavas
  contempt for, 174
  in monasteries, 183, 290
  philosophical discussion by, 289
Vaishnavism in Bengal, 182, 290
Vallabhacharya sect, 180ff
Vamachara, 249
Vedic religion
  character of, 84
  reconstruction of, 62
Vedic rituals, 62
Vedic sacrifices in inscriptions, 45, 48
Vedic texts, authority of, 62
Vishnu
  group at Udayagiri, 51
  in inscriptions, 45
  origin of cult, 89
Vishnu Purana and Krishna, 269
Vishnu-dharmohara Purana, 263ff
Vitality of Hinduism, 121
Vocabulary of Hinduism, 67ff
Vratas, 157

West (contemporary) and Hinduism, 8
Western approach to Hinduism, 2ff
Widow (Hindu), 171, 197
Wilkins, Charles, translator of the *Gita*, 5, 107
Wilkins, W. J., views on Hinduism, 10, 110, 123
Wilson, H. H., works on Hinduism, 108, 172, 175ff
Women's rites, 159
Woodroffe, Sir John, on Tantra, 251ff
Word, Hindu conception, 217
Wordsworth, W. quotation from, 319, 329
Worldly character of Hinduism, 11ff
Worldly life and Hinduism, 186ff

INDEX

Worldly prosperity, Hindu prayer for, 14

Yuan-Chwang, 56

Zeus, 79, 85
  devotion to, 222
  in mythology, 221
Zodiacal signs, significance of, 203